PSYCHOLOGY RESEARCH PROGRESS SERIES

PSYCHOLOGICAL SCIENTIFIC PERSPECTIVES ON OUT-OF-BODY AND NEAR-DEATH EXPERIENCES

PSYCHOLOGY RESEARCH PROGRESS SERIES

Suicide and the Creative Arts
Steven Stack and David Lester (Editors)
2009. ISBN 978-1-60741-958-7

Jung Today: Volume 1- Adulthood
Francesco Bisagni , Nadia Fina and Caterina Vezzoli (Editors)
2009. ISBN 978-1-60741-893-1

Psychological Scientific Perspectives on Out-of-Body and Near-Death Experiences
Craig D. Murray (Editor)
2009. ISBN 978-1-60741-705-7

PSYCHOLOGY RESEARCH PROGRESS SERIES

PSYCHOLOGICAL SCIENTIFIC PERSPECTIVES ON OUT-OF-BODY AND NEAR-DEATH EXPERIENCES

CRAIG D. MURRAY
EDITOR

Nova Science Publishers, Inc.
New York

For permission to use material from this book please contact us:
Telephone 631-231-7269; Fax 631-231-8175
Web Site: http://www.novapublishers.com

LIBRARY OF CONGRESS CATALOGING-IN-PUBLICATION DATA

Psychological scientific perspectives on out of body and near death experiences / [edited by] Craig D. Murray.

p. cm.

Includes bibliographical references and index.

ISBN 978-1-60741-705-7 (hardcover)

1. Astral projection. 2. Near-death experiences. I. Murray, Craig D.

BF1389.A7P75 2009

133.9--dc22 2009018006

Published by Nova Science Publishers, Inc. ✦ New York

CONTENTS

Acknowledgements		**vii**
Introduction	Introduction to Psychological Scientific Perspectives on Out-of-Body and Near-Death Experiences *Craig D. Murray*	**ix**
Chapter 1	Early and Modern Developments in the Psychological Approach to Out-of-Body Experiences *Carlos S. Alvarado*	**1**
Chapter 2	A Psychological Theory of the Out-of-Body Experience *Susan J. Blackmore*	**23**
Chapter 3	The Disembodied Self: An Empirical Study of Dissociation and the Out-of-Body Experience *Harvey J. Irwin*	**37**
Chapter 4	Psychological Theories of the OBE Under Scrutiny: (Commentaries on Blackmore and Irwin) *Susan J. Blackmore, Harvey J. Irwin, Jerome J. Tobacyk, Etzel Cardeña and Devin B. Terhune, David Wilde, Kathryn Gow, Pascal Le Maléfan and Renaud Evrard*	**53**
Chapter 5	Understanding the Out-of-Body Experience from a Neuroscientific Perspective *Jane E. Aspell and Olaf Blanke*	**73**
Chapter 6	Out-of-Body Experiences in the Context of Hypnosis: Phenomenology, Methodology, and Neurophysiology *Devin Blair Terhune and Etzel Cardeña*	**89**
Chapter 7	Managing Anomalous Experience: Meaning Making and the OBE *Craig D. Murray, David J. Wilde and Joanne Murray*	**105**
Chapter 8	Prevalence, Phenomenology and Biopsychosocial Aspects of the Near-Death Experience *John Belanti, Karuppiah Jagadheesan and Mahendra Perera*	**117**

Chapter 9 Near-Death Experiences, Out-of-Body Experiences and Social Scientific Paradigms **129**
James McClenon

Chapter 10 The 'Urashima Effect': A Cultural Illusion? A Japanese Perspective on Death, Life and the Near-Death Experience **145**
Ornella Corazza

Chapter 11 Out-of-Body and Near-Death Experiences as Evidence for Externalization or Survival **159**
John Palmer

Chapter 12 Endless Consciousness: A Concept Based on Scientific Studies on Near-Death Experience **171**
Pim van Lommel

Chapter 13 Near-Death Experiences and the Brain **187**
Christopher C. French

Chapter 14 Finding Meaning in Near-Death Experiences **205**
Craig D. Murray, David J. Wilde and Joanne Murray

Notes on Contributors **221**

Index **225**

ACKNOWLEDGEMENTS

I would like to thank all those who have contributed in various ways in the production of this book. Jezz Fox is deserving of particular mention. Some years ago he helped foster my interest in the topic of anomalous experience in general, and out-of-body and near-death experiences in particular, and I have enjoyed working with him on these topics enormously. I also owe a large debt of gratitude to The Bial Foundation, who have been a generous funder of my research in these areas. Two of the chapters included in this collection (chapter 2, Blackmore, and chapter 3, Irwin) have previously been published in the *Journal of Parapsychology* and I would like to thank the Rhine Centre for granting permission to reproduce these here. An earlier version of chapter 1 (Alvarado) was previously published in the *Journal of Psychology*, and I would like to thank the Helen Dwight Reid Educational Foundation for permission to include an updated version in this collection. Several people assisted me in reviewing the papers included in this collection, and I would therefore like to thank Donna Lloyd, Chris Roe, Devin Terhune and David Wilde for their careful consideration of draft manuscripts and for the valuable feedback given to contributing authors. Thanks are also due to Joanne Murray who provided valuable editorial assistance. I would like to express a special thank you to the authors included in this collection for their enthusiastic and valuable contributions, and for their sheer hard work in producing these. I'd like also to thank my partner Jo, for her tremendous support of my work over the years. A final mention is reserved for my children, Jade, Emma, Isaac and Daniel, because I love them so, because I know it will make them smile to see their names printed here, and so they might finally understand exactly what it was that I was doing for all that time they saw me sitting at the computer.

In: Psychological Scientific Perspectives on Out of Body … ISBN: 978-1-60741-705-7
Editor: Craig D. Murray

Introduction

INTRODUCTION TO PSYCHOLOGICAL SCIENTIFIC PERSPECTIVES ON OUT-OF-BODY AND NEAR-DEATH EXPERIENCES

Craig D. Murray

When I began my first full-time academic post some years ago I found myself in a psychology department where a sizeable amount of research could be described as belonging to the field of parapsychology. Up to then, most of my own research had been on the topic of embodiment, and in particular on phantom limbs and artificial limb use as experienced by people with amputations or congenital limb absences. In an attempt to find some common ground with my colleagues I considered what I knew about parapsychology (very little) and if there were any overlapping topics of mutual concern. The example which came to mind fairly quickly was that of out-of-body experiences (OBEs), and the OBE aspect of some near-death experiences (NDEs). My own interest in embodiment was to understand its phenomenological experience in health, illness and disability, and the very notion of an OBE seemed paradoxical to me. How was it that someone could report an experience of being disembodied, yet still report sights, sounds and other sensorial experiences which seemed to rely on the sense organs of the body? With my interest sufficiently stirred I began to look further into the available literature on the topics with the intention of producing a phenomenological account of the OBE.

Several years on from embarking on research in these areas what I have perhaps found most surprising is not the large body of work which already exists on these topics, nor the sheer range of explanatory theories advanced and branches of the psychological sciences which have explored them, but the resistance in academia, particularly in psychology where one might expect there to be most interest, to considering such topics as legitimate areas of research inquiry. Why might this be the case? In part, I would argue this is because the subject matter is considered frivolous, even though the experiences referred to are often of profound significance for the person having them (see, for example, chapters 7 and 14 in this volume). These topic areas are dismissed because (I would argue erroneously so and without due attention) they are assumed to be unimportant, idiosyncratic, and unable to illuminate more important theoretical considerations. In short, the questions which such experiences raise are not considered to be worthy of the investment of time and energy to answer. (I think it is worth pointing out that to members of the general public such experiences often seem fascinating, and they are frequently curious about the types of questions surrounding them that psychology often seems reluctant to address.)

Related to the above, I would argue that any mention of 'parapsychology' has developed unwelcome connotations: it has become somewhat of a 'toxic' label by which it is assumed that the researcher has a particular position, one which is unscientific, incredulous, naïve or childish, and just plain wrong. In turn, research attention to topic areas which have traditionally been addressed in the field of parapsychology suffer from the same malady. However, I would argue that this is erroneous on two counts. First, in fact, researchers working in academic parapsychology include both those who propose that there is evidence for phenomena which is not currently accepted or explainable in terms of accepted scientific theories (such as the survival of consciousness following bodily death, telepathy, and so on), as well as researchers who argue that what might appear to be, or could be advanced, as evidence of such phenomena is actually not, and that current scientific understanding can adequately explain, or be developed to explain, such phenomena. There are also researchers who would claim to be agnostic in regards to this issue. Second, regardless of which of these positions characterize the researcher's personal standpoint, the academic arguments by these researchers are invariably made with reference to evidence, and involve scientific scrutiny, appropriate evaluation and interpretation. Doubtless, it is the nature and adequacy of each of these components of researchers' arguments which becomes the source of debate between proponents of different theories. Regardless of this, it is the perception that academics outside of the field have of it, rather than the actual reality, that is important in creating a climate conducive for, or receptive to, such work. This perception is perhaps behind a recent and growing trend for researchers to label their research interest as anomalous psychology rather than parapsychology, as they attempt to distance themselves from the negative connotations of the term, or as a statement of their stance as 'skeptics' of paranormal phenomena.

This brings me back to the resistance in academia to considering certain topics as legitimate areas of research inquiry. As stated earlier, one of my initial (and continuing) areas of research concern focused on phantom limb phenomena. This refers to the experience whereby a person with an amputated limb may still experience vivid sensations that the limb is still present, and is now, but has not always been, a well-recognized feature of such persons' experience. However, it is often stated that Silas Weir Mitchell, a physician who coined the term 'phantom limb' in the late 19th century, first published an article on the topic in a popular magazine under a pseudonym in order to avoid the ridicule of his colleagues had he published it under his own name in a medical journal. I draw upon this example as a parallel to writing about or researching OBEs and NDEs today, where the culture of academia often makes it difficult for researchers to apply themselves to such issues. Perhaps Weir Mitchell's peers thought reports of phantom limbs were frivolous, unimportant, idiosyncratic, and unable to illuminate more important theoretical considerations. However, they have since proven important in illuminating theories of the body schema and, similarly, OBEs have begun to inform thinking on the integration of the body schema and the brain regions responsible for this (see, for example, chapters 5, 6 and 13 in this volume). The point here is that the realm of human experience, including the unusual or anomalous, is deserving of attention, and when science in general, and psychology in particular, chooses not to address these areas, they not only fail to address significant aspect of human experience, but they fail in their claim to be unbiased, objective, and, indeed, scientific.

To this end my own use of the term 'Psychological Scientific Perspectives' in the title of this book is deliberate. It not only allows several branches of psychology and psychology-related disciplines to be included within this collection, but it boldly asserts the scientific merit and relevance of the material presented herein. Not that the material presented herein is a unified collection in support of one particular explanatory theory of the OBE or NDE. On the contrary, the contributors herein advance different theoretical frameworks for understanding the available research on these topics, and often arrive at different interpretations of the same research data (contrast, for example, the discussion of the case of Pam Reynolds as evidence for veridical NDEs as presented in chapter 13 with that in chapters 11 and 12). The fields of medicine, neuropsychology and neuroscience, parapsychology, psychology, and sociology, which are included here under the rubric 'Psychological Scientific Perspectives', are all represented herein by the researchers who have contributed to the chapters in this volume. These researchers have different epistemological understandings of the OBE and NDE, interpret evidence in different ways, and elaborate different levels of explanatory theories to account for the phenomena that comprise the related and overlapping topic areas that are OBEs and NDEs. It is for the reader to assess the arguments presented within them.

This volume begins with a chapter by Carlos Alvarado (Early and Modern Developments in the Psychological Approach to Out-of-Body Experiences), who provides a review of psychological approaches to out-of-body experiences (OBEs) since the nineteenth century to the present. Here he demonstrates how the field of parapsychology has contributed to the development of the psychological approach to OBE. This is followed by two chapters which each present a psychological theory of the OBE. In chapter 2 (A Psychological Theory of the Out-of-Body Experience) Susan Blackmore presents a cognitive theory which accounts for the OBE as a product of models of reality which are produced by the brain, with an OBE model being constructed through schematic memory models when there is a lack of sensory input which is usually responsible for producing such a model of reality. Next, Harvey Irwin (chapter 3, The Disembodied Self: An Empirical Study of Dissociation and the Out-of-Body Experience) presents a dissociational theory of the OBE in which he explains its occurrence as due to dissociation between the sense of self and the processing of somatic events. Both Blackmore's and Irwin's chapters have previously been published as peer-reviewed journal articles and are reproduced here for two important reasons. The first relates to their importance as explanatory models of the OBE within the field. Both authors have made significant contributions to the topic of OBEs, and these specific papers have been chosen as particularly good examples of their work for the purposes of this volume. However, given that neither of these papers are recent publications (Blackmore's is now 25 years old, and Irwin's 9), their inclusion here is made more relevant by the new commentaries that are not only provided by both of these authors, but by the peer commentary from key researchers in the field provided in chapter 4 (Psychological Theories of the OBE Under Scrutiny: Commentaries on Blackmore and Irwin). The presentation of these key theories alongside this commentary, then, provides a valuable opportunity to reflect on the continued relevance of these theories.

Chapters 5 and 6 focus on neuroscientific explanations of the OBE. In the first of these (Understanding the Out-Of-Body Experience from a Neuroscientific Perspective) Jane Aspell and Olaf Blanke argue that the scientific understanding of the bodily self can be informed by the study of OBEs. Aspects of the self are experienced as spatially distinct from the physical body during these experiences, so that the study of what causes people to dissociate in an OBE, alongside the examination of how aspects of the bodily self relate to behavior and neural processing in healthy persons, will provide important insights into how these aspects of self are related phenomenally, behaviorally and neurally. Following this Devin Terhune and Etzel Cardeña (Out-Of-Body Experiences in the Context of Hypnosis: Phenomenology, Methodology, and Neurophysiology) present a review and theoretical integration of the phenomenology and neurophysiology of spontaneous and experimentally-induced OBEs during hypnosis in which they argue for the utility of hypnosis as an instrumental method for the experimental induction and manipulation of these experiences.

In chapter 7 (Managing Anomalous Experience: Meaning Making and the OBE) Craig Murray, David Wilde and Joanne Murray present a qualitative, phenomenological analysis of the experiences of OBE participants. Their work highlights the utility of idiographic, phenomenological work in identifying the subtle personal and social contributors which influence how the OBE is psychologically managed and integrated.

Moving on to the the related and overlapping topic area of near-death experiences, and continuing with contributions which highlight the synergies between these research areas, in chapter 8 (Prevalence, Phenomenology and Biopsychosocial Aspects of the Near-Death Experience) John Belanti, Karuppiah Jagadheesan and Mahendra Perera discuss the key elements of the NDE, the cultural variation in NDE reports, and the potential neurobiological mechanisms which are considered to underlie these experiences. This is followed by James McClenon (chapter 9, Near-Death Experiences, Out-of-body Experiences and Social Scientific Paradigms) who argues that NDEs have universal elements with a physiological basis, that universal NDE elements occur with equal frequency in "emergency" NDEs compared to "non-emergency" OBEs, and that the incidence of NDE/OBEs is correlated with a variety of related anomalous experiences. In addition, he advances 'ritual healing theory' to describe how genes allowing anomalous experience have contributed to the evolutionary development of religious sentiment.

In chapter 10 (The 'Urashima Effect': A cultural illusion? A Japanese Perspective on Death, Life and the Near-Death Experiences) Ornella Corazza explores the near-death phenomenon from a cross-cultural point of view, focusing in particular on NDEs reported in Japanese participants. Here, she proposes that a Japanese perspective on life and death provides 'a middle way' between reductionist and dualist theories that have been used to date to explain the NDE.

The argument for a survivalist interpretation of OBEs and NDEs is considered by John Palmer and Pim van Lommel in chapters 11 (Out-of-body and Near-Death Experiences as Evidence for Externalization or Survival) and 12 respectively (Endless Consciousness: A Concept Based on Scientific Studies on Near-Death Experience). Palmer reviews research studies that could be interpreted as providing evidence for survival of death, either directly (NDEs) or indirectly through separation of the mind from the body (OBEs). Although highlighting potential problems in the robustness of this evidence, he argues that the NDE evidence 'increases the subjective probability of survival'. Van Lommel focuses in particular on several prospective studies on NDEs in survivors of cardiac arrest. He argues that the current materialistic view of the relationship between the brain and consciousness held by most physicians, philosophers and psychologists does not enable a full understanding of NDE phenomena, that there are good reasons to conclude that consciousness does not always coincide with the functioning of our brain, meaning that consciousness can sometimes be experienced separately from the body.

In contrast to the above survivalist interpretation of NDE data, Chris French (chapter 13, Near-Death Experiences and the Brain) presents an overview of neuroscientific approaches to the near-death experience (NDE), and argues that recent claims that findings from NDE studies constitute a major challenge to the central assumptions of modern neuroscience are flawed. Rather, he suggests that such claims are based upon misconceptions and misrepresentations of previous research. His conclusion is that, while in need of further refinement, the neuroscientific approach holds the most promise with respect to understanding the NDE.

This volume concludes with an analysis by Craig Murray, David Wilde and Joanne Murray (chapter 14, Finding Meaning in Near-Death Experiences) of how meanings are attributed to the NDE by experients. In particular they highlight how experients come to new understandings of their lives as a result of their NDE, the challenges the NDE, or elements therein, have on the individual's sense of self and how they maintain and develop that self in the years following their NDE.

Taken together, the chapters in this collection span the current debates and interpretation of OBE and NDE phenomena, and these are provided both by researchers with established significant contributions to these areas as well as those who are at the forefront of current, developing work. Although these researchers may arrive at different interpretations (including focussing on different levels of interpretation), as well as advancing different theories in regards to the occurrence of the OBE and NDE, they are united in their consideration of these areas as important, significant features of human experience, and as able to illuminate important theoretical considerations in the psychological sciences – and beyond.

In: Psychological Scientific Perspectives on Out of Body … ISBN: 978-1-60741-705-7
Editor: Craig D. Murray

Chapter 1

Early and Modern Developments in the Psychological Approach to Out-of-Body Experiences[1]

Carlos S. Alvarado[2]

Abstract

This is a review of psychological approaches to out-of-body experiences (OBEs) since the nineteenth century. Some of the work discussed includes explanations of OBEs based on dissociation, telepathic hallucinations, and psycho-dynamic factors. Important developments in the modern period include the appearance of both formal psychological OBE theories and research examining psychological correlates of OBEs, including absorption, imagery, schizotypy, and dream and parapsychological experiences. The development of the psychological approach to OBE studies has been influenced by the field of parapsychology, and, particularly in recent times, by the interest in imagery and altered states of consciousness and dissociation in psychology during the last three decades.

Introduction

For many years, the psychological, psychiatric, and parapsychological literatures have included discussions of out-of-body experiences (OBEs) (Alvarado, 1989), a phenomenon in

---

[1] This chapter is an updated version of : Alvarado, C. (1992). Thee psychological approach to out-of-body experiences: A review of early and modern developments, Journal of Psychology, 126, 237-250. Reprinted with permission of the Helen Dwight Reid Educational Foundation. Published by Heldref Publications, 1319 Eighteenth St., NW, Washington, DC 20036-1802. Copyright © 1992.

[2] This is a revised version of a previously published paper (Alvarado, 1992). I wish to thank Susan J. Blackmore and Harvey J. Irwin for useful suggestions for improvement of the original article. Nancy L. Zingrone offered substantial editorial suggestions for the revision of the original and present version of the paper. The first edition of the paper was funded by the Parapsychology Foundation, and the second by the Society for Psychical Research.

which "the center of consciousness appears to the experient to occupy temporarily a position which is spatially remote from his/her body" (Irwin, 1985, p. 5). The OBE has a varied phenomenology, but, as seen in the research literature, some of its reported features consist of sensations of floating, seeing one's own body from a distance, and seeming to travel to distant locations (Alvarado, 1984; Alvarado & Zingrone, 1999; Gabbard & Twemlow, 1984; Green, 1968).

Traditionally, OBE theories and explanatory concepts have been divided into two main camps. Some have proposed that the experience represents a transcendance of the physical body in the sense that there is a projection of "something"—a subtle body or some non-physical aspect of personality—out of the physical body (Muldoon & Carrington, 1951; Woodhouse, 1994), or that the mind is able to function in nonphysical space (Carr, 2008; Poynton, 2001). Others have defended a psychological stance by which the OBE is explained as an imaginal experience. As Irwin has stated, in this approach there is an attempt to relate the OBE "to certain psychological and neurophysiological events. Within [this] group, different patterns of emphases are given to the contribution of normal, abnormal, and paranormal processes" (Irwin, 1985, p. 219). Palmer (1978) has argued that it is possible to discuss the psychology of the OBE without rejecting a projection model. However, most people defending psychological concepts to explain OBEs clearly reject the idea of projection (for reviews of the above-mentioned ideas see Alvarado, 1989, 2000, in press; Blackmore, 1982a; Irwin, 1985).

As I will discuss later in this chapter, there has been an increase of interest in the psychology of OBEs, particularly from the 1980s onward. The topic has already been reviewed over the years in books and articles (Alvarado, 1986b, 1988, 2000; Gabbard & Twemlow, 1994; Irwin, 1985; Irwin & Watt, 2007). However, there is a need for a more general overview of the subject to provide a global perspective of the psychological study of OBEs that does not repeat the content of these previously mentioned publications. The purpose of this chapter is to briefly review trends in the psychological study and conceptualization of the OBE from the nineteenth-century forward, and not to discuss findings or methodological issues.

I have organized the material into chronological periods. To some extent, these divisions are arbitrary, and although they will be useful to the presentation, they do not represent definitive developmental periods or an attempt to do a history of this aspect of OBE studies. Readers should also keep the following caveats in mind: The ideas presented here refer to a wide variety of OBE types (e.g., extremely vivid and unvivid OBEs) as well as to OBEs that occurred in different contexts. Although most of the OBEs relevant to this discussion occurred spontaneously, some were induced or occurred in experimental contexts. Other concepts have been developed from examinations of hypnotically induced OBEs or OBEs in which apparitions of the person having the experience were reported. I have tried to clearly distinguish these differences but have been unable to do so in all cases, as some of the original documents did not provide enough information. Additionally, for the sake of length I have excluded from the paper research centering on psychophysiological processes (e.g.. Burt, 1968, pp. 79-80; McCreery & Claridge, 1996b; Osis & Mitchell, 1977; Tart, 1967,1968), as well as speculations on the involvement of tempoparietal junction pathology related to vestibular processes (e.g., Blanke, Landis, Spinelli & Seeck, 2004; Blanke & Mohr, 2005; Brandt, Brechtelsbauer, Bien & Reimers, 2005), or other neurophysiological speculations (e.g., Brugger, Regard & Landis, 1997; McCreery, 1997; Nelson, Mattingle &

Schmitt, 2007).[3] I will also omit a detailed discussion of near-death experiences (NDEs), due to the fact that not all of these experiences include the OBE component (e.g., Ring, 1980; Van Lommel, van Wees, Meyers & Elfferich, 2001).

Nineteenth Century

Several early writers believed that the OBE was an illusory experience. Physician Alexandre Brierre de Boismont commented in his book *Hallucinations: Or, the Rational History of Apparitions, Visions, Dreams, Ecstasy, Magnetism, and Somnambulism* on Lutheran Protestant visionary Jean Engelbrecht's apparent NDE in which "he imagined that he had visited both heaven and hell" (Brierre de Boismont, 1853, p. 214). This "visit," as well as subsequent visions and auditory experiences were seen by the author as part of the condition of ecstasy. He wrote:

> The state of ecstasy being a phenomenon of extreme nervous excitability, it is clear that it must be manifested at all periods when the mind has been agitated by fanaticism, and by a belief which brings in its train either ardent hopes or strong fears . . . . But if the psychological history of man proves that, whenever he is exposed to a permanent moral excitation, his organization becomes susceptible of experiencing the phenomenon of ecstasy, it is essential to establish a distinction of the highest importance between the ecstasy that I shall call physiological and a morbid ecstasy. In other words, we believe that ecstasy may have no influence on the reason, and is but a very exalted state of enthusiasm, whilst it may also occasion reprehensible and unreasonable actions (p. 215).

Lawyer A.S. Morin (1860) discussed the topic in the context of the magnetic somnambulistic performances typical of mesmerism. He argued that the separation of the soul from the body was impossible because this would end in death. In his view such pretended voyages involving perceptions of distant places were imaginary (pp. 261-262, this, and other translations, are mine). Morin reminded his readers that "somnabulism is but a variety of sleep" (p. 262) in which the person dreams, and the dream produces material from the imagination (p. 262). The dreamer also confuses the real and the unreal in oniric travels. He wrote:

> The somnambule, while the crisis lasts, equally confuses illusion and reality. Because while awake he loses recollection, he is incapable of rectifying the errors into which he falls using his own judgement; so that with a new crisis, he is led towards the same topic . . . , he figures, as during the first time, that he really travelled to the places visited by his thought; he will have the same impressions than those of the first peregrinations; he will not hesitate to likewise declare real one or the other (p. 262).

Another discussion came from the spiritualist literature. In his book, *Spirit Before Our Eyes,* William H. Harrison (1879) stated his belief in the travel of the spirit in OBEs and other experiences. But he also argued for other explanations. Harrison stated that some dreams of visiting distant places, even if veridical, may not be the travels of the spirit. This could be a

[3] For critiques of some of this work see Kelly et al. (2007), and Long and Holden (2007).

case of clairvoyance or of a "dreamer seeing that which a spirit or mortal en rapport with him thought" (p. 146). This difficulty of interpretation is illustrated in the book by a case in which a person who was unconscious remembered later veridical details of a funeral he could not attend (p. 148). In Harrison's view: "He might have seen the funeral by being present at it in the spirit; he might have seen it by clairvoyance; or he might have seen that which was in the mind of a departed spirit who was present at the funeral of his own body" (p. 148).

Other interesting speculations appeared in the work of members of the Society for Psychical Research (SPR), which was founded in London in 1882.[4] Many of the SPR's prominent members published relevant speculations about psychological aspects of OBEs. The majority of these writings were published in a literature devoted to discussions of telepathic hallucinations, particularly visual ones. One of these writers, Edmund Gurney, posited in the classic psychical research study *Phantasms of the Living*, that spontaneous OBEs were hallucinatory experiences. He wrote: "The sense of being 'out of the body' ... is a known form of pathologic experience, or,—as I should regard it—of hallucination" (Gurney, Myers, & Podmore, 1886, Vol. 1, p. 288).

Gurney was referring to OBEs with no reported veridical or ESP component. For cases of the veridical type, especially reciprocal apparitions, or cases in which another person reported perceiving the OB-experient as an apparition (e.g., Gurney et al. , 1886, Vol. 2, pp. 159-160; Sidgwick, 1891, pp. 41-45),[5] Gurney held that the experience was a manifestation of a telepathic interaction process in which "each of the parties might receive a telepathic impulse from the other, and so each be at once agent and percipient" (Gurney et al., 1886, Vol. 2, p. 153). Others, such as Podmore (1894, pp. 301-302) and Sidgwick (1891, pp. 45-46), supported this concept.

Neither Gurney nor other writers on the topic detailed the probable process involved. They only implied the following: A mutual telepathic influence of two persons at a distance from each other caused one to see the apparition of the other in his or her own physical location and the other to experience the illusion that he or she was at the location in which the apparition was perceived.

Other writers speculated about the meaning of hypnotically induced experiences of visiting distant locations. Commenting on these cases of "traveling clairvoyance,"[6] physiologist Charles Richet (1887) wrote in *L'homme et l'intelligence* that it was a "mistake to believe that such dreams are real, and that the vision corresponds to the existence of exterior things" (p. 178). Rather, Richet asserted that tales of traveling to distant places were the product of an overexcited imagination coupled with memory images in the somnambulistic condition. This explanation was not unusual if we consider that explanations of the phenomena of hypnosis (and other psychological anomalies) using the concepts of hallucination, imagination, and memory were common in the nineteenth century (Blakeman, 1849; Brierre de Boismont, 1853; Carpenter, 1874).

---

[4] The SPR was an important—one may say unique—English organization that, during the nineteenth century, was devoted to the study of thought-transference, apparitions, and mediumship (Gauld, 1968), as well as to the varieties of dissociation and the subconscious mind (Alvarado, 2002).

[5] While reciprocal experiences by definition mean that two persons have had connecting experiences it is important to realize that not all reciprocal cases presented by Gurney et al. (1886) involved OBEs.

[6] For examples of traveling clairvoyance, see Haddock (1851, pp. 105-108), Hands (1845), and Sidgwick (1891, pp. 49-52, 53-62).

In a discussion of the role of hypnosis in the induction of traveling clairvoyance, psychical researcher Frank Podmore (1894) wrote that, in such cases, it has "generally been suggested to the hypnotised subject that he was actually present at the scene which he was desired to describe. It is possible that this suggestion … may have had some influence in determining the pictorial form which the telepathic impression assume in such cases, as it has certainly led the percipient himself and the bystanders in many cases to believe in an extra-corporeal visitation of the scenes described." (p. 338)

Podmore suggested that the hypnotic induction procedure influenced the expression of hypnotic and telepathic imagery in an out of body form.

EARLY TWENTIETH CENTURY TO 1940

Philosopher and psychical researcher James H. Hyslop (1912) made some interesting points on the possible psychological origin of OBEs in a review of an autobiographical account of self-induced OBEs and other recurrent experiences (Turvey, n.d.). Hyslop was not impressed by the out of body experiencer's conviction of being out of their body because, he argued, similar sensations were common in dreams:

> As dreams are subconscious affairs, if we suppose that clairvoyance is a subconscious phenomenon … we may well understand how the feelings of being where the events are under observation would take place and be associated with the feeling or knowledge of one's immediate and real environment. Suppose the information is transmitted from a distance by an observer not hampered by the bodily limitation, the subliminal which knows nothing of the bodily environment might have no other standard of locality than that of the transmitted images. (p. 513)

Hyslop contended that the subliminal mind reorganized ESP-acquired information into a hallucination of being in a different physical location, close to a distant agent.

Other concepts were presented by French psychical researchers to explain spontaneous OBEs. In his well-known *Traité de métapsychique*, Charles Richet (1922) referred to the "complete subjectivity of the phenomena of bilocation" (p. 703) and considered an OBE case nothing but a dream (p. 703). Some years later, in an article entitled "La Vision de Soi," Eugène Osty (1930) thought that OBEs were hallucinations, "the creation of the imagination" (p. 197). Following Sollier (1903), Osty believed that loss of bodily sensibility produced the feeling that the thinking self was exteriorized from the body. This "illusion of exteriorization of the self" takes place due to the "objectivation of the visual mental representation of the body . . . ." (p. 193, all quotes). OBEs, like autoscopy, were considered by Osty to be hallucinatory creations depending on temporary disturbances of sensibility, judgement, and imagination.[7] But he admitted that some veridical cases, those with "paranormal knowledge" (p. 196), required the concept of a telepathic hallucination to be explained. Such a process

[7] Attempts to explain autoscopy have included the concept of visual transformation of cenesthesic sensations (e.g., Buvet, 1902; Sollier, 1903, pp. 134-136). Quartier speculated that an OBE he had perhaps could be explained as "the dramatization, in visual form, of cenesthesic sensations …" (quoted in Osty, 1930, p. 191). Similar ideas regarding OBEs appeared in later publications (Burt, 1968, pp. 79-80; Capel, 1978, p. 55; Maire, 1933, p. 71).

was produced by a combination of the imaginative capacity of the experiencer and that part of the psyche responsible for paranormal phenomena. Osty believed this idea was plausible because hallucinations of the self were an "eclipse of the conscious [mind], which is favorable . . . to supernormal knowledge" (p. 197). In a later paper in which he was critical of the idea of etheric bodies, Osty (1933) stated: "With a little imagination everything is explained!" (p. 34).

In his book *Les métapsychoses* physician P. Thomas Bret (1939) had a variety of explanations for OBEs, including the projection of physical, but subtle doubles. But he felt that some OBE reports were dreams that represented the beliefs of the experiencers (p. 153) and "hallucinatory manifestations of ideas that the subject has during the waking state" (p. 164). Writing about the "journeys" of the hypnotized Bret argued: "It is not the self, the primary personality of the hypnotized one that makes the so-called voyage, but the secondary hypnotic personality" (p. 198). In his view the hypnotizer directs the ESP potential of the person so as to produce a "personification" in the form of the spirit of the hypnotized individual.

Maire (1933) and de Vesme (1934, 1938) also conceptualized OBEs as subjective phenomena. The author of a book review published in the *Journal of the Society for Psychical Research*, criticized "etheric body" interpretations of OBEs. He stated that considerable evidence existed to show that the mind formed "non-factual images and impressions of bodily location" (p. 212) easily produced by hypnosis (Richmond, 1940, p. 212).

Others with different ideas explored the veridical perceptual potential of OBEs in induced hypnotic experiences, obtaining suggestive results (Cornillier, 1920/1921; Durville, 1909), although from the reports it is not clear if Durville's experimental subjects had the experience of being out of their bodies. Veridical perceptions were considered important by case collectors to combat the hallucinatory explanation of OBEs (Bozzano, 1934/1937, p. 41).

1941-1970

A prominent SPR member, G. N. M. Tyrrell, strongly supported psychological explanations of OBEs. He thought that OB sensations were unconscious constructs, hallucinations, or "mediating vehicles" that brought paranormally acquired information to the conscious part of the mind (Tyrrell, 1946). In another publication, Tyrrell (1942/1953) tried to explain reciprocal apparitions and other OBEs in the context of his theory of apparitions. The theory stated that mid-levels of personality of different individuals communicated with each other through ESP to create an apparitional drama. These levels were referred to as the "producer," in charge of presenting the basic idea to be expressed by the "executor" or "stage carpenter" as an hallucination. As Tyrrell wrote about visual perception of a distant location during a spontaneous OBE:

> The whole scene … is described as if seen from a particular point in space, and gives the impression that the clairvoyant is standing in the room and looking round exactly as a person materially present in the room would do. I suggest this is an elaborate piece of dramatization, and that the clairvoyant is not present as an observer at all. The whole scene … is a dramatic construct worked out by the mid-level producer of the clairvoyant's personality in conjunction with the producers of other persons who possess the relevant information. These producers …

> create an idea-pattern between them, which is given sensory expression by the executor or stage carpenter belonging to the clairvoyant's personality. In the construction of this idea-pattern, some of the items are ... telepathically acquired, and some [are] supplied by the clairvoyant's own ideas and expectations. All the sense-data composing the scene are correlated with astonishing skill to present this scene as viewed from a particular point in space ... (1942/1953, p. 120)

It is interesting that Tyrrell conceptualized the experience as constructed with ESP-acquired information and also with psychological aspects of the subject's personality, such as ideas and expectations. Tyrrell (1946) had pointed out elsewhere the importance of the interaction between psychological and ESP factors in the manifestation of ESP-acquired information, an idea widely discussed by English SPR members (Gurney et al., 1886, Vol. 1, pp. 519-573; Sidgwick, 1923) and by other psychical researchers from the continent (Bozzano, 1907; Warcollier, 1929). His ideas can be considered an elaborate version (with more details on hypothetical subconscious processes) of previously mentioned ideas of reciprocal apparitions. In fact, none of the preceding concepts were as detailed as his.

Other writers mentioned the potential importance to understanding the OBE of variables such as body image (Hebb, 1960, p. 741; Lhermitte, 1957), and vividness of visual imagery (Burt, 1968, p. 80). Lukianowicz (1958) described OBEs as experiences of "pretending character, resembling the make believe nature of the imaginary companions in children" (p. 210).

Some of the speculations were along psychodynamic lines. Fodor (1959) interpreted a patient's OBE reports as dramatizations of the fear of death (p. 175), and a reenactment of a birth fantasy (p. 177). Medlicott (1958) considered the hallucinations of a patient, including OBEs, as a "vivid dramatization of conflict and of her strong transference relationship" (p. 672).

Carl G. Jung brought the point of view of analytical psychology into play in his discussion of personal "visions" and an OBE during near-death circumstances (Jung, 1963, p. 296). He saw such experiences as part of a process of "individuation." This was defined by him as "becoming a single, homogeneous being, and, in so far as 'individuality' embraces our innermost, last, and incomparable uniqueness, it also implies becoming one's own self. We could therefore translate individuation as 'coming to selfhood' or 'self-realization' " (Jung, 1953, p. 171). Also in the Jungian tradition, Jaffe (1963) saw the OBE, as well as the concept of the double, as an expression of archetypal images. She wrote regarding a spontaneous OBE case: "From the psychological point of view we could say that she, or her ego, plunged into the unconscious, and that her journey was actually a journey to an inner psychic realm in which the outer world and the contents of time . . . exist miraculously together in a spaceless and timeless state" (p. 158).

In his book *The Psychology of the Occult* critic D.H. Rawcliffe (1952) figured that the OBE was a type of autoscopic hallucination. When a person saw his or her image, there was a simultaneous "vivid delusion that this hallucinatory image is in fact his real self!" (p. 117). He went on to say that "most of the subjects who have actually experienced 'out-of-the body' hallucinations are psychasthenics or hysterics. ... Many such reported experiences are probably due to the delusions of incipient paranoia" (p. 123).

Others affirmed in the parapsychological literature that, up to the moment of writing, they did not think a good case had been made to consider OBEs as requiring anything other than psychological explanations (Broad, 1959, p. 76; Eastman, 1962, p. 292). As Gardner. Murphy wrote in his book *Challenge of Psychical Research*, OBEs are "not very far from the known terrain of general psychology, which we are beginning to understand more and more without recourse to the paranormal" (Murphy with Dale, 1961, p. 287). Fortunately, these views did not discourage the following work.

An innovative contribution was Celia Green's (1968) widely cited study of spontaneous OBEs entitled *Out-of-the-Body Experiences*. She analyzed the perception reported by her study participants, classifying the variety of sensory modalities appearing in the experiences. Most experiencers had a "greater than usual degree of mental clarity" (p. 81), and some experienced various emotions such as surprise and fear. Green also presented a few cases of OBEs in which the "subject reports obtaining information which was not previously known to him, and which would have been inaccesible to a normal observer in the position of his physical body" (p. 120). In the study these experiences were more common during accidents or illness in a hospital.

These veridical perceptions, studied because they suggest that the experience is more than a hallucination, have been researched by others. Sociologist Hornell Hart (1954) published some new cases in which there were reports of veridical perceptions (see also a case reported by Stratton, 1957). A few years later psychologist Charles T. Tart (1967, 1968) conducted experiments with gifted subjects in which they were tested for their ability to perceive targets during OBEs. One of the studies, in which a woman correctly perceived a five digit number, has become a classic of the modern OBE literature (Tart, 1968).

1970 TO THE PRESENT

In a recent paper published in *Science* the OBE was labelled an illusory experience (Ehrsson, 2007). In fact, psychological concepts reducing the OBE to mental constructs have proliferated in this time period. Horowitz (1970, p. 25) postulated that the cause of OBEs lay in distortions of the body image. Reed (1974, p. 125) suggested that ego-splitting reactions to cope with the loss of love underlay the experience, whereas Ehrenwald (1974) saw the OBE as a regression of the ego in response to a death threat or to the concept of death (see also Le Maléfan, 2005). Among other explanations were residual effects of birth experiences (Honegger, 1983), archetypal images (Fischer, 1975, p. 223), aspects of the fantasy-prone personality (Wilson & Barber, 1983), and "variant interpretations" of lucid dreams (LaBerge, 1985, p. 206).

While several writers have argued that the features of the OBE are different from those of autoscopy (Gabbard & Twemlow, 1984; Irwin, 1985; Kelly et al., 2007), others suggest that autoscopy and OBEs share similar underlying neurological processes (Blanke & Mohr, 2005; Brugger, Regard & Landis, 1997).

Recent writers have considered OBEs as examples of dissociation. For example, Putnam (1989, pp. 21-22) included OBEs in a discussion of "dissociative disorders not included in DSM-II." According to Sanders, McRoberts, and Tollefson (1989): "Dissociative experiences may occur spontaneously as adaptive responses to extreme or prolonged or inescapable stress. For example, a violent sexual assault may provoke a spontaneous out-of-body experience …" (pp. 21-22). More recently psychologists Harvey J. Irwin (2000) and Craig Murray and Jezz

Fox (2005a) have proposed dissociational models of the OBE. Irwin (1996) has stated: "In normal circumstances, our sensory processing of kinesthetic and somaesthetic stimuli serves to maintain the assumption that 'consciousness', or the thinking and perceiving self, is 'in' the physical body. That is, somatic processing ordinarily is integrated with a sense of self. Such is not the case during an OBE. In this sense, the OBE is a dissociative event simply by definition" (p. 158).

Several other writers presented a multitude of ideas, each resting on the assumption that the experience was a psychological construction, albeit accomplished by various means and for a variety of reasons (Brent, 1979; Capel, 1978; Dane, 1975-1976; Del Vecchio, 1981; Gabbard & Twemlow, 1984; pp. 238-240; Ivnisky, 1984; Zusne & Jones, 1982, pp. 137-143).[8]

Perhaps the most important conceptual development has been the presentation of the first formal psychological OBE theories, that is, theories that attempt to relate the OBE to other psychological processes and that present specific predictions. In his theory, Palmer (1978) suggested that the OBE was a response to a body image change perceived to be an unconscious threat to individual identity. He posited that the experience was just one of several alternatives available to reestablish identity (others could be fainting or lucid dreams). The OBE then was an attempt to prevent the threat from reaching consciousness and causing anxiety.

Blackmore (1984a) proposed that an individual's cognitive system created models of reality based on sensory input. Other models using the internal resources of the organism could also be created, but only one model, the most coherent and stable one, could be used by the system at one time. When certain conditions (e.g., stress, sensory deprivation) disrupted the sensory input model, other models took over the system, using resources such as memory and imagination. If one of these models became stronger than the one based on sensory input, it was adopted by the system as the new view of reality. Because bird's eye views are common in imagination, the OBE could be one of these models of reality.[9]

Irwin (1985, pp. 307-323) explained the out of body sensation as an interaction between absorption (or attentional) processes and loss of contact with somatic processes. When external and somatic sensory input was attenuated, the sensation of disconnection to the body could he experienced. Two other cognitive factors were also considered important: preconscious process transformation of the idea of a disembodied consciousness into a "passive, generalized somaesthetic image of a static floating self" (p. 310); and a synesthelic transformation of the somaesthetic image into other sensory modes (e.g., visual and kinesthetic) to account for various aspects of OBE phenomenology. More recently, Irwin (2000) has extended his model to include interactions between dissociation and other factors such as changes in somatic stimuli, synesthesia, and needs:

---

[8] Several psychological speculations have also been presented to explain near-death experiences (e.g., Noyes, 1972; for discussons see Greyson, 1983; Grosso, 1983).

[9] Ideas similar to Blackmore's about the importance of sensory input changes to explain altered states of consciousness have been discussed in the modern (Ludgwig, 1966) and in the old literature. An example of the latter is Prichard's (1837, p. 287) discussion of the action of the imagination during altered states induced by sensory withdrawal. An anonymous (1866/n.d.) author affirmed that the projection of the soul occurs when a "pathological, or simply a physiological cause, produces a total or partial inactivity of the organs of sensation and movement" (p. 22). The more complete the inactivity of the body, the greater the degree of projection.

> Circumstances associated with extreme (either high or low) levels of cortical arousal evoke a state of strong absorption, particularly in the case of a person with a requisite level of absorption capacity and need for absorbing experiences. Alternatively, high absorption may be induced deliberately by the experient. If this state of absorbed mentation is paralleled by a dissociation from somatic (somaesthetic and kinesthetic) stimuli, an OBE may occur . . . .
>
> In instances where the development of the state of somatic dissociation is gradual, the imminent loss of all somatic contact may be signaled by certain innate biological warning signals, the so-called OBE-onset sensations.
>
> The continued orientation of attention away from both exteroceptive and somatic stimuli effectively suspends support for the socially conditioned assumption that the perceiving self is "in" the physical body, fostering the impression that consciousness no longer is tied spatially to the body. This abstract, nonverbal idea of a disembodied consciousness is coded by the cognitive processing system into a passive, generalized somaesthetic image of a static floating self . . . . By means of the dissociative process of synesthesia the somaesthetic image also may be transformed into a visual image, given a basic level of visuospatial skills in the experient.
>
> Strong absorption in this image is a basis for the OBE's perceptual realism. The somaesthetic image also may be transformed into a more dynamic, kinesthetic form, and the experient will have the impression of being able to move in the imaginal out-of-body environment . . . .
>
> The perceived content of the out-of-body environment is governed by short-term needs. A life-threatening situation, for example, may prompt imagery about a paradisial environment; the nature of the latter is held to be a product of social conditioning, although the precise sources of these paradisial stereotypes have yet to be identified fully . . . . Because dissociation is psi conducive it is possible that the out-of-body imagery could incorporate extrasensory information and thereby feature a degree of veridicality not expected of mere fantasy . . . . Eventual dissipation of somatic dissociation or a diversion of attention to somatic or exteroceptive processes brings the individual's OBE to an end (pp. 272-273).[10]

Other developments were studies of special populations such as readers of a New Age magazine (Alvarado & Zingrone, 1999), young children (Blackmore & Wooffitt, 1990), members of an organization concerned with psychic phenomena (Kohr, 1980), and hospital patients (Olson, 1988). More important were the beginnings of systematic studies of psychological correlates of OBEs. This line of research has included surveys of spontaneous OBEs in which investigators have studied the relationship between the experience and personality variables (Alvarado, Zingrone & Dalton, 1998-99; Irwin, 1981a; Gabbard & Twemlow, 1984; Myers, Austrin, Grisso, & Nickesson, 1983; Parra, 2008; Tobacyk & Mitchell, 1987), imaginal and attentional capacities, including imagery (Alvarado & Zingrone, 1994; Blackmore, 1982c, 1987; Myers et al., 1983; Stanford, 1987), and attitudes, altered states of consciousness, and other experiences (Alvarado, Zingrone & Dalton, 1998-99; Blackmore, 1982b; Irwin, 1988; Kohr, 1980; Olson, 1988; Palmer, 1979).

Following on previous speculations of the relationship of OBEs to dissociation, this period presents the first empirical studies of the topic, most of which have shown significant positive results (Alvarado & Zingrone, 1997b; Gow, Lang & Chant, 2004; Irwin, 2000;

[10] Ideas such as Irwin's are somewhat related to previous discussions about the source of subjective anomalous experiences like hallucinations. There is a long tradition of attempts to explain hallucinations as the effect of internal physiological sensations (Azouvi, 1984), as seen in the concept of "visceral hallucinations" (e.g., Tamburini, 1901). Kellog (1897, p. 152) speculated on cenesthesic sensations as a factor affecting cortical centers supposed to project hallucinations. See also note 7.

Murray & Fox, 2005a, 2006; Parra, 2008; Richards, 1991). Many have speculated on the possibility that the OBE is a form of depersonalization (Whitlock, 1978). Marlene Steinberg (1995) asserted that "one of the most common forms of depersonalization is the out-of-body experience" (p. 94). According to some authors: "Depersonalization involves an unpleasant sense of self-observation, an exagerated hyperalertness of one's self. The split between the observing and the acting self can, at its most extreme, become an out-of-body experience, although for most people its not" (Simeon & Abugel, 2006, p. 63). Only a few studies have explored the relationship between depersonalization experiences and OBEs, finding positive relationships (Alvarado & Zingrone, 1997b; Wolfradt & Watzke, 1999), thus transcending the purely theoretical speculations and the clinical observations that predominate in the literature.

Another innovation is the exploration of relationships with absorption (Alvarado & Zingrone, 1997a; Glicksohn, 1990; Irwin, 1980, 1981b, 1985; Parra, 2008), fantasy proneness (Alvarado & Zingrone, 1994; Gow, Lang & Chant, 2004; Parra, 2008), hypnotic susceptibility (Pekala, Kumar, & Cummings, 1992; Spanos & Moretti, 1988), schizotypy (McCreery & Claridge, 1995, 1996a, 2002; Parra, 2008; Wolfradt & Watzke, 1999), body image and other body aspects (Murray & Fox, 2005a, 2005b, 2006; Murray, Wilde & Fox, 2006; Terhune, 2006), hallucinations (McCreery & Claridge, 1995, 1996a, 2002; Parra, 2008), trauma (Irwin, 1996), dreams (Alvarado & Zingrone, 1999, 2007-08; Blackmore, 1982c; Levitan, LaBerge, De Gracia & Zimbardo, 1999; Palmer, 1979), and parapsychological experiences (Alvarado & Zingrone, 1999, 2007-08; Alvarado, Zingrone & Dalton, 1998-99; Kohr, 1980; Palmer, 1979). It has been suggested that some psychological processes may be related to specific OBE characteristics (Alvarado, 1997; Blackmore, 1984a; Honegger, 1983), but only few studies have explored this possibility (Alvarado, 1984; Alvarado & Zingrone, 1999, 2003; Irwin, 1985, p. 273).

While there has been much work with the aftereffects of NDEs (e.g., Flynn, 1986), there is less about OBEs. The existing studies consist of asking experiencers for different types of changes of attitudes and values (Alvarado & Zingrone, 2003; Blackmore, 1984b; Brelaz de Castro, 1998; Gabbard & Twemlow, 1984; Osis, 1979; Tiberi, 1993).

Continuing the earlier work of Green (1968), other students of spontaneous OBEs have reported on aspects of the OBE such as emotions (Tiberi, 1993), and the variety and features of OBE vision and other sensory modalities (Alvarado, 1984; Giovetti, 1983; Holden, 1989; Osis, 1979). There have been some discussions of veridical perceptions during OBEs (Alvarado, 1982, 1983), an important area that may illuminate the perceptual and cognitive processes that are possible during the experience. Some spontaneous experiences have been discussed in relation to experiences in people close to death (Ring & Lawrence, 1993; Sartori, Badham, & Fenwick, 2006), as well as in other conditions (Giovetti, 1983; Myers et al., 1983; Palmer, 1979). The latter refer to survey questions that have not been followed up and which may not indicate veridicality (Alvarado, 1986a). Furthermore, several laboratory studies have tested for veridical perceptions during OBEs (Morris et al, 1978; Osis, 1975; Osis & McCormick, 1980; Palmer & Vassar, 1974; Palmer & Lieberman, 1975; for a review see Alvarado, 1982).

A few researchers have reported experimental studies concerning other variables. This includes the exploration of interactions of psychological correlates such as expectancies, OBE induction procedure, and imagery (e.g., Palmer & Lieberman, 1975; Palmer & Vassar, 1974); concern with the issue of an afterlife in relation to similarity of the subjects' OBEs to those produced spontaneously (Smith & Irwin, 1981); and processing of visual stimuli by the physical body during the OBE; and emotional reactions to the experience (Nash, Lynn, & Stanley, 1984).

CONCLUSION

The psychological approach to OBEs is not new, but extends back at least to the nineteenth century. In this review I have identified some trends in the OBE literature. One of them is the realization that parapsychology has contributed significantly to the study of OBEs. A good number of the publications discussed here were written by parapsychologists or published in the parapsychological literature, particularly before 2000. This explains the emphasis on ESP processes one finds in the ideas of such individuals as Gurney, Hyslop, Tyrrell, Tart, Osis, and Palmer. This state of affairs has changed from the 1980s on as the topic started to be examined in relation to cognitive and personality variables, as well as a variety of phenomena such as dreams and parapsychological experiences, several of which have been published in psychology journals (e.g., Alvarado, Zingrone, & Dalton, 1998-99; Blackmore, 1987; McCreery & Claridge, 2002; Murray & Fox, 2005a). But, as the work of Blackmore and Irwin shows, the study of the psychology of OBEs owes much to the parapsychological context, not to mention the documentation of the existence of the experience in previous times (see Alvarado, 1989, in press). This is largely the case because individuals involved in parapsychology are by definition interested in unusual mental phenomena and in the possibility of finding evidence for the existence of the mind independent of the physical body.

As usually happens in research fields, there are some differences of emphasis and detail between the earlier and the most recent research. As is to be expected, more recent theoretical concepts today are more detailed than the early ones had been. More importantly, the recent period shows an unprecedented interest in the OBE as a psychological experience, and in research exploring such topic. The differences reflect methodological, and particularly, theoretical change in psychology and parapsychology. The development of psychodynamic concepts of OBEs, for example, follows the rapid development of dynamic psychiatry during the 20th century (Ellenberger, 1970).

It is largely after 1980 that one finds most of the attempts to study empirically psychological correlates of OBEs. This is due in part to the impact of interests and developments in psychological measurement (McReynolds, 2001), and the rise of modern cognitive psychology (Gardner, 1987), transpersonal psychology (Chinen, 1996), and the New Age movement (Hanegraaff, 1998), which brought attention to unusual phenomena. Interest in OBE research was also part of the modern attention of psychology to imagery, dreams, dissociation, and, more generally, to states of consciousness (Baruss, 2003; Farthing, 1992; Ross, 1996). In a period when many psychologists were studying dreams, the hypnagogic state, hypnosis, and meditation (Ludwig, 1966; Tart, 1969; Wolman & Ullman, 1986), it was not surprising that OBEs received more scientific attention.

In the parapsychological literature, though on a smaller scale, similar issues were addressed, that is, some parapsychologists turned their attention to altered states of consciousness (Alvarado, 1998; Honorton, 1977; Parker, 1975, 2003) and to imagery (George & Krippner, 1984). With this as a background, it is reasonable to assume that the interest in

OBEs during the modern period increased because the experience was seen as a variation of, or as related to, the above-mentioned psychological variables or states of consciousness.

Regardless of all of this interest in the psychology of OBEs both in the past as well as in recent times, researchers have conducted little programmatic research. Nor have they systematically tested the predictions of the few models that have attempted to account for OBEs (for an exception see Irwin, 1985). In fact most of the attempts to explain the OBE psychologically have remained at the level of conjecture, such as assuming it is a hallucination, or depersonalization. Furthermore, there has been a lack of attempts to conduct studies to assess the importance of different factors—such as imagery, dissociation, trauma, and dreams—using multivariate analyses in a single study.

The panoramic view I have presented also shows that there is a need for studies of other topics. Two possible lines of research are the after-effects of OBEs and the relationship of the experience to psychopathology. Another important topic is the perceptions reported during the OBE. Regardless of the descriptive work already reported with spontaneous experiences about such aspects as the frequency of sensory modalities and the quality of the perceptions (e.g., Alvarado, 1984; Green, 1968), there is the issue of veridical perceptions (Alvarado, 1982, 1983). Future studies along this line or work—admittedly controversial in many circles—has the potential of providing further evidence for the possibility that the experience has aspects that are not hallucinatory. Unfortunately this aspect of the OBE remains sadly forgotten due to worldviews that define such features as absurd or impossible.

Perhaps all of this lack of research may be expected in an underdeveloped and neglected field such as that of OBE studies. But it is to be hoped that future research will be shaped around specific models and that it can refine and replicate previous findings in order to further develop our understanding of the psychological aspects of OBEs.

REFERENCES

Alvarado, C. S. (1982). ESP during out-of-body experiences: A review of experimental studies. Journal of Parapsychology, *46*, 209-230.

Alvarado, C. S. (1983). ESP and out-of-body experiences: A review of spontaneous studies. Parapsychology Review, *4*(4), 1, 1-13.

Alvarado, C. S. (1984). Phenomenological aspects of out-of-body experiences: A report of three studies. *Journal of the American Society for Psychical Research, 78*, 219-240.

Alvarado, C. S. (1986a). ESP during out-of-body experiences: A research and methodological note. *Journal of the Society for Psychical Research, 53*, 393-397.

Alvarado, C. S. (1986b). Research on spontaneous out-of-body experiences: A review of modern developments, 1960-1984. In B. Shapin & L. Coly (Eds.), *Current trends in psi research* (pp. 140-167). New York: Parapsychology Foundation.

Alvarado, C. S. (1988). Aspectos psicológicos de las experiencias fuera dcl cuerpo: Revisión de estudios de casos espontáneos [Psychological aspects of out-of-body experiences: A review of spontaneous case studies]. *Revista Puertorriqueña de Psicología, 5*, 31-43.

Alvarado, C. S. (1989). Trends in the study of out-of-body experiences: An overview of developments since the nineteenth century. *Journal of Scientific Exploration, 3*, 27-42.

Alvarado, C. S. (1992). The psychological approach to out-of-body experiences: A review of early and modern developments. *Journal of Psychology, 126*, 237-250.

Alvarado, C. S. (1997). *Mapping the characteristics of out-of-body experiences. Journal of the American Society for Psychical Research, 91*, 13-30.

Alvarado, C. S. (1998). ESP and altered states of consciousness: An overview of conceptual and research trends. *Journal of Parapsychology, 62*, 27-63.

Alvarado, C. S. (2000). Out-of-body experiences. In E. Cardeña, S.J. Lynn, & S. Krippner (Eds.), *Varieties of anomalous experiences* (pp. 183-218). Washington, DC: American Psychological Association.

Alvarado, C. S. (2002). Dissociation in Britain during the late nineteenth century: The Society for Psychical Research, 1882-1900. *Journal of Trauma and Dissociation, 3*, 9-33.

Alvarado, C. S. (in press). The spirit in out-of-body experiences: Historical and conceptual notes. In *Spirituality, Science and the Paranormal.* Bloomfield, CT: Academy of Spirituality and Paranormal Studies.

Alvarado, C. S., & Zingrone, N. L. (1994). Individual differences in aura vision: Relationship to visual imagery and imaginative-fantasy experiences. *European Journal of Parapsychology, 10*, 1-30.

Alvarado, C. S., & Zingrone, N. L. (1997a). Relación entre la experiencia fuera del cuerpo y la absorción: Estudios con participantes Puertorriqueños y Norteamericanos [Relationship between out-of-body experiences and absorption: Studies with Puerto Rican and North American participants]. *Revista Argentina de Psicología Paranormal, 8*, 249-261.

Alvarado, C.S., & Zingrone, N.L. (1997b). Out-of-body experiences and dissociation. Paper presented at the 40th Annual Convention of the Parapsychological Association, August, Brighton, England.

Alvarado, C. S., & Zingrone, N. L. (1999). Out-of-body experiences among readers of a Spanish New Age magazine. *Journal of the Society for Psychical Research, 63*, 65-85.

Alvarado, C. S., & Zingrone, N. L. (2003). Exploring the factors related to the aftereffects of out-of-body experiences. *Journal of the Society for Psychical Research, 67*, 161-183.

Alvarado, C. S., & Zingrone, N. L. (2007-08). Interrelationships of psychic experiences, dream recall and lucid dreams in a survey with Spanish participants. *Imagination, Cognition and Personality, 27*, 63-69.

Alvarado, C.S., Zingrone, N. L., & Dalton, K. (1998-99). Out-of-body experiences: Alterations of consciousness and the five-factor model of personality. *Imagination, Cognition and Personality, 18*, 297-317.

Anonymous. (n.d.). A jovem cataleptic da Suabia: Estudo psicológico [The cataleptic youngster of Suabia: A psychological study]. *Revista Espírita, 9*, 17-23. (Original work published in French 1866)

Azouvi, F. (1984). Des sensations internes aux hallucinations corporelles: De Cabanis a Lélut [Internal sensations of corporeal hallucinations: From Cabanis to Lelut]. *Revue internationale d'histoire de la psychiatric, 2*, 5-19.

Baruss, I. (2003). *Alterations of consciousness: An empirical analysis for social scientists.* Washington, DC: American Psychological Association.

Blackmore, S. J. (1982a). *Beyond the body: An investigation of out-of-body experiences.* London: Heinemann.

Blackmore, S. J. (1982b). Have you ever had an OBE?: The wording of the question. *Journal of the Society for Psychical Research, 51*, 292-302.

Blackmore, S. J. (1982c). Out of-the-body experiences, lucid dreams and imagery: Two surveys. *Journal of the American Society for Psychical Research, 76*, 301-317.

Blackmore, S. J. (1984a). A psychological theory of the out-of-body experience. *Journal of Parapsychology, 48*, 201-218.

Blackmore, S. J. (1984b). A postal survey of OBEs and other experiences. *Journal of the Society for Psychical Research, 52*, 225-244.

Blackmore, S. J. (1987). Where am I? Perspectives in imagery and the out-of-body experience. *Journal of Mental Imagery, 11*, 53-66.

Blackmore, S. J., & Wooffitt, R. C. (1990). Out-of-the body experiences in young children. *Journal of the Society for Psychical Research, 56*, 155-158.

Blakeman, R. (1849). *A philosophical essay on credulity and superstition.* New York: D. Appleton.

Blanke, O., Landis, T., Spinelli, L., & Seeck, M. (2004). Out-of-body experience and autoscopy of neurological origin. *Brain, 127*, 243-258.

Blanke, O., & Mohr, C. (2005). Out-of-body experience, heautoscopy, and autoscopic hallucination of neurological origin: Implications for neurocognitive mechanisms of corporeal awareness and self consciousness. *Brain Research Reviews, 50*, 184-199.

Bozzano, E. (1907). Symbolism and metapsychical phenomena. *Annals of Psychical Science, 6*, 235-259.

Bozzano, E. (1937). *Les phénomènes de bilocation.* Paris: Jean Meyer. (Original work published, 1934)

Brandt, C., Brechtelsbauer, D., Bien, C.G., Reiners, K. (2005). "Out-of-body experience" als mögliches Anfallssymptom bei einem Patienten mit rechtsparietaler Läsion [Out-of-body experience as possible seizure symptom in a patient with a right parietal lesion]. *Nervenarzt , 76*, 1259-1262.

Brelaz de Castro, J.F. (1998). Experiencias fuera del cuerpo: Una encuesta sobre estudiantes universitarios en Brasil [Out of body experiences: A survey of university students in Brazil]. *Revista Argentina de Psicología Paranormal, 9*, 11-27.

Brent, S. B. (1979). Deliberately induced, premortem, out-of-body experiences: An experimental and theoretical approach. In R. Kastenbaum (Ed.), *Between life and death* (pp. 89-123). New York: Springer.

Bret, P. T. (1939). *Les métapsychoses: La métapsychorragie, la télépathie, la hantise. Vol. 1: Introduction et la métapsychorragie fantasmale* [The metapsychoses: Metapsychorrhagy, telepathy, hauntings. Vol. 1: Introduction and phantasmal Metapsychorrhagy. Paris: J. B. Baillière.

Brierre de Boismont, A. (1853). *Hallucinations: Or, the rational history of apparitions. visions, dreams, ecstasy, magnetism, and somnambulism* (translated from the second French edition). Philadelphia: Lindsay and Blakiston. (First edition published in French 1845)

Broad, C. D. (1959). Dreaming and some of its implications. *Proceedings of the Society for Psychical Research, 52*, 53-78.

Brugger, P., Regard, M., & Landis, T. (1997). Illusory reduplication of one's own body: Phenomenology and classification of autoscopic phenomena. *Cognitive Neuropsychiatry, 2*, 19-38.

Burt, C. (1968). *Psychology and psychical research.* London: Society for Psychical Research.

Buvet, J. B. (1902). L'auto-represéntation organique ou hallucination cenesthesique dans l'hysterie [Organic auto-representation or cenesthesic hallucinations in hysteria]. *Gazette des hospitaux, 75*, 1305-1308.

Capel, M. (1978). Las experiencias extracorporales: Revisión de la casuística y algunas aportaciones explicativas [Extracorporal experiences: A review of cases and some suggested explanations. *Psi Comunicación, 4*, 49-71.

Carpenter, W. B. (1874). *Principles of mental physiology*. New York: D. Appleton.

Carr, B. (2008). Worlds apart? Can psychical research bridge the gulf between matter and mind? *Proceedings of the Society for Psychical Research, 59*, 1-96.

Chinen, A. B. (1996). The emergence of transpersonal psychiatry. In B.W. Scotton, A.B. Chinen, & J.R. Battista (Eds.), *Textbook of transpersonal psychiatry and psychology* (pp. 9-18). New York: Basic Books.

Cornillier, P.-E. (1921). *The survival of the soul and its evolution after death.* London: Kegan, Paul, Trench, Trübner. (First published in French, 1920).

Dane, L. (1975-1976). Astral travel: A psychological overview. *Journal of Altered States of Consciousness, 2*, 249-258.

Del Vecchio, L. (1981). L'expérience de hors-corps: Indice de pathologi ou d'actualisation de soi? [The out of body experience: Indication of pathology or of self- actualization?] *Bulletin Psilog, 1*(1), 10-11.

Durville, H. (1909). *Le fantôme des vivants.* Paris: Librairie du Magnétisme.

Eastman, M. (1962). Out-of-the-body experiences. *Proceedings of the Society for Psychical Research, 53*, 287-309.

Ehrenwald, J. (1974). Out-of-the-body experiences and the denial of death. *Journal of Nervous and Mental Disease, 159*, 227-233.

Ehrsson, H. H. (2007). The experimental induction of out-of-body experiences. *Science, 317*, 1048.

Ellenberger, H. F. (1970). *The discovery of the unconscious*. New York: Basic Books.

Farthing, G. W. (1992). *The psychology of consciousness.* Englewood Cliffs, NJ: Prentice Hall.

Fischer, R. (1975). Cartography of inner spaces. In R. K. Siegel and L. J. West (Eds.), Hallucinations: Behavior, experience, and theory (pp. 197-239). New York: Wiley.

Flynn, C. P. (1986). *After the beyond: Human transformation and the near-death experience.* Englewood Cliffs, NJ: Prentice-Hall.

Fodor, N. (1959). *The haunted mind.* New York: Helix Press.

Gabbard, G. O., & Twemlow, S. W. (1984). *With the eyes of the mind: An empirical analysis of out-of-body states*. New York: Praeger.

Gardner, H. (1987). *The mind's new science: A history of the cognitive revolution.* New York: Basic Books

Gauld, A. (1968). *The founders of psychical research.* London: Routledge & Kegan Paul.

Giovetti, P. (1983). *Viaggi senza corpo* [Travels without the body] Milano: Armenia.

Glicksohn, J. (1990). Belief in the paranormal and subjective paranormal experience. *Personality and Individual Differences, 11*, 675-683.

George, L., & Krippner, S. (1984). Mental imagery and psi phenomena: A review. In S. Krippner (Ed.), *Advances in parapsychological research 4* (pp. 64-82). Jefferson, NC: McFarland.

Gow, K., Lang, T., & Chant, D. (2004). Fantasy proneness, paranormal beliefs and personality features in out-of-body experiences. *Contemporary Hypnosis, 27*, 107-125.

Green, C. (1968). *Out-of-the-body experiences*. London: Hamish Hamilton.

Greyson, B. (1983). The psychodynamics of near-death experiences. *Journal of Nervous and Mental Disease, 171*, 376-381.

Greyson, B. (2000). Dissociation in people who have had near-death experiences: Out of their bodies or out of their minds? *Lancet, 355*, 460-463.

Grosso, M. (1983). Jung, parapsychology, and the near-death experience: Toward a transpersonal paradigm. *Anabiosis, 3*, 3-38.

Gurney, E., Myers, F. W. H., & Podmore, F. (1886). *Phantasms of the living* (2 vols.). London: Trübner.

Haddock, J. W. (1851). *Somnolism & psycheism* (2nd rev. ed.). London: James S. Hodson. (First edition published 1849)

Hands, W. (1845). Case of Ellen Dawson. *Zoist, 3*, 226-236

Hanegraaf, W. J. (1998). *New Age religion and Western culture: Esotericism in the mirror of secular thought.* Albany, NY: State University of New York Press.

Harrison, W. (1879). *Spirits before our eyes*. London: W.H. Harrison.

Hart, H. (1954). ESP projection: Spontaneous cases and the experimental method. *Journal of the American Society for Psychical Research, 48*, 121-146.

Hebb, D. O. (1960). The American revolution. *American Psychologist, 15*, 735-745.

Holden, J. M. (1989). Visual perception during naturalistic near-death out-of body experiences. *Journal of Near-Death Studies, 7*, 107-120.

Honegger, B. (1983). The OBE as a near-birth experience. In W. G. Roll (Ed.), *Research in parapsychology 1982* (pp. 230-231). Metuchen, NJ: Scarecrow Press.

Honorton, C. (1977). Psi and internal attention states. In B. B. Wolman (Ed.), *Handbook of parapsychology* (pp. 435-472). New York: Van Nostrand Reinhold.

Horowitz, M. J. (1970). *Image formation and cognition.* New York: Appleton-Century-Crofts.

Hyslop, J. H. (1912). A review, a record and a discussion. *Journal of the American Society for Psychical Research, 6*, 490-516.

Irwin, H. J. (1980). Out of the body down under: Some cognitive characteristics of Australian students reporting OBEs. *Journal of the Society for Psychical Research, 50*, 448-459.

Irwin, H. J. (1981a). The psychological function of out-of-body experiences: So who needs the out-of-body experience? *Journal of Nervous and Mental Disease, 169*, 244-248.

Irwin, H. J. (1981b). Some psychological dimensions of the out-of-body experience. *Parapsychology Review, 12*(4), 1-4.

Irwin, H. J. (1985). *Flight of mind: A psychological study of the out-of-body experience.* Metuchen, NJ: Scarecrow Press.

Irwin, H. J. (1988). Out-of-body experiences and attitudes to life and death. *Journal of the American Society for Psychical Research, 82*, 237-251.

Irwin, H. J. (1996). Childhood antecedents of out-of-body and déjà vu experiences. *Journal of the American Society for Psychical Research, 90*, 157-173

Irwin, H. J. (2000). The disembodied self: An empirical study of dissociation and the out-of-body experience. *Journal of Parapsychology, 64*, 261-277.

Irwin, H. J., & Watt, C. A. (2007). *An introduction to parapsychology* (5th ed.). Jefferson, NC: McFarland.

Ivnisky, D. (1984). Estudio de las experiencias de "salirse del cuerpo": Algunas consideraciones [The study of experiences of "leaving the body": Some considerations. *Cuadernos de Parapsicologia, 17*(2), 15-18.

Jaffe, A. (1963). *Apparitions and precognition.* New Hyde Park, NY: University Books.

Jung, C. G. (1953). Two essays on analytical psychology. In H. Read, M. Fordham, & G. Adler (Eds.), *The collected works of C. G. Jung* (Vol. 7, pp. 119-239). New York: Pantheon Books.

Jung, C. G. (1963). *Memories, dreams, reflections* (edited by A. Jaffe). New York: Vantage Books.

Kellog, T. H. (1897). A *text-book on mental diseases.* New York: William Wood.

Kelly, E., Kelly, E.W., Crabtree, A., Gauld, A., Grosso, M., & Greyson, B. (2007). *Irreducible mind: Toward a psychology for the 21st century.* Lanham, MD: Rowman & Littlefield.

Kohr, R. L. (1980). A survey of psi experiences among members of a special population. *Journal of the American Society for Psychical Research, 74*, 395-411.

LaBerge, S. (1985). *Lucid dreaming.* Los Angeles: Tarcher.

Le Maléfan, P. (2005). La « sortie hors du corps » est-elle pensable par nos modèles cliniques et psychopathologiques ? Essai de clinique d'une marge: A propos d'un cas [Is "leaving the body" acceptable by our clinical and psychopathological model? Clinical essay of the margin: About a case]. *L'Evolution psychiatrique, 70*, 513-534.

Levitan, L., LaBerge, S., DeGracia, D.J., & Zimbardo, P. G. (1999). Out-of-body experiences, dreams, and REM sleep. *Sleep and Hypnosis, 1*, 186-196.

Lhermitte, J. (1957). Bilocation phenomena in neuropathology. *Proceedings of four conferences of parapsychological studies* (pp. 168-169). New York: Parapsychology Foundation.

Long, J., & Holden, J. M. (2007). Does the arousal system contribute to near-death and out-of-body experiences? A summary and response. *Journal of Near-Death Studies, 25*, 135-169.

Ludwig, A. M. (1966). Altered states of consciousness. *Archives of General Psychiatry, 15*, 225-234.

Lukianowicz. N. (1958). Autoscopic phenomena. *A.M.A. Archives of Neurology and Psychiatry, 80*, 199-220.

Maire, M. (1933). Chronique: L'exteriorisation de la conscience: Argument en favour du spiritisme? [Chronique: Exteriorization of consciousness: An argument in favor of spiritism?] *Revue métapsychique*, No. 1, 65-71.

McCreery, C. (1997). Hallucinations and arousability: Pointers to a theory of psychosis. In G. Claridge (Ed.), *Schizotypy: Implications for illness and health* (pp. 252-273). New York: Oxford University Press.

McCreery, C., & Claridge, G. (1996). Out-of-body experiences and personality. *Journal of the Society for Psychical Research, 60*, 129-148.

McCreery, C., & Claridge, G. (1996a). A study of hallucination in normal states: I. Self report data. *Personality and Individual Differences, 21*, 739-747.

McCreery, C., & Claridge, G. (1996b). A study of hallucination in normal states: II. Electrophysiological data. *Personality and Individual Differences, 21*, 749-758.

McCreery, C., & Claridge, G. (2002). Healthy schizotypy: The case of out-of-the-body experiences. *Personality and Individual Differences, 22*, 141-154.

McReynolds, P. (2001). History of psychological assessment. In W.E. Craighead & C.B. Nemeroff (Eds.), *The Corsini encyclopedia of psychology and behavioral science* (pp. 1284-1288). New York: Wiley.

Medlicott, R. W. (1958). An inquiry into the significance of hallucinations with special reference to their occurrence in the sane. *International Record of Medicine, 171*, 664-677.

Morin, A.S. (1860). *Du magnétisme et des sciences occultes* [Magnetism and occult sciences] Paris: Germer Baillière.

Morris, R.L., Harary, S.B., Janis, J., Hartwell, J., & Roll, W.G. (1978). Studies of communication during out-of-body experiences. *Journal of the American Society for Psychical Research, 72*, 1-21.

Muldoon, S.J., & Carrington, H. (1951). *The phenomena of astral projection.* London: Rider.

Murphy, G., with Dale, L. A. (1961). *Challenge of psychical research.* New York: Harper & Row.

Murray, C., & Fox, J. (2005a). Dissociational body experiences: Differences between respondents with and without prior out-of-body experiences. *British Journal of Psychology, 96*, 441-456.

Murray, C.D., & Fox, J. (2005b). The out-of-body experience and body image: Differences between experients and non-experients. *Journal of Nervous and Mental Disease, 193*, 70-72.

Murray, C., & Fox, J. (2006). Differences in body image between people reporting near-death and spontaneous out-of-body experiences. *Journal of the Society for Psychical Research, 70*, 98-109.

Murray, C., Wilde, D., & Fox, J. (2006). Self-concept and body investment in out-of-body experients. *European Journal of Parapsychology, 21*, 27-37.

Myers, S. A., Austrin, H. R., Grisso, J. T., & Nickesson, R. C. (1983). Personality characteristics as related to the out-of-body experience. *Journal of Parapsychology, 47*, 131-144.

Nash, M. R., Lynn, S. J., & Stanley, S. M. (1984). The direct hypnotic suggestion of altered mind/body perception. *American Journal of Clinical Hypnosis, 27*, 95- 102.

Nelson, K. R., Mattingle, M., & Schmitt, F. A. (2007). Out-of-body experience and arousal. *Neurology, 68*, 794-795.

Noyes, R. (1972). The experience of dying. *Psychiatry, 35*, 174-184.

Olson, M. (1988). The incidence of out-of-body experiences in hospitalized patients. *Journal of Near-Death Studies, 6*, 169-174.

Osis, K. (1975). Perceptual experiments on out-of-body experiences. In J. D. Morris, W. G. Roll, & R. L. Morris (Eds.), *Research in parapsychology 1974* (pp. 53-55). Metuchen, NJ: Scarecrow Press.

Osis, K. (1979). Insider's view of the OBE: A questionnaire study. In W.G. Roll (Ed.), *Research in parapsychology 1978* (pp. 50-52). Metuchen, NJ: Scarecrow Press. (Abstract)

Osis, K., & McCormick, D. (1980). Kinetic effects at the oestensible location of an out-of-body projection during perceptual testing. *Journal of the American Society for Psychical Research, 74*, 319-329.

Osis, K., & Mitchell, J. L. (1977). Physiological correlates of reported out-of-body experiences. *Journal of the Society for Psychical Research, 49*, 525-536.

Osty, E. (1930). La vision de soi [Seeing the self). *Revue métapsychique*, No. 3, 185-197.

Osty, E. (1933). Transmission de pensée expérimentale et télépathie spontanée [Experimental thought transmission and spontaneous telepathy]. *Revue métapsychique*, No. 1, 1-40.

Palmer, J. (1978). The out-of-body experience: A psychological theory. *Parapsychology Review, 9*(5), 19-22.

Palmer, J. (1979). A community mail survey of psychic experiences. *Journal of the American Society for Psychical Research, 73*, 221-251.

Palmer, J., & Lieberman, R. (1975). The influence of psychological set on ESP and out-of-body experiences. *Journal of the American Society for Psychical Research, 69*,193-213.

Palmer, J., & Vassar, C. (1974). ESP and out-of-the-body experiences: An exploratory study. *Journal of the American Society for Psychical Research, 68*, 257-280.

Parker, A. (1975). *States of mind: ESP and altered states of consciousness.* New York: Taplinger.

Parker, A. (2003). Psi and altered states. In L. Storm & M. Thalbourne (Eds.), *Parapsychology in the 21st Century* (pp. 65-89). Jefferson, NC: McFarland.

Parra, A. (2008). Esperienze fuori del corpo ed esperienze allucinatorie: Un approccio psicologico [Our-of-body experiences and hallucinatory experiences: A psychological approach]. *Quaderni di Parapsicologia, 39*, 32-51.

Pekala, R.J., Kumar, V.K., & Cummings, J. (1992). Types of high hypnotically susceptible individuals and reported attitudes and experiences of the paranormal and the anomalous. *Journal of the American Society for Psychical Research, 86*, 135-150.

Podmore, F. (1894). *Apparitions and thought-transference.* London: Walter Scott.

Poynton, J. (2001). *Challenges of out-of-body experience: Does psychical research fully met them? Journal of the Society for Psychical Research, 65*, 194-206.

Prichard, J. C. (1837). *A treatise on insanity and other disorders affecting the mind.* Philadelphia: Haswell, Barrington, and Haswell.

Putnam, F. W. (1989). *Diagnosis and treatment of multiple personality disorder.* New York: Guilford Press.

Rawcliffe, D. H. (1952). *The psychology of the occult.* London: Derricke Ridway.

Reed, G. (1974). *The psychology of anomalous experience.* Boston: Houghton-Mifflin.

Richards, D.G. (1991). A study of the correlation between subjective psychic experiences and dissociative experiences. *Dissociation, 4*, 83-91.

Richet, C. (1887*). L' homme et l' intelligence* (2nd ed.) [Man and intelligence]. Paris: Félix Alcan. (First edition published 1884)

Richet, C. (1922). *Traité de métapsychique* [Treatise on metapsychics]. Paris: Félix Alcan.

Richmond, K. (1940). Review of Why I do Believe in Survival, by B. A. Collins. *Journal of the Society for Psychical Research, 31*, 210-213.

Ring, K. (1980). *Life at Death: A scientific investigation of the near-death experience.* New York: Coward, McCann & Geoghegan.

Ring, K., & Lawrence, M. (1993). Further evidence for veridical perception during near-death experience. *Journal of Near-Death Studies, 11*, 223-229.

Ross, C. A. (1996). History, phenomenology, and epidemiology of dissociation. In L.K. Michelson and W.J. Ray (Eds.), *Handbook of dissociation: Theoretical, Empirical, and clinical perspectives* (pp. 3-24). New York: Plenum Press.

Sanders, B., McRoberts, G., & Tollefson, C. (1989). Childhood stress and dissociation in a college population. *Dissociation, 2*, 17-23.

Sartori, P., Badham, P., & Fenwick, P. (2006). A prospectively near-death experience with corroborated out-of-body perceptions and unexplained healing. *Journal of Near-Death Studies, 25*, 69-84.

Sidgwick, Mrs. H. (1891). On the evidence for clairvoyance. *Proceedings of the Society for Psychical Research, 7*, 30-99.

Sidgwick, Mrs. H. (1923). On hindrances and complications in telepathic communication. *Proceedings of the Society for Psychical Research, 34*, 28-69.

Simeon, D., & Abugel, J. (2006). *Feeling unreal: Depersonalization disorder and the loss of the self.* Oxford: Oxford University Press.

Smith, P., & Irwin, H. (1981). Out-of-body experiences, needs and the experimental approach: A laboratory study. *Parapsychology Review, 12*(3), 1-4.

Sollier, P. (1903). *Les phénomènes d'autoscopie* [The phenomena of autoscopy]. Paris: Félix Alcan.

Spanos, N. P., & Moretti, P. (1988). Correlates of mystical and diabolical experiences in a sample of female university students. *Journal for the Scientific Study of Religion, 27*, 106-116.

Stanford, R. G. (1987). The out-of-body experience as an imaginal journey: The developmental perspective. *Journal of Parapsychology, 51*, 137-155.

Steinberg, M. (1995). *Handbook for the assessment of dissociation: A clinical guide.* Washington, DC: American Psychiatric Press.

Stratton, F. J. M. (1957). Correspondence: An out-of-the-body experience combined with ESP. *Journal for the Society for Psychical Research, 39*, 92-97.

Tamburini, A. (1901). Les aberrations de la conscience viscerale [The aberrations of the visceral consciousness). In P. Janet (Ed.), *IVe congrès international de psychologie* (pp. 216-220). Paris: Félix Alcan.

Tart, C.T. (1967). A second psychophysiological study of out-of-the body experiences in a gifted subject. *International Journal of Parapsychology, 9*, 251-258.

Tart, C.T. (1968). A psychophysiological study of out-of-the body experiences in a selected subject. *Journal of the American Society for Psychical Research, 62*, 3-27.

Tart, C. T. (Ed.). (1969). *Altered states of consciousness.* New York: Wiley.

Tobacyk, J. S., & Mitchell, T. P. (1987). The out-of-body experience and personality adjustment. *Journal of Nervous and Mental Disease, 175*, 367-370.

Terhune, D.B. (2006). Dissociative alterations in body image among individuals reporting out-of-body experiences: A conceptual replication. *Perceptual and Motor Skills, 103*, 76-80.

Tiberi, E. (1993). Extrasomatic emotions. *Journal of Near-Death Studies, 11*, 149-170.

Turvey, V. N. (n.d., ca 1911). *The beginnings of seership.* London: Stead's.

Tyrrell, G. N. M. (1946). The modus operandi of paranormal cognition. *Proceedings of the Society for Psychical Research, 48*, 65-120.

Tyrrell, G. N. M. (1953). *Apparitions.* London: Gerald Duckworth. (Original work published 1942)

Van Lommel, P., van Wees, R., Meyers, V., & Elfferich, I. (2001). Near-death experience in survivors of cardiac arrest: A prospective study in the Netherlands. *Lancet, 358,* 2039-2045.

de Vesme, C. (1934). Chronique: A propos de 'bilocation' [Chronicle: A propos of 'bilocation'). *Revue métapsychique,* No. 4, 274-275.

de Vesme. C. (1938). Review of The Case for Astral Projection. by S. J. Muldoon. *Revue métapsychique,* No. 3, 224-225.

Warcollier, R. (1929). La télépathie: Ses rapports avec le subconscient et l'inconscient [Telepathy: Its relationship to the subconscious and the unconscious). *Revue métapsychique,* No. 4, 270-287.

Whitlock, F. A. (1978). The psychiatry and psychopathology of paranormal phenomena. *Australian and New Zealand Journal of Psychiatry, 12,* 11-19.

Wilson, S. C., & Barber, T. X. (1983). The fantasy-prone personality: Implications for understanding imagery, hypnosis, and parapsychological phenomena. In A. A. Sheikh (Ed.), *Imagery: Current theory, research, and application* (pp. 340-387). New York: Wiley.

Wolfradt, U., & Watzke, S. (1999). Deliberate out-of-body experiences, depersonalization, schizotypal traits, and thinking styles. *Journal of the American Society for Psychical Research, 93,* 249-257.

Wolman, B. B., & Ullman, M. (Eds.). (1986). *Handbook of states of consciousness.* New York: Van Nostrand Reinhold.

Woodhouse, M. (1994). Out-of-body experiences and the mind-body problem. *New Ideas in Psychology, 12,* 1-17.

Zusne, L., & Jones, W. H. (1982). *Anomalistic psychology.* Hillsdale, NJ: Lawrence Erlbaum.

In: Psychological Scientific Perspectives on Out of Body … ISBN: 978-1-60741-705-7
Editor: Craig D. Murray

Chapter 2

A Psychological Theory of the Out-of-Body Experience[1]

Susan J. Blackmore

Abstract

A psychological theory of the out-of-body experience (OBE) is presented. It suggests that altered states of consciousness (ASCs) in general and OBEs in particular are best understood in terms of "models of reality." Two central proposals are that (1) the cognitive system builds many models at once but at any time one and only one is taken to represent external "reality" and that (2) this is the most complex, stable, or coherent model. Normally the chosen model is built largely from sensory input, but when deprived of sensory information, under stress and so on, this can break down, allowing other models to take over. In an attempt to regain input control, the cognitive system may build the best model it can of the surroundings it thinks it should be seeing. This has to be built from information in memory and imagination. Memory models are often more abstract and schematic than perceptual models and may take a bird's-eye view. The theory suggests that if such a model becomes more stable than the input model, it takes over as "reality." The imagined world then seems real, and an OBE has occurred. The phenomenology of the OBE is discussed in light of this theory, and some testable predictions are made. Other ASCs are briefly considered.

In a recent review of psychological models of the out-of-body experience (OBE), Rogo (1982) argues that none of the models are sufficiently developed to provide a valid alternative to paranormal or ecsomatic models. In particular, he argues that none of them can explain much of the phenomenology of the OBE. In an attempt to rectify this situation, I would like to present a psychological theory of the OBE that may go some way toward meeting Rogo's objections. I shall try to present it as clearly and in as much detail as possible so that it can more easily be open to criticism and empirical test.

---

[1] This chapter originally appeared in the Journal of Parapsychology (Blackmore, S.J. (1984) A Psychological Theory of the Out-of-body Experience. Journal of Parapsychology, *48*, 201-218.) The editor would like to express thanks to John Palmer and the Rhine Research Center for permission to reprint this material here.

I shall start by treating the OBE as one of many possible, more or less discrete, altered states of consciousness (ASCs). However, there is no generally acceptable theory of ASCs that provides even the hope of an explanation for the OBE.

We might first ask what is altered in an altered state, but even this is very hard to answer. Theories of consciousness do not provide much help. They tend to be highly reductionistic, very vague, or aimed at aspects irrelevant to ASCs (e.g., Underwood & Stevens, 1979, 1981; Valle & von Eckartsberg, 1981). Research specifically on ASCs has also often been mainly reductionistic, relating reported states to measurable physiological variables, drugs given, or other induction procedures (see, e.g., Davidson & Davidson, 1980). This is important work, but limited. For example, if we know that EEG patterns are altered in an OBE, this is useful but does not tell us anything about what the OBE is like. If different ASCs are associated with the same EEG patterns, it is also clear that the EEG is useless as a means of identifying or defining the state. Similarly, reducing an ASC to simple learning or habituation processes (e.g., Neher, 1980) is interesting, but again limited. Rather different is Tart's (1980) "systems approach to ASCs." He discusses the processes that might be involved in the maintenance and disruption of discrete states of consciousness, but he has not applied these ideas to a detailed theory of the OBE.

To get closer to understanding the OBE as an altered state, we need to be very careful about the level of explanation at which we begin. Any problem can be tackled at different levels of explanation. In the case of much of cognitive psychology, there are now explanatory models at several levels and hopes of integrating them into fuller theories (see, for example, Marr, 1982). Such success has not come solely by starting at the bottom and working up. Indeed, Dennet (1983) has argued that starting at the top has usually been more productive, although both are necessary. I suggest that in the case of the OBE in particular (and ASCs in general) we have not been starting in the most fruitful place. We need to look to a much higher level of explanation than we have been doing. I suggest that a productive level of explanation to begin at is the "model of reality" that a person holds at any given time.

I hope to show that by starting in this way we can understand how the OBE may come about under certain circumstances, why it takes the form it does, and why it is a relatively discrete ASC. In addition, I think this approach has implications for other ASCs, but I shall not discuss these in detail here.

I shall now explain what I mean by a model of reality. People are self-modeling systems. Indeed, one of the main tasks of the brain is to construct models of ourselves in our environment. These include the temporary models that are built in perception, as well as long-term models that are built up in memory over a lifetime. And of course each interacts with the other.

Perception is a model-building process that uses information from memory and the constructive powers of imagination to provide workable models of a complex and rapidly changing world. It is essential to realize, as psychologists have long been realizing, that little about the outside world is "given" or obvious. All the incoming information has to be transformed, analyzed, and used to construct models of what is "out there." Models are constructed at many different levels, from the primitive models in the periphery to the more complex, integrated central models. The latter contribute to memory, both in the remembering of specific events and in the building-up of generalized models of the world, or cognitive maps.

The same can be said of our perception of self. We have long-term models of the kind of person we see ourselves to be (self-image) and what our bodies are like (body image), and we have a constantly changing model of our own bodies (also referred to as the body image). For the coordination of movements and perception, it is obviously essential that we have such an effective and rapidly updated model of our own body. This is built up from somatosensory information, visual, and other sensory input and memory.

The body image has usually been discussed independently of the processes of perception, but I think it is important to realize that the end product of our normal perceiving processes is a model of what is out there with our own body firmly placed within it. I am not just seeing my keyboard and screen before me, and the room beyond, but I am also implicitly aware of my own position relative to these things. "I" am in my constructed world.

The position of this "I" is m most interesting. I have equated it with the body because that is mostly how it seems. We more or less take it for granted most of the time that we sit somewhere in our heads; for most people, somewhere behind the eyes. But of course we must realize that this, too, is a construction. It is a very useful construction to have because it gives us the most economical and comprehensible model of the perceived world. Since, for humans, vision is predominant, it makes sense that we seem to be looking out of our eyes, but of course when we are listening intently for something or doing some very fine or skilled task with our hands or with a fine tool, we may find this habitual position changing. The body image may even extend to the edge of our car! Whatever the model of self we have at any given time, we must bear in mind that it too is a constructed part of our model of reality.

Superficially, it seems obvious that when we build perceptual models of the world, we are modeling what is "really" there; in other words, we are building models of reality. But, in fact, this may not be obvious at all. I do not mean to allude here to philosophical issues involving the status of any world out there. Rather, I wish to point out that, as far as the brain is concerned, it is not necessarily obvious what is real and what is not. After all, the brain is constantly engaged in all kinds of modeling processes. Some models are better or more stable than others, some are based more on sensory input, and some on internal processes of thinking. With all this mass of activity going on, the brain has to decide which of its models represents external reality - a mistake could be very costly.

It is very interesting to speculate about how this might be done. The longer I do so the more difficult and interesting the question becomes. Might we take each object or thought one by one and decide on some criterion whether it is real or not? This would be extremely inefficient, aside from the fact that there is no obvious, or even best, way of dividing the world into objects in the first place. And this is even more problematic for "thoughts."

Perhaps we might simply distinguish things on the basis of whether they are derived from sensory input or not. However, this is no easier. Any model constructed from sensory input is not just that and nothing more. Certainly, at the most peripheral levels a great deal of analysis is done without recourse to stored information, but even things like the crucial analysis of depth involves learned depth cues, and any modeling of objects involves recalled information about previous objects seen. The model that results from perception is not just the result of sensory input.

Also, imagined models are not always entirely imagined. We may start a train of thought because of something we see, or we may elaborate perceptions in our imagination and be quite sure that they are "thoughts" and not "reality." If both thoughts and perceptions involve varying mixtures of sensory input and recalled information, then this cannot be used as the criterion for reality. So what is?

I suggest that we will get on better by looking at the problem from the higher level of complete integrated models of the world. At any one time, there are probably several such models being constructed. For example, at the moment I have a model (to which I am paying little attention) of the room around me and myself sitting at the keyboard. I also have a complex mental structure representing the chapter I am trying to write and all the many things I hope to say. From time to time, I also have thoughts about what I am going to have for lunch and whether I have left the heating on or not. These may be brief, but they are quite complex and involve images of the kitchen the rest of the house, or tins of baked beans, or whatever. Now, all the time, although I am concentrating on the writing, I have no trouble in knowing which model represents the world out there, and I do not confuse one model with another.

I suggest that it is between these kinds of complete models that the brain makes its decisions about reality. This strategy immediately benefits from the fact that such models are internally coherent but have relatively little connection with each other. Unlike vaguely conceptualized "objects" or "thoughts," we can see that at this higher level the models are fairly distinct. So let us suppose that it is at this level that the brain makes its decisions about what is real.

It is interesting to note that in the extremely complex task of perception, or for that matter any cognitive task, the brain is generally helped if it can impose constraints on its processes. For example, in vision, knowing that objects generally do not have discontinuities in both depth and illumination at the same place aids in the perception of edges. Assuming that the rigidity of moving objects aids movement perception, and knowing about the trajectories of falling objects helps in tracking rapid movement. On a much higher level, a useful constraint is the assumption that there is only one external reality. So it is a sensible strategy for the brain to assume that there can be only one model of reality. Accordingly, it chooses the best candidate and, if you like, accords that candidate "reality status." Other models can be labeled thinking, imagining, or whatever.

I suggest, and this is central to the theory, that at any given time one, and only one, model is held to represent reality.

The system must then choose which one. I suggest that this is normally a very easy choice. One model, the one derived largely from sensory input, is relatively complex, stable, and coherent as compared with any of the others. It is constantly fed by new input that is either consistent with the model or can be made so with relatively little difficulty. It also behaves in ways that we have learned to associate with reality. In the case in which we are "lost in thought," we still do not normally confuse that thought with external reality. If we have any doubt about which model should be "real," we need only attend to sensory input, and more detail will confirm and extend the input-based model but not the others.

Note that I have not specified the precise criteria for selecting reality models, but only indicated the kinds of thing they might be (such as stability, complexity, and so on). If the theory proves to be useful, the criteria used will have to be investigated. For the moment I shall assume that the criterion is one of stability; that the most stable model is taken to represent the external world.

Note also that I am assuming a system in which models are built at many different levels. If the system is functioning effectively, there should be no incompatibility between the higher level models, built on expectation, memory, and so on (and involving a lot of top-down processing) and the lower level models built up from the analysis of input (from bottom-up processing). In fact, the former should be good models of the latter. When the two do not coincide, the models will be unstable and unlikely to gain reality status.

It is then important to consider how the system copes with such discrepancies when they arise. Minor discrepancies will arise all the time because we live in a rapidly changing world. The model appropriate to a moment ago, or that based on expectation of change, will rarely be an entirely adequate model of the current situation. Also, errors will creep in either from high-level modeling (wrong guesses, unjustified expectations, and so on) or from noisy input.

The system then has the choice of either ignoring the input concerned or updating the model so as to incorporate it. Either action may be appropriate, depending on the source of the discrepancy. At any time, there may be a criterion in force that defines just how much discrepancy is going to be allowed between the model and the input. In other words, how much checking of aberrant input or updating of the model will be carried out? When there is plenty of capacity to spare, the criterion will be strict and almost all discrepancies quickly eliminated so that the reality model is as good a reflection of input as possible. Under less favorable circumstances, greater discrepancies may be allowed.

We have now reached the stage of being able to see how the cognitive system might sustain a stable, input-driven, model of reality that is not confused with the many other models that may be being - constructed at the same time. We may now consider what happens under conditions that are less than ideal; particularly, what happens if there is a lot of noise in the system or if sensory input is greatly reduced.

First, let us consider the case of excessive noise. The system is very good at coping with a certain amount of noise. There is a lot of redundancy that allows for internal checking at many levels. If noise results in a wrong decision about some input, then often this will produce discrepancies of the sort already mentioned. The error can usually be identified by checking against other input or against models at other levels. If it is identified as being due to noise, then it can be ignored. However, if the whole system is very noisy, then it may become very difficult to correct errors. It may then be necessary to shift to a laxer criterion and to allow more discrepancies to go uncorrected. After all, the system cannot expend all its capacity on correcting them when this gets harder and harder to do.

This strategy may let one get by until things improve. However, it may mean increasing oddities in the model. These may be of the sort I often experience, like briefly thinking I see my cat asleep before I realize that it is only a pile of papers. Or they may be more severe and reach the extent of being hallucinations. At the extreme, the higher level models may lose touch entirely with the input and cease to be an effective model of reality. This situation may be expected, for example, when someone is badly deprived of deep, taking certain drugs, under extreme stress, or close to death. If this happens the input-driven model of reality has broken down.

A similar extreme may be seen with reducing sensory input, for example, in sensory isolation experiments, in very boring environments, or in sleep (a special case to which I shall return). Somatosensory input, which is necessary for maintaining the current body image, may be reduced simply by keeping still for a long time. Or it may be distorted by habituation (Neher, 1980), so that erroneous, as well as inadequate, information is available. In such cases, the input-driven model must necessarily become impoverished. It may need to rely more than usual on information from memory to keep it stable. And, most important, correcting errors becomes harder if there is less input against which to check them. The result is that greater discrepancies may arise between model and input (that is, between lower and higher level models). Again, there may arise a situation in which the current reality model does not represent the input at all well. What does the system do now?

Obviously it is important to get back to a good input-controlled model as soon as possible; otherwise, effective behavior cannot be maintained. To do this, one may try out various alterations to the current model in the hope that one of these may reduce the discrepancies and get the model back to input control. If this works, one probably will not notice anything amiss. However, what if it does not? The attempt to alter the model may shift it yet further away from a reasonable representation of the outside world. In this case, the system has to do something more drastic.

If the model is allowed to degenerate further, one of the other models going on at the time, for example, my speculations about what to have for lunch, may actually become more coherent, stable, and complex than this degraded input-based model. It would then take over reality status, and I would be hallucinating baked beans. This is awful strategy for an organism that wants to survive!

An alternative is to start from the beginning again and build a new input-controlled model. Normally, this would be easy and could start from the results of input processing. In a sense, this is happening all the time as the models are constantly updated. However, in this case, we have very noisy or inadequate input; so we cannot do this. The alternative is to build a model only from the top down, and this means relying heavily on information from memory. It is here that, finally, we come to the OBE.

Suppose that the system builds the best model it can of what it thinks it should be seeing. It can go on the last effective model it had before the breakdown occurred, add to that the changes based on movements known to have occurred, or actions taken, and construct a new model with the aid of information from memory. This new model may be a fairly good approximation of, for example, me sitting at my desk, but it will differ in important ways from any normal input-driven model.

It is important to note the ways in which memory models differ from perceptual ones. The processes of perception involve building successive representations of the outside world. Marr (1982) describes these as progressing from a viewer-centered to a more object-centered representation. The retinal image from which visual perception starts is viewer-centered in the sense that all objects are represented as seen from that specific viewpoint. However, moving up the system, the effect of the processing is to make the representation more and more independent of that location. Round objects seen at an angle are represented as ellipses in the retinal image, but as circles higher up the system, and so on. In the end, you “see” round plates and square tables. Indeed, you "see" rectangular rooms even though you see them from the inside.

Memory models can be seen as taking this process even further (see, for example, Bartlett, 1932; Neisser, 1976). When you remember scenes, on the whole they are represented in a version that preserves the essential features of the objects seen, without preserving all the detail of each view. This is a far more economical and useful way of storing the information. Sometimes a bird's-eye representation is used. As Siegel (1977) has suggested, try remembering the last time you were at the seaside. Do you see yourself as though from above as a spectator, or do you reconstruct what you saw at the time? You may in fact do either, but there is no doubt that many memory representations involve viewpoints never actually experienced. They may be kind of all-round views in which you look from no particular place at all or they may in some other way be generalized versions of the many views actually seen. This makes sense because it would take far too much storage (and quite unnecessarily) to remember all the different complex views you ever saw. A generalized or schematic model may contain all the essential information and be far more useful.

These features of memory models are found in research on cognitive maps (see, for example, Liben, Patterson, & Newcombe, 1981). The cognitive map is the memory model we all have of locations we know well. It is not at all like a map on paper of course. For example, try to imagine taking the route from your home to work, or to the shops. You can do this in several ways. You may see everything passing by as you see it when you actually travel, but of course this is extremely slow and laborious and involves a lot of processing. You may instead prefer to fly or float above the streets and see them pass below you. Most people can do this easily. Although they have never actually flown this way, their memory representation is such that this is a surprisingly easy way of presenting the information. In fact, if you have a well-structured cognitive map, you may be able to, as it were, see the whole thing at once as you fly. Finally, you may simply imagine yourself first in one place, and then, instantaneously, find yourself at the other.

In trying this exercise, you will learn much about memory representations. You will probably find that there are lots of errors both of omission and commission. Buildings you don't know very well will have a convincing looking number of windows, but stop to count them and you will find you cannot. You will see signs or advertisements along the streets but may not be able to read them. If you check against the actual street you may find you have added likely looking side roads or smoothed out curves. All this is a result of your building up the best representation you can on the available information.

Also, if you try looking through the buildings, you will find they can be transparent. If you know what the inside looks like, you can probably see it without having to imagine going in through the door. Indeed, you may be able to pass happily through the walls and floors of your cognitive buildings. Finally, of course, you may manipulate these images within the constraints of your ability to imagine. If you have good imagination you may remove buildings, plant trees, turn building sites into parks, or anything you like to think of. This is the world of the imagination. It is quite different from the world of perception.

Now this is the stuff out of which our lost perceptual modeler must build the new model of reality. Let us suppose that I am to reconstruct a model of myself sitting at my desk and typing. It is possible that I will be able to construct a sufficiently viewer-centered image to mimic an input-driven model. If there is also enough input, then the two may coincide, and "reality" will have been restored. If this happens I may not even notice, or I may just feel that things seemed momentarily a bit funny. However, it is more likely that if I have very little input to go on (as we are assuming) and I build my model from memory, it will be something like a cognitive map seen in a bird's-eye view. In other words, I will see myself sitting at my desk and typing, but I will see myself from above or behind, just as in my memory representations.

This model will not be an adequate representation of the input (or the results of the bottom-up processing). However, it may be fairly stable and complex. If there is just a little sensory input, some of this may even be incorporated and help to stabilize the erroneous model. Auditory input is particularly effective here because it can provide a link to what is happening without being anything like as position-dependent as visual input is. The model thus created may be good enough to be considered as reality by the system. It may be more stable and convincing than any other current model. So, just like the normal input-driven model, it becomes "reality." This is, I propose, an OBE.

I believe that this interpretation of the OBE makes sense of a great deal of what we know about the experience. First, one of the most persistent problems is in accounting for why the OBE seems so real. If it is "just imagination," it shouldn't seem like reality. But of course, in the case I have described, the out-of-the-body (OB) model has achieved reality status because it is the best possible substitute for the missing input-driven model. Everything seems real because it *is* real, in exactly the same sense as anything ever seems real.

Second, it accounts for why sensory deprivation, relaxation, illness, and certain drugs so often precipitate OBEs. On this theory, it is essential that the input-driven model be incapacitated before the OBE model can take over. At the most extreme, of course, this can happen near death. There may also be other reasons for adopting an OB perspective during extreme fear, illness, or when near death. Reinterpretation of pain as belonging to a different body is one. The denial of death (Ehrenwald, 1974) or the desire to be something more than just a perishable body are others. Under suitable conditions, these factors may tip the balance toward the OB state. The theory can also make sense of the training techniques that emphasize relaxation, control of imagery, and concentration (see Blackmore, 1982). If an OBE is to be induced voluntarily, it is not enough just to want to be "out of body." It is necessary to shift the balance of stability away from the input model and toward some internally generated one. Relaxation and immobility may reduce somatosensory input; good imagery control helps to build an alternative viewpoint; and concentration helps one to keep attending to that rather than flipping back to input.

Third, this interpretation explains the many features that the OB world has in common with the cognitive map (see Blackmore, 1978): the ability to move through solid objects, the errors of omission and commission, and the stylized nature of many things seen out of the body. Most interesting to me is that it accounts for the thought-responsive nature of the OB world. Occultists, magicians, and astral travelers have long described the astral world as a thought-created world and one responsive to imagination (e.g., Muldoon & Carrington, 1929). On this theory, this is just what we should expect. Indeed, one can even make sense of seemingly obscure features like Muldoon's three traveling speeds in the astral. They match pretty closely the three ways of traveling through the cognitive map which I described earlier.

The thought-created nature of the OB world gives rise both to its vast potential and to its limitations. For example, odd features of the OBE, such as the difficulty of turning on lights, may be explained in terms of the limitations of imagery. It may be difficult to effect all at once the sudden increase in complexity of the model required for a change from darkness to light.

In these ways, I think we can see that a lot of the phenomenology of the OBE does begin to make sense.

We may now ask why the experience seems to be relatively discrete. According to this theory, it is because intermediate states are unstable. If the OB model of reality has a viewpoint very different from normal, it is unlikely to shift back to input control and is therefore highly stable as long as the conditions allow. On the other hand, if the viewpoint is only slightly away from normal, there is a good chance of its getting close enough to fit with sensory input and so to shift back. Such intermediate states are therefore highly unstable, and it is this which produces the apparent discreteness of the OBE.

If at any time during an OBE, sensory input adequately reasserts itself, it will be obvious to the system that the new input-based model is preferable. The temporary memory model will be dropped or rapidly modified, and the experience will suddenly end with a flip back to the normal viewpoint. This is commonly, though not invariably, what happens at the end of OBEs. Remember that the cognitive system is always trying to maintain an input-controlled model of reality. This is why OBEs are relatively rare, do not usually last long, and are hard to bring about voluntarily.

The reader may now be asking whether this theory is any improvement over previous ones. I suggest that it has a theoretical advantage over the ecsomatic theories. It seems to make sense of much of the phenomenology of OBEs, while fitting in with what is known about cognitive processes, and without the terrible logical problems confronted by the ecsomatic theories (see Blackmore, 1982). For this reason alone, I would argue that it is to be preferred.

I believe it also has advantages over other psychological theories. The most important of these is Palmer's (1978) theory. Very briefly, Palmer posits that the OBE is triggered by a change in a person's body concept, which in turn threatens his self-concept. The threat activates unconscious (primary) processes that seek to reestablish the sense of self-identity. The OBE is just one of the forms this reestablishment may take.

The theories agree to the extent that the OBE may be triggered by a change in body concept - according to the present theory, this is one aspect of the breakdown of the input-controlled model. However, they diverge considerably at this point. The main problem with Palmer's theory, as I see it, is that his appeal to primary processes fails to specify why the new self-concept should involve viewing the world from a location outside the body; in other words, an OBE. It cannot (at least in its present form) answer questions such as why the viewpoint is often above the body or why the OB world is like it is. In other words, as Rogo suggested, it cannot account for the phenomenology of the OBE. As I have already explained, I believe the present theory can at least begin to do this.

That being the case, the final test is the predictions that the theory makes. I shall give a few examples of testable predictions from it and try to point out where these differ from the predictions of other theories. Undoubtedly others could be derived.

The OB world is supposed, on this theory, to be the best construction that imagination and memory can produce. A general prediction, therefore, is that the OB world should resemble constructions from memory. This is not central to any other theory of the OBE but is compatible with any of the "psychological theories."

This general prediction may apply to almost any aspect, but one specific example is that of viewpoint. According to this theory, we should expect two things. First, we should expect most OBEs to start from viewpoints that are most easily constructed in imagination. It is known that many OBEs begin with a viewpoint above and slightly behind the head (e.g., Crookall, 1961; Green, 1968; Muldoon & Carrington, 1951). However, no detailed study has been made of this feature of OBEs or of which viewpoints are easiest to imagine. A comparison of these two would provide a simple test.

Second, people who have had OBEs might be expected to be better at creating these different-viewpoint images than are people who have not. In a previous experiment (Blackmore, 1983), I tried to find out whether OBEers more often remembered scenes as though from above, rather than eye level, and whether they could easily switch from one to the other. There was no evidence that they were more likely to recall scenes from above, but they did claim to find it easier to switch viewpoints. A better test of this hypothesis would be to use the actual present scene, that is, to test people's ability to switch imagined viewpoints within the room they are actually in. 'We would expect the easiest viewpoints to be those commonly adopted in OBEs, and that OBEers should find the task easier than others. If this were found, it could not provide evidence against any of the other theories; but it is at least a specific test derived from this one.

Other aspects of the same general prediction concern the effects of thought on the OB world. Those things that are easy or difficult to do in imagination should correspond to those that are easy or difficult when "out of the body." An example already given is that of turning on electric lights. This requires a fast and detailed increase in imagery, which may explain why it is so difficult in both lucid dreams and OBEs. But turning off lights, or turning on other electrical appliances, need not involve so much imagery and should be easier in OBEs. Other examples might be performing skilled actions of various kinds or watching the behavior of falling, breaking, or fast-moving objects.

There has been much debate about whether psychological theories of the OBE in general predict better imagery among OBEers (see, for example, Irwin 1981a, 1981b; Palmer, 1981). This theory does predict such a relationship, but with reservations. First of all, it leads to slightly different predictions in the case of spontaneous OBEs as opposed to deliberately induced ones. For the former, the prevailing conditions may be more important, whereas in the latter, imagery and other skills play much more of a role. Note that this dichotomy is not the same as that between natural and enforced OBEs, proposed by Crookall (1961) and tested by Alvarado (1981).

Let me clarify this. According to the theory, two things are needed for an OBE to occur: the breakdown of the input-controlled model and the construction of, and replacement by, an imagery-based one.

Factors that promote either of these are conducive to an OBE. A spontaneous OBE usually occurs when sensory input is low or the system is very noisy. If these conditions are powerful enough to destroy the input-controlled model, then it will not matter too much how good the imagery is in the alternative model. So imagery, while it may be helpful, is less likely to be a determining factor in whether the switch of models occurs.

In a deliberate OBE, on the other hand, it is necessary to make both changes deliberately, that is, to ignore or block out the good input-controlled model and to substitute for it an entirely imagery-based model. In this case (unless one is extremely good at blocking out input), good imagery will be essential.

I would therefore predict that any correlation of OBEs with imagery skills should be greater for deliberately induced OBEs. Irwin (personal communication, 1981) has tried to find this difference in some of his data, but unsuccessfully. I intend to look for it in future studies, but the problem is the rarity of self-induced OBEs. This prediction would not, as far as I can see, be made by any other theory of the OBE.

Still on the subject of imagery, it is not at all clear which aspects of imagery are most relevant. Vividness and control of imagery have generally not been found to be related to having OBEs (see, for example, Blackmore, 1982), but these may not be the most relevant aspects. For example, spatial imagery skills may be more important (Blackmore, 1983; Cook & Irwin, 1983). On this theory, the complexity or detail of imagery may be more important than vividness. More specific predictions about imagery would follow if we could specify precisely the criteria used for selecting reality models. If they were, in fact, stability, complexity, and coherence, then we should expect those aspects of imagery to be the ones important for having OBEs. This is obviously an area for further investigation.

The other skill necessary for deliberately inducing OBEs is the ability to ignore or block out sensory input. In common with other theories, the present one predicts that people who can do this should more easily have OBEs: but again, it predicts that this is more important for deliberate than spontaneous OBEs. This may well relate to Irwin's (1981a) finding that OBErs tended to have a higher absorption score than did non-OBErs. It is the ability to remain absorbed in an alternative model that makes it more likely to gain reality status.

To summarize these predictions briefly, I suggest that, generally, features of the OBE should correspond to those of models built from memory and imagination. For example, common OB positions should correspond to those positions from which it is easiest to visualize scenes. Tasks that are easy to perform in imagination should also be easy in the OB state and vice versa. In addition, people who are likely to have OBEs should be good at visualizing scenes from alternative positions. Those who can induce OBEs voluntarily also need to be good at ignoring sensory input and have vivid and well-controlled imagery. Although some of these predictions are common to other theories, others are more specific, and their investigation could provide a basis for testing the theory presented here.

Finally, I would like to mention, briefly, some other ASCs. The theory I have outlined predicts, in general, that whenever the input-controlled model is inadequate, some other, internally generated, model may take over as reality. This occurs commonly in sleep.

During NREM sleep there may be so little processing going on that every model is weak and unstructured, but in REM sleep one is in the curious position of being without adequate sensory input or even the need for an input-based model. Nevertheless, there is sufficient arousal for complex models to be built. According to the theory, whichever model is the most complex, coherent, or stable will take over reality status and seem absolutely real at the time. On your awaking, the input-controlled model is reinstated, and you may look back and wonder how on earth this crazy model ever seemed real! This is surely the common experience of dreaming. It prompts the question of why OBEs usually continue to seem real even after they end. I think the answer is that the OBE involves a self that is continuous with that of normal waking. With respect to memory, thinking skills, and so on, you seem to be just the same person as usual. In these respects, "you" do not change when the OBE ends. In a dream, by contrast, you do not typically have access to much of your normal memory about who and where you are and do not think in the same way. The dream is, in this sense, quite discontinuous with waking life.

In this light, it is interesting to consider what happens if, during sleep, you manage to access some of that normal memory and build a model that says that you are asleep and dreaming. This may take two forms. One is a model of yourself as a body lying in bed, and this is then equivalent to an OBE. The other is the realization that you are dreaming so that you, modeled after your usual waking self, can use and manipulate the dream. Both of these are very hard to sustain because there is so little sensory input to stabilize them, and they demand concentration and large amounts of information from memory, which may not be readily available during sleep. I have suggested elsewhere (Irwin and Blackmore, in press) that this approach may be a productive way of looking at lucid dreaming and the related experiences of flying dreams and false awakenings. These states are similar in many ways to the OBE and on recollection seem more “real” than ordinary dreams do. However, while the

OBE is always in dangers of giving way to an input-driven model, these dream states are more likely to give way to other (less lucid) dream models.

Finally, and more speculatively, this approach may have implications for understanding mystical states of various kinds, and states achieved through mental disciplines and meditation. For example, in several kinds of meditation, one learns to ignore sensory input almost totally while maintaining sufficient arousal for complex modeling. One of the hardest things to do must be to maintain a reality model of nothing at all when the system is madly trying to make models from input. If you can do this, you have great control over models of reality and hence great potential.

In some kinds of open meditation, one attends to sensory input but in quite a different way from normal. One does not evaluate or elaborate on input in the same way, or build it into complex structures to make sense of it. The result is that you can be acutely aware of far, far more than normal, but at a much simpler level of elaboration. In both these cases, I think we may get closer to understanding what the state is like if we ask what the model of reality is like rather than looking at physiology or other bodily changes.

Similarly, there are some states of realization that I think can be approached in this way. What if you achieve a state in which your model of reality is a model of the whole world with yourself as nothing special within it, or a model of yourself as a grain of sand, or a hair on the head of an infinite God, or indeed a model so simple that it defies verbal description? I suggest that if any of these becomes reality, in a condition of alert wakefulness, a person is going to be changed by the experience. Again, we must look at the level of the model of reality if we are to see why.

I believe this approach can also shed new light on the traditional higher worlds and other planes, even the astral planes of occult lore. Many adepts of various disciplines and many spontaneous OBEers have described "other worlds" with remarkable consistency. This consistency is often used as evidence that these worlds have independent existence or are of "real substance" (Rogo, 1983). I suggest instead that these worlds reflect the possible models of realty that we, with our particular kind of cognitive system, are capable of constructing. The potential for such worlds is constrained by the constraints of that system, and it is by understanding this that we shall be able to understand these other worlds of the imagination. There have been many attempts at building maps of these spaces, or maps of consciousness (e.g., Fischer, 1975; Metzner, 1971; von Eckartsberg, 1981).[1] This theory may be able to provide a new map by understanding just how some models of reality are closer to others whereas some are far apart, and which can be reached by which routes.

These further speculations may not help us at all in understanding the OBE. Indeed, they are premature when the theory has not even been tested in its simplest applications. However, I present them as part of my case that we should look at ASCs in general, and OBEs in particular, in terms of a person's model of reality.

[1] The term map is used here in two different senses. First there is the cognitive map, which refers to a hypothetical internal representation of the physical world. Second, there are maps of consciousness or of experience, which are built (usually by psychologists) to describe variations in experience. The two should not be confused, as they have been, for example, by von Eckartsberg (1981).

REFERENCES

Alvarado, C.S. (1981). Phenomenological differences between natural and enforced out-of-the-body experiences: A reanalysis of Crookall's findings. *Theta, 9(4),* 10-11.

Bartlett, F. C. (1932). *Remembering.* London: Cambridge University Press.

Blackmore. S. J. (1978). *Parapsychology and out-the-body experiences.* London: Society for Psychical Research.

Blackmore. S.J. (1982). *Beyond the body* London: Heinemann.

Blackmore S.J . (1983). Imagery and the OBE [Abstract]. In W. G. Roll, J. Beloff, & R. A. White (Eds.), *Research in Parapsychology,* 1982 (pp. 231-232). Metuchen, N.J.: Scarecrow Press.

Cook, A.M., & Irwin, H. J. (1983). Visuospatial skills and the out-of-body experience. *Journal of Parapsychology, 47,* 23-35.

Crookall, R. (1961). *The study and practice of astral projection.* London: Aquarian Press.

Davidson, J. M., & Davidson, R. J. (1980). *The psychobiology of consciousness.* New York and London: Plenum Press.

Dennett, D. (1983). Artificial intelligence and the strategies of psychological investigation. In J. Miller (Ed.), *States of mind.* London: The British Broadcasting Corporation.

Ehrenwald, J. (1974). Out-of-the-body experiences and the denial of death. *Journal of Nervous and Mental Disease, 159,* 227-233.

Fischer, R. (1975). Cartography of inner space. In R. K. Siegel & L. J. West (Eds.), *Hallucinations.* New York, Wiley.

Green C. E. (1968). *Out-of-the-body experiences.* London. Hamish Hamilton.

Irwin, H. J. (1981a). Some psychological dimensions of the OBE. *Parapsychology Review, 12(4),* 1-6.

Irwin, H. J. (1981b). Letter to the Editor. *Journal of the Society for Research, 51,* 118-120.

Irwin, H.J., & Blackmore, S.J. (1988). Out-of-body experiences and dream lucidity: Two views. In J. Gackenbach & S. La Berge (Eds.), *Lucid dreaming: New research on consciousness during sleep.* New York: Plenum.

Liben, L.S., Patterson, A.H., & Newcombe N. (Eds.) (1981). *Spatial Representations and behavior across the life span.* New York: Academic Press

Marr, D. (1982). *Vision.* San Francisco: W. H. Freeman.

Metzner, R. (1971). *Maps of consciousness.* London: Collier-Macmillan.

Muldoon, S. & Carrington, H. (1929). *The projection of the astral body.* London: Rider.

Muldoon, S. & Carrington, H. (1951). *The phenomena of astral projections.* London: Rider.

Neher, A. (1980). *The psychology of transcendence.* Englewood Cliffs, NJ: Prentice Hall.

Neisser, U. (1976). *Cognition and reality.* San Francisco: *W.* H. Freeman,

Palmer, J. (1978). The out-of-body experience: A psychological theory. *Parapsychology Review, 9 (5),* 19-22.

Palmer, J. (1981). Letter to the Editor. *Journal of* the *Society for Psychical Research, 51,* 35-36.

Row, D. S. (1982). Psychological models of the out-of-body experience. *Journal of Parapsychology, 46,* 29-45.

Row, D. S. (1983). *Leaving the body.* Englewood Cliffs, NJ: Prentice Hall.

Siegel, R. (1977). Hallucinations. *Scientific American, 237,* 132-140.

Tart, C. T. (1980). A systems approach to altered states of consciousness. In J. M. Davidson & R. J. Davidson, *The psychobiology of consciousness.* (pp. 243-269). New York and London: Plenum Press.

Underwood, G. & Stevens, R. (1979). *Aspects of consciousness* (Vol, 1). London: Academic Press.

Underwood, G. & Stevens, R. (1981). *Aspects of consciousness* (Vol.2). London: Academic Press.

Valler, R.S., & Von Eckartsberg, R. (Eds.) (1981). *The metaphors of consciousness,* Ne w York and London: Plenum Press.

Von Eckartsberg, R. (1981). Maps of the mind. In R. S. Valle & R. Von Eckartsberg (Eds.), *The metaphors of consciousness.* New York and London, Plenum Press.

In: Psychological Scientific Perspectives on Out of Body … ISBN: 978-1-60741-705-7
Editor: Craig D. Murray ©2009 Nova Science Publishers, Inc.

Chapter 3

THE DISEMBODIED SELF: AN EMPIRICAL STUDY OF DISSOCIATION AND THE OUT-OF-BODY EXPERIENCE[1]

Harvey J. Irwin

ABSTRACT

Recent developments in the study of dissociation prompted a re-examination of the nature of the out-of-body experience (OBE). A questionnaire survey of Australian university students addressed the relation between the OBE and nonpathological dissociation (psychological absorption), pathological mental dissociation, and pathological somatoform dissociation. Both the occurrence of the OBE and the frequency of OBEs were found to be predicted by somatoform dissociation. The findings are discussed with reference to the extent to which the OBE should be considered a pathological phenomenon. A dissociational theory of the OBE is formulated; this depicts the experience as a dissociation between the sense of self and the processing of somatic events.

INTRODUCTION

The out-of-body experience (OBE) is one in which "the center of consciousness appears to the experient to occupy temporarily a position which is spatially remote from his/her body" (Irwin, 1985, p. 5). In the book Flight of Mind, written some 15 years ago (Irwin, 1985), I advanced a theoretical account of the OBE that stressed the involvement of various features of the cognitive--personality construct known as psychological absorption. Absorption is a state of strong engrossment in one's mentation and has been defined formally as "a 'total' attention, involving a full commitment of available perceptual, motoric, imaginative and ideational resources to a unified representation of the attentional object" (Tellegen &

[1] This chapter originally appeared in the Journal of Parapsychology (The Disembodied Self: An Empirical Study of Dissociation and the Out-Of-Body Experience. Journal of Parapsychology, *64(3)*, 261-276.) The editor would like to express thanks to John Palmer and the Rhine Research Center for permission to reprint this material here.

Atkinson, 1974, p.274). Most other behavioral scientists at the time were inclined to designate the OBE as an instance of depersonalization (e.g., Whitlock, 1978). Since the late 1980s a resurgence of research interest in the topic of dissociation (Spiegel & Cardena, 1991) has served to repositi on both psychological absorption and depersonalization in the broader context of dissociative processes, reinstating their original conceptualization by Pierre Janet in the 19th century (Janet, 1889; van der Hart & Friedman, 1989). It is therefore timely to reconsider the OBE in relation to the concept of dissociation.

Mental processes such as thoughts, memories, feelings, and the sense of identity ordinarily are integrated. Spiegel and Cardena (1991) described dissociation as a structured separation of these processes; that is, one cognitive process may appear to proceed independently of another such process when ordinarily one might expect the two processes to be intrinsically linked. By way of illustration, in the relatively common dissociative state known as "highway hypnosis" drivers may become so engrossed in their daydreams or other mentation during a long journey that the mental processes associated with driving evidently are dissociated from consciousness; nonetheless, the "vehicle steering" mental processes evidently continue to be executed, given that the road is successfully navigated. For many people in the general population this type of dissociative experience is reportedly a familiar part of everyday life (Ross, Joshi, & Currie, 1990), although in some cases dissociative processes may become more pathological, possibly to the extent that they constitute one of the psychological dysfunctions known formally as the dissociative disorders (Spiegel, 1991/1993).

In phenomenological terms the OBE entails an experient's (henceforth, OBE-er's) impression that the self has separated from the body, and on this ground the OBE is designated a parapsychological experience, that is, one in which it seems to the experient that a paranormal phenomenon is involved (Irwin, 1999a). It is uncertain, however, that a paranormal process actually does underlie the OBE. Indeed, despite creative attempts to demonstrate experimentally the paranormality of the experience (e.g., Osis, 1975) it is doubtful that a conclusive study to this end can be designed (Blackmore, 1994). For this reason many researchers have opted to investigate the OBE as a psychological event that coincidentally may or may not be conducive to extrasensory awareness (Alvarado, 1992). It is in this context that there arises the notion of the OBE as a dissociative phenomenon.

In normal circumstances a person's sensory processing of kinesthetic and somaesthetic stimuli may serve to maintain the assumption that consciousness, or the thinking and perceiving self, is "in" the physical body; that is, somatic processing ordinarily is integrated with a sense of self. Such is not the case during an OBE. In this sense the OBE has been deemed a dissociative event simply by definition (e.g., Spiegel & Cardena, 1991; Steinberg, 1991/1993). On the other hand, the OBE cannot adequately be explained by declaring it to be an instance of dissociation. Rather, a dissociational theory of the OBE would have to specify how the functional separation of particular cognitive processes might account for all the diverse aspects of the experience's phenomenology. The present study was in part intended to provide some empirical justification for the development of a dissociational theory of the OBE.

In seeking to relate the OBE to dissociation it is important at the outset to appreciate that dissociation is not a unidimensional domain. An adequate acknowledgment of this fact has emerged only in the last few years. Researchers previously had assumed that dissociative tendencies form an intrinsic continuum, ranging from very low levels in some members of the general population to very high levels among dissociative-disordered patients (e.g., Ross, 1989). Although it was evident that some dissociative phenomena (e.g., psychological absorption) were much more common than others (e.g., depersonalization), the concept of a "dissociative continuum" (Spiegel, 1963) had long been a premise of the empirical investigation of the dissociative domain. Recent research nevertheless suggests that the assumption of a unitary dissociative continuum is erroneous, or at least an oversimplification.

Waller and his colleagues (Waller, Putnam, & Carlson, 1996; Waller & Ross, 1997) have identified two distinct types of dissociation, only one of which is dimensional. Using the statistical approach of taxometric analysis, Waller et al. (1996) found that pathological dissociative experiences, such as depersonalization and dissociative amnesia, are in fact taxonic; that is, people can be dichotomized into two distinct groups according to whether they have had such experiences. This taxonic form of dissociation does not constitute a continuum. Although scores on Waller et al.'s index of pathological dissociation (the Dissociative Experiences Scale--Taxon) are numerically continuous, the underlying factor is inherently classlike rather than traitlike. In addition, pathological dissociation evidently has no genetic component (Waller & Ross, 1997) and seems at least in part to be a product of severe childhood trauma (Irwin, 1999b; Kroll, Fiszdon, & Crosby, 1996).

Waller et al. (1996) also identified a second, nonpathological type of dissociation that evidently does constitute a continuum. According to Frank Putnam (personal communication, April 19, 1996), this dimensional type of dissociation is best indexed by experiences of psychological absorption. The capacity to achieve this state of high engrossment in experience shows the statistical characteristics of a personality trait or dimension (Tellegen & Atkinson, 1974) and is believed to have a normal distribution in the general population. Psychological absorption is closely related to fantasy proneness (Wilson & Barber, 1983) and indeed, the two constructs might not be truly discriminable (Lynn & Rhue, 1988). Thus, nonpathological dissociation might usefully be thought of as a capacity for imaginative involvement. The nonpathological dissociative trait is also reported to have a substantial genetic component (Finkel & McGue, 1997; Tellegen et al., 1988), although it certainly is not immune from environmental influence (Vanderlinden, van Dyck, Vandereycken, & Vertommen, 1993).

Although there is a need for independent replication of Wailer et al.'s (1996) findings, in the present context it may be noted that there is some evidence that the OBE is correlated with these two types of dissociative tendencies. In a series of studies in the 1980s I established that OBE-ers presented with a relatively high capacity for psychological absorption (Irwin, 1980, 1985)--and, conversely, people with high absorption capacity were relatively susceptible to an experimental OBE-induction technique (Irwin, 1981). The link between OBEs and absorption has been replicated by researchers in other countries (Glicksohn, 1990; Myers, Austrin, Grisso, & Nickeson, 1983). In addition, fantasy proneness is reported to be higher among OBE-ers than among nonexperients or "non-OBE-ers" (Hunt, Gervais, Shearing-Johns, & Travis, 1992; Myers et al., 1983; Wilson & Barber, 1983). It would seem, therefore, that a capacity for nonpathological dissociation is a factor in the occurrence of the OBE. This interpretation ac cords with several aspects of the phenomenology of the experience (Irwin, 1985).

The relation between OBEs and pathological dissociative tendencies has been given scant empirical scrutiny, despite the fact that most psychiatrists and psychologists classify the OBE as an instance of depersonalization, that is, of pathological dissociation (Steinberg, 1995).

Thus, generally speaking, researchers have not sought to establish that OBE-ers as a group are marked by pathological dissociative tendencies (apart from the "symptom" of the OBE itself). Alvarado and Zingrone (1997), however, found Waller et al.'s (1996) DES-T index of pathological dissociation to discriminate between OBE-ers and non-OBE-ers better than did a set of mainly absorption items. This is a most important finding for the construction of theories of the OBE, and one of the primary objectives of the present study was to try and replicate the result obtained by Alvarado and Zingrone.

It would seem, however, that there is even more to the dissociation domain than the distinction between pathological and nonpathological dissociation documented by Waller et al. (1996). Contemporary North American researchers construe dissociation in terms of mental functions. Thus, Spiegel and Cardena (1991, p. 367) defined dissociation as "a structured separation of mental processes." Janet's (1889, 1907/1965) original formulation of the concept of dissociation, on the other hand, was applicable to both psyche and soma. According to Janet, dissociation could result in an alteration of bodily, or somatic, functions as well as mental processes (Nijenhuis & van der Hart, 1999).

Some European researchers have now revived the notion of dissociative processes related to somatic states and functions. Nijenhuis and his coworkers (Nijenhuis, 1999; Nijenhuis, Spinhoven, van Dyck, van der Hart, & Vanderlinden, 1996, 1998b; Nijenhuis & van der Hart, 1999) have operationalized this facet of dissociative processes in the concept of somatoform dissociation, defined as "dissociation which is manifested in a loss of the normal integration of somatoform components of experience, bodily reactions and functions" (Nijenhuis, Spinhoven, van Dyck, van der Hart, & Vanderlinden, 1998a, p. 713). While acknowledging that mental and physiological processes are intrinsically interrelated, Nijenhuis maintains that there is a clear phenomenological distinction between the manifestations of mental (or psychological) dissociation and those of somatoform dissociation and that researchers' neglect of the latter needs to be redressed. In many instances of somatoform dissociation there is a "deficit symptom," or loss of somatic function, that has no evident organic basis; for example, a person may report numbness (anesthesia) in a part of the body or the loss of a sensory function (e.g., so-called hysterical blindness). Somatoform dissociation can also comprise a "positive symptom" or addition to somatic functions, such as psychosomatic pain or tics.

Nijenhuis and his colleagues (Nijenhuis, 1999; Nijenhuis et al., 1996, 1998b) have demonstrated the construct of somatoform dissociation to be psychometrically coherent. In addition, these researchers have gathered evidence to suggest that somatoform dissociation is pathological in nature; for example, somatoform dissociation correlates more strongly with pathological (mental) dissociation than with nonpathological dissociation (absorption) and has been found to be related to a history of severe childhood trauma (Nijenhuis, 1999; Nijenhuis et al, 1996, 1998a). Nonetheless, the correlation between somatoform dissociation and (other) pathological dissociation is about .7 (Nijenhuis et al., 1996); that is, barely half (.7 squared = .49) of the common variance is accounted for. Thus, although somatoform dissociation may be pathological, it seems to be both qualitatively (phenomenologically) and quantitatively distinct from pathological mental dissociation.

An investigation of the relation between the OBE and dissociative tendencies therefore should take due account of somatoform dissociation in addition to both pathological mental dissociation (henceforth referred to simply as pathological dissociation) and nonpathological dissociation (psychological absorption). To date no research has sought to examine the OBE in relation to somatoform dissociation. Nonetheless, there is a clear rationale for undertaking such a project. As indicated earlier, the argument for the potential relevance of dissociative processes to the OBE is that at a phenomenological level the OBE appears to entail a dissociation between sensory processing of somatic (somaesthetic and kinesthetic) events and the sense of self or identity. This interpretation of the OBE seems fundamentally to implicate somatoform dissociative processes. Note there is no necessary suggestion here that somatoform dissociation would be the sole type of dissociative mechanism involved in the OBE, but there is ample justification to include somatoform dissociation in an investigation of the nature of the OBE.

In summary, the objective of the study was to investigate the relation between OBE occurrence and three facets of dissociation, namely, pathological, nonpathological, and somatoform dissociative tendencies.

METHOD

Participants

The study was undertaken as a postal questionnaire survey of adults enrolled in an off-campus introductory psychology course taught through the University of New England, Australia. Students in this course generally are of mature age; most are in paid employment, some are homemakers. Survey forms were completed by 113 students. The sample comprised 28 men and 85 women, ranging in age from 19 to 64 years (M = 35.6, Mdn = 33, SD = 10.34).

Materials

The survey inventory contained three questionnaires. One was a brief form surveying demographic variables and OBEs; the other two were related to dissociative tendencies. Each of these will be described in turn.

The first questionnaire asked respondents for their gender and age; these items were included not only to ascertain basic sample characteristics but also because there are some reports suggesting that proneness to dissociation may vary with gender and age (Irwin, 1994; Ross, Ryan, Anderson, Ross, & Hardy, 1989; Torem, Hermanowski, & Curdue, 1992). Participants also were asked if they had had OBEs and, if so, how many. The item surveying the occurrence of OBEs was one originally devised by Palmer (1979):

I have had an experience in which I felt that "I" was located "outside of" or "away from" my physical body; that is, the feeling that my consciousness, mind, or center of awareness was at a different place than my physical body. (If in doubt, please answer "False" (p. 231).

Proneness to both pathological and nonpathological dissociation was measured by the DES, developed by Bernstein and Putnam (Bernstein & Putnam, 1986; Carlson & Putnam, 1993). The DES is a 28-item self-report measure indexing the frequency of various experiences of dissociative phenomena in the respondent's daily life. For example, one item concerns looking into a mirror and not recognizing oneself (an instance of pathological dissociation); another item concerns lack of awareness of nearby events while watching television or a movie (an instance of psychological absorption). With the version of the DES used in this study, for each item the participant is instructed to circle a number on a 21-point scale (that ranges from 0 to 100 in 5% increments) so as to indicate the percentage of time he or she has the nominated dissociative experience. The DES has been shown to have good reliability (Cronbach's [alpha] = .95, test-retest reliability = .79-.96; Carlson & Putnam, 1993; Frischholz et al., 1990), and its con current and discriminative validity has been extensively documented (Carlson & Putnam, 1993; Frischholz et al., 1991; van IJzendoorn & Schuengel, 1996).

For the purposes of this project the DES was used to generate two scores for each participant. One score, based on eight items of the scale, indexed the pathological form of dissociation (the DES-T; Waller et al., 1996). The second score, derived from 12 DES items in the case of nonclinical samples (Ross, Ellason, & Anderson, 1995), is a measure of psychological absorption, the key nonpathological dimension of the dissociative domain. Scores on both of these facets of dissociation are computed as the mean of responses to the component items and thus can range from 0 to 100. On each scale high scores signify strong (pathological or nonpathological) dissociative tendencies.

Proneness to somatoform dissociation was measured by the Somatoform Dissociation Questionnaire (SDQ-20; Nijenhuis, 1999; Nijenhuis et al., 1996, 1998b). The SDQ-20 comprises 20 items relating to physical symptoms and bodily experiences indicative of somatoform dissociation (e.g., "My body, or a part of it, is insensitive to pain"). On each item respondents are asked to indicate on a 5-point scale (1 = not at all to 5 = extremely) the extent to which the statement is applicable. A total score is computed as the sum of ratings over the 20 items and thus can range from 20 to 100, with high scores taken to indicate substantial proneness to somatoform dissociation. The SDQ-20 has been shown to have good reliability (Cronbach's [alpha] = .95-.96) as well as impressive factorial purity, and its convergent and discriminative validity has been adequately documented (Nijenhuis, 1999; Nijenhuis et al., 1996, 1998b).

Procedure

A "plain language" statement was attached to the front of the inventory mailed to potential participants. This statement described the topic of the study and stressed that participation was voluntary and anonymous. Participants were not required to put their names on any of the survey forms; the plain-language statement explained that the return of the completed form would in itself be taken to signify students' informed consent to participate in the project. An appeal was made to participants to respond to all questionnaire items as spontaneously and openly as possible. Participants returned their completed forms in a stamped envelope supplied by me.

Results

Preliminary comment is appropriate on the scoring of the DES-T as an index of pathological dissociation. One of the items of the DES relating to depersonalization, Item 7, has some affinity with the OBE:

Some people sometimes have the experience of feeling as though they are standing next to themselves or watching themselves do something and they actually see themselves as if they were looking at another person. Circle a number to show what percentage of the time this happens to you (p. 231).

There is some cause for debate as to whether this item should be included in the DES-T index when testing if pathological dissociative tendencies are related to the OBE. On the one hand, inclusion of the item might be seen as using an item about OBEs to predict the occurrence of OBEs. On the other hand, exclusion of the item might be seen to compromise the breadth and the psychometric integrity of the DES-T as a measure of pathological dissociation. In the following statistical analyses Item 7 of the DES was retained as a component of the DES-T score. Two points nevertheless should be noted in this regard. First, and most pragmatically, when this item was excluded from the DES-T score no substantial difference in the pattern of statistical results was found. Second, it may be stressed that the experience addressed by Item 7 of the DES is not identical to the OBE. Thus, the item also accommodates the autoscopic hallucination in which a person sees his or her own "double" but does not have an impression of bei ng outside the body (Dening & Berrios, 1994; Lukianowicz, 1958). Conversely, some OBE-ers do not report seeing their physical body during the experience and would respond in the negative to Item 7. Indeed, for the present sample 59% of OBE-ers gave a rating of zero on Item 7, and 16% of non-OBE-ers gave a rating greater than zero, which is contrary to the view that this item addresses nothing other than the OBE. Although a positive relation certainly obtains between the two variables (for a simplified 2 x 2 contingency table chi squared [1, N = 113] = 8.78, Cramer's V = .28, p< .005), there can be no reasonable claim of a simple equivalence between OBEs and the experiences tapped by Item 7 of the DES.

Of the 113 people in the sample 44 acknowledged having had an OBE. This level of incidence (38.9%) is broadly comparable to data for similar samples I have surveyed throughout the 1980s and in the 1990s (Irwin, 1985, 1988, 1996). The estimated number of OBEs reported by experients ranged from 1 to 100. Descriptive statistics (mean and standard deviation) on the independent variables are given in Table 1.

To assess the relation between dissociative tendencies and the occurrence of the OBE, a standard logistic regression analysis was undertaken with DES Absorption, DES-T, SDQ-20, gender, and age as predictors of OBE-er status. A logistic regression determines which variables serve differentially to predict group membership (in this case, OBE-ers and non-OBE-ers) and is especially useful when one or more of the individual predictor variables is not normally distributed (Tabachnick & Fidell, 1996), as is the case here; in a standard logistic regression analysis all predictor variables are entered simultaneously. The analysis, conducted with SPSS software (SPSS, Inc., 1995), evidenced a significant multivariate result (-2 log likelihood = 129.3, goodness of fit = 108.2, chi-squared [5, N = 113] = 21.75, p = .0006), that is, the set of independent variables predicted group membership to a significantly better degree than a model in which the difference between groups was a simple constant. No problems with multicollinearity of independent variables were found (Tabachnick & Fidell, 1996, p. 618). A summary of the analysis is given in Table 2; this shows the regression coefficients and their standard errors, the results of Wald's test with the associated degrees of freedom and level of significance, and the multivariate correlations. According to the associated classification matrix, the logistic regression equation correctly identified 34% (15 of 44) of OBE-ers in the sample and 91% (63 of 69) of non-OBE-ers. The only predictor variable independently to discriminate OBE-ers from non-OBE-ers was the SDQ-20 (R = .162, p = .015).

TABLE 1. DESCRIPTIVE STATISTICS ON RESEARCH MEASURES FOR THE COMPLETE SAMPLE (N = 113), OUT-OF-BODY EXPERIENTS (OBE-ERS, N= 44), AND NONEXPERIENTS (NON-OBE-ERS, N = 69)

	Full sample		OBE-ers		Non-OBE-ers	
Variable	M	SD	M	SD	M	SD
Nonpathological dissociation (DES Absorption)	15.28	14.31	19.51	16.42	12.58	12.17
Pathological dissociation (DES-T)	4.94	8.91	8.28	12.56	2.80	4.39
Somatoform dissociation (SDQ-20)	23.36	5.80	25.91	8.13	21.74	2.59
Age (years)	35.64	10.34	33.68	9.74	36.89	10.59
No. OBEs	3.38	13.54	8.64	20.76	0.0	0.0

Note. DES = Dissociative Experiences Scale; DES-T = Dissociative Experiences Scale - Taxon; SDQ-2O = Somatoform Dissociation Questionaire.

TABLE 2. STANDARD LOGISTIC REGRESSION OF NONPATHOLOGICAL DISSOCIATION (DES ABSORPTION), PATHOLOGICAL DISSOCIATION (DES-T), SOMATOFORM DISSOCIATION (SDQ-20), GENDER, AND AGE ON OBE OCCURRENCE (OBE-ERS VS NON-OBE-ERS) (N = 113)

Variable	B	SE	Wald	df	p	R
DES Absorption	- .021	.027	.569	1	.451	.000
DES-T	.088	.063	1.912	1	.167	.000
SDQ-20	.163	.067	5.940	1	.015	.162
Gender (female)	-.648	.483	1.799	1	.180*	.000
Age	-.015	.022	.486	1	.486	.000

Note. *N* = 113. Intercept = -3.605. OBE = out-of-body experience; DES = Dissociative Experiences Scale; DES-T = Dissociative Experiences Scale-Taxon; SDQ-20 = Somatoform Dissociation Questionnaire. *In the original article the p value for gender is shown incorrectly as .018.

A further analysis was undertaken to assess the extent to which dissociative tendencies predicted the number of OBEs that respondents estimated they had had. To this end, a standard multiple regression analysis was used to assess the predictability of OBE frequency from the independent variables of DES Absorption, DES-T, SDQ-20, age, and gender; all nonexperients of course were scored as having zero OBEs. Because the frequency distributions of OBE frequency and dissociation scores were substantially skewed, an inverse transformation was first applied to these variables. In a standard multiple regression all independent variables enter into the regression equation simultaneously; this is the recommended method when there are insufficient theoretical grounds for controlling the order of entry of variables (Tabachnick & Fidell, 1996). Again, analysis was conducted using SPSS software (SPSS, Inc., 1995).

Table 3 presents the unstandardized regression coefficients and intercept; the standardized regression coefficients; the semipartial correlations; and R, R squared, and adjusted R squared. By way of explanation, a semipartial correlation represents the contribution of a given independent variable to R squaured when the contribution of other independent variables is removed from both the dependent variable and the particular independent variable; thus, a semipartial correlation coefficient is a useful indicator of the unique contribution of the independent variable to the total variance of the dependent variable (Tabachnick & Fidell, 1996). In addition, given that the various types of dissociative tendencies are likely to intercorrelate, it is important to inspect so-called tolerance statistics (Tabachnick & Fidell, 1996) and ensure that intercorrelations among predictor variables do not compromise the analysis. All tolerance statistics in the regression were well above zero, ranging from .51 to .97; multicollinearity of transformed predictor variables therefore was of no practical concern (Darlington, 1990).

TABLE 3. STANDARD MULTIPLE REGRESSION OF NONPATHOLOGICAL DISSOCIATION (DES ABSORPTION), PATHOLOGICAL DISSOCIATION (DES-T), SOMATOFORM DISSOCIATION (SDQ-20), GENDER, AND AGE ON OBE FREQUENCY

Variable	B	?	p	sr.squared (unique)
DES Absorption	-.059	-.020	.851	
DES-T	.127	.131	.272	
SDQ-20	20.129	395	.000	.107
Gender (female)	.123	.149	.086	
Age	.0007	.019	.830	

Note. N = 113. Intercept = -1.516; *R squared* = .23; *Adjusted R squared* = .19; R = .48; p < .0001. DES = Dissociative Experiences Scale; DES-T = Dissociative Experiences Scale - Taxon; SDQ-20 = Somatoform Dissociation Questionnaire; OBE = out-of-body experience.

The multiple correlation R for the regression was significantly different from zero, R= .48, F(5, 107) = 6.38, p<.0001; that is, OBE frequency was significantly related to the set of independent variables. Altogether, 23% (or 19% adjusted) of the variability in the number of OBEs was predicted by scores on the measures of dissociation, gender, and age. Only one of the independent variables contributed significantly to the prediction of OBE frequency, namely, the SDQ-20 (*sr* squared = .107, p = .0002).

Discussion

The findings of this study support the view that the OBE is related to dissociative phenomena. The logistic regression analysis of the predictors of OBE occurrence identified somatoform dissociation as the only independently significant contributor to the regression equation. The pivotal role of somatoform dissociation was confirmed in the regression analysis of OBE frequency; here the sole variable independently predictive of OBE frequency was somatoform dissociation.

To the extent that somatoform dissociation is a fundamentally pathological process (Nijenhuis et al., 1998a), the study is broadly supportive of Alvarado and Zingrone's (1997) report that the OBE is related to pathological dissociation. In addition, the latter finding is advanced by the present study in its indications that the particular type of pathological dissociative tendency most pertinent to OBE occurrence is somatoform in nature. This observation is reminiscent of Wickramasekera's (1993) impression that there is a link between parapsychological experiences more generally and susceptibility to stress-related somatic symptoms. In essence, it seems that people who have OBEs, especially those who have many OBEs, tend to be characterized by a persistent proneness to dissociate in the somatic domain.

Caution must nevertheless be exercised against overpathologizing the OBE on the basis of these findings. It would certainly be overstating the case to claim that the OBE represents a deficit somatoform symptom. It must be remembered that the SDQ-20, the index of somatoform dissociation used in this study, was intentionally designed to comprise items about specifically pathological somatoform symptoms (Nijenhuis et al., 1996). Not all somatoform dissociation, however, may be pathological; like mental dissociation, somatoform dissociation might range in form from pathological to nonpathological. The present findings may well implicate pathological dissociation and specifically pathological somatoform dissociation in both the occurrence and frequency of the OBE, but there may also exist some less pathological somatoform dissociative tendencies that underlie cases in which a person only has one or two OBEs or has "milder" forms of OBE. (for more on the latter, see Jacobs & Bovasso, 1996). Further research into t his possibility is impeded by the current unavailability of a measure of nonpathological somatoform dissociative tendencies. In any event, at present it is appropriate to place more emphasis on the somatoform quality than the pathological quality of the dissociative tendencies associated with the OBE.

It must also be emphasized that the effect sizes found in the study are by no means large: For OBE occurrence, only 34% of OBE-ers (but 91% of non-OBE-ers) were correctly classified, and for OBE frequency the multivariate R for the regression equation was .48. The moderate effect sizes might be explained in part by the fact that some nonexperients with high dissociative tendencies might well have an OBE at some time in the future; that is, dissociation might be more strongly related to an individual's capacity to have OBEs than the present research design is able to demonstrate. A more likely explanation, however, is that there are factors in addition to dissociative tendencies that have a bearing on whether a person will have (or will report having) an OBE. A few other personality characteristics and cognitive skills have been identified (for a review see Irwin, 1999a), but there remains a need for substantial further empirical investigation in this regard.

As I have argued elsewhere (Irwin, 1985) a theoretical account of the OBE must comprise more than a mere specification of factors that explain why the person feels as if the self is exteriorized during the experience. There are many other facets of the phenomenology of the OBE, and an adequate theory must address these subjective events, too. With this in mind I now offer an outline of a theory that (somewhat speculatively) reformulates my earlier account (Irwin, 1985) in terms of the dissociative domain. The following model is essentially a dissociational theory of the OBE.

The origins of the OBE are hypothesized to lie in a confluence of dissociative factors. Circumstances associated with extreme (either high or low) levels of cortical arousal evoke a state of strong absorption, particularly in the case of a person with a requisite level of absorption capacity and need for absorbing experiences. Alternatively, high absorption may be induced deliberately by the experient. If this state of absorbed mentation is paralleled by a dissociation from somatic (somaesthetic and kinesthetic) stimuli, an OBE may occur. People who are prone to this type of somatoform dissociation may generally be said to have tendencies toward depersonalization. There may nevertheless be various pathological and nonpathological factors underlying this propensity (Jacobs & Bovasso, 1996), and the OBE therefore should not automatically be construed as a pathological symptom.

In instances where the development of the state of somatic dissociation is gradual, the imminent loss of all somatic contact may be signaled by certain innate biological warning signals, the so-called OBE-onset sensations.

The continued orientation of attention away from both exteroceptive and somatic stimuli effectively suspends support for the socially conditioned assumption that the perceiving self is "in" the physical body, fostering the impression that consciousness no longer is tied spatially to the body. This abstract, nonverbal idea of a disembodied consciousness is coded by the cognitive processing system into a passive, generalized somaesthetic image of a static floating self. Consciousness of that image corresponds to the so-called asensory OBE. By means of the dissociative process of synesthesia the somaesthetic image also may be transformed into a visual image, given a basic level of visuospatial skills in the experient.

Strong absorption in this image is a basis for the OBE's perceptual realism. The somaesthetic image also may be transformed into a more dynamic, kinesthetic form, and the experient will have the impression of being able to move in the imaginal out-of-body environment. The somatic imagery entailed in this transformation is held to underlie the phenomenon of the parasomatic form. A drawing of attention back to the physical body's state also may be expressed synesthetically by way of the image of the astral cord.

The perceived content of the out-of-body environment is governed by short-term needs. A life-threatening situation, for example, may prompt imagery about a paradisial environment; the nature of the latter is held to be a product of social conditioning, although the precise sources of these paradisial stereotypes have yet to be identified fully (see Irwin, 1987). Because dissociation is psi conducive it is possible that the out-of-body imagery could incorporate extrasensory information and thereby feature a degree of veridicality not expected of mere fantasy; empirical documentation of extrasensory elements in spontaneous OBEs, however, is not yet convincing. Eventual dissipation of somatic dissociation or a diversion of attention to somatic or exteroceptive processes brings the individual's OBE to an end.

The above outline of a dissociational theory of the OBE is offered not as a definitive description but as a constructive stimulus to further research effort. One issue for research in this context is the extent to which the three types of dissociative tendencies help to illuminate individual phenomenological features of the OBE.

References

Alvarado, C. S. (1992). The psychological approach to out-of-body experiences: A review of early and modern development. *Journal of Psychology, 126,* 237-250.

Alvarado, C. S., & Zingrone, N. L. (1997). Out-of-body experiences and dissociation. Proceedings of presented papers: *The Parapsychological Association 40th Annual Convention*, 11-25.

Bernstein, E. M., & Putnam, F. W. (1986). Development, reliability, and validity of a dissociation scale. *Journal of Nervous and Mental Disease, 174,* 727-735.

Blackmore, S.J. (1994). Exploring cognition during out-of body experiences. *Proceedings of presented papers: The Parapsychological Association 40th Annual Convention*, 65-71.

Carlson, E. B., & Putnam, F. W. (1993). An update on the Dissociative Experiences Scale. *Dissociation, 6,* 16-27.

Darlington, R. B. (1990). *Regression and linear models*. New York: McGraw-Hill.

Dening, T. R., & Berrios, G. E. (1994). Autoscopic phenomena. *British Journal of Psychiatry, 165,* 808-817.

Finkel, D., & Mogue, M. (1997). Sex differences and nonadditivity in heritability of the Multidimensional Personality Questionnaire scales. *Journal of Personality and Social Psychology, 72,* 929-938.

Frischholz, E.J., Braun, B. G., Sachs, R. G., Hopkins, L., Shaeffer, D. M., Lewis, J., Leavitt, F., Pasquotto, J. N., & Schwartz, D. R. (1990). The Dissociative Experiences Scale: Further replication and validation. *Dissociation, 3,* 151-153.

Frischholz, E.J., Braun, B. G., Sachs, R. G., Schwartz, D. R., Lewis, J., Shaeffer, D., Westergaard, C., & Pasquotto, J. (1991). Construct validity of the Dissociative Experiences Scale (DES): I. The relation between the DES and other self-report measures of dissociation. *Dissociation, 4,* 185-188.

Glicksohn, J. (1990). Belief in the paranormal and subjective paranormal experience. *Personality and Individual Differences, 11,* 675-683.

Hunt, H. T., Gervais, A., Shearing-Johns, S., & Travis F. (1992). Transpersonal experiences in childhood: An exploratory empirical study of selected adult groups. *Perceptual & Motor Skills, 75,* 1135-1153.

Irwin, H. J. (1980). Out of the body Down Under: Some cognitive characteristics of Australian students reporting OOBEs. *Journal of the Society for Psychical Research, 50,* 448-459.

Irwin, H.J. (1981). Some psychological dimensions of the out-of-body experience. *Parapsychology Review, 12(4),* 1-6.

Irwin, H.J. (1985). *Flight of mind: A psychological study of the out-of body experience.* Metuchen, NJ: Scarecrow Press.

Irwin, H.J. (1987). Images of heaven. *Parapsychology Review, 18(1),* 1-4.

Irwin, H.J. (1988). Out-of-body experiences and attitudes to life and death. Journal of the *American Society for Psychical Research, 82,*237-251.

Irwin, H.J. (1994). Proneness to dissociation and traumatic childhood events. *Journal of Nervous and Mental Disease, 182,* 456-460.

Irwin, H.J. (1996). Childhood antecedents of out-of-body and deja vu experiences. *Journal of the American Society for Psychical Research, 90,* 157-173.

Irwin, H.J. (1999a). *An introduction to parapsychology* (3rd ed.). Jefferson, NC: McFarland.

Irwin, H.J. (1999b). Pathological and nonpathological dissociation: The relevance of childhood trauma. *Journal of Psychology: Interdisciplinary and Applied, 130,* 157-164.

Jacobs, J. R., & Bovasso, G. (1996). A profile analysis of psychopathology in clusters of depersonalization types. *Dissociation, 9,* 169-175.

Janet, P. (1889). *L'automatisme psychologique* [Psychological automatism]. Paris: Felix Alcan.

Janet, P. (1965). *The major symptoms of hysteria* (2nd ed.). New York: Hafner. (Original work published 1907)

Kroll, J., Fiszdon, J., & Crosby, R. D. (1996). Childhood abuse and three measures of altered states of consciousness (dissociation, absorption and mysticism) in a female outpatient sample. *Journal of Personality Disorders, 10,* 345-354.

Lukianowicz, N. (1958). *Autoscopic phenomena.* AMA Archives of Neurology and Psychiatry, 80, 199-220.

Lynn, S.J., & Rhue, J. W. (1988). Fantasy proneness: Hypnosis, developmental antecedents, and psychopathology. *American Psychologist, 43,* 35-44.

Myers, S. A., Austrin, H. R., Grisso, J. T., & Nickerson, R. C. (1983). Personality characteristics as related to the out-of-body experience. *Journal of Parapsychology, 47,* 131-144.

Nijenhuis, E. R. S. (1999). *Somatoform dissociation: Phenomena, measurement, and theoretical issues.* Assen, The Netherlands: van Gorcum.

Nijenhuis, E. R. S., Spinhoven, P., Van Dyck, R., Van Der Hart, O., & Vanderlinden, J. (1996). The development and psychometric characteristics of the Somatoform Dissociation Questionnaire (SDQ-20). *Journal of Nervous and Mental Disease, 184,* 688-694.

Nijenhuis, E. R. S., Spinhoven, P., Van Dyck, R., Van Der Hart, O., & Vanderlinden, J. (1998a). Degree of somatoform and psychological dissociation in dissociative disorder is correlated with reported trauma. *Journal of Traumatic Stress, 11,* 711-730.

Nijenhuis, E. R. S., Spinhoven, P., Van Dyck, R, Van Der Hart, O., & Vanderlinden, J. (1998b). Psychometric characteristics of the Somatoform Dissociation Questionnaire: A replication study. *Psychotherapy and Psychosomatics,* 67, 17-23.

Nijenhuis, E. R. S., & Van Der Hart, O. (1999). Somatoform dissociative phenomena: A Janetian perspective. In J. M. Goodwin & R. Attias (Eds.), *Splintered reflections: Images of the body in trauma.* New York: Basic Books.

Osis, K. (1975). Perceptual experiments on out-of-body experiences [Abstract]. In J. D. Morris, W. C. Roll, & R. L. Morris (Eds.), *Research in parapsychology* 1974 (pp. 53-55). Metuchen, NJ: Scarecrow Press.

Palmer, J. (1979). A community mall survey of psychic experiences. *Journal of the American Society for Psychical Research, 73,* 221-251.

Ross, C. A. (1989). Multiple personality disorder: Diagnosis, clinical features, and treatment. New York: Wiley.

Ross, C. A., Ellason, J. W., & Anderson, G. (1995). A factor analysis of the Dissociative Experiences Scale (DES) in dissociative identity disorder. *Dissociation, 8,* 229-235.

Ross, C. A., Joshi, S., & Currie, R. (1990). Dissociative experiences in the general population. *American Journal of Psychiatry, 147,* 1547-1552.

Ross, C. A., Ryan, L., Anderson, G., Ross, D., & Hardy, L. (1989). Dissociative experiences in adolescents and college students. *Dissociation, 2,* 239-242.

Spiegel, D. (Ed.). (1993). *Dissociative disorders: A clinical review.* Lutherville, MD: Sidran Press. (Original work published 1991)

Spiegel, D., & Cardena, E. (1991). Disintegrated experience: The dissociative disorders revisited. *Journal of Abnormal Psychology, 100,* 366-378.

Spiegel, H. (1963). The dissociation-association continuum. *Journal of Nervous and Mental Disease, 136,* 374-378.

SPSS, Inc. (1995). *SPSS* [Computer software]. Chicago: Author.

Steinberg, M. (1993). The spectrum of depersonalization: Assessment and treatment. In D. Spiegel (Ed.), *Dissociative disorders: A clinical review* (pp. 79-103). Lutherville, MD: Sidran Press. (Original work published 1991.)

Steinberg, M. (1995). *Handbook for the assessment of dissociation: A clinical guide.* Washington, DC: American Psychiatric Press.

Tabachnick, B. G., & Fidell, L. S. (1996). *Using multivariate statistics* (3rd ed.). New York: HarperCollins.

Tellegen, A., & Atkinson, G. (1974). Openness to absorbing and self-altering experiences ("absorption"), a trait related to hypnotic susceptibility. *Journal of Abnormal Psychology 83,* 268-277.

Tellegen, A., Lykken, D. T., Bouchard, T.J., Wilcox, K.J., Segal, N. L., & Rich, S. (1988). Personality similarity in twins reared apart and together. *Journal of Personality and Social Psychology, 54,* 1031-1039.

Torem, M. S., Hermanowski, R. W., & Curdue, K.J. (1992). Dissociative phenomena and age. *Stress Medicine, 8,* 23-25.

Van Der Hart, O., & Friedman, B. (1989). A reader's guide to Pierre Janet on dissociation: A neglected intellectual heritage. *Dissociation, 2,* 3-16.

Vanderlinden, J., Van Dyck, R., Vandereycken, W., & Vertommen, H. (1993). Dissociation and traumatic experiences in the general population of the Netherlands. *Hospital and Community Psychiatry, 44,* 786-788.

Van Ijzendoorn, M. H., & Schuengel, C. (1996). The measurement of dissociation in normal and clinical populations: Meta-analytic validation of the Dissociative Experiences Scale (DES). *Clinical Psychology Review, 16,* 365-382.

Waller, N. G., Putnam, F. W., & Carlson, E. B. (1996). Types of dissociation and dissociative types: A taxometric analysis of dissociative experiences. *Psychological Methods, 1,* 300-321.

Waller, N. G., & Ross, C. A. (1997). The prevalence and biometric structure of pathological dissociation in the general population: Taxometric and behavior genetic findings. *Journal of Abnormal Psychology, 106,* 499-510.

Whitlock, F. A. (1978). The psychiatry and psychopathology of paranormal phenomena. *Australian and New Zealand Journal of Psychiatry*, 12, 11-19.

Wickramasekera, I. (1993). Is hypnotic ability a risk factor for subjective (verbal report) psi, somatization, and health care costs? In L. Coly & J. D. S. McMahon (Eds.), *Psi and Clinical Practice* (pp. 184-197). New York: Parapsychology Foundation.

Wilson, S. C., & Barber, T. X. (1983). The fantasy-prone personality: Implications for understanding imagery, hypnosis, and parapsychological phenomena In A. A. Sheikh (Ed.), *Imagery: Current theory, research, and application* (pp. 340-387). New York: Wiley.

In: Psychological Scientific Perspectives on Out of Body ... ISBN: 978-1-60741-705-7
Editor: Craig D. Murray

Chapter 4

Psychological Theories of the OBE Under Scrutiny

Commentaries on Blackmore and Irwin

Postscript to 'A Psychological Theory of the Out-of-Body Experience'

Susan J. Blackmore

Twenty-five years after it was written, I rather nervously reread my own paper and was struck by two things. First was how much the psychology of mind and consciousness has changed in the intervening years, and second was how well the basic idea behind the theory still holds up.

Since then, the 1980s computer-inspired cognitive psychology has given way to a much richer science of the mind, from neuroscience and brain scanning to the multi-disciplinary field of consciousness studies. In particular, enactive theories of perception have exposed deep philosophical problems with the notion of representation, and replaced the idea that what we experience is the contents of a mental model with the idea that seeing is a kind of activity – we experience what we are doing (O'Regan & Noë 2001, Noë 2005). I have contributed in a small way to this change with experiments on change blindness (Blackmore *et. al.,* 1995) and my arguments that consciousness is neither a stream nor a container with contents (Blackmore, 2002, 2003).

In this context my cavalier use of such terms as "cognitive system" and "successive representations" seems naïve. Even so, the theory does not depend on using these precise terms, and still makes sense in the light of more subtle notions of modeling and representation developed since then.

I originally conceived the theory because of my own dramatic out-of-body experience (Blackmore, 1970). At first I assumed that my spirit had left my body, or my astral body had projected into the astral planes, but after much research and exploration I rejected those ideas, and began to wonder, instead, about the very nature of self. Most of us feel as though we are an inner self inhabiting our body and looking out from behind the eyes, but from a neuroscience point of view this inner self has to be a fiction. So what is going on? Around that time I began to practice Zen meditation, and this tradition also emphasizes the illusory nature of the self we think we are. So if this perceiving, located self is a fiction, could it be that a different fiction might sometimes be constructed – one that seems to be looking down on the world from a bird's eye view instead of looking out from inside the head?

The rest of the theory follows from there. Looking at the OBE this way led me to ask both how the normal fiction of a located self is created, and when and why it might be replaced with a bird's eye view. I speculated that although we can think about, imagine, remember and perceive many things at once, we normally have no trouble distinguishing between our own thoughts and the actual world. This is because our perceptions are integrated with our body image into a complex, stable and coherent unity that I called the "model of reality". This model of reality seems real not because of any particular distinguishing features but simply because it is currently the most stable and coherent model we have. This means that it might be replaced by an alternative view either because it is weakened or disrupted, or because something else becomes even more complex and stable (or both). The alternative could be a model constructed from memory and imagination, and we know that memories are often imagined in a bird's eye view.

This made sense of the conditions under which spontaneous OBEs occur, the methods used to induce them, and the skills of the people most likely to have them. I made various predictions from the theory; that common OB locations would be those most easily imagined, that people with skill at imagining from different locations would be more likely to have OBEs; and that people who can induce OBEs at will should also be good at ignoring sensory input.

In this 1984 paper I reported some of my earliest findings confirming these predictions, and soon afterwards completed further research. I found that people reporting deliberate OBEs also reported better dream control skills, while those who had spontaneous OBEs were more likely to have mystical experiences (Blackmore, 1986a). In a further three studies I found that OBErs are more likely to use an observer perspective (or bird's eye view) in recalling dreams (though not when recalling actual events). This was also found by Irwin (1986). In experiments asking people to switch viewpoints in their imagination, OBErs were more easily able to do this, and they reported clearer and more vivid imagery from different viewpoints (Blackmore, 1987).

My suggestion that inducing an OBE requires the ability to ignore input was also confirmed by research showing that OBErs score higher on the scale of "absorption", a measure of how easily people become absorbed in books, films, or music to the exclusion of the outside world (Gabbard & Twemlow, 1984, Irwin, 1986). I also found that the incidence of OBEs among schizophrenics is no different from that in a control group (Blackmore, 1986b), providing evidence against the popular idea that there is something pathological about having an OBE.

After this I turned to research on near-death experiences (Blackmore, 1993), which very often include OBEs, but then I stopped all my research on these topics – mainly because so little was happening in the field. It was therefore a great surprise to find, in this new century, that at last progress was being made again, using new techniques.

In 2002 Blanke and his colleagues described how they induced an OBE repeatedly in a patient being treated for epilepsy, by electrically stimulating her right angular gyrus. This confirmed the early accidental findings of Wilder Penfield (1955) and has subsequently been repeated by another team treating a patient with tinnitus (Ridder, et al 2007). The stimulation also induced other distortions of the body image suggesting, as I would expect, that OBEs "may reflect a failure by the brain to integrate complex somatosensory and vestibular information" (Blanke *et. al.*, 2002).

Blanke and Arzy (2005) argued that OBEs are related to a failure to integrate multisensory information at the temporo-parietal junction, leading to disruption of the body image and other aspects of self-processing, and further research confirmed that ambiguous input from sensory systems is indeed implicated in OBEs (Blanke *et. al.*, 2004). In addition, this same brain area was found to be selectively activated when healthy volunteers imagined themselves in typical OBE positions (Blanke *et al* 2005). With a completely different approach Lenggenhager and colleagues (2007) induced experiences somewhat like OBEs, including seeing a virtual body and mislocalizing the self, by using conflicting visual and somatosensory input in a virtual reality set up.

I could never have predicted which brain areas were involved in OBEs, but otherwise these findings are just what I would have expected: they show how the normally stable model of self in the world can be weakened, giving other viewpoints a chance to take over and seem real.

I find these new researches very exciting. One of the things that depressed me most in my decades of research is the tendency for people (and the media) to divide theories of OBEs and NDEs into two black-and-white types. On the one hand are the "good" (or "spiritual") theories – OBEs mean the spirit can leave the body, NDEs are a glimpse of life after death. On the other hand are the "bad" (or "boring", or "reductionist") theories – OBEs and NDEs don't exist or are "just hallucinations", horrible scientists are denying people's life-changing experiences.

Now, at last, we have research linking OBEs to measurable brain processes, to other experiences, and to research on the mystery of consciousness. We can confidently say that OBEs really do happen, they really do change people's lives, and they are exciting and interesting to study. But rather than telling us about spirits, souls or astral bodies, they reveal something much more interesting about the illusion of being me.

REFERENCES

Blackmore, S. (1970). Out-of-the-Body, explained away, but it was so real. http://www.issc-taste.org/arc/dbo.cgi?set=expom&id=00075&ss=1

Blackmore, S.J. (1986a). Spontaneous and deliberate OBEs: A questionnaire survey. *Journal of the Society for Psychical Research*, *53*, 218-224.

Blackmore, S.J. (1986b). Out-of-body experiences in schizophrenia: a questionnaire survey. *Journal of Nervous and Mental Disease*, *174*, 615-619.

Blackmore, S.J. (1987). Where am I?: Perspectives in imagery, and the out-of-body experience. *Journal of Mental Imagery*, *11*, 53-66.

Blackmore, S.J. (1993). *Dying to Live: Science and the near death experience* London, Grafton, and Buffalo, N.Y., Prometheus.

Blackmore, S.J. (2002). There is no stream of consciousness. *Journal of Consciousness Studies, 9,* 17-28.

Blackmore, S. (2003). *Consciousness: An introduction*, London, Hodder & Stoughton

Blackmore, S.J., Brelstaff, G., Nelson, K., & Troscianko, T. (1995). Is the richness of our visual world an illusion? Transsaccadic memory for complex scenes. *Perception, 24,* 1075-1081.

Blanke, O., & Arzy, S. (2005). The out-of-body experience: Disturbed self-processing at the temporo-parietal junction. *The Neuroscientist, 11,* 16-24.

Blanke, O., Ortigue, S., Landis, T., & Seeck, M. (2002). Stimulating illusory own-body perceptions. *Nature, 419,* 269-70

Blanke, O., Landis, T., Spinelli, L., & Seeck, M. (2004). Out-of-body experience and autoscopy of neurological origin. *Brain, 127,* 243-258.

Blanke, O., Mohr, C. Michel, C.M., Pascual-Leone, A., Brugger, P., Seeck, M.,

Gabbard, G.O., & Twemlow, S.W. (1984). *With the eyes of the mind,* New York, Praeger

Irwin, H.J. (1986). Perceptual perspective of visual imagery in OBEs, dreams and reminiscence. *Journal of the Society for Psychical Research, 53,* 210-217.

Lenggenhager, B., Tadi, T., Metzinger, T., & Blanke, O. (2007). Video ergo sum: Manipulating bodily self-consciousness. *Science, 317,* 1096 - 1099.

Noë, A. (2005). *Action in perception*, Cambridge, MA, MIT Press

O'Regan, J.K., & Noë, A. (2001). A sensorimotor account of vision and visual consciousness. *Behavioural and Brain Sciences, 24(5),* 939-1011.

Penfield,W. (1955). The role of the temporal cortex in certain psychical phenomena. *The Journal of Mental Science, 101,* 451-465.

De Ridder, D. Van Laere, K., Dupont, P., Menovsky, T. & Van de Heyning, P. (2007). Visualizing Out-of-Body Experience in the Brain. *New England Journal of Medicine, 357,* 1829 – 1833.

POSTSCRIPT TO 'THE DISEMBODIED SELF: AN EMPIRICAL STUDY OF DISSOCIATION AND THE OUT-OF-BODY EXPERIENCE'

Harvey J. Irwin

The identification of the out-of-body experience as a dissociative phenomenon is not new. Early suggestions of this kind, however, seemed to have had an implicit intention not so much to explain the OBE, but rather, to explain it away; as the experience was attributed to a mundane psychological process, not only was there no evident need to appeal to the paranormal or fanciful mystical connotations, but it appeared any further discussion and research was rendered almost superfluous. Be that as it may, labeling an experience is not the same as explaining it, so the OBE did warrant closer theoretical and empirical scrutiny.

My initial analysis of the phenomenological characteristics of the OBE (Irwin, 1985) identified several dissociative processes that could potentially illuminate the way in which this experience unfolded. Perhaps in part because of the lack of appropriate psychometric instruments in the mid 1980s my analysis regrettably did not lead to a rush of incisive empirical investigations, but in the following decade measures of dissociation, and in particular of somatoform dissociation, were developed and these innovations encouraged me to undertake both a dissociational investigation of the near-death experience (Irwin, 1993) and the study reported in the present contribution to this book.

The findings of the latter project have since been independently replicated and constructively extended (Gow, Lang, & Chant, 2004; Murray & Fox, 2005a,b; Terhune, 2006). Further support for the dissociational model may be gleaned from research on the neurosensory bases of embodiment or the impression that the self is located within one's bodily borders. A complex of proprioceptive, motor, vestibular, and visual systems has been found to underlie one's assumption of embodiment (for a recent review see Giummarra, Gibson, Georgiou-Karistianis, & Bradshaw, 2008), and in this regard it is notable that a series of studies by Blanke and his colleagues (e.g., Blanke, 2004; Blanke & Arzy, 2005; Blanke, Ortigue, Landis, & Seeck, 2002) suggests a failure to integrate information across these systems is associated with proneness to OBEs. Although Blanke's findings more commonly are used to buttress a neurological depiction of the OBE they might be interpreted also in a dissociational context, given that contemporary accounts of dissociation give specific emphasis to disturbances in the integration of cognitive processes (e.g., see Giesbrecht, Lynn, Lilienfeld, & Merckelbach, 2008; Spiegel & Cardeña, 1991). A dissociational model of the out-of-body experience therefore looks increasingly viable.

References

Blanke, O. (2004). Out of body experiences and their neural basis. *British Medical Journal, 329,* 1415–1416.

Blanke, O., & Arzy, S. (2005). The out-of-body experience: Disturbed self-processing at the temporo-parietal junction. *Neuroscientist, 11,* 16–24.

Blanke, O., Ortigue, S., Landis, T., & Seeck, M. (2002). Stimulating illusory own-body perceptions. *Nature, 419(6904),* 269–270.

Giesbrecht, T., Lynn, S. J., Lilienfeld, S. O., & Merckelbach, H. (2008). Cognitive processes in dissociation: An analysis of core theoretical assumptions. *Psychological Bulletin, 134,* 617–647.

Giummarra, M. J., Gibson, S. J., Georgiou-Karistianis, N., & Bradshaw, J. L. (2008). Mechanisms underlying embodiment, disembodiment and loss of embodiment. *Neuroscience and Biobehavioral Review, 32,* 143–160.

Gow, K., Lang, T., & Chant, D. (2004). Fantasy proneness, paranormal beliefs and personality features in out-of-body experiences. *Contemporary Hypnosis, 21,* 107-125.

Irwin, H. J. (1993). The near-death experience as a dissociative phenomenon: An empirical assessment. *Journal of Near-Death Experiences, 12,* 95-103.

Murray, C., & Fox, J. (2005a). Dissociational body experiences: Differences between respondents with and without prior out-of-body experiences. *British Journal of Psychology*, 96, 441-456.

Murray, C., & Fox, J. (2005b). The out-of body experience and body image: Differences between experients and nonexperients. *Journal of Nervous and Mental Disease, 193,* 70-72.

Spiegel, D., & Cardeña, E. (1991). Disintegrated experience: The dissociative disorders revisited. *Journal of Abnormal Psychology, 100,* 366-378.

Terhune, D.B. (2006). Dissociative alterations in body image among individuals reporting out-of-body experiences: A conceptual replication. *Perceptual and Motor Skills, 103,* 76-80.

PRELIMINARY EVIDENCE SUGGESTING A TYPOLOGICAL MODEL OF THE OUT-OF-BODY EXPERIENCE

Jerome J. Tobacyk

The papers by Blackmore (1984, A psychological theory of the out-of-body experience) and Irwin (2000; The disembodied self: An empirical study of dissociation and the out-of-body experience), reproduced in Chapters 2 and 3 of this volume, both represent important contributions to the psychological study and explanation of the out-of-body experience (OBE). Both papers significantly contributed to the continuing naturalization of the OBE by proposing theories of the OBE as a natural process amenable to scientific explanation within the framework of cognitive and personality psychology. The two papers differ somewhat in epistemic strategy in that Blackmore emphasizes a deductive (i.e., top-down) approach to theory construction (with some proposals for empirical investigation included at the end), whereas Irwin employs a more inductive (i.e., bottom-up) approach to theory construction. Irwin begins with a review of empirical research concerning absorption and the OBE, then introduces dissociation as an explanatory construct, reports empirical tests of normal and pathological dissociation processes in relation to the OBE, and finally presents a dissociation-based theory of the OBE that is consistent with his empirical findings. Blackmore's cognitive theory of the OBE reflects a relatively high level of abstraction (i.e., person as model-builder) and can be viewed as a meta-theory within which Irwin's more specific dissociation-based theory can be nested.

The focus of this commentary is a discussion of an implication of Irwin's (2000) paper. It is proposed that there may be qualitatively different types of OBE reporters, with these different types perhaps characterized by different causal mechanisms and by different personality correlates. Therefore, the class of OBE reporters might be not be a homogeneous group, but rather may be comprised of different subgroups, with each subgroup characterized by different personality profiles perhaps reflecting different causal mechanisms and correlates of the OBE. This conclusion is based on statistical information reported in Irwin's paper that may not have been previously discussed.

In Irwin's contribution, Table 1 lists standard descriptive statistics for three dissociation measures: (1) the Dissociative Experiences Scale-Absorption (DES-A), a measure of absorption that reflects a non-pathological dissociative process; (2) the Dissociative Experiences Scale-Taxon (DES-T), a measure of pathological dissociation; and (3) the

Somatoform Dissociation Questionnaire (SDQ-20), a measure of pathological somatoform dissociation. In Irwin's Table 1 are listed standard deviations for the full sample (n = 113), for the OBE group (n = 44), and for the Non-OBE group n = 69). As indicated in Table A below, one striking feature of Irwin's descriptive statistics concerns the relatively large group differences in variability on the three dissociation measures, as indicated by the group standard deviations. For all three dissociation measures, but particularly for the two measures of pathological dissociation, the DES-T and the SDQ-20, the standard deviations are considerably greater (two to three times greater) for the OBE group compared to the Non-OBE group.

Table A also presents the results of F tests that test the differences between the standard deviations of the OBE group compared to those of the Non-OBE group on the three dissociation measures. As indicated in Table A, the standard deviations of the OBE group are significantly greater (i.e., indicate significantly greater variability) on both measures of pathological dissociation — the DES-T and the SDQ-20 — than the Non-OBE group, suggesting considerable variability in pathological dissociation tendencies within the OBE group.

From this finding, it is reasonable to speculate that the significantly greater variability in the OBE group may indicate that a subgroup of OBE reporters record relatively low scores (or moderate scores) on the two measures of pathological dissociation (DES-T & SDQ-20), whereas a different subgroup of OBE reporters record relatively high scores on these same two measures.

Table A. Results of F tests comparing the standard deviations of the OBE group versus the Non-OBE group on the three dissociation measures

Instrument/Construct	OBE Group-Standard Deviation	Non-OBE Group - Standard Deviation	F test	p level
DES-Absorption (Non-pathological Dissociation)	16.42	12.17	1.35	ns
DES-T (Pathological Dissociation)	12.56	4.39	2.86	$p < .01$
SDQ-20 (Pathological Somatoform Dissociation)	8.13	2.59	3.14	$p < .01$

N OBE group = 44, N Non-OBE group = 69; df_1 F = 43, df_2 F = 68

The possibility of a typology of OBE reporters, with high levels of pathological dissociation characterizing one subset of OBE reporters, may be a productive question for future research. This interpretation is guarded because at least two interpretations are possible:

1. A response set explanation: There may be a subset of OBE reporters who tend to endorse relatively rare subjective experiences, in this case both OBEs and the events described in the DES-T and the SDQ-20.
2. An OBE typological explanation: There may be qualitatively different types of veridical OBE reporters, perhaps reflecting different causal mechanisms or different predispositional personality characteristics.

The notion of a typological model of the OBE is also consistent with Irwin's findings that a logistic regression using the three dissociation measures as predictors correctly identified only 34% (15 of 44) of the OBE reporters in his sample, whereas it correctly identified 91% (63 of 69) of non-OBE reporters. The relatively modest predictability of membership in the OBE group by the measures of dissociation may be due to the OBE group being comprised of two (or more) subgroups of qualitatively different OBE reporters—only one subgroup being characterized by high levels of pathological somatoform dissociation.

In summary regarding Irwin's paper, pathological dissociation may be only one of various dispositional characteristics predisposing a person toward experiencing an OBE. Alternatively, there may be qualitatively different forms of OBEs that may be differentiated by the varying underlying predisposing factors and causal mechanisms (e.g., absorption or normal dissociation versus pathological dissociation). Thus, the same kind of OBEs may occur through different mechanisms—or there may be qualitatively (and perhaps experientially) different forms of OBEs characterized by different causal mechanisms. Profile analyses of OBE reporters based on a battery of personality measures, including personal information based on interviews, would provide evidence germane to the hypothesis of different OBE typologies.

Psychological research has provided considerable information regarding both general principles and individual differences concerning the OBE (See Irwin & Watt, 2007 for a review). As an illustration of general principles: over 90% of OBEs are characterized as visual and over 90% of OBE experiences occur during states of physical inactivity. Such general principles provide important clues about the nature of OBEs. As an illustration of individual differences, personality characteristics significantly associated with OBEs (that may be predispositional) include: absorption, dissociation, and fantasy proneness). However, a deeper understanding of the OBE also requires explanation at a biological level, by articulating the structural and dynamic brain processes associated with this experience.

The investigation of the OBE is particularly challenging because a deep understanding of the OBE is closely linked to the solution of several significant philosophical problems. First, a deep explanation of the OBE must be nested within valid definitions of both consciousness (i.e., subjective experience) and the self—definitions of these phenomena still appear intractable. Second, a deep explanation of the OBE requires a solution to one of the "easy" problems of consciousness (Chalmers, 1995). In this sense, an "easy" problem is the articulation of the neural structures, biochemical processes, and pathway activations that characterize the OBE. This is considered an "easy" problem because, in principle, it appears potentially solvable by the application of empirical scientific methods, though its solution is not likely in our lifetime. It is important to note that a solution to this "easy" problem regarding the OBE would provide correlative information about what neural structures and activities are associated with the OBE. However, it would not answer the "hard" question of consciousness (Chalmers, 1995) concerning how and why material brain events give rise to the conscious subjective experience (i.e., qualia) of an OBE happening to *me* (i.e., an experiencing self). Given a human brain comprised of billions of neurons, trillions of synapses, and virtually countless recursive connections and pathways, a solution of even the "easy" problem appears a very ambitious goal.

REFERENCES

Blackmore, S. J. (1984). A psychological theory of the out-of-body experience. *Journal of Parapsychology, 48,* 201-218.

Chalmers, D. (1995). Facing up to the problem of consciousness. *Journal of Consciousness Studies, 2 (3),* 200-219.

Irwin, H. J. (2000). The disembodied self: An empirical study of dissociation and the out-of-body experience. *Journal of Parapsychology, 64,* 261-277.

Irwin, H. J., & Watt, C. A. (2007). *An introduction to parapsychology.* (5th ed.). Jefferson, N.C.: McFarland & Co.

FLIGHTS OF FANCY?

Etzel Cardeña and Devin B. Terhune

The theoretical models of Blackmore (1984) and Irwin (2000) have provided fruitful speculation and received support from other researchers (Alvarado, 2000). The two models are complementary in that Blackmore emphasizes the ontology of the OBE (a constructed model of reality dependent on memory and imagination), whereas Irwin underlines mediating processes such as the interaction between losing contact with bodily sensation, absorption, and somatoform dissociation. In this commentary, we will develop a point mentioned mostly in passing by both authors, namely the possible connection between attentional processes, psychopathology, and OBEs.

Overall, there is no clear indication that OBEs are associated with most forms of psychopathology. One exception is the relation between 'happy schizotypy' and OBEs (McCreery & Claridge, 1995), but the former, which can be seen as the propensity to experience unusual experiences independently of distress or dysfunction, may be more fruitfully considered as a personality trait rather than as an indicator of psychopathology (McCreery & Claridge, 2002). The other, more challenging, exception is the positive correlation between somatoform dissociation and OBEs (Irwin, 2000). Even so, two points can be made. The first, as noted by Irwin himself, is that the relationship between those two variables is very small, such that somatoform dissociation explains relatively little variance in the incidence of OBEs (R^2 = .16). The second one, hinted at by Blackmore (1994), is that there may be different processes at play in the case of induced versus spontaneous OBEs, a distinction similar to that made by Pierre Janet (1976/1919) between spontaneous and induced somnambulism. Janet used the former term to refer to spontaneous dissociative experiences frequently reported by distressed, traumatized individuals in their daily lives, whereas the latter occurred among psychological healthy individuals within a structured setting such as hypnosis.

With respect to his ideas about spontaneous dissociative phenomena related to trauma, there is ample evidence that they may occur transiently around the time of trauma, or become chronic in the case of severe or long-lasting traumatization (for a review see Cardeña, Butler, & Spiegel, 2003). As for "induced" dissociation among healthy individuals, consider the results of a study with highly hypnotizable individuals, who had been previously screened for psychological health (Cardeña, 2005). Without exception, all of them reported spontaneous experiences of floating, falling, the "mind separating from the body," or flying away from their physical bodies.

How can one explain these diverse findings? First, the fact that some people tend to experience OBEs whereas others do not probably involves the interaction between genetic and environmental factors. With respect to the former, Irwin (2000) mentions one article that had not found a genetic contribution for dissociation. However, two later and methodologically superior studies have since found evidence for such a genetic contribution (Becker-Blease et al., 2004; Jang, Paris, Zweig-Frank, & Livesley, 1998). This predisposition may then interact with environmental circumstances that elicit absorptive processes. One of them, of course, is hypnosis, in which there are implicit and explicit suggestions to focus one's attention, but meditation and other focusing techniques, as well as performance of activities whose requisite behavior is easily automatized (e.g., running), can also elicit a sense of detachment from the body (Cardeña, 2005; Holroyd, 2003). Another context is the experience of trauma, in which circumstances often demand a somewhat sustained focus of attention, as hypnosis procedures also elicit. For instance, in one study experients of an intense earthquake reported greater attention focusing and perceptions of detachment from their bodies and other psychological processes such as emotions, around the time of trauma than four months later (Cardeña & Spiegel, 1993). In the case of early, severe, and/or chronic traumatization, dissociative processes may become a coping mechanism rather than just a transient reaction. A more general model for hypnotizability and dissociation also posits pathological and non-pathological paths of development (Carlson & Putnam, 1989).

Finally, there is also evidence, supportive of both Blackmore's and Irwin's models, that scant or extreme afferent stimulation may make an OBE more likely. In the aforementioned hypnosis study with high responders (Cardeña, 2005), participants were more likely to experience increased body image changes when they were lying down motionless than when they were pedaling a stationary bike, and strenuous and repetitive running can produce OBEs among some people (Morgan, 1993). In either case, the ordinary sense of the "ecological" self is disrupted by either lack of stimulation or repetitive stimulation, which can produce neuronal habituation (cf. Neisser, 1988; Tart, 1975); thus a different model of the body in relationship to the environment may ensue.

A full model of OBEs, including the extent to which they are associated with pathological conditions, requires a discussion of cultural variables such as expectations and interpretations of reality (Cardeña, 1999) and of possible anomalous acquisition of information during an OBE (Alvarado, 2000), but space limitations prevents us from considering these issues here. OBEs are intrinsically interesting for those who have them, but also provide important insights about the fragility of our conceptions of the (embodied) self, whether altered or not.

REFERENCES

Alvarado, C. (2000). Out-of-body experiences. In E. Cardeña, S. J. Lynn, & S. Krippner (Eds.), *Varieties of anomalous experience* (pp. 183-218). Washington, DC: American Psychological Association.

Becker-Blease K. A., Deater-Deckard, K., Eley, T., Freyd, J. J., Stevenson, J., & Plomin, R. (2004). A genetic analysis of individual differences in dissociative behaviors in childhood and adolescence. *Journal of Child Psychology and Psychiatry, 45,* 522–532.

Blackmore, S. J. (1984). A psychological theory of the out-of-body experience. *Journal of Parapsychology, 48,* 201-218.

Cardeña, E. (1999). Culture, and psychopathology. The hidden dimensions in T. X. Barber's theory. *Contemporary Hypnosis, 16,* 132-138.

Cardeña, E. (2005). The phenomenology of deep hypnosis: Quiescent and physically active. *International Journal of Clinical and Experimental Hypnosis, 53,* 37-59.

Cardeña, E., Butler, L. D., & Spiegel, D. (2003). Stress disorders. In G. Stricker & T. Widiger, (Eds.) *Handbook of psychology*. Volume 8. (pp. 229-249). New York: John Wiley.

Cardeña, E., & Spiegel D. (1993). Dissociative reactions to the Bay Area Earthquake. *American Journal of Psychiatry, 150,* 474-478.

Carlson, E. B., & Putnam F. (1989). Integrating research on dissociation and hypnotizability. *Dissociation, 2,* 32-38.

Holroyd, J. (2003). The science of meditation and the state of hypnosis. *American Journal of Clinical Hypnosis, 46,* 109-128.

Irwin, H. J. (2000). The disembodied self: An empirical study of dissociation and the out-of-body experience. *Journal of Parapsychology, 64,* 261-277.

Janet, P (1976). *Psychological healing. Volume 1.* New York: Arno Press. (Originally published 1919)

Jang, K. L., Paris, J., Zweig-Frank, H., & Livesley, W. J. (1998). Twin study of dissociative experience. *Journal of Nervous and Mental Diseases, 186,* 345–351.

McCreery, C., & Claridge, G. (1995). Out-of-the-Body Experiences and Personality. *Journal of the Society for Psychical Research, 60(838),* 129-148.

McCreery, C., & Claridge, G. (2002). Healthy schizotypy: The case of out-of-body experiences. *Personality and Individual Differences, 32,* 141-154.

Morgan, W. P. (1993). Hypnosis and sport psychology. In J. W. Rhue, S. J. Lynn, I. Kirsch (Eds.) *Handbook of clinical hypnosis* (pp. 649-670). Washington, D. C.: American Psychological Association.

Neisser, U. (1988). Five kinds of self-knowledge. *Philosophical Psychology, 1,* 35-59.

Tart, C. T. (1975). *States of consciousness.* New York: E. P. Dutton.

TAKING THE PSYCHOLOGICAL APPROACH: BLACKMORE AND IRWIN IN CONTEXT

David Wilde

By far the most dominant of all the theoretical perspectives postulated in OBE research history is the psychological explanation (Alvarado, 2000). Alvarado has put forward two main reasons for this; firstly, the psychological approach is more open to systematic scientific testing than its ecsomatic[1] counterpart, and, secondly it broadens the investigative interest of the experience to those studying cognition and perception, as well as other areas of psychology, such as, personality and psychopathology. As it stands today, there are now several psychological theories, taking very different approaches, however, in this commentary, I shall summarize the two theories reproduced in the two preceding chapters, namely Susan Blackmore's (1984) cognitive-perceptual theory and Harvey Irwin's (1985; 2000) theory of dissociation.

Blackmore's (1984) theory has it that the cognitive system continuously creates various models of reality based on the memories of the percipient and sensory impressions received from the external world. Blackmore argued that the system allows for only one of these models to dominate consciousness at any one particular time; the dominant model is usually based on the level of congruity with the prevailing sensory information (Irwin & Watt, 2007). However, there are times when the sensory input to the cognitive system undergoes changes radical enough to challenge the sensory based model of reality; such changes can be brought about by stress or sensory reduction, and this explains why OBEs can occur under conditions such as sensory deprivation, relaxation, illness, and drug use. During these periods of sensory disruption, the cognitive system then favors a model of reality based on memory and imagination. The OBE is but one of these resultant models; others may be lucid dreaming, perceptual distortions and mystical experiences (Alvarado, 2000).

Irwin (1981) initially developed a synesthetic theory of the OBE owing to the role that this 'cross modal experiencing' seems to play within such experiences. This was later revised (Irwin, 2000) to incorporate other psychological factors, such as absorption. Irwin's theories were driven by what he saw as an exclusive focus by previous theorists on explaining why an experient needs to experience their self as separate from their physical body and a corresponding failure to pay attention to the richly diverse phenomenological components of the experient's accounts. Irwin's theory postulated that dissociation occurs between somatic inputs in cases where cross-modal (synaesthestic) processing takes place. When such a reduction or breakdown of somatic processing takes place, the assumption of the perceiving self as contained within the body is then undermined. This can lead to an abstract perception of a disembodied self/consciousness and a resultant cognitive representation of "...a passive, generalized somaesthetic image of a static floating self" (Irwin, 2000, p. 272). It is important to note that the experient needs to be experiencing a relatively high level of psychological

[1] The general idea underlying ecsomatic theories of OBEs is that the OBE is veridical, that is, something detaches and travels away from the physical body and subsequently returns, often with a very clear memory of what has happened during the excursion, and possibly with a recollection of information not previously known that could ostensibly only have been gathered extra-sensorially

absorption in parallel with a somatic dissociative experience for the OBE to occur. The powerful realism of the OBE is explained by Irwin as a product of the strong absorption processes at work during the experience, as well as playing a certain role in directing the experient's attention further away from their somatic sensations once the process begins.

Both Blackmore's and Irwin's theories had a distinct advantage over their predecessors (e.g. Freudian theories, such as, Palmer, 1978; Rank, 1971) in that they generate eminently testable hypotheses using scientific methods. This was an important move forward in the study of OBEs as it opened up the potential for a much wider range of research to be carried out, such as, the experimental induction and testing of OBEs in the laboratory, and survey and questionnaire based studies, which aimed to profile the personalities of OB experients (OBErs). Results from this work have provided a wealth of valuable information. These two theories also share fundamental similarities in that sensory disruption between input and experience is central to both theories, and both emphasize the role played by a person's visio-spatial skills in the onset and maintenance of the experience.

However, the two theories differ somewhat in the empirical support for each model. For instance, one of the strongest claims Blackmore made to support her theory is that OBErs have greater visual imagery skills than non-OB experients (non-OBErs). This hypothesis has been tested by several researchers over the last twenty or so years. Blackmore (1987) herself found that OBErs did indeed have greater visio-spatial skills than non-OBErs and were more adept at changing their imagery viewpoints than non-OBErs. This latter result was also supported by Cook and Irwin (1983) who found that OBErs were superior to non-OBErs when asked to imagine a particular scene from differing viewpoints. The results of these studies would suggest some consistency between theory and real life experience, given the rich visual imagery component of the experience, and that some OB induction techniques place emphasis on the ability to visualize either target locations or destinations (e.g. Buhlman, 1996) or a target object, such as a cube, at various distances from behind closed eyes (e.g. Monroe, 1971). Blackmore also argued that those who deliberately induced OBEs would have greater visual imagery skills than those who have OBEs spontaneously due to the greater demand on those skills. Again, she found support for this in a study comparing spontaneous OBErs and OBErs who induce their experience deliberately, with the inducers scoring higher on measure of dream control skills (Blackmore, 1986).

However, the theory's predictions have at times lacked some precision. Murray, Fox, and Wilde (2005) noted that precisely which visual imagery skills OBErs are expected to be better at has not been made explicit. OBErs taking part in Irwin's (1980) study were found to be no more habitual 'visualizers' than those in the normal population, and scored lower than would be expected on a measure of vividness of visual imagery. Blackmore (1983) also assessed OBErs and non-OBErs on a measure of vividness of imagery and found no differences between the two groups. Similarly, she found no differences between another OBE and non-OBE sample on Gordon's (1949) Control of Imagery Questionnaire, leading her to conclude that, "in general vividness of imagery does not seem to be a good predictor of the people who have these [OBE] experiences" (Blackmore, 1983, p. 242).

Irwin's theory by contrast enjoys some robust support concerning two of its main assumptions; namely the roles played by psychological absorption and dissociation. With regards to the role absorption plays in the OBE, several significant positive findings have been made by Irwin himself using Tellegen's Absorption Scale (Tellegen & Atkinson, 1974) as the main measuring tool (Irwin, 1980; 1981; 1985), and others (Dalton, Zingrone, &

Alvarado, 1999; Glicksohn, 1990; Myers, Austrin, Grisso, & Nickeson, 1983). Studies that have used the Tellegen Absorption Scale have also been instrumental in demonstrating a positive correlation between the scale's synesthesic elements and OBEs (Irwin, 1985; McCreery & Claridge, 1995). However, other studies have found non-significant relationships (Gabbard & Twemlow, 1984; Spanos & Moretti, 1988).

Concerning the disruption to somatic input necessary for OBErs to have their experience, a particular form of dissociation, somatoform dissociation, has more recently become of interest to OBE researchers. This has been defined by Nijenhuis, Spinhoven, Van Dyck, Van der Hart, and Vanderlinden (1998, p. 713) as, "dissociation which is manifested in a loss of the normal integration of somatoform components of experience, bodily reactions and functions". To test how this might apply to his own theory, Irwin (2000) administered the Somatoform Dissociation Questionnaire (SDQ-20) (Nijenhuis, Spinhoven, van Dyke, van der Hart, & Vanderlinden, 1996), Dissociation Experiences Scale (DES) (Bernstein & Putnam, 1986) and the DES-T (a sub-scale of the DES which taps into pathological dissociation) to a sample of 113 participants. He found that somatoform dissociation was the only significant variable that discriminated between OBErs and non-OBErs. These results have been supported more recently in a series of studies by Murray and Fox who found evidence to show that OBErs score significantly higher on measures of somatoform dissociation than non-OBErs (Murray & Fox, 2005a, 2005b, 2006).

In closing, it can be said that both Blackmore's and Irwin's theories have contributed significantly to the study of OBEs. They have provided the OBE researcher with a wide range of intriguing research questions, many of which have yet to be satisfactorily answered. Blackmore's theory views the OBE as a purely psychological event–essentially a psychological misinterpretation of a subjective experience that didn't actually take place–and as such makes a bold statement about the veridicality of the OBE, which, of course, may not sit well with some theorists and probably most experients, too. However, being cognitive in nature, it enabled researchers to focus more specifically on hitherto unexplored aspects of the experience, such as sleep related phenomena and the aforementioned visio-spatial mechanisms.

As noted earlier one of the central elements to both Blackmore's and Irwin's theories is that the OBE is seen to be triggered by a disruption of somatic input. In Blackmore's theory it is the degradation or loss of somatic input that triggers the OBE. However, by focusing on psychological absorption and dissociation, and in particular the role of somatoform dissociation, Irwin's theory also suggests that there could be wider social, perceptual and affective dimensions that may be correlated with the OBE phenomenon. Conversely, it must be noted that much of this kind of work is correlational in nature, and as such, is limited to what it can say about causes and effects related to the OBE. On the other hand, Irwin's theory is perhaps more encompassing as an explanation of the phenomena as it describes both 'positive' and 'deficit' dissociative processes are related to the OBE phenomenon. It is a more general dissociative model of OBEs which includes social and affective dimensions as well as perceptual ones, as well as suggesting that there are pre-existing differences with regards to body image between OBE and non-OBE experients, which are susceptible to 'positive' and 'deficit' dissociative processes.

REFERENCES

Alvarado, C. S. (2000). Out-of-body experiences. In E. Cardeña, S. J. Lynn & S. C. Krippner (Eds.), *Varieties of anomalous experience: Examining the scientific evidence* (pp. 183-218): American Psychological Association.

Bernstein, E. M., & Putnam, F. W. (1986). Development, reliability, and validity of a dissociation scale. *Journal of Nervous and Mental Disease, 174,* 727-735.

Blackmore, S. J. (1983). Imagery and the OBE. In W. G. Roll, J. Beloff & R. A. White (Eds.), *Research in parapsychology, 1982* (pp. 231-232). Metuchen, N. J.: Scarecrow.

Blackmore, S. J. (1984). A psychological theory of the out-of-body experience. *Journal of Parapsychology, 48,* 201-218.

Blackmore, S. J. (1986). Spontaneous and deliberate OBEs: A questionnaire survey. *Journal of the Society for Psychical Research, 53(802),* 218-224.

Blackmore, S. J. (1987). Where am I? Perspectives in imagery and the out-of-body experience. *Journal of Mental Imagery, 11,* 53-66.

Buhlman, W. (1996). *Adventures beyond the Body: How to experience out-of-body travel.* New York: HarperCollins.

Cook, A. M., & Irwin, H. J. (1983). Visuospatial skills and the out-of-body experience. *Journal of Parapsychology, 47,* 23-35.

Dalton, K., Zingrone, N. L., & Alvarado, C. S. (1999). *Exploring out-of-body experiences, dissociation, absorption, and alteration of consciousness in the ganzfeld with a creative population.* Paper presented at the 42nd Annual Convention of the Parapsychological Association, Stanford University, Palo Alto, CA.

Gabbard, G. O., & Twemlow, S. W. (1984). *With the eyes of the mind: An empirical analysis of out-of-body sStates.* New York: Praeger Scientific.

Glicksohn, J. (1990). Belief in the paranormal and subjective paranormal experience. *Personality and Individual Differences, 11,* 675-683.

Gordon, R. (1949). An investigation into some of the factors that favour the formation of stereotyped images. *British Journal of Psychology, 39,* 156-167.

Irwin, H. J. (1980). Out-of-the-body down under: some cognitive characteristics of Australian students reporting OOBEs. *Journal of the Society for Psychical Research, 50(785),* 448-459.

Irwin, H. J. (1981). The psychological function of out-of-body experiences: so who needs the out-of-body experience? *Journal of Nervous and Mental Disease, 169(4),* 244-248.

Irwin, H. J. (1985). *Flight of mind: A psychological study of the out-of-body experience.* Metuchen, NJ: Scarecrow Press.

Irwin, H. J. (2000). The disembodied self: An empirical study of dissociation and the out-of-body experience. *Journal of Parapsychology, 64,* 261-277.

Irwin, H. J., & Watt, C. (2007). Out-of-body experiences. In *An Introduction to Parapsychology* (5th Revised edition ed.). Jefferson, NC: McFarland & Co Inc.

McCreery, C., & Claridge, G. (1995). Out-of-the-body experiences and personality. *Journal of the Society for Psychical Research, 60(838),* 129-148.

Monroe, R. (1971). *Journeys out of the body.* New York: Doubleday.

Murray, C. D., & Fox, J. (2005a). Dissociational body experiences: Differences between respondents with and without prior out-of-body experiences. *British Journal of Psychology, 96,* 441-456.

Murray, C. D., & Fox, J. (2005b). The out-of-body experience and body image: Differences between experients and non-experients. *Journal of Nervous and Mental Disease, 193(1),* 70-72.

Murray, C. D., & Fox, J. (2006). Differences in body image between people reporting near-death and spontaneous out-of-body experiences. *Journal of the Society for Psychical Research, 70(2),* 98-109.

Murray, C. D., Fox, J., & Wilde, D. J. (2005). *The relationship between belief in the paranormal and performance on a visual imagery task: Do out-of-body experients have better visual imagery skills than non-experients?* Paper presented at the 29th International Conference of the Society for Psychical Research, Bath, UK.

Myers, S. A., Austrin, H. R., Grisso, J. T., & Nickeson, R. C. (1983). Personality characteristics as related to the out-of-body experience. *Journal of Parapsychology, 47,* 131-144.

Nijenhuis, E. R. S., Spinhoven, P., Van Dyck, R., Van der Hart, O., & Vanderlinden, J. (1998). Degree of somatoform and psychological dissociation in dissociative disorders is correlated with reported trauma. *Journal of Traumatic Stress, 11,* 711-773.

Nijenhuis, E. R. S., Spinhoven, P., van Dyke, R., van der Hart, O., & Vanderlinden, J. (1996). The development and psychometric characteristics of the somatoform dissociation questionnaire. *Journal of Nervous and Mental Disease, 184(11),* 688-694.

Palmer, J. (1978). The out-of-the body experience: A psychological theory. *Parapsychology Review, 95,* 19-22.

Rank, O. (1971). *The Double: A psychoanalytic study.* Chapel Hill: University of North Carolina Press.

Spanos, N. P., & Moretti, P. (1988). Correlates of mystical and diabolical experiences in a sample of female university students. *Journal for the Scientific Study of Religion, 27,* 106-116.

Tellegen, A., & Atkinson, G. (1974). Openness to absorbing and self-altering experiences ("absorption"), a trait related to hypnotic susceptibility. *Journal of Abnormal Psychology, 83,* 268-277.

Attempts to Explain OBEs by Susan Blackmore and Harvey Irwin

Kathryn Gow

Out of Body Experiences (OBEs) have been defined as many things and have been reported in most cultures across time. Research into out-of-body experiences appears to have commenced in earnest in the late 1970s. There are the believer, experiencer and non-believer camps. While both Blackmore and Irwin appear to be skeptics, it could be conjectured that there must have been some belief underlying their interest in order to pursue their research studies at a period in psychology history when researchers were considered to be slightly "odd" to be engaged in such endeavors.

It should be noted that the two chapters included in this book by Susan Blackmore (see Chapter 2) and Harvey Irwin (see Chapter 3) represent a small sample of the extent and breadth of their work in paranormal psychology. The material in these chapters focus on theoretical conjectures of their early scientific thinking which formed the basis for a lot of later research which spanned a number of anomalous experiences and it is for this specific reason that they have been included here, as their currency remains strong today.

Susan Blackmore is one of the most convincing and entertaining skeptics in the area of paranormal psychology, who in her research into paranormal and anomalous phenomena, sets out to explore one more possibility that perhaps just this time, there might be some truth in the claims of the believers. The difficulty for those researchers who would like to retain some modicum of belief in anomalous experiences, such as OBEs, is that Blackmore is so "darned" objective and logical and hopelessly intellectually brilliant.

Her approach to understanding what goes on in the mind of a believer of OBEs is that there is a breakdown in the reality of what the senses say is happening and what is actually happening. Although much maligned at times in the research area, the Neuro Linguistic Programming method on analyzing strategies (e.g., Bandler & Grinder, 1975) of thinking and behaving in terms of installation and processing of events adds credence to what Blackmore suggests. Indeed, her model is so intellectually acceptable that it holds perchance for the false memories debate, even perhaps for exploring the much more entrenched foundations of our society such as the belief in history as being a true record of what has happened at different times in various places (Gow, 2005; Lewandowsky & Stritzke, 2008); that is, we come to believe in something that is not real, but that has been constructed and then installed into our memory banks as real. Reading and absorbing what Blackmore lays out for us requires careful reading and deductions on our part.

In terms of dealing with the OBE as an altered state of consciousness, there are few people who doubt that this is really the case; it is in fact a state of consciousness which is altered from the normal state of awareness. However, this does not hold scientifically in terms of it being a false experience. Several of the OBEs are similar in description to those mystical experiences equated with the Holy Grail experiences, perhaps encountered only once in a lifetime (Gow, 2006).

Irwin taps into the concept of dissociation in this type of experience (one of the correlates of hypnotizability), in chapter 3. Gow, Lang and Chant (2004) report on Irwin's (1985) earlier published cross-modal (synesthetic) theory of OBE which combines features of somatoform dissociation and psychological absorption, suggesting that psychological absorption may generate the sensation of body separation resulting from exclusion of somatic input. Gow et al (2004) confirmed for their OBE experients, that somatoform dissociation displayed a moderate positive relationship with both absorption and dissociation The study by Alvarado (1986) supports both Blackmore's and Irwin's models relating absorption and visuo-spatial abilities to OBEs. Irwin (1985) and McCreery et al. (1995) have provided evidence that synesthesia-like items from Tellegen's Absorption scale are positively correlated with OBEs.

It is also Irwin who investigates the factors of belief and personality as well as the effects of trance like phenomena in OBEs. Irwin (1996), along with others (Twemlow, 1997; Wilson & Barber, 1983) has researched the concept that experiencers of OBEs tend to have a greater ability to fantasize and imagine, and he outlines the basis on which this relationship rests, in his chapter in this book.

Others have followed the leadership of Irwin in exploring the relationship of paranormal belief (and a range of other variables such as fantasy proneness, dissociation, personality variables) in OBEs and other anomalous experiences such as past lives, alien abductions, near death and general anomalous and paranormal experiences (Gow, Lane & Chant, 2003; Murphy, & Lester, 1976; Pekala, Kumor & Marcano, 1995) all attempting to shed light on how people have come to believe in anomalous experiences. Generally there has been evidence that believers and experiencers score higher on fantasy proneness, dissociation and absorption (though not always to the same extent) than non-believers.

So where to from here? Regardless of what researchers do to understand why people have, and believe in the reality of their, OBE experiences, Blackmore argues that the model of reality that wins out in the end for the actual experiencer is that which seems to be the "most complex, stable, or coherent model". However, even vacillating believers are unable to dismiss the very real experiences they have had in relation to their out- of- body experiences.

The Sceptics Society offer awards to researchers to disprove reports of such anomalous experiences, but their model of the world must, at some stage of their lives, had to have encompassed some type of experience from which to base their arguments against. How else could they know what people are talking about in relation to anomalous experiences?

Both Blackmore and Irwin have afforded us many years of their working lives to investigate experiences that give people hope that "there is something else out there"; each person's faith in the unseen varies, but we all have beliefs in some things that are yet to be proven. Why else would scientists be given money to find cures and to invent new problem solving devices to save the world?

References

Alvarado, C.S. (1986). ESP during spontaneous out-of-body experiences: A research and methodological note. *Journal of the Society for Psychical Research, 53,* 393-397.

Bandler, R. & Grinder, J. (1975). *The structure of magic.* Palo Alto, CA: Science and Behavior Books.

Gow, K.M. (2005). *Memories of abuse in and out of hypnosis: Where are we now?* Paper presented at the 35th Annual Congress of the Australian Society of Hypnosis: Expect the unexpected. Sydney, New South Wales, 14th- 18th September.

Gow, K., Lane, A., & Chant, D. (2003). Personality characteristics, beliefs and the near-death experience. *Australian Journal of Clinical and Experimental Hypnosis, 31(2),* 128-152.

Gow, K., Lang, T., & Chant, D. (2004). Fantasy proneness, paranormal beliefs and personality features in out-of-body experiences. *Contemporary Hypnosis, 21(3),* 107-125.

Gow, K.M. (2006). The 'Holy Grail' experience or heightened awareness? *The Indo-Pacific Journal of Phenomenology, 6 (1),* 1-10.

Irwin, H. J. (1985). *Flight of mind: A psychological study of the out-of-body experience.* Metuchen, NJ: Scarecrow Press.

Lewandowsky, S & Stritzke, W. G. K., (2008). Misinformation and the 'War on Terror': When Memory Turns Fiction into Fact. In Stritzke, W. G. K., Lewandowsky, S.,

Denemark, D., Morgan, F., & Clare, J. (Eds.) *Terrorism and torture: An interdisciplinary perspective.* Cambridge, UK: Cambridge University Press.

McCreery, C., & Claridge, G. (1995). Out-of-the-body experiences and personality. *Journal of the Society for Psychical Research, 60,* 129-148.

Murphy, K., & Lester, D. (1976). A search for correlates of belief in ESP. *Psychological Reports, 38,* 82.

Pekala, R. J., Kumor, V. K., & Marcano, G. (1995). Anomalous/Paranormal experiences, hypnotic susceptibility, and dissociation. *Journal of the American Society for Psychical Research, 89(4),* 313-332.

Twemlow, S.W. (1997). Epilogue: Personality file. In R.Monroe (Ed.), *Journeys out of the body* (pp. 275-280). Garden City, NY: Doubleday.

Wilson, S.C., & Barber, T.X. (1983). The fantasy prone personality: Implications for understanding imagery, hypnosis, and parapsychological phenomena. In A.A. sheikh (Ed.), *Imagery: Current theory, research, and application* (pp. 340-387). New York: Wiley.

Comments on Two Anglo-Saxon Theories of the 'Exit Outside the Body'

Pascal Le Maléfan and Renaud Evrard

Susan Blackmore doubtless produced one of the first coherent and testable models of the out-of-body experience (OBE) on purely psychological grounds. However, before developing our commentary, we briefly note our preferred use of the expression "exit outside the body" to the term "out-of-body experience" (OBE), because the latter connotes parapsychology and the paranormal. We are situated for our part in a clinical approach of the specular identity. The specular identity implies a time of splitting during its constitution, and the impression of going out of ones physical envelope and seeing oneself remote would come to verify it again.

Blackmore's hypotheses regarding how the cognitive system could supply an alternative but sufficiently stable version of reality provides a plausible explanation of how one may come to have the sensation of being outside one's own body. This sensation would thus not be pathological, although rare, but would correspond at a minimal level to a mostly accidental or incidental short-circuit of the usual cognitive system, but with the possibility that this experience could be voluntarily induced by training, in a manner close to that of the mystic state.

As with every model, Blackmore's is reductionist, in spite of its relevance. It lacks some of the explanatory power of a more structural perspective that can gain understanding of the meaning of the experience of the exit outside the body and which considers how the sensation "to have gone out of one's own body" and to see it remotely might support the subject in a critical or exceptional moment, by decomposing the coordinates of its identification. This structural perspective also has the advantage, quite as Blackmore did with her model, and to a degree with Irwin, to postulate that everyone, as the mystic, can be subject of this experience. But, if there is no a priori reason to psychopathologize the phenomenon, it is nevertheless not a commonplace experience because it comes from a clinical practice of the extreme and implies a psychic work around the issue of self-unity. So, if for certain subjects this experience will live and will be remembered in the elation, it is not without being in charge of a latent degree of strangeness or fear, for which this elation tries to stitch, with more or less success.

This a priori absence of pathological character of the exit outside the body makes inappropriate the use of the term of dissociation, even somatoform dissociation, such as Irwin employed it following Janet. It seems too much connoted and a source of confusion, in particular with psychotic phenomena. It seems more adequate to propose that we are in the register of disjunction, which exactly uncrosses two types of identification such as Lacan's (1977) theory helps to conceive them: the imaginary or specular identification, whose prototype is the recognition of one's image in the mirror, and the symbolic identification, that proceeds from the link between this image and the name introduced in the field of the Other to appoint the subject. During an exit outside the body, there is precisely persistence of the recognition of one's own body, but as remote, and, besides, this perception is not at once harrowing. That is why this experience does not pertain systematically neither to a pathology of the body-image or of bodily schema, nor to a psychopathologic ailment, and differs from a neurological breach on one hand and from a heautoscopy on another hand.

REFERENCE

Lacan, J. (1977). *Ecrits : A selection.* W.W Norton & Co, Inc., New York.

In: Psychological Scientific Perspectives on Out of Body... ISBN: 978-1-60741-705-7
Editor: Craig D. Murray

Chapter 5

UNDERSTANDING THE OUT-OF-BODY EXPERIENCE FROM A NEUROSCIENTIFIC PERSPECTIVE

Jane E. Aspell and Olaf Blanke

ABSTRACT

The self is a multifaceted entity. Studies of the self as it relates to the body (the 'bodily self') have revealed three crucial aspects of bodily self-consciousness: (1) ownership (2) self-location and (3) visuo-spatial perspective. The normal bodily self includes the representation of an owned body (1), and the self is experienced as being localized within this owned body (embodied), at a definite location in space (2). Moreover, in healthy humans, the external world is experienced *from* this location, i.e. consciousness has an inherent visuo-spatial perspective (3) whose origin normally coincides with self-location. Scientists have only very recently begun to investigate the links between these different aspects and their underlying neural bases (Arzy, Seeck, Ortigue, Spinelli, & Blanke, 2006a; Aspell, Lenggenhager, & Blanke, 2009; Ehrsson, 2007; Ehrsson & Petkova, 2008; Lenggenhager, Mouthon, & Blanke, 2009; Lenggenhager, Tadi, Metzinger, & Blanke, 2007). Here we argue that the scientific understanding of the bodily self can be informed by the study of OBEs because these aspects of the self are experienced as spatially distinct from the physical body during these experiences (Blanke, Landis, Spinelli, & Seeck, 2004). How is it possible that these features of the bodily self can 'come apart' in an OBE? The study of what causes them to dissociate in an OBE and the examination of how these aspects of the bodily self relate to behavior and neural processing in healthy subjects will provide important insights into how these aspects of self are related: phenomenally, behaviorally and neurally.

INTRODUCTION

If you ever had the experience of lying in bed, about to fall asleep, when suddenly you had the distinct impression of floating up near the ceiling and looking back down at your body on the bed, then it is likely that you had an out-of-body experience (OBE). Here is a description of an OBE by Sylvan Muldoon, one of the first authors to describe his own OBEs (and those of others) in great detail: *"I was floating in the very air, rigidly horizontal, a few feet above the bed [...] I was moving toward the ceiling, horizontal and powerless [...] I managed to turn around and there [...] was another 'me' lying quietly upon the bed"* (Muldoon & Carrington, 1929) (Fig.1).

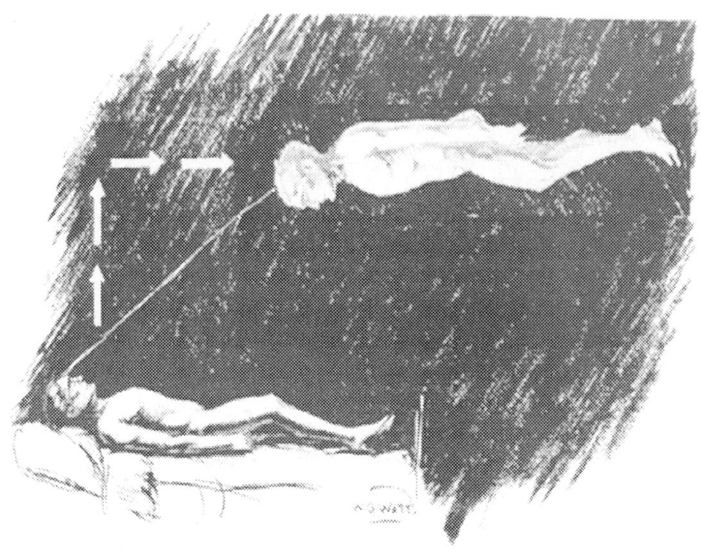

Figure 1. Depiction of the phenomenology of the OBE with elevated self-location (the light upper body), visuo-spatial perspective, and autoscopy (the body shown on the bed). [Modified version of a figure from (Muldoon & Carrington, 1929)]

OBEs are bizarre departures from normal human experience but they are much more than a mere curiosity for science and the humanities: an OBE is effectively a breakdown of the bodily self, thus the study of this phenomenon is likely to lead to insights into the bodily foundations of self-consciousness. OBEs can be characterized by three phenomenological elements: the impression (1) that the self is localized outside one's body (disembodiment or extracorporeal self-location), (2) of seeing the world from an extracorporeal and elevated perspective, and (3) of seeing one's own body from this perspective (Blanke et al., 2004; Irwin, 1985). OBEs are striking phenomena because they challenge our everyday experience of the spatial unity of self and body,: the experience of a "real me" that 'resides' in my body and is the subject or "I" of experience and thought (Blackmore, 1982).

OBEs have been reported since time immemorial and have been estimated to occur in about 5% of the general population (Blackmore, 1982; Irwin, 1985). OBEs also occur in various medical conditions (Blanke et al., 2004), and several precipitating factors have been determined including certain types of neurological and psychiatric disease. In healthy subjects they may also occur during hypnagogic and hypnopompic hallucinations (Cheyne & Girard, 2009; Terhune, 2009). They can also occur in cases of awareness during general anesthesia, sensory deprivation, marijuana use, rapid body position changes (as during falls or car accidents) and extreme fear (Bünning & Blanke, 2005). To date, only a few neurological and neuroscientific investigations have been carried out on OBEs, probably because, in general, they occur spontaneously, are of short duration, and happen only once or twice in a lifetime

(Irwin, 1985). Investigations of neurological patients with OBEs have several advantages as OBEs in patients may occur repeatedly, sometimes in quick succession, and in rare instances can be induced by electrical stimulation of the brain (Blanke, Ortigue, Landis, & Seeck, 2002; De Ridder, Van Laere, Dupont, Menovsky, & Van de Heyning, 2007; Penfield, 1955). An individual undergoing an OBE usually experiences a dissociation between his self-location and his visuo-spatial perspective with respect to the felt and/or seen location of his own body – in other words, he perceives his own body (and the world) from a spatial location that does not coincide with the felt and seen position of his body (Blanke et al., 2004; Blanke & Mohr, 2005; Brugger, Regard, & Landis, 1997). In OBEs the origin of the visuo-spatial perspective is co-localized with self-location (as it is for healthy subjects), but the body is experienced at a different location. What causes this dissociation of unity between self and body? In this chapter we will present a description of the neurology and neuroscience of OBEs and we will argue that studying OBEs and their involved brain mechanisms provide unique opportunities for gaining a scientific understanding of the bodily self. We will also present recent findings from studies with healthy subjects which have sought to simulate, via controlled experimental manipulations, some of the aspects of the out-of-body experience, in order to understand the role of multisensory integration in OBEs and more generally, in bodily self-representation.

The Out-of-Body Experience: Etiology and Anatomy

Out-of-body experiences have been reported to occur in various generalized and focal diseases of the central nervous system. OBEs associated with focal damage typically occur in cases of epilepsy, traumatic brain injury, vascular brain damage and migraine (Devinsky, Feldmann, Burrowes, & Bromfield, 1989; Kölmel, 1985; Lippman, 1953; Todd & Dewhurst, 1955). Generalized neurological etiologies include generalized epilepsy, cerebral infections (e.g. meningitis and encephalitis) and intoxication (Blanke et al., 2004; Brugger et al., 1997; Dening & Berrios, 1994; Devinsky et al., 1989; Hécaen & Ajuriaguerra, 1952; Lhermitte, 1939). OBEs of focal origin mainly implicate posterior regions of the brain and some authors have suggested a primary involvement of either the temporal or parietal lobe (Blanke et al., 2004; Devinsky et al., 1989; Hécaen & Ajuriaguerra, 1952; Todd & Dewhurst, 1955). There is no consensus on whether the left or right hemisphere is more involved in OBEs: some authors found no hemispheric predominance (Dening & Berrios, 1994; Devinsky et al., 1989; Hécaen & Ajuriaguerra, 1952) but others have suggested that the right hemisphere is more implicated (Brugger et al., 1997; Grüsser & Landis, 1991). More recently, Blanke and colleagues (Blanke et al., 2004) argued for a crucial role for the cortex at the temporo-parietal junction (TPJ; Fig.2) of the right hemisphere. The crucial role of the right TPJ has been suggested because lesion overlap in several patients with OBEs centered on this region (Blanke et al., 2004; Blanke & Mohr, 2005), electrical stimulation of this region can give rise to OBE-like experiences (Blanke et al., 2002; De Ridder et al., 2007; Penfield & Erickson, 1941), and because the TPJ is activated during mental imagery of disembodied self-location (Arzy, Thut, Mohr, Michel, & Blanke, 2006b).

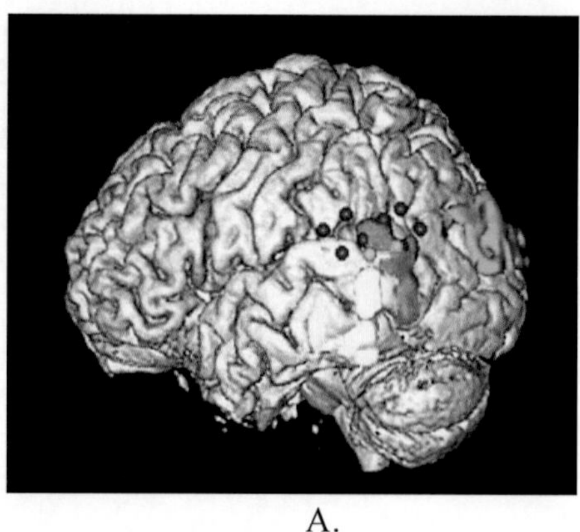

A.

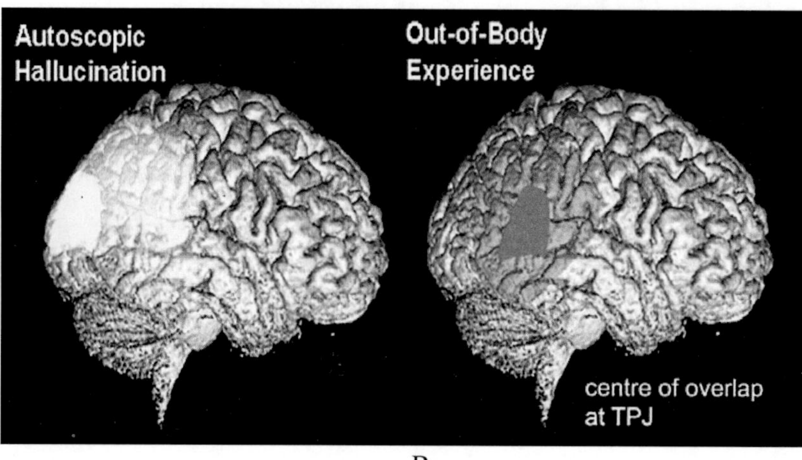

B.

Figure 2(A). Mean lesion overlap analysis of five patients from (Blanke et al., 2004). Each color represents a different patient Mean overlap analysis is centered on the TPJ. [Modified version of a figure from (Blanke et al., 2004)] (B) - Mean lesion locations in patients with autoscopic hallucinations and out-of-body experiences. Lesion locations of eight patients with autoscopic hallucination (Blanke & Castillo, 2007) are represented by the light yellow color with the region of maximum overlap - in a dark yellow color – centering on temporo-occpital and parieto-occipital cortex. In contrast, the centre of lesion overlap for a group of patients with OBEs (Blanke & Mohr, 2005) is at the temporo-parietal junction (dark pink color). [Modified version of a figure from (Blanke & Castillo, 2007)]

Other work suggests that damage to certain subcortical structures such as the brainstem and the spinal cord may also be associated with OBEs. OBEs frequently occur during dreams (Green, 1968; Muldoon & Carrington, 1929) and it has been hypothesized that the generalized paralysis that occurs during REM-sleep dreams might be a precipitating factor of such OBEs (Bünning & Blanke, 2005). In keeping with this, other studies found that subjects with near death experiences that include OBEs commonly have sleep paralysis (Nelson, Mattingly, Lee, & Schmitt, 2006; Nelson, Mattingly, & Schmitt, 2007; see also Dieguez & Blanke, 2008). It has also been speculated that bodily mechanisms related to abnormal motor and somatosensory signals may lead to OBEs during general anesthesia (Bünning & Blanke, 2005). In general anesthesia, somatosensory and motor signals from the body are disturbed due to the application of muscle relaxants while the patient is in a state of partial awareness. The resulting conflicting condition (partial awareness combined with abnormal somatosensory and motor signals) has been proposed as one of the main patho-mechanisms for awareness during general anesthesia (Blacher, 1975; Moerman, Bonke, & Oosting, 1993; Sandin, Enlund, Samuelsson, & Lennmarken, 2000; Spitellie, Holmes, & Domino, 2002) and might also account for OBEs in these circumstances (Bünning & Blanke, 2005). Thus, disturbed somatosensory and sensorimotor signals from large parts of the body in (1) tetraplegia with severe somatosensory loss, (2) general anesthesia (Moerman et al., 1993), and (3) during sleep paralysis (Nelson et al., 2006) seem to disturb the integration of multisensory body-related information in personal space due to interference with brainstem, spinal cord and peripheral nervous system signaling information from the somatosensory and motor systems. As REM intrusions or sleep paralysis have been linked to damage or interference with brainstem mechanisms, the recent observation of an OBE following a spinal cord lesion (Overney, Arzy, & Blanke, 2009) implicates cervical spinal cord mechanisms. OBEs during general anesthesia and in patients suffering from Guillan-Barré syndrome (Cochen et al., 2005) even point to the implication of the peripheral nervous system.

Multisensory Dis-Integration in OBEs

The anatomical, phenomenological and behavioral data collected from patients has led to the hypothesis that the abnormal perceptions in OBEs are due to selective deficits in integrating multisensory body-related information into a single coherent neural representation of one's body and its position in extra-personal space (Blanke et al., 2004; Blanke & Mohr, 2005). This theory extended previous propositions made for the related phenomena of phantom limb sensations (Brugger, 2002; Brugger et al., 1997) and synesthesia (Irwin, 1985). Furthermore, the OBE deficits have been attributed to abnormal processing at the TPJ, as mentioned earlier, TPJ lesions are found in patients with OBEs (Blanke et al., 2004; Blanke & Mohr, 2005) and neuroimaging studies (Arzy et al., 2006b; Blanke et al., 2005; Vallar et al., 1999) have shown that this region plays an important role in multisensory integration, embodiment and in generating an egocentric perspective in healthy subjects (see also Bremmer, Schlack, Duhamel, Graf, & Fink, 2001; Calvert, Campbell, & Brammer, 2000; and Leube et al., 2003).

More precisely, Blanke and colleagues (Blanke et al., 2004; Blanke & Mohr, 2005) have proposed that OBEs occur when there is (1) a disintegration in own-body (personal) space because of incongruent tactile, proprioceptive and visual inputs alongside (2) a disintegration between personal and extrapersonal space due to incongruent vestibular and visual inputs. They further suggested that the phenomenological variation between different types of autoscopic phenomena - the group of illusions that affect the experience of the entire body and include OBEs, heautoscopy and autoscopic hallucination - can be explained by different levels of vestibular disturbance. Vestibular dysfunction is greatest in OBEs, which are strongly associated with feelings of floating and elevation (usually absent in autoscopic hallucinations (Blanke et al., 2004)). During autoscopic hallucinations patients see their body in extrapersonal space, but there is no disembodiment and no self-attribution (ownership) of the illusory extracorporeal body (Blanke et al., 2004; Brugger et al., 1997). The pronounced vestibular disturbance in OBEs fits with the greater implication of the TPJ in this disorder (Blanke & Mohr, 2005; Lopez, Halje, & Blanke, 2008), as the core region of vestibular cortex is located in the TPJ (Brandt & Dieterich, 1999; Fasold et al., 2002; Lobel, Kleine, Bihan, Leroy-Willig, & Berthoz, 1998).

Empirical Studies of the Bodily Self in Healthy Subjects

How can the relations between the different aspects of the bodily self that are dissociated in OBEs be investigated in healthy subjects in the research laboratory? Two groups (Ehrsson, 2007; Lenggenhager et al., 2007) separately developed novel techniques to dissociate (1) the location of the physical body, (2) the location of the self (self-location), (3) the location of the origin of the visuo-spatial perspective, and (4) self-identification. Both groups utilized congruent and incongruent visual-tactile stimulation to alter these four aspects of bodily self-consciousness, thereby extending a protocol similar to that used in a related corporeal illusion - the rubber hand illusion (RHI; Botvinick & Cohen, 1998) - to the full body (see Fig. 3). The general idea in these full body studies is to mislead subjects about where they experience their body and/or self to be, and/or with what location and which body they self-identify with. To achieve this, a visual (real-time video) image of their body was presented via a head-mounted-display (HMD) that was linked to a video camera that filmed their back from behind (Fig. 3). They were thus able to see themselves from an 'outside' or third-person perspective, as though they were viewing their own body from the visuo-spatial perspective of the camera. In one study (Lenggenhager et al., 2007), subjects viewed the video image of themselves (the 'virtual body') while they were stroked on their back with a stick. This stroking was felt and also seen, and the seen stroking was either synchronous with the felt stroking (i.e. the touch was seen on the same part on the body as where it was simultaneously felt) or was asynchronous with it (when a video delay was added). The stroking manipulation thus generated either congruent (synchronous) or incongruent (asynchronous) visuo-tactile stimulation, and this has been shown to affect the perception of hand ownership and hand location in the RHI (Botvinick & Cohen, 1998). It was found that (1) the illusion of self-identification with the virtual body (i.e. global ownership, the feeling that 'the virtual body is my body') and (2) the referral of touch ('feeling the touch of the stick where I saw it touching my virtual body') were stronger when subjects were stroked synchronously than when they were stroked asynchronously (Lenggenhager et al., 2007). Self-location was also measured by passively displacing the body of the blindfolded subjects after the stroking period and then asking them to walk back to the original position. Note that, as predicted, self-location was experienced at a position that was closer to the virtual body, as if subjects were located "in front" of the position where they had been standing during the experiment. This ensemble of measures has been termed the full body illusion (FBI).

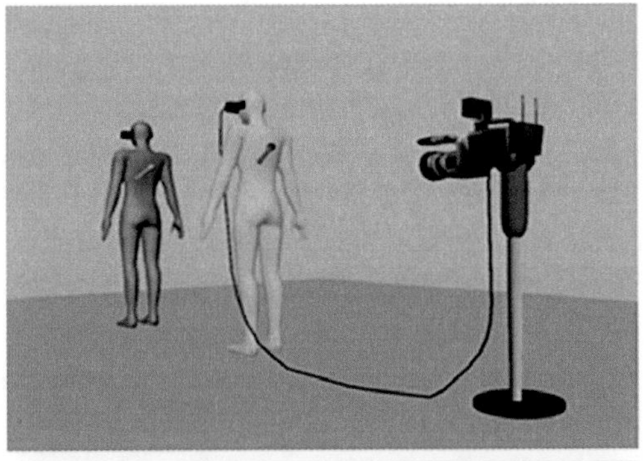

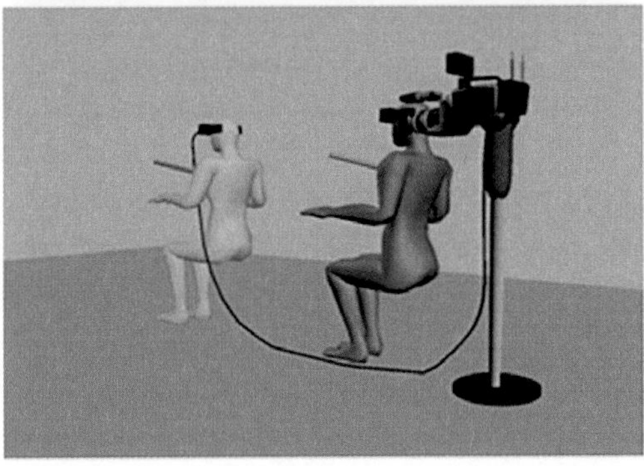

Figure 3. Experimental set-up in synchronous (back) stroking condition in (Lenggenhager et al., 2007) [top panel] and in synchronous (chest) stroking condition in (Ehrsson, 2007) [bottom panel]. In both panels the physical body of the subject is light-colored and the dark-colored body indicates the hypothesized location of the perceived body (bodily self). [Modified version of a figure from (Lenggenhager et al., 2009)]

In a related study (Ehrsson, 2007) subjects were stroked on their chest (Fig. 3). They were seated while they viewed themselves (via an HMD) from behind, and they could see a stick moving (synchronous or asynchronous with the touch) just below the camera's lens. In this case, subjects (1) felt that the stick they saw was touching their real chest, (2) self-identified with the camera's location and felt that looking at the virtual body was like viewing the body of someone else. Self-location was not quantified in this study by using the drift measure as in (Lenggenhager et al., 2007); instead, a threatening stimulus was presented to the apparent location of the origin of the visuo-spatial perspective (just below the camera). The skin conductance response to a swinging hammer (approaching the camera) was found to be higher during synchronous stroking than during asynchronous, providing implicit physiological evidence that subjects identified and localized themselves to the position of the camera.

There were several differences in bodily experiences in these two similar set-ups, and it is worth considering what may account for these. Meyer (Meyer, 2008) proposed (in a response to these studies) that in both set-ups the brain may use at least four different sources of information to generate the conscious experience of self-location and self-identification: (1) where the body is seen (2) where the world is seen from (the origin of the visuo-spatial perspective) (3) where the touch is seen to occur and (4) where the touch is felt to occur. (Although Meyer separates (1) and (3) it is not clear that these can be classified as different cues/sources of information). These four 'cues' do not correspond in the experimental set-ups (but of course in everyday life, they usually do). Meyer argued that the most important of these cues (for the conscious experience of self-location) might be where the touch is *seen* to occur (i.e. where the stroking stick is seen). He concluded this because, firstly, in neither set-up did self-location (measured by drift (Lenggenhager et al., 2007) and/or questionnaire scores (Ehrsson, 2007) exactly coincide with the location where the touch was felt (i.e. where the physical body was located). Secondly, the seen location of the virtual body biased self-location in one study (Lenggenhager et al., 2007) but not in the other (Ehrsson, 2007), and thirdly, the location of the visuo-spatial perspective corresponded to self-location in Ehrsson (2007) but not in Lenggenhager et al. (2007). However, in both cases, self-location coincided with (or more accurately, was biased towards) the location where the touch was seen to occur (i.e. the seen location of the stroking stick).

It is not very surprising that the tactile sense appears to have the weakest role in determining self-location. Touch, after all, cannot give any reliable information regarding the location of the body in external space, except via tactile contact with external surfaces. There is, however, an additional important point to consider regarding the four cues. As pointed out by Blanke et al.'s (Blanke, Metzinger, & Lenggenhager, 2008) response to (Meyer, 2008), self-location was biased towards the virtual body more when the seen stroking was synchronous with the felt stroking than when it was asynchronous. Thus, the congruence between tactile and visual input is an additional important factor in determining self-location in this context. It seems that when vision and touch are incongruent, the influence of the 'visual information about stroking' is weaker and not pre-eminent as Meyer implies. Thus in the asynchronous condition, subjects' self-location is closer to where the touch is felt (i.e. where their physical body is actually located) than it is in the synchronous condition.

It should be cautioned that, since different methods were used in these studies (Ehrsson, 2007; Lenggenhager et al., 2007) it is difficult to make meaningful, direct comparisons between them. A recent paper (Lenggenhager et al., 2009) sought to directly compare the approaches presented in these studies by using identical body positions and measures in order to quantify the conscious experience of self-identification, visuo-spatial perspective, and self-location. The authors investigated these aspects of bodily self-consciousness while subjects were tested in the supine position (as OBEs usually occur in this position (Bünning & Blanke, 2005; Green, 1968). Subjects were again fitted with an HMD that displayed a video image of their body. Their virtual body thus appeared to be located below their physical body (see Fig.4). The dependent behavioral measure for the quantification of self-location was a new one: a 'mental ball dropping' (MBD) task in which subjects had to imagine that a ball fell from their hand, and they had to press one button when they imagined that it left their grasp, and then another button when they imagined that it hit the floor. The authors proposed that MBD estimation would be greater (i.e. the time that subjects imagined it would take for the ball to reach the ground would be longer) when subjects' self-location (where they perceived their self to be) was higher from the ground than when it was closer to the ground. The prediction in this study was that, compared to asynchronous stroking, (1) synchronous back stroking would lead to a 'downward' shift in self-location (towards the virtual body, seen as though below subjects) and an increased self-identification with the virtual body and (2) synchronous chest stroking would lead to an 'upward' shift in self-location ('away' from the virtual body seen below), and a decreased self-identification with the virtual body. As predicted, self-identification with the virtual body and referral of touch to the virtual body were found to be greater during synchronous than during asynchronous *back* stroking. In contrast, during synchronous *chest* stroking there was decreased self-identification with the virtual and decreased illusory touch. The MBD time estimates (quantifying self-location) were lower for synchronous back stroking than synchronous chest stroking, suggesting that, as predicted, self-location was more biased towards the virtual body in the synchronous back stroking condition and relatively more towards the location of the visuo-spatial perspective in the synchronous chest stroking condition. This study confirmed the earlier suggestion that self-location and self identification are strongly influenced by where the stroking is seen to occur. Thus, self-location was biased towards the virtual body located as though below (or in front) when subjects were stroked on the back, and biased towards the location of the visuo-spatial perspective (behind/above the virtual body) when subjects were stroked on their chests.

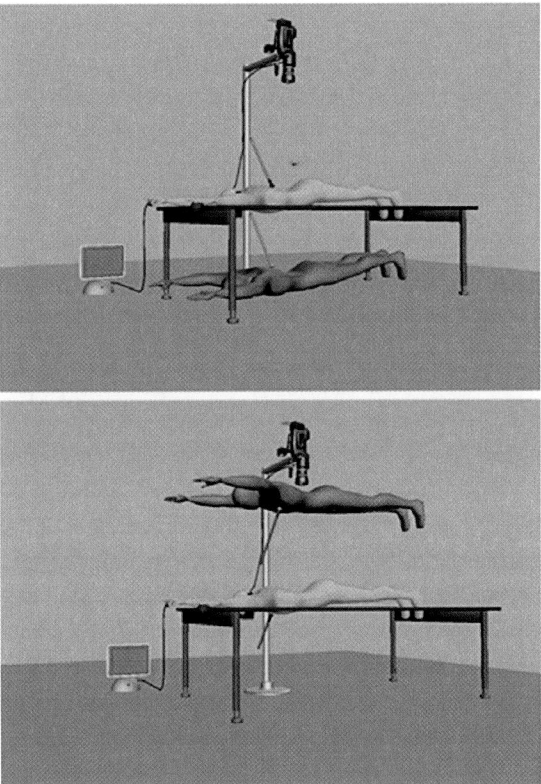

Figure 4. Experimental set-up in synchronous (back) stroking condition [top panel] and synchronous (chest) stroking condition [bottom panel] in (Lenggenhager et al., 2009). The subject was filmed from above and viewed the scene via an HMD. The light-colored body indicates where the subjects' real body was located and the dark-colored body, the hypothesized location of the perceived body (bodily self). [Modified version of a figure from (Lenggenhager et al., 2009)]

It is notable that the subjective upward drift in self-location during synchronous chest stroking was correlated with sensations of elevation and floating (as assessed by questionnaires). This suggests that when subjects adopt a relaxed prone position - synchronous visual-tactile events may interfere with vestibular processing. The importance of vestibular (otolith) input in abnormal self-location has already been demonstrated (Blanke et al., 2002; Blanke et al., 2004). Furthermore, there is evidence that vestibular cues may interfere with body and self-representation (Le Chapelain, Beis, Paysant, & Andre, 2001; Lenggenhager, Lopez, & Blanke, 2008; Sang, Jauregui-Renaud, Green, Bronstein, & Gresty, 2006). The relatively motionless prone body position of the subjects in this study would have minimized vestibular sensory updating and thus may have further contributed to the occurrence of such vestibular sensations, highlighting their potential relevance for bodily self-consciousness and OBEs (see also Lopez et al., 2008; Schwabe & Blanke, 2008).

Visuo-Tactile Integration, Ownership and Self-Identification

What explains the importance of the synchrony of tactile and visual inputs for self-location? The role of visuo-tactile congruence has been studied for a related, though not identical phenomenon: the rubber hand illusion (RHI) (Botvinick & Cohen, 1998). In the RHI, a subject watches a fake hand that is being stroked by a paintbrush in synchrony with stroking on his own (occluded) corresponding hand. This can induce the illusion that the touch is felt in the fake hand and that the fake hand 'feels like it's my hand' (illusory ownership or self-attribution (Botvinick & Cohen, 1998; Ehrsson, Spence, & Passingham, 2004; Tsakiris & Haggard, 2005)). There is also a mislocalization of the subject's hand towards the fake hand (drift). The illusory ownership, tactile mislocalization and drift are all abolished when the stroking is asynchronous (Austen, Soto-Faraco, Enns, & Kingstone, 2004; Botvinick & Cohen, 1998; Ehrsson et al., 2004; Tsakiris & Haggard, 2005). It seems that the temporal congruence of the visual-tactile events is necessary for the change in felt arm position and ownership of the rubber hand to occur.

A recent paper on the RHI (Makin, Holmes, & Ehrsson, 2008) proposed an explanatory model that implicates the role of multimodal integration within peri-hand space. In this model, visual information about hand position is weighted more highly (especially when the hand is not moving) than information from other modalities (most likely because vision is superior at representing spatial location than proprioception). Because of the dominance of vision, the brushstrokes that are seen to occur on the rubber hand are processed as though they are occurring near the real hand, i.e. the central representation of the location of the hand is shifted towards the rubber hand (Lloyd, 2007). Given the temporal congruence of the seen and felt stroking these inputs are integrated together as a coherent multisensory event in spatial co-ordinates that are shifted towards those of the rubber hand. The authors propose that this may result in the sensation of touch being referred to the rubber hand. According to this model, it is the referral of touch that induces the feeling of ownership for the rubber hand. It should be noted that this direction of causality, although plausible in principle, has yet to be verified experimentally. Note also that the size of the drift is generally quite small compared to the actual distance between the fake and real hand.

It is possible that similar mechanisms could explain some aspects of the 'full body illusion' (FBI), but there are likely to be several important conceptual, behavioral, and neurobiological differences. The finding that in the FBI there appears to be referral of touch to a virtual body viewed as though at a distance of two meters away is in contrast to the finding that the RHI is abolished simply by changing the posture of the rubber hand to an implausible one (Tsakiris & Haggard, 2005). Viewing one's body from an external perspective at two meters distance is even less 'anatomically plausible' than a rubber hand with a misaligned posture, therefore it is perhaps surprising that the FBI occurs under such conditions. But perhaps this illustrates that the constraints operating in the FBI are in certain ways markedly different to those operating in the RHI. They appear similar in that there is a dependence of the strength of both illusions on the temporal congruence between seen and felt stroking. However, the constraints regarding the spatial relations between the location of the origin of the visuo-spatial perspective and the rubber hand are different to those between the location of the origin of the visuo-spatial perspective and the location of the seen virtual body. Moreover, in the RHI it is the hand with respect to the bodily self that is mislocalized. In the FBI the entire body (in effect, the bodily self) is mislocalized within external space. It is therefore to be expected that the spatial constraints operating in these two illusions should differ. Could it be that the 'volume' of peripersonal space (including personal space) is 'relocated' within extrapersonal space during the FBI? What exactly is the role of vestibular cues in these changes, and how do these changes relate to other aspects of the self, such as cognitive and conceptual aspects (Blanke & Metzinger, 2009)? At present we can only make very preliminary speculations.

The Multimodal First- Person Perspective

We have seen how the visuo-spatial perspective can be dissociated from self-location in healthy subjects (Lenggenhager et al., 2007), has this also been reported in patients with own body illusions such as OBEs and autoscopic hallucinations? A recent neurological study (De Ridder et al., 2007) showed that after a patient (with tinnitus) received electrical brain stimulation at the right TPJ he experienced an OBE during which his self-location was dissociated from his visuo-spatial perspective. The patient visually perceived the environment from his normal visuo-spatial perspective and not from a disembodied perspective, as is classically reported by people with OBEs. Furthermore, patients with heautoscopy – another type of autoscopic phenomenon - may experience two rapidly alternating visuo-spatial perspectives (and self-locations), leaving them confused about where their self is localized (Blanke et al., 2004; Brugger, Agosti, Regard, Wieser, & Landis, 1994). In such patients, the visuo-spatial perspective may sometimes even be experienced at two positions at the same time and this is often associated with feelings of bi-location: the experience of a duplicated or split self (i.e. not 'just' a split between body and self as in OBEs; see also Lopez et al., 2008). The visuo-spatial perspective is perhaps the only perspective that usually comes to mind, and yet vision is not the only modality with an inherent 'perspectivalness' (Metzinger, 2003; Metzinger, Rahul, & Bikas, 2007) – there is also an auditory perspective (and also "perspectives" based primarily on proprioceptive and motor signals; (Schwabe & Blanke, 2008)). Sounds are heard as occurring in spatial locations that are always in spatial relation to the bodily self. Again, in healthy subjects the auditory perspective and visual perspective are spatially congruent, and yet patients with heautoscopy may describe spatial incongruence between both perspectives (for further examples and discussion see (Blanke et al., 2004; Blanke & Metzinger, 2009).

Conclusion

Studies of OBEs have strongly influenced our scientific thinking on the nature of bodily self-consciousness. They have highlighted the fact that bodily self-consciousness can be broken down into several components, and the phenomenology of OBEs demonstrates that these components are dissociable, suggesting that they may have distinct neural bases. The investigation of OBEs has therefore inspired the first empirical studies on the global bodily self and the experimental findings so far have shown that it is also possible to dissociate the components of the bodily self - to a lesser extent - in healthy subjects. The systematic manipulation of the multisensory cues that the brain uses to create a representation of self-location and identity has begun to reveal the differing importance of these cues and the mechanisms underlying their integration. Future studies will seek to develop experimental settings in which the bodily self can be manipulated to an even greater degree in healthy subjects. In this way we may come to learn about the limits of bodily self-representation. It will also be important for future studies to characterize the neural correlates of the behavioral changes induced in the FBI paradigms. This will help us better understand the role of the TPJ as well as the roles of other cortical and subcortical brain regions in bodily self-consciousness. Patient and electrical stimulation studies, along with mental imagery studies, have implicated the TPJ, but it remains to be seen whether this area is activated in healthy subjects during full body illusions.

Will it ever be possible to experimentally induce full-blown OBEs in healthy subjects? OBEs have previously been induced using direct brain stimulation in neurological patients (Blanke et al., 2002; De Ridder et al., 2007; Penfield, 1955), but these clinical examinations can only be carried out in a highly selective patient population, and related techniques, such as transcranial magnetic stimulation do not induce similar effects (Blanke & Thut, 2007). Blackmore (Blackmore, 1982, 1984) has listed a number of behavioral procedures that may induce OBEs, and it may be interesting for future empirical research to employ some of these "induction" methods in a systematic manner in combination with scientific experiments. It is important to note that OBEs were not actually induced in the previously reported studies that used video-projection (Ehrsson, 2007; Lenggenhager et al., 2009; Lenggenhager et al., 2007), although there were measurable changes to bodily self-consciousness in these experiments. What changes to the experimental methods will be necessary to induce something even closer to an OBE? We believe that virtual reality technology, robotics, and techniques from the field of vestibular physiology will be important. The use of these techniques may also make it possible to study the effects of such procedures on other aspects of self, such as the cognitive and conceptual aspects that have typically been studied using self-reports and questionnaires, and that have been reported to be associated with the occurrence of OBEs (Blackmore, 1984; Irwin, 1985; Murray & Fox, 2005). For example, it has been shown that the occurrence of OBEs is associated with psychological absorption (engrossment in mental experience) and dissociation (Glickson, 1990; Irwin, 1985, 2000; Murray & Fox, 2005; Richards, 1991). Such findings suggest that there may be a pre-existing difference in the bodily experience of people who have had an OBE and those who have not had one. Murray and Fox (Murray & Fox, 2005) have argued that OBEs are more likely to occur in people who have a weaker than average sense of embodiment, i.e. a generalized dissociation between their sense of self and their body.

Many questions remain unanswered. Is there a spatial limit over which referral of touch to a virtual body can occur? What other modalities - apart from tactile - could be mislocalized during full body illusions? What is the role of sensorimotor contingencies? What role does interoception - the brain's representation of the heartbeat, blood pressure, the digestive system etc. - play in bodily self-consciousness? And how do the exteroceptive senses like vision and audition interact with interoception in the construction of the self and the self-centered world? Answering these questions will lead us closer to a tantalizing and important goal: a neuroscientific model of the 'I' of experience and thought and of our identity across a lifetime.

REFERENCES

Arzy, S., Seeck, M., Ortigue, S., Spinelli, L., & Blanke, O. (2006a). Induction of an illusory shadow person. *Nature, 443(7109),* 287-287.

Arzy, S., Thut, G., Mohr, C., Michel, C. M., & Blanke, O. (2006b). Neural Basis of Embodiment: Distinct Contributions of Temporoparietal Junction and Extrastriate Body Area. *Journal of Neuroscience, 26(31),* 8074-8081.

Aspell, J. E., Lenggenhager, B., & Blanke, O. (2009). Keeping in touch with one's self: multisensory mechanisms of self-consciousness. *submitted.*

Austen, E., Soto-Faraco, S., Enns, J., & Kingstone, A. (2004). Mislocalizations of touch to a fake hand. *Cognitive, Affective and Behavioral Neuroscience, 4,* 170-181.

Blacher, R. S. (1975). On awakening paralyzed during surgery. A syndrome of traumatic neurosis. *Journal of the American Medical Association, 234(1),* 67-68.

Blackmore, S. (1982). *Beyond the body. An investigation of out-of-body experiences.* London: Heinemann.

Blackmore, S. (1984). A psychological theory of the out-of-body experience. *Journal of Parapsychology, 48,* 201-218.

Blanke, O., & Castillo, V. (2007). Clinical neuroimaging in epileptic patients with autoscopic hallucinations and out-of-body experiences. *Epileptologie, 24,* 90-95.

Blanke, O., Landis, T., Spinelli, L., & Seeck, M. (2004). Out-of-body experience and autoscopy of neurological origin. *Brain, 127(2),* 243-258.

Blanke, O., & Metzinger, T. (2009). Full-body illusions and minimal phenomenal selfhood. *Trends in Cognitive Sciences, 13(1),* 7-13.

Blanke, O., Metzinger, T., & Lenggenhager, B. (2008). Response to Kaspar Meyer's E-Letter. *Science E-letter.*

Blanke, O., & Mohr, C. (2005). Out-of-body experience, heautoscopy, and autoscopic hallucination of neurological origin: Implications for neurocognitive mechanisms of corporeal awareness and self-consciousness. *Brain Research Reviews, 50(1),* 184-199.

Blanke, O., Mohr, C., Michel, C., Pascual-Leone, A., Brugger, P., Seeck, M., et al. (2005). Linking Out-of-Body Experience and Self Processing to Mental Own-Body Imagery at the Temporoparietal Junction. *Journal of Neuroscience, 25(3),* 550-557.

Blanke, O., Ortigue, S., Landis, T., & Seeck, M. (2002). Neuropsychology: Stimulating illusory own-body perceptions. *Nature, 419(6904),* 269-270.

Blanke, O., & Thut, G. (2007). Inducing out of body experiences. In G. Della Sala (Ed.), *Tall Tales* Oxford: Oxford University Press.

Botvinick, M., & Cohen, J. (1998). Rubber hands /`feel/' touch that eyes see. *Nature, 391*(6669), 756-756.

Brandt, T., & Dieterich, M. (1999). The vestibular cortex: Its locations, functions, and disorders. *Annals of the New York Academy of Science, 871(1),* 293-312.

Bremmer, F., Schlack, A., Duhamel, J.-R., Graf, W., & Fink, G. R. (2001). Space coding in primate posterior parietal cortex. *NeuroImage, 14(1),* S46-S51.

Brugger, P. (2002). Reflective mirrors: Perspective-taking in autoscopic phenomena. *Cognitive Neuropsychiatry, 7,* 179-194.

Brugger, P., Agosti, R., Regard, M., Wieser, H., & Landis, T. (1994). Heautoscopy, epilepsy, and suicide. *Journal of Neurology, Neurosurgery, and Psychiatry, 57(7),* 838-839.

Brugger, P., Regard, M., & Landis, T. (1997). Illusory reduplication of one's own body: Phenomenology and classification of autoscopic phenomena. *Cognitive Neuropsychiatry, 2(1),* 19-38.

Bünning, S., & Blanke, O. (2005). The out-of body experience: precipitating factors and neural correlates. In *Progress in Brain Research* (Vol. 150, pp. 331-350): Elsevier.

Calvert, G. A., Campbell, R., & Brammer, M. J. (2000). Evidence from functional magnetic resonance imaging of crossmodal binding in the human heteromodal cortex. *Current Biology, 10(11),* 649-657.

Cheyne, J. A., & Girard, T. A. (2009). The body unbound: Vestibular-motor hallucinations and out-of-body experiences. *Cortex, 45(2),* 201-215.

Cochen, V., Arnulf, I., Demeret, S., Neulat, M. L., Gourlet, V., Drouot, X., et al. (2005). Vivid dreams, hallucinations, psychosis and REM sleep in Guillain-Barre syndrome. *Brain, 128(11),* 2535-2545.

De Ridder, D., Van Laere, K., Dupont, P., Menovsky, T., & Van de Heyning, P. (2007). Visualizing out-of-body experience in the brain. *The New England Journal of Medicine, 357(18),* 1829-1833.

Dening, T. R., & Berrios, G. E. (1994). Autoscopic phenomena. *The British Journal of Psychiatry, 165(6),* 808-817.

Devinsky, O., Feldmann, E., Burrowes, K., & Bromfield, E. (1989). Autoscopic phenomena with seizures. *Archives of Neurology, 46(10),* 1080-1088.

Dieguez, S., & Blanke, O. (2008). Leaving body and life behind. Out-of-body and near–death experiences. In Tononi & Laureys (Eds.), *The neurology of consciousness*: MIT Press.

Ehrsson, H. (2007). The experimental induction of out-of-body experiences. *Science, 317(5841),* 1048.

Ehrsson, H., & Petkova, V. (2008). If I were you: Perceptual illusion of body swapping. *PLoS ONE, 3(12),* e3832.

Ehrsson, H., Spence, C., & Passingham, R. (2004). That's my hand! Activity in premotor cortex reflects feeling of ownership of a limb. *Science, 305(5685),* 875-877.

Fasold, O., von Brevern, M., Kuhberg, M., Ploner, C. J., Villringer, A., Lempert, T., et al. (2002). Human vestibular cortex as identified with caloric stimulation in functional magnetic resonance imaging. *NeuroImage, 17(3),* 1384-1393.

Glickson, J. (1990). Belief in the paranormal and subjective paranormal experience. *Personality and Individual Differences, 11,* 675-683.

Green, C. (1968). *Out-of-body experiences*. Oxford: Institute of Psychophysical Research.

Grüsser, O., & Landis, T. (1991). The splitting of 'I' and 'me': heautoscopy and related phenomena. . In O. Grüsser & T. Landis (Eds.), *Visual agnosias and other disturbances of visual perception and cognition* (pp. 297-303). Amsterdam: MacMillan.

Hécaen, H., & Ajuriaguerra, J. (1952). *Méconnaissances et hallucinations corporelles: intégration et désintégration de la somatognosie* Paris: Masson.

Irwin, H. (1985). *Flight of mind: A psychological study of the out-of-body experience.* Metuche, NJ: Scarecrow Press.

Irwin, H. (2000). The disembodied self: An empirical study of dissociation and the out-of-body experience. *Journal of Parapsychology, 64,* 261-276.

Kölmel, H. (1985). Complex visual hallucinations in the hemianopic field. *Journal of Neurology, Neurosurgery and Psychiatry, 48,* 29-38.

Le Chapelain, L., Beis, J. M., Paysant, J., & Andre, J. M. (2001). Vestibular caloric stimulation evokes phantom limb illusions in patients with paraplegia. *Spinal Cord, 39(2),* 85-87.

Lenggenhager, B., Lopez, C., & Blanke, O. (2008). Influence of galvanic vestibular stimulation on egocentric and object-based mental transformations. *Experimental Brain Research, 184,* 211-221.

Lenggenhager, B., Mouthon, M., & Blanke, O. (2009). Spatial aspects of bodily self-consciousness. *Consciousness and Cognition, In Press, Corrected Proof.*

Lenggenhager, B., Tadi, T., Metzinger, T., & Blanke, O. (2007). Video ergo sum: Manipulating bodily self-consciousness. *Science, 317(5841),* 1096-1099.

Leube, D. T., Knoblich, G., Erb, M., Grodd, W., Bartels, M., & Kircher, T. T. J. (2003). The neural correlates of perceiving one's own movements. *NeuroImage, 20(4),* 2084-2090.

Lhermitte, J. (1939). Les phenomènes héautoscopiques, les hallucinations spéculaires et autoscopiques. . In *L'image de notre corps* (pp. 170-227). Paris: L'Harmattan.

Lippman, C. (1953). Hallucinations of physical duality in migraine. *Journal of Nervous and Mental Disease, 117,* 345-350.

Lloyd, D. M. (2007). Spatial limits on referred touch to an alien limb may reflect boundaries of visuo-tactile peripersonal space surrounding the hand. *Brain and Cognition, 64(1),* 104-109.

Lobel, E., Kleine, J. F., Bihan, D. L., Leroy-Willig, A., & Berthoz, A. (1998). Functional MRI of galvanic vestibular stimulation. *Journal of Neurophysiology, 80(5),* 2699-2709.

Lopez, C., Halje, P., & Blanke, O. (2008). Body ownership and embodiment: Vestibular and multisensory mechanisms. *Neurophysiologie Clinique/Clinical Neurophysiology, 38(3),* 149-161.

Makin, T. R., Holmes, N. P., & Ehrsson, H. H. (2008). On the other hand: Dummy hands and peripersonal space. *Behavioral Brain Research, 191(1),* 1-10.

Metzinger, T. (2003). *Being No One. The Self-Model Theory of Subjectivity*: MIT Press, USA.

Metzinger, T., Rahul, B., & Bikas, K. C. (2007). Empirical perspectives from the self-model theory of subjectivity: a brief summary with examples. In *Progress in Brain Research* (Vol. Volume 168, pp. 215-245, 273-278): Elsevier.

Meyer, K. (2008). How does the brain localize the self? *Science, E-letter*

Moerman, N., Bonke, B., & Oosting, J. (1993). Awareness and recall during general anesthesia: Facts and feelings. *Anesthesiology, 79(3),* 454-464.

Muldoon, S., & Carrington, H. (1929). *The Projection of the Astral Body*. London: Rider & Co.

Murray, C., & Fox, J. (2005). Dissociational body experiences: differences between respondents with and without prior out-of-body experiences. *British Journal of Psychology, 96,* 441-456.

Nelson, K. R., Mattingly, M., Lee, S. A., & Schmitt, F. A. (2006). Does the arousal system contribute to near death experience? *Neurology, 66(7),* 1003-1009.

Nelson, K. R., Mattingly, M., & Schmitt, F. A. (2007). Out-of-body experience and arousal. *Neurology, 68(10),* 794-795.

Overney, L. S., Arzy, S., & Blanke, O. (2009). Deficient mental own-body imagery in a neurological patient with out-of-body experiences due to cannabis use. *Cortex, 45(2),* 228-235.

Penfield, W. (1955). The 29th Maudsley Lecture - the Role of the Temporal Cortex in Certain Psychical Phenomena. *Journal of Mental Science, 101(424),* 451-465.

Penfield, W., & Erickson, T. (1941). *Epilepsy and Cerebral Localization*: Charles C. Thomas.

Richards, D. (1991). A study of the correlation between subjective psychic experiences and dissociate experiences. *Dissociation, 4,* 83-91.

Sandin, R. H., Enlund, G., Samuelsson, P., & Lennmarken, C. (2000). Awareness during anesthesia: a prospective case study. *The Lancet, 355(9205),* 707-711.

Sang, F. Y., Jauregui-Renaud, K., Green, D. A., Bronstein, A. M., & Gresty, M. A. (2006). Depersonalisation/derealisation symptoms in vestibular disease. *The Journal of Neurology, Neurosurgery, and Psychiatry, 77(6),* 760-766.

Schwabe, L., & Blanke, O. (2008). The vestibular component in out-of-body experiences: a computational approach. *Frontiers in Human Neuroscience, in press.*

Spitellie, P., Holmes, M., & Domino, K. (2002). Awareness during anesthesia. *Anesthesiology clinics of North America, 20(3),* 555-570.

Terhune, D. B. (2009). The incidence and determinants of visual phenomenology during out-of-body experiences. *Cortex, 45(2),* 236-242.

Todd, J., & Dewhurst, K. (1955). The double: its psychopathology and psycho-physiology. *Journal of Nervous and Mental Disorders, 122,* 47-55.

Tsakiris, M., & Haggard, P. (2005). The rubber hand illusion revisited: Visuotactile integration and self-attribution. *Journal of Experimental Psychology-Human Perception and Performance, 31(1),* 80-91.

Vallar, G., Lobel, E., Galati, G., Berthoz, A., Pizzamiglio, L., & Le Bihan, D. (1999). A fronto-parietal system for computing the egocentric spatial frame of reference in humans. *Experimental Brain Research, 124(3),* 281-286.

In: Psychological Scientific Perspectives on Out of Body… ISBN: 978-1-60741-705-7
Editor: Craig D. Murray

Chapter 6

Out-of-Body Experiences in the Context of Hypnosis: Phenomenology, Methodology, and Neurophysiology

Devin Blair Terhune and Etzel Cardeña

Abstract

Out-of-body experiences (OBEs) are characterized by disruptions between normally integrated subsystems that modulate the visuo-spatial representation of embodied consciousness. Similar disruptions in the coordination of cognitive processes, and corresponding alterations in cortical functional connectivity, have been observed in highly suggestible individuals following a hypnotic induction and after specific hypnotic suggestions. Such individuals more frequently report OBEs during their daily lives and spontaneously following a hypnotic induction than those who are low in suggestibility. They are also capable of experiencing OBEs following corresponding hypnotic suggestions. We present a review and theoretical integration of the phenomenology and neurophysiology of spontaneous and experimentally-induced OBEs during hypnosis and conclude by arguing for the utility of hypnosis as an instrumental method for the experimental induction and manipulation of these experiences.

Introduction

The out-of-body experience (OBE) consists of a disruption in the process of multisensory integration that gives rise to embodied consciousness, that is, the perceived spatial localization of our phenomenal sense of awareness to our physical body (Blanke & Mohr, 2005; Brugger, 2006; Irwin, 2007). That the OBE is reflective of such a disruption is a central feature of both cognitive theories of this phenomenon that have invoked dissociative processes (Irwin, 2000) and neurological models that emphasize the role of deficient multisensory integration (Blanke & Mohr, 2005).

In attempting to discern the phenomenology and mechanisms of a particular experience, it is pragmatic to consider who reports the experience most frequently and the conditions that most commonly give rise to the experience. Highly suggestible (HS) individuals, that is, those who exhibit high suggestibility following a hypnotic induction, report a greater prevalence of spontaneous OBEs than their low suggestible (LS) counterparts (Kumar & Pekala, 2001). HS individuals also frequently report spontaneous OBEs following a hypnotic induction (e.g., Cardeña, 2005) and can experience OBEs when administered corresponding suggestions (Nash, Lynn, & Stanley, 1984; Röder, Michal, Overbeck, van de Ven, & Linden, 2007). Thus, it is worthwhile to consider OBEs from within the domain of hypnosis. In what follows, we examine the fundamental features of OBEs, hypnotic responding, and their relationship. We next describe research concerning spontaneous and experimentally induced OBEs during hypnosis with specific reference to their phenomenology and neurophysiological mechanisms. Finally, we advocate for the use of hypnotic suggestion as a means of studying OBEs.

PHENOMENA

OBEs can be regarded as emergent phenomena in the sense that they are comprised of multiple phenomenological components that often occur independently of one another, but in conjunction constitute the OBE. In this section, we present a brief overview of these features of OBEs, the principal features of hypnosis and hypnotic responding, and their relationship.

Out-of-Body Experiences

OBEs are anomalous perceptual experiences in which one's phenomenal centre of awareness appears to be in a remote spatial location from one's physical body (Blanke, Landis, Spinelli, & Seeck, 2004; Brugger, 2006; Irwin, 2007). This experience is characterized by an overwhelming impression that one's phenomenal self is detached or disconnected from one's physical body and a corresponding locus of perception that deviates from the spatial location of the physical body (Irwin, 1985). It has been argued that OBEs possess three phenomenological components: a sense of disembodiment wherein one's centre of awareness appears to be in a physically independent location from one's body; autoscopy, in which one has a visual perception of one's physical body (i.e., the sense of seeing oneself), and a distant visuo-spatial perspective wherein one perceives one's body from a physical distance (Blanke & Mohr, 2005). The prevalence of OBEs varies from 10 to 50% in the general population (Alvarado, 2000) and they tend to occur under conditions of low or high arousal, such as daydreaming or exposure to a physical trauma, respectively (Irwin, 1985).

Bodily experiences ranging from awareness and ownership to movement and position depend on the coordinated interaction between body schema and body image representations (Giummarra, Gibson, Georgiou-Karistianis, & Bradshaw, 2008). Body schema refers to the unconscious representation of the body that underlies non-conscious motor movements and posture, whereas body image is the conscious representation comprised of perceptual experience of, conceptual understanding of, and emotional attitude toward, the body (Gallagher & Cole, 1995; see also Giummarra, et al., 2008). The experience of embodiment and spatial localization of one's body requires a match between the perceived (positional) representation of one's body (the efference copy) and its actual position as communicated by proprioceptive, vestibular, and visual information. OBEs appear to occur when there is a mismatch between one's body image representation and the body's actual position. The angular gyrus of the right temporoparietal junction (TPJ) has been repeatedly implicated in mental own-body transformations and in the integration of proprioceptive, vestibular, and visual information giving rise to embodied consciousness, suggesting that OBEs result from deficient multisensory integration in this region (Blanke et al., 2005).

Hypnosis and Hypnotic Suggestibility

Hypnosis consists of a social interaction between two individuals (or the same individual in the case of self-hypnosis) in which an experimenter or clinician administers a hypnotic induction, involving instructions to focus one's attention and become hypnotized, followed by a series of suggestions to the participant or patient, for alterations in the latter's attention, emotion, somatic functioning, and/or behavior. Responsiveness to hypnotic suggestions varies considerably in the general population with approximately 10 to 15% of participants falling in the range of high hypnotic suggestibility (Perry, Nadon, & Button, 1992). HS individuals are able to experience a variety of cognitive-perceptual suggestions including agnosia and auditory and visual hallucinations (McConkey & Barnier, 2004). The cognitive and neurophysiological mechanisms underlying hypnosis and hypnotic responding remain the subject of debate (Barnier, Mitchell, & Dienes, 2008; Lynn, Kirsch, & Hallquist, 2008; Woody & Sadler, 2008), but there is converging evidence that a hypnotic induction effects a reduction in left frontal lobe activity and a concomitant weakening of executive functions in HS individuals (Egner & Raz, 2007), but has the converse effect in LS individuals (Cardeña et al., 2008)..

OBEs and Hypnotic Suggestibility

Although few studies have directly targeted the relationship between the prevalence of OBEs and hypnotic suggestibility, it has been found that individuals specifically reporting spontaneous OBEs in their daily lives exhibit increased hypnotic suggestibility (e.g., Spanos & Moretti, 1988). Before turning to OBEs experienced during hypnosis it is valuable to consider the roots of this relationship.

A variable that appears to be critically involved in the incidence of OBEs, and that may parallel the mechanisms underlying hypnosis, is somatoform dissociation. Psychoform (or cognitive) dissociation involves a disruption between normally integrated processes governing affect, attention, identity, and/or memory (e.g., Spiegel & Cardeña, 1991). In contrast, somatoform dissociation refers to a disruption of the processes that give rise to bodily sensation, control, and a unified representation of one's body (Cardeña, 1997; Nijenhuis, 2004; Maaranen et al., 2005) and is believed to be reflected in such diverse symptoms as non-epileptic seizure-like events, conversion blindness, and other functional symptoms that lack organic (i.e. neurological) causes (e.g., Litwin & Cardeña, 2000). Irwin (2000) found that self-reported somatoform dissociative symptomatology significantly discriminated individuals who had experienced OBEs from those who hadn't (see also Gow,

Lang, & Chant, 2004; Murray & Fox, 2005a, 2005b). The former group has also been observed to exhibit greater alterations in bodily awareness and body image during procedures intent on manipulating awareness of environmental and endogenous stimuli (Murray & Fox, 2005a; Terhune, 2006). Importantly, Roelofs and colleagues (2002) reported that patients diagnosed with conversion disorder, a psychogenic condition characterized by impaired motor or sensory functioning, exhibited higher hypnotic suggestibility than two control groups (but see also Goldstein, Drew, Mellers, Mitchell-O'Malley, & Oakley, 2000; Litwin & Cardeña, 2000).

Previous research suggests that HS individuals and those reporting OBEs possess a heightened tendency for dissociating representations of the body from awareness, which in turn leads to profound alterations in their perception of the body. Individuals reporting OBEs appear to have a liminal body image representation in which bodily awareness and bodily boundaries are hypersensitive to environmental manipulations (Murray & Fox, 2005b). OBEs, or features thereof, may also occur when one's body is under threat such as in physically traumatic situations (Irwin, 1985), conditions provoking social anxiety (Spurr & Stopa, 2003), or sleep paralysis (e.g., Girard & Cheyne, 2004). These conditions are associated with bodily-focused attention (Brown, Poliakoff, & Kirkman, 2007; Cardeña & Spiegel, 1993) and are conducive to peritraumatic somatoform dissociation (e.g., tonic immobility; Nijenhuis, van der Hart, Kruger, & Steele, 2004; Pitman, Van der Kolk, Orr, & Greenberg, 1990). These two contexts may facilitate OBEs through different mechanisms, an idea that we return to later in this chapter.

OBEs During Hypnosis

The occurrence of spontaneous OBEs outside of a laboratory context limits their systematic experimental investigation. It follows that a perennial labor has been the development of an experimental analogue of the OBE or an experimental procedure that facilitates such experiences (Alvarado, 2000). We will now describe in turn the incidence and phenomenology of spontaneous and hypnotically-suggested OBEs, speculate on their cognitive and neurophysiological mechanisms in these distinct contexts, and argue for the instrumental value of utilizing hypnosis for the experimental induction and manipulation of OBEs.

Spontaneous OBEs During Hypnosis

Spontaneous experiential responses to a hypnotic induction represent an important area of study in the domain of hypnosis. Such experiences are presumed to be neither the product of specific suggestions nor artifactual of the respective hypnotic induction used. Although most studies use traditional relaxation-based hypnotic inductions (e.g., Pekala & Kumar, 2007), some studies (Cardeña, 2005; Cardeña et al., 2008) have used a 'neutral' hypnotic induction procedure wherein individuals are only instructed to enter a deep state of hypnosis (Edmonston, 1991; Kihlstrom & Edmonston, 1971) and have yielded comparable findings.

Alterations in body image and vestibular hallucinations represent a common and arguably core component of the phenomenological response to a hypnotic induction. In some cases these perceptual alterations can develop into heautoscopic disembodiment in which vestibular illusions give rise to the sense of being in a different physical location from the body. In an early report, Schneck (1950) noted the spontaneous occurrence of feelings of numbness, perceived (illusory) movement of the body, changes in the size of appendages, and vestibular hallucinations (e.g., 'spinning'), as have many other authors (for a review see Cardeña, 2005). More recently, Rainville et al. (1999, 2002) found that a hypnotic induction facilitated a reduction in bodily awareness in HS individuals. Attenuated awareness and other alterations in bodily experience are relatively common among moderately suggestible and HS individuals during hypnosis (Cardeña, 2005; Pekala & Kumar, 2007). HS individuals, however, seem to 'graduate' to a higher level of response involving more pronounced cognitive, affective, and perceptual alterations, which may be facilitated in part by attenuated bodily and environmental awareness (Cardeña, 2005; Cardeña et al., 2008; Pekala & Kumar, 2007).

The other two features of OBEs – a distanced visuo-spatial perspective and autoscopy – are less frequent or have not been observed in isolation during hypnosis. Both authors have repeatedly observed HS individuals reporting feeling as though their locus of perception was in a spatial position removed from their physical bodies, but it is unclear whether this experience can occur in the absence of a sense of disembodiment and accompanying vestibular hallucinations. Alteration in one's locus of perception is not isolated to the experience of endogenous stimuli. Many authors (e.g., Schneck, 1986) have noted that clients or participants will spontaneously experience the hypnotist as being at a much further distance than in reality. To our knowledge, there are no reports of isolated spontaneous autoscopy during hypnosis. This perceptual phenomenon appears to be an artifact of other features of the OBE (see below). An increase in spontaneous visual imagery (and accompanying increased activation in posterior occipital visual cortical areas) is frequently found in HS individuals during hypnosis (Cardeña et al., 2008; Rainville, 1999, 2002). An induction appears to produce a shift in some HS individuals from a lexical to an imagic mode of cognition (e.g., Nash, 2008) that may facilitate, and be necessary for, the experience of autoscopy and other visual phenomenological features of an OBE when occurring in conjunction with disembodiment.

These perceptual alterations commonly occur in conjunction and give rise to spontaneous OBEs during hypnosis. Such OBEs have received scant attention by experimental hypnosis researchers and thus it is difficult to gauge their prevalence among HS individuals (Meyerson & Gelkopf, 2004). Among a group of these individuals, Cardeña (2005) found that all of them experienced various vestibular hallucinations (e.g., floating) or a sense of disembodiment during hypnosis. Notably, although some individuals reported perceptions of the room from a remote spatial position, none experienced autoscopy. Given that hypnosis often produces positive affective responses in HS individuals (Cardeña et al., 2008), it is worth noting that spontaneous OBEs occurring during hypnotherapy may also have productive therapeutic consequences (Meyerson & Gelkopf, 2004; contrast with Nash et al., 1984).

The continua-like properties of OBEs should be acknowledged. A distanced visuo-spatial perspective and autoscopy do not appear to spontaneously occur during hypnosis in the absence of disembodiment and accompanying vestibular hallucinations. Vestibular hallucinations seem to represent relatively 'low level' features of the OBE that in turn give rise to more complex features including a verisimilar exterior locus of perception and autoscopy. Multiple studies have described OB-type vestibular hallucinations that are devoid of autoscopy (Cheyne & Girard, 2009; Terhune, 2009). Blanke et al. (2002) similarly found that mild electrical stimulation of the TPJ induced vestibular hallucinations resembling disembodiment, but visual perceptual features of OBEs were only produced by stimulation of greater magnitude. Vestibular hallucinations experienced spontaneously by HS individuals following a hypnotic induction may be a precursor to spontaneous OBEs, whose occurrence requires more severe disruptions of subsystems regulating the representation of the body in space.

It is useful to contrast hypnosis with the conditions under which people commonly experience OBEs. Spontaneous OBEs appear to more frequently occur at the extremes of arousal (Irwin, 1985). Seeing as how hypnosis is most commonly induced when the participant is in a physically restful state (but see Banyai & Hilgard, 1976; Cardeña, 2005), we might suspect that spontaneous hypnotic OBEs share more phenomenological resemblance to spontaneous OBEs occurring under low arousal conditions such as resting in a supine position. Such physical conditions provoke reduced attention to the physical body and can promote minor alterations in somatic, kinaesthetic, and vestibular perception. Lack of bodily stimulation can give rise to a sense of disembodiment, which may in turn trigger autoscopy. A notable feature of the cognitive conditions preceding OBEs under physically active conditions is engagement in a monotonous task whose requisite behavior is easy to automatize (Irwin, 2007). A greater proneness for automatization of behavior in HS individuals (Egner & Raz, 2007; Laurence, Beaulieau-Prévost, & du Chéné, 2008) may contribute to the increased frequency of OBEs in their daily lives and following a hypnotic induction.

Experimentally-Produced OBEs During Hypnosis

Hypnotic suggestion is often experimentally used in an instrumental manner to study particular affective, cognitive, or perceptual phenomena (Cox & Bryant, 2008; Oakley, 2006; Reyher, 1962). Such an approach provides a rich experimental environment within which OBEs can be induced and subjected to experimental manipulation. We are unaware of any studies that have directly used hypnotic suggestion to induce disembodiment, an exterior locus of perception, or autoscopy in isolation. However, it is plausible that it could be used to induce these perceptual features of OBEs. Dening and Berrios (1994), for instance, presented a case in which autoscopy appears to have been triggered by suggestion. Hypnotic suggestion has been used to induce visual hallucinations of human forms, as well as altered visual perception of one's own face (Barnier et al., 2008), and could feasibly be used to induce autoscopic hallucinations.

Two studies have used hypnotic suggestion in HS individuals to experimentally induce OBEs. Nash et al. (1984) administered hypnotic suggestions to HS individuals and a control group for floating out of the body, seeing one's own physical body and environmental objects in the room, and maintaining a disembodied locus of perception at a distant location in the room. Nash et al. (1984) reported that nine of the fourteen (64%) HS individuals reported having OBEs. Notably, eight of these individuals (89%) experienced negative affective concomitants of the OBE including anxiety, dizziness, spinning, headaches, and nausea. These symptoms were in stark contrast with the suggestions administered to participants, which included repeated references to positive affective experiences.

More recently, Röder and colleagues (2007) used hypnotic suggestion to induce OBEs to study the neural correlates of depersonalization and its impact on pain perception. HS participants were administered a suggestion for disembodiment and concurrent autoscopy; contrast conditions included relaxation-based hypnotic suggestions for analgesia, and a non-hypnotic eyes-closed resting period. In all conditions participants were exposed to a noxious stimulus presented to the right wrist. In addition to facilitating reduced pain reports, the hypnotic depersonalization condition, relative to the two other conditions, was associated with reduced activation in the TPJ. Röder et al. (2007) also found reduced activation in ipsilateral medial prefrontal cortex (PFC) during the depersonalization condition.

These studies clearly demonstrate that hypnotic suggestion can be used to induce OBEs. Pointing to the practical utility of this approach, more than half of the sample of HS individuals in Nash et al. (1984) was capable of experiencing OBEs. Röder et al. (2007) found that hypnotically-suggested OBEs were associated with cortical activation in the same region that has been previously claimed to govern these experiences (Blanke et al., 2004, 2005). This strongly suggests that the mechanisms underlying suggested OBEs parallel those that give rise to these experiences in other contexts. Accordingly, Röder et al.'s study goes a long way towards addressing concerns as to the reality of hypnotically-suggested OBEs (e.g., Irwin, 1989). A limitation of these experiments is that neither involved a comprehensive assessment of the experiential features of suggested OBEs. Future research needs to more closely consider the phenomenology of hypnotically-suggested OBEs and its resemblance to spontaneous OBEs and those produced by other procedures (e.g., Ehrsson, 2007; McCreery & Claridge, 1996).

Cognitive and Neurophysiological Mechanisms of Hypnotic OBEs

In this section we consider the mechanisms of OBEs occurring spontaneously during hypnosis and those induced by hypnotic suggestion. Based on the available empirical evidence, we speculate about these mechanisms from within the recent dual process model of dissociation (Holmes et al., 2005) and neurological model of OBEs advanced by Blanke and colleagues (Blanke & Mohr, 2005; Blanke et al., 2004, 2005), but extend them to highlight the operational role of the PFC.

Embedded within the construct of somatoform dissociation are two distinct processes that effect different symptomatology: detachment and compartmentalization (Cardeña, 1997; Holmes et al., 2005). Detachment is argued to be manifested during instances in which one experiences qualitatively reduced awareness of an aspect of oneself (e.g., one's body) or the environment. Compartmentalization refers to a process in which subsystems of consciousness that are normally integrated exhibit a functional disconnectedness. A hallmark concomitant of compartmentalization is the perceived inability to control processes or actions that are normally amenable to control (e.g., motor movements). We propose that spontaneous hypnotic OBEs exemplify detachment. In such cases, attention focused on inner (e.g., imaginal) experience and directed away from a stationary body leads to reduced bodily awareness and perceptual alterations, culminating in a sense of disembodiment. Compensatory mechanisms that seek to realign vestibular and visual representations of the body trigger visual environmental hallucinations and autoscopy. Hypnotically-suggested OBEs, in contrast, are the result of compartmentalization, in which a suggestion instigates a top-down process of structured disruption between processes governing vestibular, visual, and self-specific information, resulting in a mismatch between one's body image representation and actual position of one's body.

Recent neurological research converges on the importance of the angular gyrus in the right TPJ for the occurrence of OBEs (Blanke et al., 2002). This region has been implicated in mental own-body visual transformations and plays an essential role in the integration of multisensory information (Blanke et al., 2005). Direct electrical stimulation of this region has been found to trigger component features of OBEs (Blanke et al., 2002). Cumulatively, these and related findings have been taken to support the hypothesis that OBEs result from deficient integration of multisensory (proprioceptive, vestibular, and visual) information in the TPJ (Blanke & Mohr, 2005; see also Simeon, Guralnik, Hazlet, Spiegel-Cohen, Hollander, & Buchsbaum, 2000). We maintain that hypnotic OBEs occur through a similar process. As would be predicted by this account, the study by Röder et al. (2007) indicates that hypnotically-suggested OBEs result from increased (and potentially altered) processing in this region. In order to account for hypnotic OBEs, however, it is necessary to extend this model by considering the role of the PFC in facilitating these experiences.

The PFC plays a central role in the organization of cortical functioning. PFC structures are responsible for executive functions, including higher-order attention, planning and execution of behavior, as well as response monitoring and inhibition (Miller & Cohen, 2001). Because of its supervisory role in executive functions, the PFC has connections to regions throughout the cortex. We will here focus on two PFC functions, production of a unified sense of self and executive inhibition, and the dependence of embodied consciousness on cortical synchronization between the PFC and TPJ.

A number of studies indicate that a hypnotic induction effects a reduction in frontal lobe activity, and executive functions, in HS individuals (Gruzelier, 2006; Jamieson & Woody, 2007). Research suggests that a coordinated network of cortical regions including medial PFC give rise to the sense of self (e.g., Kelley et al., 2002). We contend that the impact of a hypnotic induction on PFC function may lead to deactivation of the medial PFC resulting in an alteration in the sense of self that may contribute to the phenomenology of the hypnotic OBE. This feature, so we would like to argue, will be shared by spontaneous and experimentally-induced OBEs. It is noteworthy that activity in this region was reduced during hypnotically-suggested OBEs relative to the two other conditions in the Röder et al. (2007) study. Although the exact process by which frontal activity is reduced during a hypnotic induction is poorly understood, it may occur through a weakening of the supervisory attentional system (Woody & Bowers, 1994) and the concurrent posterior shift in the center of cortical 'gravity' or activity and corresponding heightened absorption in visual imagery (Cardeña et al., 2008; Isotani et al., 2001; Rainville et al., 1999, 2002).

Various cognitive functions require the synchronization of a distributed cortical network of neuronal assemblies that have particular functional properties (Ward, 2003). Semi-stable reduction in functional connectivity between normally integrated cortical regions has been found in a variety of psychopathological conditions (e.g., Saito et al., 1998). Similarly, transient macrostates (seconds to minutes) of cortical functional disconnectivity have been implicated in a variety of altered states of consciousness (Vaitl et al., 2005). One study has demonstrated that a hypnotic induction triggers a decoupling of the PFC structures regulating executive attention in HS individuals (Egner et al., 2005). Reduced cortical synchronization at a global level or between frontal and parietal regions in HS individuals has been found to underlie spontaneous experiential sequelae of a hypnotic induction (Cardeña et al., 2008) and hypnotically-suggested hallucinations (Vaitl et al., 2005). Accordingly, along with the local deficient integration of multisensory information in the TPJ (Blanke et al., 2004, 2005), we propose that spontaneous and suggested OBEs during hypnosis are mediated by a reduction in synchronized oscillatory activity between frontal (medial PFC) and parietal (TPJ) regions. This reduction may underlie the altered sense of self that is commonly experienced by HS individuals during hypnosis and which forms an integral part of the OBE. It may also contribute to a sense of disembodiment and other features of OBEs. Evidence indicates that this prediction applies to non-hypnotic OBEs. Easton, Blanke, and Mohr (2009) found that individuals reporting OBEs exhibited impaired task-switching in a mental-rotation task, suggesting that they exhibit impaired connectivity in frontal-parietal networks. This baseline reduced functional connectivity may predispose these individuals to macrostates characterized by reduced awareness and disembodiment. HS individuals have also been found to exhibit reduced global cortical synchronization at baseline (Isotani et al., 2001).

A further concern are the neural correlates of the differential mechanisms of detachment and compartmentalization giving rise to spontaneous and suggested OBEs during hypnosis, respectively. As mentioned, in contrast with the bottom-up process of detachment that triggers a sense of disembodiment that cascades into the perceived adoption of a remote perceptual locus and autoscopy in spontaneous hypnotic OBEs, we argue that hypnotic suggestion induces OBEs through the top-down process of compartmentalization (see also Oakley, 1999; Woody & Sadler, 2008). We maintain that hypnotically-suggested OBEs occur through the inhibition of frontal-parietal synchronization by right hemisphere PFC structures. One PFC candidate is the orbitofrontal cortex, which has been implicated in previous studies on inhibitory hypnotic suggestions (Halligan et al., 2000; Mendelsohn et al., 2008; Ward, Oakley, Frackowiak, & Halligan, 2003). Contrary to this prediction, Röder et al. (2007) did not find increased activation in the right PFC during suggested OBEs relative to control conditions. However, the other conditions in their experiment, suggestions for relaxing and disattending from a noxious stimulus and a waking control condition, both of which are likely to be associated with greater PFC activity relative to a resting hypnosis condition (Gruzelier, 2006), were not suitable for testing this prediction. An appropriate control would be a hypnosis condition in which no suggestions are administered. Outside of the hypnotic context, we would clearly only expect right PFC activity in OBEs that are purposely induced with the aid of frontally-governed mechanisms of executive inhibition.

Hypnotic Suggestion as an Experimental Instrument

There is growing evidence demonstrating the efficacy of hypnotic suggestion as an instrumental tool for the induction of experimental analogues of pathological conditions and other anomalous perceptual experiences (Oakley, 2006). The foregoing sections specifically demonstrate its utility in the study of OBEs. Here we elaborate on the value of using hypnosis in such an instrumental manner, but also acknowledge the limitations and restrictions upon experimentation that this method necessarily entails.

Many of the benefits of using hypnotic suggestion can be gleaned from our contemporary knowledge of hypnotic responding. The great intra-subject reliability in hypnotic suggestibility (Piccione, Hilgard, & Zimbardo, 1989) ensures that hypnotic suggestion could be repeatedly used with the same participants to induce OBEs (Irwin, 1989). Hypnotic suggestions can be promptly cancelled allowing for suitable within-group control conditions and participant comfort in case of negative affective sequelae (Nash et al., 1984). Hypnosis may grant the unique opportunity of contrasting spontaneous and experimentally-induced OBEs in a within-groups design. Furthermore, HS individuals who are not responsive to an OBE suggestion can be included as a control group in experimental research to partial out the influence of hypnotic suggestibility.

The experimental induction of OBEs via hypnotic suggestion also confers the possibility of systematically manipulating features of these experiences and thereby may allow for assessments of predictions that have hitherto been untested. Hypnotic suggestion, for instance, could be used to contrast the neurophysiological correlates of disembodiment with those of the OBE. Hypnotic suggestion could be used to induce full-body paralysis and could be systematically altered along with bodily position (Cheyne, 2002; Irwin, 2007) to examine the conditions under which paralysis may trigger vestibular hallucinations and OBEs. Terhune (2009) made a series of predictions by which visual and non-visual (or 'out-of-body feelings' [Cheyne & Girard, 2009]) OBEs could be discriminated. Variable inclusion of suggestions for autoscopic and environmental visual hallucinations during experimentally-produced OBEs would allow for unequivocal tests of these predictions. Finally, hypnosis could be used in conjunction with other techniques (Ehrsson, 2007; Lenggenhager, Tadi, Metzinger, & Blanke, 2007) to examine the extent to which hypnotic suggestion could terminate some of the features induced by these procedures; this, in turn, may further allow us to understand the role of different cortical regions in the manifestation of OBEs.

Although hypnotic suggestion is an efficacious methodological tool that could feasibly be used to make substantive contributions to our understanding of OBEs, it does possess limitations that require careful consideration. The hypnotic context carries with it numerous expectations in the minds of participants and the influence of demand characteristics upon hypnotic responding is well documented (Spanos, 1986). Because of their heightened suggestibility, HS individuals are more susceptible to the influence conveyed by socially-transmitted implicit demands and cues embedded within the experimental protocol. In addition, a number of studies suggest that HS individuals do not experience hypnotic suggestions via uniform mechanisms (Barber, 1999; Brown & Oakley, 2004; De Pascalis, Bellusci, Gallo, Magurano, & Chen, 2004); this, in turn, may compromise studies of the neural correlates of particular hypnotic phenomena (Woody & McConkey, 2003).

Conclusion

In this chapter we have reviewed the extant literature on the relationship between OBEs and hypnotic suggestibility with particular reference to studies that have actively investigated spontaneous and experimentally-induced OBEs during hypnosis. This research indicates that the hypnotic context is a worthwhile environment within which to study OBEs. The phenomenological features of spontaneous and suggested hypnotic OBEs have not been thoroughly examined so it is unclear how they may differ from one another and from OBEs occurring in other contexts. The neural response to a hypnotically-suggested OBE, however, is remarkably consistent with recent neurological research on OBEs and demonstrates the efficacy of utilizing hypnotic suggestion for inducing OBEs under laboratory conditions. Although no study to date has attempted such an endeavor, hypnotic suggestion also offers the possibility of systematically manipulating the features of OBEs in an experimental environment. We have assumed that hypnotic OBEs occur through relatively similar mechanisms as those in other contexts, but we have attempted to extend, and tailor to the hypnotic context, previous neurophenomenological accounts of OBEs by emphasizing the role of the PFC. In recent years, hypnotic suggestion has been instrumentally used for experimental studies exploring a variety of attentional, emotional, and perceptual phenomena (Oakley, 2006). We hope that hypnosis will be more broadly considered as a method by which OBEs can be experimentally studied as its use is likely to lead to substantive contributions to our understanding of this most unusual of experiences.

REFERENCES

Alvarado, C.S. (2000). Out-of-body experiences. In E. Cardeña, S.J. Lynn, & S. Krippner (Eds.), *Varieties of anomalous experience: Examining the scientific evidence* (pp. 183-218). Washington, DC: American Psychological Association.

Banyai, E.I., & Hilgard, E.R. (1976). A comparison of active-alert hypnotic induction with traditional relaxation induction. *Journal of Abnormal Psychology, 85*, 218-224.

Barber, T.X. (1999). A comprehensive three-dimensional theory of hypnosis. In I. Kirsch, A. Capafons, E. Cardeña-Buelna, & S. Amigó (Eds.), *Clinical hypnosis and self-regulation: Cognitive-behavioral perspectives* (pp. 21-48). Washington, DC, US: American Psychological Association.

Barnier, A.J., Cox, R.E., O'Connor, A., Coltheart, M., Langdon, R., Breen, N., & Turner, M. (2008). Developing hypnotic analogues of clinical delusions: Mirrored-self misidentification. *Cognitive Neuropsychiatry, 13*, 406-430.

Barnier, A.J., Dienes, Z., & Mitchell, C.A. (2008). How hypnosis happens: New cognitive theories of hypnotic responding. In M.R. Nash & A.J. Barnier (Eds.), *The Oxford handbook of hypnosis: Theory, research and practice* (pp. 141-177). Oxford: Oxford University Press.

Blanke, O., Ortigue, S., Landis, T., & Seeck, M. (2002). Stimulating illusory own-body perceptions. *Nature, 419*, 269-70.

Blanke, O., Landis, T., Spinelli, L., & Seeck, M. (2004). Out-of-body experience and autoscopy of neurological origin. *Brain, 127*, 243-58.

Blanke, O., Mohr, C., Michel, C.M., Pascual-Leone, A., Brugger, P., & Seeck, M., et al. (2005). Linking out-of body experience and self processing to mental own-body imagery at the temporoparietal junction. *Journal of Neuroscience, 25*, 550–557.

Blanke, O., & Mohr, C. (2005). Out-of-body experience, heautoscopy, and autoscopic hallucination of neurological origin Implications for neurocognitive mechanisms of corporeal awareness and self-consciousness. *Brain Research Brain Research Reviews, 50*, 184-99.

Brown, R.J., & Oakley, D.A. (2004). An integrative cognitive theory of hypnosis and high hypnotizability. In M. Heap, R.J. Brown, & D.A. Oakley (Eds.), *The highly hypnotizable person: Theoretical, experimental and clinical issues* (pp. 152-186). NY: Routledge.

Brown, R.J., Poliakoff, E., Kirkman, M.A. (2007). Somatoform dissociation and somatosensory amplification are differentially associated with attention to the tactile modality following exposure to body-related stimuli. *Journal of Psychosomatic Research, 62*, 159-165

Brugger, P. (2006). From phantom limb to phantom body: Varieties of extracorporeal awareness. In G. Knoblich, I.M. Thornton, M. Grosjean, & M. Shiffrar (Eds), *Human body perception: From the inside out* (pp. 171–209). Oxford: Oxford University Press.

Cardeña, E. (1997). The etiologies of dissociation. In S. Powers & S. Krippner (Eds.), *Broken images, broken selves: Dissociative narratives in clinical practice* (pp. 61-87). NY: Brunner.

Cardeña, E. (2005). The phenomenology of deep hypnosis: Quiescent and physically active. *International Journal of Clinical and Experimental Hypnosis, 53*, 37-59.

Cardeña, E., Lehmann, D., Jönsson, P, Terhune, D.B., & Faber, P. (March, 2008). *Electrocortical activity during deep hypnosis and hypnotic responding*. Poster presented at the 7th Simpósio da Fundaçao Bial. Porto, Portugal.

Cardeña, E., & Spiegel D. (1993). Dissociative reactions to the Bay Area Earthquake. *American Journal of Psychiatry, 150,* 474-478.

Cheyne, J.A. (2002). Situational factors affecting sleep paralysis and associated hallucinations: Position and timing effects. *Journal of Sleep Research, 11*, 169-177.

Cheyne, J.A., & Girard, T.A. (2009). The body unbound: Vestibular-motor hallucinations and out-of-body experiences. *Cortex*, 45, 201-215.

Cox, R.E., & Bryant, R.A. (2008). Advances in hypnosis research: Methods, designs and contributions of intrinsic and instrumental hypnosis. In M.R. Nash & A. Barnier (Eds.), *The Oxford handbook of hypnosis: Theory, research and practice* (pp. 311-336). Oxford: Oxford University Press.

De Pascalis, V., Bellusci, A., Gallo, C., Magurano, M.R., & Chen, A.C. (2004). Pain-reduction strategies in hypnotic context and hypnosis: ERPs and SCRs during a secondary auditory task. *International Journal of Clinical and Experimental Hypnosis, 52*, 343-63.

Dening, T.R., & Berrios, G.E. (1994). Autoscopic phenomena. *British Journal of Psychiatry, 165*, 808-817.

Easton, S., Blanke, O., & Mohr, C. (2009). A putative implication for fronto-parietal connectivity in out-of-body experiences. *Cortex, 45*, 216-227.

Edmonston, W.E. Jr. (1991). Anesis. In S.J. Lynn & J.W. Rhue (Eds.), *Theories of hypnosis: Current models and perspectives* (pp. 197-237). NY: Guilford Press.

Egner, T., & Raz, A. (2007). Cognitive control processes and hypnosis. In. G.A. Jamieson (Ed.), (2007). *Hypnosis and conscious states: The cognitive neuroscience perspective.* NY: Oxford University Press.

Egner, T., Jamieson, G.A., & Gruzelier, J. (2005). Hypnosis decouples cognitive control from conflict monitoring processes of the frontal lobe. *Neuroimage, 27*, 969-978.

Ehrsson, H.H. (2007). The experimental induction of out-of-body experiences. *Science, 317*, 1048.

Gallagher, S., & Cole, J. (1995). Body image and body schema in a deafferented subject. *Journal of Mind and Behaviour, 16*, 369–390.

Girard, T.A., & Cheyne, J.A. (2004). Individual differences in lateralisation of hallucinations associated with sleep paralysis. *Laterality: Asymmetries of Body, Brain and Cognition, 9,* 93-111.

Giummarra, M.J., Gibson, S.J., Georgiou-Karistianis, N., & Bradshaw, J.L. (2008). Mechanisms underlying embodiment, disembodiment and loss of embodiment. *Neuroscience & Biobehavioral Reviews, 32*, 143-160.

Goldstein, .L, Drew, C., Mellers, J., Mitchell-O'Malley, S, & Oakley D. (2000). Dissociation, hypnotizability, coping styles and health locus of control: Characteristics of pseudoseizure patients, *Seizure, 9*, 314-322.

Gow, K., Lang, T., & Chant, D. (2004). Fantasy proneness, paranormal beliefs and personality features in out-of-body experiences. *Contemporary Hypnosis*, *21*, 107-125.

Gruzelier, J.H. (2006). Frontal functions, connectivity and neural efficiency underpinning hypnosis and hypnotic susceptibility. *Contemporary Hypnosis*, *23*, 15-32.

Halligan, P.W., Athwal, B.S., Oakley, D.A., & Frackowiak, R.S. (2000). Imaging hypnotic paralysis: implications for conversion hysteria. *Lancet* , *355*, 986–987.

Holmes, E.A., Brown, R.J., Mansell, W., Fearon, R.P., Hunter, E.C.M., Frasquilho, F., & Oakley, D.A. (2005). Are there two qualitatively distinct forms of dissociation? A review and some clinical implications. *Clinical Psychology Review*, *25*, 1-23

Irwin, H.J. (1985). *Flight of mind: A psychological stuffy of the out-of-body experience*. Metuchen, NJ: Scarecrow Press.

Irwin, H.J. (1989). Hypnotic induction of the out-of-body experience. *Australian Journal of Clinical Hypnotherapy and Hypnosis*, *10*, 1-7.

Irwin, H.J. (2000). The disembodied self: an empirical study of dissociation and the out-of-body experience. *Journal of Parapsychology*, *64*, 261–276.

Irwin, H.J., &Watt. C.A (2007). *Introduction to parapsychology*. 5th ed. Jefferson, NC: McFarland.

Isotani, T., Lehmann, D., Pascual-Marqui, R.D., Kochi, K., Wackermann, J., Saito, N., Yagyu, T., Kinoshita, T., & Sasada, K. (2001). EEG source localization and global dimensional complexity in high- and low- hypnotizable subjects: A pilot study. *Neuropsychobiology*, *44*, 192-198.

Jamieson, G.A., & Woody, E. (2007). Dissociated control as a paradigm for cognitive neuroscience research and theorizing in hypnosis. In G.A. Jamieson (Ed.), *Hypnosis and conscious states: The cognitive neuroscience perspective* (pp. 111-128). NY: Oxford University Press.

Kelley, W.M., Macrae, C.N., Wyland, C.I., Caglar, S., Inati, S., & Heatherton, T.F. (2002). Finding the self? An event-related fMRI study. *Journal of Cognitive Neuroscience, 14*, 785-794.

Kihlstrom, J.F., & Edmonston, W.E. (1971). Alterations in consciousness in neutral hypnosis: Distortions in semantic space. *American Journal of Clinical Hypnosis*, *13*, 243-248.

Kumar, V.K., & Pekala, R.J. (2001). Relation of hypnosis-specific attitudes and behaviors to paranormal beliefs and experiences. In J. Houran, & R. Lange (Eds), *Hauntings and Poltergeists: Multidisciplinary Perspectives* (pp 260-279). Jefferson, NC: McFarland.

Laurence, J.-R., Beaulieu-Prévost, D., & Due Chéné, T. (2008). Measuring and understanding individual differences in hypnotizability. In M.R. Nash & A.J. Barnier (Eds.), *The Oxford handbook of hypnosis: Theory, research and practice* (pp. 225-253). Oxford: Oxford University Press.

Lenggenhager, B., Tadi, T., Metzinger, T., & Blanke, O. (2007). Video ergo sum: manipulating bodily self-consciousness. *Science*, *317*, 1096-9.

Litwin, R., & Cardeña, E. (2000). Demographic and seizure variables, but not hypnotizability or dissociation, differentiated psychogenic from organic seizures. *Journal of Trauma and Dissociation, 1,* 99-122.

Lynn, S.J., Kirsch, I., & Hallquist, M.N. (2008). Social cognitive theories of hypnosis. In M.R. Nash & A. Barnier (Eds.), *The Oxford Handbook of Hypnosis: Theory, Research and Practice* (pp. 111-139). Oxford: Oxford University Press.

Maaranen, P., Tanskanen, A., Haatainen, K., Honkalampi, K., Koivumaa-Hankanen, H., Hintikka, J., et al. (2005). The relationship between psychological and somatoform dissociation in the general population. *Journal of Nervous and Mental Disease, 193*, 690-692.

McConkey, K.M., & Barner, A.J. (2004). High hypnotizability: Unity and diversity in behavior and experience. In M. Heap, R.J. Brown & D.A. Oakley (Eds.), *The highly hypnotizable person: Theoretical, experimental and clinical issues* (pp. 61-84). London, U.K.: Brunner-Routledge.

McCreery, C., & Claridge, G. (1996). A study of hallucination in normal subjects – II: Electrophysiological data. *Personality and Individual Differences, 21*: 749–758.

Mendelsohn, A., Chalamish, Y., Solomonovich, A., & Dudai, Y. (2008). Mesmerizing memories: Brain substrates of episodic memory suppression in posthypnotic amnesia. *Neuron, 57*, 159-170.

Meyerson, J., & Gelkopf, M. (2004). Therapeutic utilization of spontaneous out-of-body experiences in hypnotherapy. *American Journal of Psychotherapy, 58*, 90-102.

Miller, E.K., & Cohen, J.D. (2001). An integrative theory of prefrontal cortex function. *Annual Review of Neuroscience, 24*, 167-202.

Murray, C.D., & Fox, J. (2005a). The out-of-body experience and body image: Differences between experients and nonexperients. *Journal of Nervous and Mental Disease, 193*, 70–72.

Murray, C.D., & Fox, J. (2005b). Dissociational body experiences: Differences between respondents with and without prior out-of-body-experiences. *British Journal of Psychology, 96,* 441-56.

Nash, M.R. (2008). A psychoanalytic theory of hypnosis: A clinically informed approach. In M.R. Nash & A.J. Barnier (Eds.), *The Oxford handbook of hypnosis: Theory, research and practice* (pp. 201-223). Oxford: Oxford University Press.

Nash, M.R., Lynn, S.J., & Stanley, S.M. (1984). The direct hypnotic suggestion of altered mind/body perception. *American Journal of Clinical Hypnosis, 27*, 95-102.

Nijenhuis, E.R.S. (2004). *Somatoform dissociation: Phenomena, measurement, & theoretical issues*. NY: W.W. Norton & Co.

Nijenhuis, E.R.S., van der Hart, O., Kruger, K., & Steele, K. (2004). Somatoform dissociation, reported abuse and animal defence-like reactions. *Australian and New Zealand Journal of Psychiatry, 38*, 678-686

Oakley, D.A. (1999). Hypnosis and conversion hysteria: A unifying model. *Cognitive Neuropsychiatry, 4*, 243-265.

Oakley, D.A. (2006). Hypnosis as a tool in research: Experimental psychopathology. *Contemporary Hypnosis, 23*, 3-14.

Pekala, R.J., & Kumar, V.K. (2007). An empirical-phenomenological approach to quantifying consciousness and states of consciousness: With particular reference to understanding the nature of hypnosis. In G.A. Jamieson (Ed), *Hypnosis and conscious states: The cognitive neuroscience perspective*. (pp. 167-194). Oxford: Oxford University Press.

Perry, C., Nadon, R., & Button, J. (1992). The measurement of hypnotic ability. In E. Fromm & M. R. Nash (Eds.), *Contemporary hypnosis research* (pp. 459-490). New York: Guilford.

Piccione, C., Hilgard, E.R., & Zimbardo, P.G. (1989). On the degree of stability of measured hypnotizability over a 25-year period. *Journal of Personality and Social Psychology, 56*, 289-295

Pitman, R. K., Van der Kolk, B. A., Orr, S. P., & Greenberg, M. S. (1990). Naloxone-reversible analgesic response to combat-related stimuli in posttraumatic stress disorder. A pilot study. *Archives of General Psychiatry, 47*, 541-547.

Rainville, P., Hofbauer, R.K., Paus, T., Duncan, G.H., Bushnell, M. C., & Price, D.D. (1999). Cerebral mechanisms of hypnotic induction and suggestion. *Journal of Cognitive Neuroscience, 11*, 110-125.

Rainville, P., Hofbauer, R.K., Bushnell, M.C., Duncan, G.H., & Price, D.D. (2002). Hypnosis modulates activity in brain structures involved in the regulation of consciousness. *Journal of Cognitive Neuroscience, 14*, 887-901.

Reyher, J. (1962). A paradigm for determining the clinical relevance of hypnotically induced psychopathology. *Psychological Bulletin, 59*, 344–52.

Roelofs, K., Hoogduin, K.A.L., Keijsers, G.P.J., Näring, G.W.B., Moene, F.C., & Sandijck, P. (2002). Hypnotic susceptibility in patients with conversion disorder. *Journal of Abnormal Psychology, 111*, 390-395

Röder, C.H., Michal, M., Overbeck, G., van de Ven, V.G., & Linden, D.E.J. (2007). Pain response in depersonalization: A functional imaging study using hypnosis in healthy subjects. *Psychotherapy and Psychosomatics, 76*, 115–121.

Saito, N., Kuginuki, T., Yagyu, T., Kinoshita, T., Koenig, T., Pascual-Marqui, R.D., Kochi, K., Wackermann, J., & Lehmann, D. (1998). Global, regional, and local measures of complexity of multichannel electroencephalography in acute, neuroleptic-naive, first-break schizophrenics. *Biological Psychiatry, 43*, 794-802.

Schneck, J.M. (1950). A note on spontaneous hallucinations during hypnosis. *Psychiatric Quarterly, 24*, 492-494.

Schneck, J.M. (1986). Psychogenic micropsia and a spontaneous hypnotic auditory equivalent. *American Journal of Clinical Hypnosis, 29*, 53-58.

Simeon, D., Guralnik, O., Hazlett, E. A., Spiegel-Cohen, J., Hollander, E., & Buscbaum, M.S. (2000). Feeling unreal: A PET study of depersonalization disorder. *American Journal of Psychiatry, 157*, 1782-1788.

Spanos, N.P. (1986). Hypnotic behavior: A social-psychological interpretation of amnesia, analgesia, and "trance logic." *Behavioral and Brain Sciences, 9*, 449-467.

Spanos, N.P., & Moretti, P. (1988). Correlates of mystical and diabolical experiences in a sample of female university students. *Journal for the Scientific Study of Religion, 27*, 105-116.

Spiegel, D., & Cardeña, E. (1991). Disintegrated experience: The dissociative disorders revisited. *Journal of Abnormal Psychology, 100*, 366-78.

Spurr, J.M., & Stopa, L. (2003). The observer perspective: effects on social anxiety and performance. *Behaviour Research & Therapy, 41*, 1009-1028.

Terhune, D.B. (2006). Dissociative alterations in body image among individuals reporting out-of-body experiences: a conceptual replication. *Perceptual & Motor Skills, 103*, 76-80.

Terhune, D.B. (2009). The incidence and determinants of visual phenomenology during out-of-body experiences. *Cortex, 45*, 236-242.

Vaitl, D., Birbaumer, N., Gruzelier, J., Jamieson, G.A., Kotchoubey, B., Kübler, A., Lehmann, D., Miltner, W.H.R., Ott, U., P ütz, P., Sammer, G., Strauch, I., Strehl, U.,

Wackermann, J., & Weiss, T. (2005). Psychobiology of altered states of consciousness. *Psychological Bulletin, 131*, 98-127.

Ward, L.M. (2003). Synchronous neural oscillations and cognitive processes. *Trends in Cognitive Sciences, 7*, 553-559.

Ward, N.S., Oakley, D.A., Frackowiak, R.S., Halligan, P.W. (2003). Differential brain activations during intentionally simulated and subjectively experienced paralysis. *Cognitive Neuropsychiatry, 8*, 295-312.

Woody, E.Z., & Bowers, K.S. (1994). A frontal assault on dissociated control. In S.J. Lynn & J.W. Rhue (Eds.), *Dissociation: Clinical and theoretical perspectives* (pp. 52-79). NY: Guilford Press.

Woody, E.Z., & McConkey, K.M. (2003). What we don't know about the brain and hypnosis, but need to: A view from the Buckhorn Inn. *International Journal of Clinical and Experimental Hypnosis, 51*, 309-338.

Woody, E.Z., & Sadler, P. (2008). Dissociation theories of hypnosis. In M.R. Nash & A. Barnier (Eds.), *The Oxford handbook of hypnosis: Theory, research and practice* (pp. 81-110). Oxford: Oxford University Press.

In: Psychological Scientific Perspectives on Out of Body… ISBN: 978-1-60741-705-7
Editor: Craig D. Murray

Chapter 7

MANAGING ANOMALOUS EXPERIENCE: MEANING MAKING AND THE OBE

Craig D. Murray, David J. Wilde and Joanne Murray

ABSTRACT

A variety of anomalous experiences, including the out-of-body experience (OBE), have been reported in the research literature as enhancing, rather than indicating poor mental health. Within this chapter we report on our qualitative, phenomenological research which sought to investigate the experience of an OBE and its resultant after-effects. The findings from this work reveal how participants managed such experiences. Experients perceived their OBEs as occurring at times of personal significance and these were inextricably linked with participants' lives beyond their point of occurrence, playing an adaptive role in response to difficult life events. The process of integration was helped or hindered by the varying reactions from others to the disclosure of the OBE. We conclude that the idiographic nature of the present work is instrumental in highlighting the subtle personal and social factors that influence how the OBE is managed and integrated.

INTRODUCTION

A considerable body of psychological research has been conducted with the theoretical assumption that the out-of-body experience (OBE) is some form of hallucination (Blackmore, 1984) and that it may be linked to mental health disorders, such as depersonalization (Whitlock, 1978) or schizophrenia (Rawcliffe, 1959). However, there appears to be no evidence linking OBEs to psychosis (McCreery & Claridge, 1995) depersonalization (Twemlow, 1989) or schizophrenic body boundary disturbances (Blackmore, 1986a).

One personality variable that has received considerable research attention is that of schizotypy, in particular the fully dimensional model proposed by Claridge (1997). This model portrays schizotypy as encompassing a range of personality traits related to psychosis and schizophrenia, varying over a normally distributed continuum from psychological good health to psychological ill health (Goulding, 2004). This is distinctly different to the categorical view of the same illnesses, where someone either has the illness, or does not. Schizophrenia and psychosis, on the other hand, are considered to be breaks in normal psychological functioning, which make up a second continuum, with schizotypal personality disorder at one end and advanced schizophrenic psychosis at the other (Claridge, 1997). Claridge's model effectively decouples the concept of schizotypy from that of mental illness whilst still allowing for certain aspects of schizotypy, particularly at the higher end of the spectrum, to be causally linked to such illnesses (McCreery & Claridge, 1995).

Claridge's model comprises four factors, 1) aberrant perceptions and beliefs (sub-clinical forms of positive symptomatology), 2) cognitive disorganization with anxiety (sub-clinical forms of thought blocking and high social anxiety), 3) introvertive anhedonia (sub-clinical forms of the negative symptomatology of schizophrenia), and 4) asocial behavior, such as social non-conformity, impulsiveness and disinhibition of mood.

Evidence from research into this model suggests that schizotypy, although associated with psychopathology, may also have an adaptive value, particularly where anomalous experiences are concerned (McCreery & Claridge, 2002). For instance, McCreery and Claridge (1995) found that out-of-body experients (OBErs) scored higher on the positive factor of aberrant perceptions and beliefs than non-OBErs, moderately on neuroticism, and low on physical anhedonia and social anxiety. In another study (McCreery & Claridge, 2002) the same authors found that the only discriminating factor between OBErs and non-OBErs was the aberrant perceptions and beliefs factor.

Research on schizotypy has been extended to other anomalous experiences, some of which have been linked with OBEs. In a review of the literature, Goulding (2005) listed 18 studies conducted over a 25 year period that showed people who were believers in, or who claimed to have experienced, paranormal phenomena also scored high on measures of schizotypy. Goulding's research adds support to McCreery and Claridge's (2002) view of the healthy schizotype, which they define as people who are fully functional in everyday life "in spite of, and even in part because of, their anomalous perceptual and other experiences" (p.141).

A criticism of much of the previous work on the OBE is that it takes a largely 'top-down' approach rather than first eliciting such experiences in detail before forming testable hypotheses which would provide the best psychological insight into the phenomenon (Alvarado 1997). In particular, Alvarado and Zingrone (2003) have been critical of the lack of systematic work conducted to elicit the impact the OBE has on the experient. In so doing, research in this area has tended to overlook the relevance or the significance of the experience for the person having it.

While this previous work has added substantially to our understanding of the OBE, there is a need for an examination of the longitudinal after-effects experienced by people who have them, and the nature of those after-effects. To date there has been no in-depth examination of the lived experience of having an OBE and what meaning OBErs attribute to that experience. Such work would be expected to contribute to an understanding of how anomalous experience (or aberrant perceptions) may contribute to, or impact upon the mental well-being of such persons.

Within this chapter we report on our qualitative, phenomenological work with participants reporting prior OBEs, focusing on the meaning of these experiences and the ways in which they have been implicated in later life. Although a small body of work on the OBE has been conducted from a qualitative perspective, to date this has been largely a descriptive enterprise. This contrasts with our focus here where research outcomes arise from the application of phenomenological theory to obtain and honor a person's experiences, understandings, personal perceptions and accounts of an event by trying to enter imaginatively into that person's worldview, to attempt to gain an 'insider's perspective' (see Wilde & Murray, 2009, and Wilde & Murray, in press, for further details)

STUDY DETAIL

The phenomenological approach to the OBE here is focused upon the interpretation and meaning of such experiences, drawing out the implications for mental health issues. It makes no claim, nor do we have an interest here, with regards to whether these experiences are of 'real' veridical events.

The intense analysis of individual accounts and the examination of shared meaning, along with any nuances in these meanings, are reflective of the idiographic characteristic of much phenomenological research. To meet these requirements three participants (two males and one female) were recruited; one participant was recruited at a local paranormal annual conference day. The remaining two participants were recruited from a database of respondents who had taken part in previous research studies and who had given their contact details with the wish to take part in future research.

Mark (age 30) estimated he had had between 20 and 50 OBEs. These had begun in childhood. A typical OBE for Mark began when he experienced a variety of physical sensations usually beginning with a buzzing or vibration that ran up and down his body; a stage of sleep paralysis followed and a feeling of pressure on his chest area. This was followed by a period of light-headedness before finally he felt he had exited his physical body into the OB environment. His adult OBEs started shortly after the death of his brother and the most significant content of his OBEs were his self-believed evidential communications with his deceased brother.

Cindy (age 45) reported 2 prior OBEs. She described having floating, out-of-body sensations when she was a teenager whilst listening to music. She had her first full OBE while going to sleep when she was 20 years old, 4-5 weeks post-child birth. Cindy described the exit from her body as very quick and recalled suddenly finding herself looking down on her body as she lay in bed. She described the OB environment as similar to the physical room she was lying in, except that the walls and ceilings were transparent. She then heard a voice telling her to go back as it was 'not her time' yet. She returned to her body quickly and with force. Before waking up she then heard her (deceased) step-grandfather's voice telling her not to worry and that her baby was not well. At that point she 'woke up' feeling very frightened. The next day she took her baby to the local doctor's surgery and then later to the local hospital, where the baby was diagnosed with bronchial pneumonia.

John (age 28) reported 2 prior OBEs. He had been diagnosed with nocturnal epilepsy at the age of 10 and received medication to control it. His first OBE happened when he was 17 years old and asleep in his room. He experienced sleep paralysis, which he described as "terrifying". After the paralysis, John went back to sleep, then next remembered being out of his body, sitting on top of the bookcase in the corner of his room, looking down on himself as he lay in bed. As he looked back at his physical body the whole room seemed to come towards him and he found himself back in his body and awake again.

In the next section of this chapter we present in thematic form the findings of our analysis of the interview transcripts with the above participants.

THE SOCIAL EXPERIENCE OF SHARING THE EXPERIENCE

Both Mark and Cindy had a strong desire to share their OBEs with others as part of an attempt to better understand them. They had both encountered mixed reactions from within and outside of their family circle. By contrast, John had not tried to talk in detail about the OB aspect of his experiences as he was concerned that this might provoke derision from others. Instead he had preferred to talk about the sleep paralysis aspect of the experience which frightened and confused him, as he had thought it might indicate the recurrence of his epilepsy, despite taking medication to control it. Mark described his parents' initial reaction to hearing what he had to tell them about his first frightening OBE:

> I just explained to her [his mother] what I'd seen and me parents...they just listened to what I had to say and then they just...parents tend to dismiss things, and...they just put it down to dreams- a dream experience, so, you've had a bad dream or nightmare, erm, and then when you're that age as well you tend to accept that.

The early dismissiveness Mark experienced from his parents helped galvanize a long-term personal inhibition about talking to others about any kind of experience which might be perceived as out of the ordinary. This inhibition may have contributed to his self-declared reduced social skills and strategies in later life, particularly in regards to knowing when, how, and with whom to broach these topics. Diminished opportunities to talk about these personally significant experiences left him with long-term feelings of being undervalued, powerlessness, frustration and isolation, which had been compounded by the negative reactions he had received when he had tried to discuss his experiences within a workplace setting:

> I've found that, I think I made a mistake sometime by discussin' it in, perhaps in the workplace...People just tend to dismiss it an' go, what are y'on about, y'know...its probably because the' don't really, the' not really interested...so they just tend to sort of dismiss it y'see. But like I say, I don't think it's, the workplace is the right place to discuss it...it's quite, er, a clumsy thing to do really.

In contrast, John had never really spoken in depth to anyone else about the OB aspect of his experience, although he felt that he wanted to. Although he had a desire to talk about what he had experienced, like Mark, he felt inhibited. However, John's inhibition was made in anticipation of negative reactions from others:

> It's the sort of thing I would want to share, but I'd only tell select people that, y'know, that I could trust, they wouldn't laugh at me and that sort of thing.

All three participants had received support from a variety of sources since having their first OBEs, which had been crucial in helping them to integrate the experience. Mark's already close relationship with his mother became stronger following the death of his brother. His accounts of his OBEs, in which he described being visited by his deceased brother, were a source of comfort and healing for them and their family:

> It has a kind of positive uplifting effect on me mum and I feel a lot happier, in life…it's just a, an inner sense of peace within myself that I know me brother's spoken to me an' I've seen him and I feel real happy about that…and I think been able to share that with me mum as well, erm, is, is really good, an' other members of me family.

Outside of the family, Mark had found support and acceptance for his experiences and beliefs at a local paranormal investigation group, which he joined shortly after the death of his brother:

> I don't expect the group to just believe what I say…and I don't enforce me beliefs on anybody else erm, it's entirely up to anybody else whether they believe me or not…It's just that I feel that I want to share the experiences with other people an' see what their views and opinions are.

The sharing and accepting process within his family and with his peers at the paranormal group had helped reduce the early apprehension he had felt about his OBEs. Beyond being a source of comfort for himself and his mother, there was a wider social implication in that he felt more confident and independent and enjoyed being a part of something to which he had something to contribute. This had raised his self-esteem, provided him with a wider social network and given him a definite sense of being more in control of his life.

However, Cindy differed from Mark and John in that she felt less inhibited about talking about her experiences and less concerned about potential negative reactions to her story. She attributed this confidence and certainty to the felt realism of her experience itself as it in some way given her a glimpse of life after death:

> It's convinced me so much, no one will tell me anything different that the, as far as I'm concerned there's another side and that is it…I'm a hundred percent about that.

The Positive Impact of the OBE

Each participant spoke resolutely for the positive effects the experience brought to their lives. For Mark, this was a story of recovery and healing after tragedy. The sudden tragic death of his brother in a car accident had a profoundly upsetting effect upon him and his family. Shortly after his brother's death Mark began having his OBEs in which he felt able to communicate with his deceased brother within the OB state. For him, this had provided proof that his brother was happy, having 'crossed over'. Communicating this to his mother and other family members, who accepted Mark's experiences as 'real', had in turn aided his family's healing. Therefore, an initially frightening experience became transformed and imbued with positive meaning and purpose. Mark felt that, notwithstanding the relatively recent loss of his brother, life had become better, and this he partly attributed to the after effects of having his OBEs. He considered himself to be happier and to have benefited from the experiences.

Cindy's story was also one of recovery and healing for her and of rescue for her newly born baby. From a very early age Cindy was extremely afraid of death, in particular she feared her grandparents dying as she had a close relationship with them. This fear was characterized in later life by refusing to attend her grandfather's funeral:

> I don't think I fear death…like, erm, when you are [a] young child and you hear the word death it sort of fills you with absolute dread…y'know, when my granddad died, y'know, I was pregnant at the time, I didn't, y'know, want to go and visit him because I didn't want to see someone on their death bed and there was seeing him in the coffin and things like, that because I was so scared of death, so, but I've, obviously, because of these things that have happened I'm the complete opposite end now.

Cindy also firmly believed that there was an immediate positive outcome to the OBE she had as it saved her baby's life:

> I just understood that this presence was there and it was there to sort of look after, like me and the baby…I think it was a positive experience for me. Without that the chances are, y'know, my son might've died.

John was somewhat different in that the OB aspect had had a milder positive effect than it did for Mark and Cindy. Rather, it was his fear of an aspect of his OBE – the paralysis which preceded the OBE – and its immediate association with a potential return of his epilepsy, which caused him most concern. Having now accepted and overcome this fearful aspect of the experience, John was convinced that as whole it was a positive one, which he would like to repeat:

> If I had the chance to do it again, I would, knowing that it was safe, y'know, if you could get it controlled or whatever, it doesn't scare me, the paralysis thing scared me…so, hey, I'd love to able to just turn it on, on and off, it would be great.

Placing the OBE Within a Biographical Context

John felt there had been little in the way of significant changes in his life since his first experience. The initial shock of the sleep paralysis preceding his OBE seemed to have overshadowed the OB aspect itself, which appeared to have been more quietly integrated and John made his own suggestions as to why this might be the case:

> I think maybe that's why I'm not, it's not made such a big impact 'cos I know other people that's been sleepy, y'know, there is a buzz word to describe sleep paralysis… so I think, maybe if it was, if someone had said sleep paralysis is a paranormal event that happens because of this, that and the other, then it would have had more of a, an impact.

The OBE is often viewed as a paranormal event by many lay people and some professionals. This is partly because of the implication within its name that something detaches itself (e.g. the mind, or consciousness) and travels beyond the confines of the physical body. In this study, both John and Mark shared the same view about the 'paranormality' of their OBEs. Both had prior knowledge of the paranormal and of OBEs, yet both suggested that, having experienced them, they saw them as naturally occurring events in their lives, something which they both viewed as positive life-affirming experiences. In this extract, Mark not only highlights the normality of the experience, but also minimizes the difference between himself as an OBEr and other people who may not have had OBEs:

> It feels like it's a naturally occurring experience that are a part of life, and personally I believe that they've always been there, an, and I don't believe that I'm special in the way that it only happens to me, I just, I genuinely believe that this is the case for all human beings.

Since his experiences, Mark had developed an open-minded view towards anomalous experiences and paranormal phenomena. He placed his faith in scientific research to find out the answers to the questions he had about his own, and other experiences. His experiences had been catalytic in fuelling his desire to find out more about what his experiences are and how they come about. Since the onset of his OBEs, he had begun a distance learning course about how to scientifically research the paranormal, including OBEs. An important consideration for Mark when he was seeking out a program of study was that the course should not be purely academic, but also incorporate the personal experiences of the student, thus allowing him freedom of expression and a chance to evaluate his experiences alongside known scientific data about OBEs:

> Well, the course is based on twenty modules, it's, like I say, it's a scientific based organization, which personally I think is really important because you share a lot of common ground with other people…then in some of the answers you can interpret your own belief system as well, y'know you can mix some of your experiences in with scientific knowledge.

Mark's overall feeling about his OBEs was that they had been mostly very positive and uplifting experiences. Despite the negative reactions from outside of the family, he seemed to have become resolute in his belief that his OBEs were indeed as they appeared to be. Beyond being a source of comfort for himself, his mother and family, there was a wider social implication. His OBEs had been instrumental in forging a 'new' Mark, someone who has left behind old ways of inhibition, doubt and self-consciousness, and had raised his self-esteem, provided him with access to a wider social network and afforded him a sense of being more in control of his life. The initially negative response he had had to his experiences had encouraged him to be more accepting of other's views, particularly of those who don't believe in the veridicality of his OBEs:

> I'd say it's been a very uplifting experience, erm, and a very positive experience…I would say since the experiences…I'm more conscientious about life and I've found that I want to learn more…I feel more in control of me own life and I don't worry about what other people think as much.

Cindy's OBE seemed to have played a dual role in her life. As mentioned earlier, she felt it was instrumental in warning her of her baby's impending illness and in reducing her fear of death and dying. She had an unwavering attitude towards most reactions to her story and attributed this to feeling so convinced that her OBE was completely veridical. She also attributed an increased sensitivity to death and accidents to her OBE, and felt this was a sign of having attained a spiritual connection with the world:

> When I got, when my dad died, y'know, I was, y'know, I wouldn't leave the room, I knew and the funny thing is I knew he was going to die. No one in my family, didn't even know he was ill and I just...I can sense things now really sense things...I dunno, if there's a bit of a connection somewhere in whatever it is spiritual, I feel like I've got a bit of a connection now.

Like Mark, Cindy's OBE was a catalyst for her starting to search for answers to explain what had happened to her. Her early attempts to seek out explanations and answers to her experience led her to attend a spiritualist church, and she began to avidly study areas of the paranormal and spirituality.

Discussion

Within this chapter we have examined the longitudinal after-effects experienced by people who have out-of-body experiences, and the nature of those after-effects, including the pathways people take whilst attempting to integrate their experiences, and the temporal, social and psychological factors that may impinge on the integration process. The above analysis has revealed that the OBE is both socially and affectively complex; the successful integration of which may add positively to a person's mental well-being. In this section of the paper we will discuss these findings within a theoretical context.

As discussed earlier, OBEs have sometimes been researched in the past in connection with mental illnesses. Mental disorders themselves have attracted stigma throughout history, often in the form of direct discrimination (personally, institutionally or structurally) or through social psychological processes which engage the perceptions of the person being stigmatized, for example, psychosis (MacDonald, Sauer, Howie, & Albiston, 2005), schizophrenia (Dinos, Stevens, Serfaty, Weich, & King, 2004), and bipolar disorder (Perlick et al., 2001).

Here, participants reported encounters with others in which they perceived these persons to view a person who has OBE as having something else 'wrong' with them. Such negative perceptions alone can have debilitating effects on a person's sense of identity and self-esteem. Poor experiences of self-disclosure can also have negative long-term consequences in terms of how the experience may be integrated.

To begin the process of successful integration, open and honest disclosure must be met with acceptance, empathy and understanding, particularly if it is from those perceived by the experient as a caring and trusted role model. In the research reported here, participants did find those sources of support, though not always where they might have initially expected and not always upon first disclosure.

The positive effects of successful sharing and disclosure of experiences such as OBEs have been noted by Palmer and Braud (2002), who found that scores on measures of disclosure of Exceptional Human Experiences (EHEs) positively correlated with measures of personal and existential meaning in life and psychological well-being. There was also a negative correlation with stress related physical and psychological illnesses.

All participants in the present study emphasized positive aspects of their OBEs, such as finding greater meaning and a sense of purpose in life, compassion, happiness and a reduced fear of death. Similarly, in a questionnaire survey comparing OBErs and non-OBErs, Osis (1979) found that 88% of OBErs reported having beneficial changes post-experience, such as, a deeper philosophical consideration of life and death, and a reduced fear of dying. The positive moods reported post-OBE by participants here echoes findings from McCreery and Claridge (1995). In their work on schizotypy, they found that OBErs scored higher on a measure of hypomania, which they found consistent with their model of schizotypy in that, to a certain degree, the hypomania measure was tapping into a person's tendency towards positive mood states.

Two of the three participants reported experiencing encounters with deceased individuals during their OBEs. This is particularly interesting as while extant literature suggests such experiences are a relatively common aspect of the near-death experience (during which experients feels as if they are experiencing bodily death and the continuation of consciousness outside of the body), they have not previously been reported as part of an OBE. This may be a methodological issue, in that previous structured approaches to these issues have not enabled the expression of these facets of people's experiences. However, this also leads to the question of whether it was the OBE per se or the believed communications with deceased relatives that led to the positive effects (e.g. greater acceptance of death) reported here. However, it is a common report that the perceived detachment of consciousness from the body during the OBE is sufficient to instill a belief that consciousness will continue after bodily death.

The above participants reported their experienced communication with deceased relatives as beneficial, helping them to cope with emotionally difficult situations that had happened in their lives. Similarly, McCreery and Claridge (2002) have suggested that there may be an adaptive value underlying some kinds of anomalous experiences, citing an example of someone who is experiencing post-operative pain before an OBE, who once having an OBE, then report less pain. Green and McCreery (1975) have also described what they called 'reassuring apparitions', forms of hallucination in which human figures appear which have the subsequent effect of calming a person who is experiencing a stressful life event. This finding is in part supported by the work of Palmer and Braud (2002) who found that there was a needs related aspect to the occurrence of the EHEs that their participants reported. In many instances, their participants would recall how these experiences would happen as "helper experiences just when they needed the help" (p.35).

All three of the participants in this study had prior knowledge of OBEs before they happened and had strong beliefs themselves about the nature and veridicality of the experience. The role of an experient's belief system, particularly their belief in the paranormal, has also received research attention in relation to the 'healthy schizotype' personality and the adaptive value of anomalous experiences. For instance, Williams and Irwin (1991) suggested that having a belief in the paranormal may provide individuals with a mechanism by which to accept and explain their anomalous experiences. This was supported by Schofield and Claridge (2007) who found that participants who had a framework by which to support their belief in the paranormal were less cognitively disorganized and recounted their paranormal experiences as more pleasant, which also may have a bearing on the experient's psychological well-being. The authors also suggest that persons with a weak belief framework may find the same experience alarming and unwanted. This scenario fits well with the experiences of all participants in the present study, who, despite some previous knowledge of OBEs and the paranormal before their OBEs, found their initial experiences disturbing. However, upon subsequent reflection and with at least one additional OBE a stronger belief has been forged that their experiences are veridical OBEs.

CONCLUSIONS

The present work highlights the value of qualitative, phenomenological work in understanding the experience of an OBE and its resultant after-effects. In particular, the findings from this work reveal how participants managed such experiences. Participants OBEs occurred at times of personal significance and continued to exert considerable influence in how participants made sense of their lives, including their apparent adaptive role in response to difficult life events. Although participants reported some interpersonal difficulties involving disclosure of these experiences, as a whole the findings from this work contribute to the body of literature which suggests that people who have anomalous experiences may not only continue to be fully functional in everyday life, but may derive psychological benefits from such experiences depending upon the meaning which these experiences come to be imbued with for them.

ACKNOWLEDGEMENTS

The work reported here was supported by a grant awarded by the Bial Foundation and a Parapsychological Association Research Endowment. The authors would like to express their gratitude for this support.

REFERENCES

Alvarado, C. S. (1997). Mapping the characteristics of out-of-body experiences. *Journal of the American Society for Psychical Research 91,* 15-32.

Alvarado, C. S., & Zingrone N. L. (2003). Exploring the factors related to the after-effects of out-of-body experiences. *Journal of the Society for Psychical Research, 67(3),* 161-183.

Blackmore, S. J. (1984). A psychological theory of the out-of-body experience. *Journal of Parapsychology, 48,* 201-218.

Blackmore, S. J. (1986a). Out-of-body experiences in schizophrenia: a questionnaire survey. *Journal of Nervous and Mental Disease, 174,* 615-619.

Claridge, G. (1997). Theoretical background and issues. In G. Claridge (Ed.), *Schizotypy: Implications for illness and health* (pp 3-18). Oxford: Oxford University Press.

Dinos, S., Stevens, S., Serfaty, M., Weich, S., & King, M. (2004). Stigma: the feelings and experiences of 46 people with mental illness. *British Journal of Psychiatry, 184,* 176-181.

Goulding, A. (2004). Schizotypy models in relation to subjective health and paranormal beliefs and experiences. *Personality and Individual Differences, 37,* 157-167.

Goulding, A. (2005). Healthy schizotypy in a population of paranormal believers and experients. *Personality and Individual Differences, 38,* 1069-1083.

Green, C., & McCreery, C. (1975). *Apparitions.* London: Hamish Hamilton.

MacDonald, E., Sauer, K., Howie, L., & Albiston, D. (2005). What happens to social relationships in early psychosis? A phenomenological study of young people's experiences. *Journal of Mental Health, 14(2),* 129-143.

McCreery, C., & Claridge, G. (1995). Out-of-the-body experiences and personality. *Journal of the Society for Psychical Research, 60(838),* 129-148.

McCreery, C., & Claridge, G. (2002). Healthy schizotypy: The case of out-of-body experiences. *Personality and Individual Differences, 32,* 141-154.

Osis, K. (1979). Insider's view of the OBE, a questionnaire study. In W. G. Roll, J. Beloff , & R. A. White (Eds.), *Research In Parapsychology, 1982* (pp 50-52). Metuchen, N. J.: Scarecrow.

Palmer, G., & Braud, W. (2002). Exceptional human experiences, disclosure, and a more inclusive view of physical, psychological, and spiritual well-being. *Journal of Transpersonal Psychology, 34,* 29-61.

Perlick, D. A., Rosenheck, R. A., Clarkin, J. F. Sirey, J. A., Salahi, J. L. E., Struening, E. L. & Link, B. G. (2001). Stigma as a barrier to recovery: Adverse effects of perceived stigma on social adaptation of persons diagnosed with bipolar affective disorder. *Psychiatric Services, 52(12),* 1627-1632.

Rawciffe, D. H. (1959). *Illusions and delusions of the supernatural and the occult.* New York: Dover.

Schofield, K., & Claridge, G. (2007). Paranormal experiences and mental health: Schizotypy as an underlying factor. *Personality and Individual Differences, 43,* 1908-1916.

Twemlow, S. W. (1989). Clinical approaches to the out-of-body experience. *Journal of Near-Death Studies, 8,* 29-43.

Whitlock, F. A. (1978). The psychiatry and psychopathology of paranormal phenomena. *Australian and New Zealand Journal of Psychiatry, 12,* 11-19.

Wilde, D.J. and Murray, C.D. (2009). The evolving self: finding meaning in near-death experiences using Interpretative Phenomenological Analysis. *Mental Health, Religion & Culture, 12,* 223-239.

Wilde, D.J. and Murray, C.D. (in press) Interpreting the anomalous: finding meaning in out-of-body and near-death experiences. *Qualitative Research in Psychology*

Williams, L. M., & Irwin, H. J. (1991). A study of paranormal belief, magical ideation as an index of schizotypy, and cognitive style. *Personality and Individual Differences, 12,* 1339-1348.

In: Psychological Scientific Perspectives on Out of Body... ISBN: 978-1-60741-705-7
Editor: Craig D. Murray

Chapter 8

PREVALENCE, PHENOMENOLOGY AND BIOPSYCHOSOCIAL ASPECTS OF THE NEAR-DEATH EXPERIENCE

John Belanti, Karuppiah Jagadheesan and Mahendra Perera

ABSTRACT

Near Death Experiences (NDEs) have been recorded from time immemorial and have been noted to occur in a sizeable number of the population. NDEs are experienced by some individuals faced with situations that are perceived as life threatening or potentially fatal. The key elements of an NDE are: an out of body experience (OBE); feelings of peace; meeting a being of light; meeting others; a life review; and reaching a point of no return. Fear evoking NDEs have also been described. Although there is a composite description there is a wide inter individual variation in the experiences described. There are iconic images, which are influenced by the experient's culture and religion. Within this chapter we discuss the key elements of the NDE, the cultural variation in NDE reports, and potential neurobiological mechanisms which are considered to underlie these experiences:

INTRODUCTION

Near death experiences (NDEs) have been reported from various parts of the globe. Although NDEs have been recorded in history and reported from various countries (Corazza, 2008; Peake, 2006; Roberts & Owen, 1988), these were first popularized and brought to the attention of a wider audience in English speaking countries by Dr Raymond Moody through his seminal book "Life After Life" (Moody, 1975). The book contains a comprehensive overview of the NDE, along with a typology which is still in use.

Although there are many accounts and texts written on this subject, there is a paucity of epidemiological data regarding its occurrence, especially in general populations. Gallup and Procter (1982) noted a prevalence of 15% in America, while a study from Germany (Knoblauch et. al., 2001) found the prevalence to be 4%. A general population survey in

Australia (Perera et. al., 2005), the first study know to the authors to use a structured questionnaire administered with a nationally representative sample, found that 8% of the general population reported an NDE, rising to almost one fourth of those who experienced a life threatening situation. Surveys from India (Pasricha, 1995, 2008) noted the prevalence to be 0.1% and 0.04%. However, a methodological limitation of this latter research was that data was gathered by questioning the principal resident of the selected household regarding knowledge of cases rather than directly questioning individuals. This may well explain the markedly low prevalence. A review of the prevalence in clinical studies yielded estimates of 9 – 18% in intact cohorts (Greyson, 1998). Hence, the NDE is prevalent in the general population and more common among patients. There have also been reports of NDEs from children (Morse et al, 1986; Morse & Perry, 1992). In a recent article, cardiologist and near-death research pioneer Dr Michael Sabom (2008) has added a further dimension to the NDE, by distinguishing a category called acute dying experience (ADE). In essence it can be thought of as an NDE without the mystical consciousness and an adaptive mechanism in traumatic situations (Sabom, 2008). At this stage, although such a distinction may be useful in research work, it may not be as relevant in clinical settings.

The expression of NDEs may be influenced by socio-cultural and religious factors (Belanti, et. al., 2008; Kellehear, 2008). One does need to be cognizant of the fact that not all those who have come close to dying report an NDE. There are other situations such as drug-induced states, electrical stimulation of parts of the brain or other circumstances in which some of the phenomena have been reported and are more commonly termed out-of-body experiences (Corazza, 2008). This chapter will focus on the key elements that comprise NDEs, the influence of culture on its expression and an overview of the biological underpinnings relating these to experiences.

PHENOMENOLOGY

Dr Raymond Moody's systematic investigation of NDEs has significantly contributed to an understanding the cardinal features of this phenomenon (Moody, 1975). He pooled together accounts of 150 individuals, including people who had been resuscitated after having been thought of as clinically dead, those who had come very close to physical death, and from deathbed narratives that were conveyed to him. The key components identified were: ineffability or a feeling of indescribable transcendence; hearing themselves being pronounced dead; feelings of peace and quiet; noises; an out-of-body experience; meeting others in the realm of the non-living; meeting a being of light; experiencing a review of their life; and travelling to the border or the point beyond which there was no return (to the land of the living, coming back and life thereafter). These experiences are likely to have a profound effect on the individual.

Ring (1980) expanded on the subject of NDE phenomenology with more case vignettes and commentary, while Greyson and Stevenson (1980) have summarized NDE phenomena from an analysis of three cohorts. Perhaps the most common theme that arises from these works is the experient's feeling of being outside their own body and having a 'body' as distinct from their physical body, along with being able to travel in a non-physical realm. Moving out of the body was sometimes coupled with a sensation of being pulled through a tunnel and may be accompanied by noises. Feelings of peace, equanimity, freedom from the pain and suffering (e.g., in accident victims) and transcendence are juxtaposed. NDE experients were also able to see and hear those physically present. Less common elements were the life review, which has been conceptualized as a kaleidoscopic vision of the experient's entire life being flashed before their eyes in a split second, and a feeling of being held accountable for their actions, in a non-judgmental manner. The sense of time itself may be altered with speeding up or slowing down. The 'being of light' has been described in various ways; it is said to be radiant yet non-blinding with incredible warmth, with the experient feeling irresistibly drawn towards it.

Meeting with other entities such as religious figures, deceased relatives and others not known to the individual have also been reported. The border or point of no return is reported in fewer instances in case series. The person usually finds him or herself at a place from which, if they proceed further, will result in their not being able to return to their body. Some choose to return of their own volition when they feel that there is unfinished business on earth. Others are informed that they must go back (even if they are not willing to) as their time for the return is in the future, and others have come back without any conscious decision to do so or not. Communication in a NDE is non-verbal and seems to occur by a process of thought transference. Extrasensory perceptions such as being able to see through things, which to mortal eyes seem solid, and a heightened sense of awareness, are additional features.

Knowledge of future events (Lundhal, 2001) is another reported aspect, but there is no undisputed documented evidence to substantiate this. Although the prevailing ethos of such experiences is one of peace and transcendence, there are reports of distress when the experience itself is interpreted as unpleasant, a sense of nonexistence or visualizing graphic hellish landscapes (Greyson & Bush, 1992).

Cultural Aspects

Reviewing the literature on culture and the NDE there have been writers who have explored cultural comparisons and emphasized the cultural shaping of NDEs (Belanti et al, 2008; Carr, 1993; Ellwood, 2000; Fox, 2003; Giovetti, 1982; Groth-Marnat, 1994; Kellehear, 1996, 2008; Lundahl, 2000; Murphy, 2001; Schorer, 1985). However, the impact of cultural variables on NDEs can be difficult to interpret due to the varied nature of the samples, small sample sizes, lack of objective means of collecting data, and lack of discussion of cultural context in some studies. In addition, translations of NDE narratives into the English language may lose cultural meanings that exist in the original language. At present there are no external validating criteria against which these experiences could be verified.

The NDEs reported in western cultures are predominantly highlighted by their individuality, the experience of overwhelming love and bliss in the presence of the Light compared to features that predominantly reflect a feeling of estrangement from the body, particularly evident in the Chinese studies, and in most Tibetan accounts, fear and concern about being reborn through emotional attraction to visions of their future parents (Bailey, 2001; Becker, 1981; Carr, 1993; Zhi-ying & Jian-xun, 1992). Further distinct differences between Euro-American NDEs and the literature reflected in the Tibetan books of the dead, is the emphasis on God's forgiveness and loving acceptance in contrast to Tibetan Buddhism's emphasis on Karma's fear inducing judgment (Carr, 1993). These ideational shifts can generally relate to the level of fear versus love expressed in European NDEs (Zaleski, 1987). Euro-Americans also typically report seeing a golden color light (Ring, 1980) compared with the clear light seen by Tibetans. Interestingly, this suggests that people can have differing perspectives upon events that are informed by culturally generated symbols, narratives and concepts that allow people to distinguish between what is good and bad, true and false (Ellwood, 2000). In addition, Carr (1993) and Lee (2003) highlight that over history the dominant views of the Christian Church have shaped the content of people's NDEs, and how people interpret the meaning of their lives as conditioned by religious beliefs.

In the non-Western context, the concepts of messengers accompanying the deceased person, hell and torture are commonly noted in NDEs from Thailand (Murphy, 2001). The concept of a messenger taking the individual to other realms, checking their names in a book and being returned due to them being the wrong person is noted in India (Pasricha, 1995). There appears to be an absence of tunnel sensation and life reviews are found only in certain cultures (a detailed review has been provided by Kellehear, 2008).

A personal experience of one of the authors (JB) who was a witness and survivor of the 2004 Tsunami whilst in Thailand, involved escaping from one of the waves, an experience he found similar to an NDE, although he was not unconscious or clinically dead. Features of this experience included a stillness of time, a sense of disassociation from the body whilst escaping, and having the experience of a life review where many memories came to consciousness with a deep sense of self evaluation and a sense of calmness. The experience was different to that described for the NDE in extant literature from Thailand.

Cultural variations in the concept of life and death may explain the varying emphasis on specific features in NDEs. For example, Counts (1983) notes that in a Melanesian society, death is not considered to be the natural conclusion of the life cycle, but results instead from an external source, such as sorcery, and while North Americans and Europeans commonly see a beautiful garden, the Kalai of Melanesia experience an industrialized world of factories, highways and urban sprawl. By contrast, NDE reports in Thailand and India do not include visions of 'paradise,' but instead have experiences that include visions of religious figures and the experience of Karma and judgment.

> "Yamraj (the god of death) was there sitting on a high chair with a white beard and wearing yellow clothes. He asked me, 'What do you want?' I told him that I wanted to stay there. He asked me to extend my hand. I don't remember whether he gave me something or not. Then I was pushed down and revived". (Pasricha & Stevenson, 1986, p. 167).

Interestingly, as narratives from different geographical regions with similar cultures or historical linkages between them are explored, there begins to appear common features in these NDE reports. Perhaps this reflects, at least in part, the way in which the languages and cultures of each have coalesced or influenced each other at various times (Comrie, Matthews and Polinsky, 2005). Gómez-Jeria (1993) studied NDEs in the Mapuche people in South America and explored how religious beliefs and historical events contributed to individuals' reports of NDEs. This study revealed common themes relating to a volcano where 'dead people' were found, and this theme is also reflected in Kellehear's paper (2001) describing similar features in a real-life account of a Hawaiian NDE. Furthermore, the Mapuche people describe the belief that life continues beyond death in a body that is an exact double of the body during life, preserving all the characteristics of the individual at the time of death, including the same needs. Narratives also revealed visions of deceased friends and relatives together with other people, which were common features of their NDE.

> "There was a German gentlemen reading and writing in big books. When the German saw him, he asked what he wanted. 'I am following my son,' said the old man. 'What is his name?' asked the German gentleman. 'Francisco Leufuhue.' He called the guard and ordered him to inform Francisco . . . And a distant voice answered . . . Then he passed through a wooden gate. . . He passed the next . . . another . . . and after the fourth, Francisco arrived at the German gentleman's table . . . 'Your Dad is looking for you.' Old Fermin approached his son . . . saying: 'You will receive me because I do not wish to live any more where I am living now' . . . 'No, Dad . . . it is not time for you to arrive here by your own will. When the time comes, I myself shall go to the side of the house to look for you. Then you will come. Now, go away.' At this moment, Don Fermin woke up and opened his eyes." (Calvo de Guzman, 1992, pp. 47–48, in Gómez-Jeria, 1993, pp. 220–221).

Interestingly, the vision of a 'German gentleman' in the afterlife in the above account reflects the German colonization in 1850 of the part of Chile from which this narrative came (Gómez-Jeria, 1993). Similar influences are also seen in the experience of an American who had a NDE while with Sai Baba (a venerated, holy man living in India with devotees from all parts of the globe and credited with many miraculous deeds), who reported that he was brought back to life by Sai Baba (Sandweiss, 1975).

In India comparable reports of deathbed visions have found that Indian NDEs commonly include religious visions with the person generally unwilling to follow the spiritual beings sent to take them further (Osis & Haraldson, 1977). By contrast, Americans typically had visions of deceased relatives and followed them into an after-death state (Osis & Haraldson, 1977). Further differences between the two cultures highlighted in this study were that the panoramic life reviews, tunnels, out of body experiences and transcendental elements commonly reported in Western cultural accounts were not present in Indian NDEs (Pasricha, 1993; 1995). However, Blackmore (1993) explored NDEs in India and found that there were NDE accounts comparable to those reported by Moody (1975), which included visions of tunnels, dark spaces, and bright lights, contrary to previous reports of Indian cases.

As it becomes evident that both past and current cultural environments may have some influence in shaping the content of NDE experiences, there is an Israeli account of a NDE which was culturally dissonant and reported that cultural and religious beliefs did not necessarily influence an individual's psychological processes that may have projected pre existing beliefs in their NDE (Abramovitch, 1988). In addition, the notion that the phenomenology of NDEs is not determined by a person's culture, but rather reflects that person's expectations of what death would be like, was explored in NDE narratives from Thailand (Murphy, 2001). Findings revealed clear differences in the content and themes in contrast to other accounts of NDEs, including references to Karma and to temples, monks and traditional foods were found. Interestingly, there was a sense of punishment portrayed in this experience, which could possibly be construed in a variety of ways depending upon the meaning placed upon the terms used, such as 'judgment,' 'lack of donation,' and the statement 'sentenced me to many rebirths.' (Murphy, 2001).

> "There were fried eggs, an omelette, beef curry, chicken curry, and candied eggs . . . prepared just as my mother had made them for me . . . I became thirsty. I told this woman that I wanted some water. She said that there was no water for me here, because I had never donated anything to drink to the monks or to a temple . . . I would (sic) never forget to donate cool drinks to the monks I went to visit. After a long walk with this angelic woman, I came home, where I revived. I was so thirsty." (Suwannathat, n.d., pp. 171–203, in Murphy, 2001, p. 165).

In Japan, there is literature that explores NDEs in great detail; however it is not available in the English language. The journalist Tachibana has thoroughly investigated NDEs from different frameworks to introduce the concept of NDEs in Japan in the early 90s when NDEs were not well known as a common story (Tachibana, 2000a).

Nowadays NDEs are well known and the outstanding feature Japanese people will report about an NDE is "... almost crossing a *Sanzu* River to go to the world after the death but I didn't for some reason" (Tachibana, 2000b, p. 108). Sanzu River is the river from an old folk story that went to the world after death in which people had believed in for over a thousand years as folklore combined with Buddhism. The feature of "crossing the Sanzu river" is still used as a trope of "to die" in Japanese language now. In his book, Tachibana mentions that Japanese people are still strongly influenced by that concept in their NDEs (Tachibana, 2000b). According to this, Japanese people tend to have a "river" experience, which is a motif in Greek and Roman mythology but they (the Japanese) are less likely to have a "light" experience, as reflected in western cultural accounts. There are accounts of some people experiencing the "light" after the tunnel but interestingly they do not associate it with "God", "love" or "existence of something absolute" and the light is not personalized but just one of the conditions of the environment of their NDEs, although it is supernatural and beautiful (Tachibana, 2000b).

Tachibana, then, assumes that identifying with the light experience as meeting with God or enlightenment is the reflection of the Western culture influenced by Christianity. These differences in interpretation between Japanese NDEs and Western NDEs may reflect the views of Japanese culture towards religion, as it may be part of custom and folklore activity, which differs from other cultures.

NEUROBIOLOGY

There has been growing interest in finding out neurobiological substrates and mechanisms underlying NDEs. Changes in neurotransmitters, cerebral gas composition and functional levels in certain parts of the brain are implicated in NDEs (Blackmore, 1996; Parnia & Fenwick, 2002).

Of the neural substrates, endorphins are given significant attention, particularly based on the observation that endorphins are released under stress, both physical and psychological, and that this substance is associated with a feeling of well being, acceptance and intense pleasure and modulated pain experience (Carr, 1981; 1982) Endorphins could lower seizure threshold and there has been an observation that opioid antagonist, noloxone, turned positive experiences into fearful NDEs (Judson & Wiltshaw, 1983). However, endorphin theory still remains to be confirmed. Serotonergic system and NMDA receptors are considered to have some role in NDEs (Morse et al, 1986; Jansen, 1989). Potential role of anesthetics is another area of interest, particularly in those who receive critical medical care. The observation that patients who receive anesthetics have fewer or less detailed NDEs and that NDEs have been observed in drug-free patients indicate that the underlying pathophysiology of NDEs is more than that could be explained by medication alone (Blackmore, 1996).

Changes in cerebral gas composition have been implicated in NDEs. The evidence for this proposition comes from a body of research on NDEs in cardiac arrest survivors. Parnia, et. al. (2001) reported that a majority of 11% cardiac survivors who had memories had NDEs. Later, Greyson (2003) reported that 10% of patients with cardiac arrest and 1% of other cardiac patients had NDEs. Particularly, anoxia is considered a factor, as there are brain structures (e.g., temporal lobe, limbic lobe) that are sensitive to low oxygen levels (Blackmore, 1996).

Blackmore (1996) suggested that anoxia is associated with visual cortical disinhibition and that this disinhibition related random excitation of central to peripheral visual field areas in the visual cortex creates tunnel and light experience. Carbon dioxide retention is another potential factor of interest, particularly given that high carbon dioxide levels are associated with strange experiences such as lights, visions, out-of-body and mystical experiences (Meduna, 1950). Although NDEs are observed in cardiac survivors, given that cardiac arrest is associated with significant compromise in the brain functioning, there is a suggestion that NDEs could occur either while consciousness is lost or gained (Parnia & Fenwick, 2002).

The temporal lobe and limbic system have been given considerable attention in NDE research (Blackmore, 1996). Notably, both these brain structures are sensitive to anoxia (Halgren et al, 1978; Penfield, 1955) and endorphins could lower seizure threshold in these areas (Frenk et al, 1978). Temporal lobe epilepsy in hypoxic brain is considered a possibility. Temporal lobe stimulation has been found to associate with hallucinations, memory flashbacks, body distortions and out-of-body experiences (Halgren et al, 1978; Penfield, 1955). Based on this, it was hypothesized that the NDE is a temporal lobe excitation syndrome, an adaptive response to extreme anxiety (Noyes & Kletti, 1977). There is also the suggestion that people who are prone for NDEs might have unstable temporal lobes (Ring, 1984).

Another brain area of interest is that the limbic system given its role emotions and memory (Blackmore, 1996). It has been suggested that limbic system could be connected with life review of NDEs. Blanke et al (2002) carried out an experimental stimulation of angular gyrus and noted that the patient had vestibular responses ("sinking into bed" or "falling from a height"), OBE, feeling of floating and lightness and somatic illusion. The angular gyrus is situated close to the vestibular cortex and hence it is proposed that failure to integrate complex somatosensory and vestibular information could be a neural mechanism associated with OBE and associated experiences (Blanke et al, 2002).

Neurobiological evidence indicates potential brain-based mechanisms for NDEs. Nevertheless, methodological limitations, e.g., sample selection and size, need consideration while interpreting these data. NDEs are observed in a variety of conditions such as healthy state, critically ill state, and psychologically or physically threatening situations. Hence there needs to be ongoing, carefully controlled scientific experimentation and diligent interpretation of the findings in order to elucidate more clearly the underlying biological bases of NDEs. Therefore, at this stage, neurobiological factors could be best considered potential explanatory factors rather than robust evidence for NDEs.

Conclusion

Based on the limited epidemiological studies we estimate conservatively that there would be over one million people in the world currently who have experienced an NDE. These are characterized by unusual experiences such out of body feelings, altered time sensations and other paranormal events. Peaceful feelings are common but fearful emotions too have been evoked in NDE. The experience is underpinned by upbringing, belief systems and neurobiological mechanisms but its description is limited by language. Multidisciplinary research will help furthering our understanding of such events and give us further clues to their etiology.

Acknowledgments

The authors would like to thank Ms Hanae Iwamoto for her research assistance and translation of Rinshi Taiken (Near death experience) by Takashi Tachibana.

References

Abramovitch, H. (1988). An Israeli account of a near-death experience: A case study of cultural dissonance. *Journal of Near-Death Studies, 6*, 175-184.

Bailey, L.W. (2001). A "little death": The near-death experience and Tibetan delogs. *Journal of Near-Death Studies, 19*, 139-159.

Becker, C.B. (1981). The centrality of near-death experiences in Chinese Pure Land Buddhism. *Anabiosis: The Journal of Near-Death Studies, 1*, 154-171

Belanti, J.F., Perera, M., & Jagadheesan, K. (2008). Phenomenology of near-death experiences: A cross-cultural perspective. *Transcultural Psychiatry, 45,* 121-133.

Blackmore, S. J. (1993). Near-death experiences in India: They have tunnels too. *Journal of Near-Death Studies, 11*, 205-217.

Blackmore, S.J. (1996). Near death experiences. *Journal of Royal Society of Medicine, 89,* 73-76.

Blanke, O., Ortigue, S., Landis, T., & Seeck, M. (2002). Stimulating illusory own-body perceptions. *Nature, 419,* 269.

Carr, D. (1981). Endorphins at the approach of death. *Lancet, 14,* 390.

Carr, D, (1982). Pathophysiology of stress induced limbic lobe dysfunction: a hypothesis for NDEs. *Journal of Near Death Studies, 2,* 75-89

Carr, C. (1993). Death and near-death: A comparison of Tibetan and Euro-American experiences. *Journal of Transpersonal Psychology, 25*, 59-110.

Comrie. B., Matthews, S., & Polisky, M. (2005). (Eds), *SBS Atlas of languages: The origin and development of languages throughout the world* (pp. 16 – 35). Sydney, Australia: Qarto.

Corazza, O. (2008). *Near-death experiences: Exploring the mind-body connection.*
(chapter title Journeys in the afterlife) New York: Routledge, ch.2 (pp.22-53)

Counts, D. A. (1983). Near-death and out-of-body experiences in a Melanesian society. Anabiosis: *Journal of Near-Death Studies*, 3, 115-135.

Ellwood, F. G. (2000). Religious experience, religious worldviews, and near-death studies. *Journal of Near-Death Studies, 19*, 5-21.

Frenk, H., McCarty, B.C., & Liebeskind, J.C. (1978). Different brain areas mediate the analgesic and epileptic properties of enkephalin. *Science*, 200, 335-337.

Fox, M. (2003). *Through the valley of the shadow of death: religion, spirituality and the near- death experience.* London: Routledge.

Gallup, G., & Proctor, W. (1982). *Adventures in Immortality: a look beyond the threshold of death.* New York, NY: McGraw-Hill.

Giovetti, P. (1982). Near-death and deathbed experiences: An Italian survey. *Theta, 1*, 10-13.

Gómez-Jeria, J. S. (1993). A near-death experience among the Mapuche people. *Journal of Near-Death Studies, 11*, 219-222.

Greyson B. (1998). The incidence of near-death experiences. *Medicine and Psychiatry, 1*, 92–99, 1998.

Greyson, B. (2003). Incidence and correlates of near-death experiences in a cardiac care unit. *General Hospital Psychiatry, 25,* 269-276.

Greyson, B., & Bush, N.E. (1992). Distressing near-death experiences. *Psychiatry, 55,* 95-110.

Greyson, B., & Stevenson, I. (1980). The Phenomenology of near-death experiences. *American Journal of Psychiatry, 137,* 1193-1196.

Groth-Marnat, G. (1994). Cross-cultural perspectives on the near-death experience. *Australian Parapsychological Review, 19, 7-11.*

Halgren, E., Walter R.D., Cherlow, D.G., & Crandall, P.H. (1978). Mental phenomena evoked by electrical stimulation of human hippocampal formation and amygdale. *Brain, 101,* 83-117.

Jansen, K. (1989). Near death experience and the NMDA receptor. *British Medical Journal, 298,* 1708.

Judson, I.R., & Wiltshaw, E. (1983). A near-death experience. *Lancet*, 3, 561-562.

Kellehear, A. (1996). *Experiences near death: Beyond medicine and religion.* New York. NY: Oxford University Press.

Kellehear, A. (2001). An Hawaiian near-death experience. *Journal of Near-Death Studies, 20*, 31-35.

Kellehear, A. (2008). Census of non western near-death experiences to 2005: Overview of the current data. *Journal of Near-Death Studies, 26 (4)*, 249-265.

Knoblauch, H., Schmied, I. & Schnettler, B. (2001). Different kinds of Near-Death Experience: a report on a survey of near-death experiences in Germany. *Journal of Near-Death Studies, 20,* 15-29.

Lee, R.L.M. (2003). The re-enchantment of death: Near-death, death awareness, and the new age. *Journal of Near-Death Studies, 22*, 117-131.

Lundahl, R. C. (2000). A comparison of other world perceptions by near-death experiencers and by the Marian visionaries of Medjugorie. *Journal of Near-Death Studies, 19,* 45-52.

Lundhal, C.R. (2001) Prophetic revelations in near-death experiences. *Journal of Near-Death Studies, 19, 233-239.*

Meduna, L.J. (1950). *Carbon dioxide therapy*. Springfield, USA: Charles C Thomas.

Moody, R. A. Jr. (1975). *Life after life.* Atlanta: Mockingbird Books.

Morse, M. & Perry, P. (1992). *Transformed by the light: The powerful effect of near-death experiences on people's lives.* New York: Villard Books.

Morse, M., Castillo, P., Venecia, D., Milstein, J., & Tyler, D.C. (1986). Childhood near death experiences. *American Journal of Diseases in Childhood, 140,* 1110-1114

Murphy, T. (2001). Near-death experiences in Thailand. *Journal of Near-Death Studies, 19,* 161-178.

Noyes, R., & Kletti, R. (1977). Panoramic memory: A response to the threat of death. *Omega, 8,* 181-194.

Osis, K., & Haraldson, E. (1977). Death bed observations by physicians and nurses: A cross-cultural survey. *Journal of the American Society for Physical Research, 3, 237-259.*

Parnia, S., & Fenwick, P. (2002). Near death experiences in cardiac arrest: Visions of a dying brain or visions of a new science of consciousness. *Resuscitation, 52,* 5-11.

Parnia, S., Waller, D. G., Yeates, R., & Fenwick, P. (2001). A qualitative and quantitative study of the incidence, features and aetiology of near death experiences in cardiac arrest survivors. *Resuscitation, 48(2),* 149 - 156.

Pasricha, S. (1993). A systematic survey of near-death experiences in South India. *Journal of Scientific Exploration, 7*, 161-171.

Pasricha, S. (1995). Near-death experiences in South India: A systemic survey. *Journal of Scientific Exploration, 9*, 79-88.

Pasricha, S. (2008). Near-death experiences in India: Prevalence and new features. *Journal of Near-Death Studies, 26*, 267- 282.

Pasricha, S. and Stevenson, I. (1986). Near-death experiences in India. *Journal of Nervous and Mental Disease, 174*, 165-170.

Peake, A. (2006). Is there life after death? *The extraordinary science of what happens when we die.* (pp.331-360) New Jersey: Chartwell Books Inc.

Penfield, W. (1955). The role of temporal cortex in certain psychical phenomena. *Journal of Mental Sciences, 101, 451-465.*

Perera, M., Padmasekara, G. & Belanti, J. (2005). Prevalence of Near-Death Experiences in Australia. *Journal of Near-Death Studies, 24,* 109-116.

Ring, K. (1980). *Life at death: A scientific investigation of the near-death experience.* New York: Coward, McCann and Geoghegan.

Ring, K. (1984). *Heading toward Omega: In search of the meaning of the near-death experience.* New York: Quill.

Roberts, G., & Owen, J. (1988). The Near-death Experience. *British Journal of Psychiatry, 153, 607-617.*

Sabom, M.B. (2008). The acute dying experience. *Journal of Near-Death Studies, 26*, 181-218.

Sandweiss, S.H. (1975). *Sai Baba the holy man and the psychiatrist.* India: Sri Sathya Sai Books and Publications Trust.

Saver, J.L., & Rabin, J. (1997). The neural substrates of religious experience. *Journal of Neuropsychiatry, 9,* 498-510.

Schorer, C. E. (1985). Two Native American near-death experiences. *Omega, 16*, 111-113.

Tachibana, T. (2000a). *Rinshi taiken (Near death experience)* (Vol. 1). Tokyo, Japan: Bungei Shunjusha.

Tachibana, T. (2000b). *Rinshi taiken (Near death experience)* (Vol. 2, pp 108-109). Tokyo, Japan: Bungei Shunjusha.

Zaleski, C. (1987). *Otherworld journeys: Accounts of near-death experience in medieval and modern times.* New York, NY: Oxford University Press.

Zhi-ying, F. & Jian-xun, L. (1992). Near-death experiences among survivors of the 1976 Tangshan earthquake. *Journal of Near-Death Studies, 11*, 39-48.

In: Psychological Scientific Perspectives on Out of Body... ISBN: 978-1-60741-705-7
Editor: Craig D. Murray

Chapter 9

NEAR-DEATH EXPERIENCES, OUT-OF-BODY EXPERIENCES AND SOCIAL SCIENTIFIC PARADIGMS

James McClenon

ABSTRACT

Near-death experiences (NDEs) and out-of-body experiences (OBEs) can be evaluated within social scientific paradigms. Cross-cultural comparison of NDE/OBEs, comparison of NDEs to OBEs, and analysis of variables correlated with NDE/OBEs allow assessment of social scientific theories. Data derived from this process support arguments that (1) NDEs have universal elements with physiological basis; (2) Universal NDE elements occur with equal frequency in "emergency" NDEs compared to "non-emergency" OBEs; (3) Incidence of NDE/OBEs is correlated with propensity for hypnosis, dissociation, fantasy proneness, apparitions, extrasensory perceptions, paranormal dreams, and spiritual healing. Recurring features provide a foundation for folk religious beliefs regarding spirits, souls, life after death, and magical abilities. A ritual healing theory describes how genes allowing anomalous experience contributed to the evolutionary development of religious sentiment. Hypothesized genes facilitated shamanism, humankind's first religious form. Shamanism, spanning many millennia, provided survival advantages to those with genes allowing response to ritual suggestion and these same genes facilitate anomalous, shamanic experiences such as OBE/NDEs.

INTRODUCTION

Near-death experiences (NDEs) are defined as "profound psychological events with transcendental and mystical elements, typically occurring to individuals close to death or in situations of intense physical or emotional danger" (Greyson, 2000: 315). Those reporting such episodes are termed NDErs. Out-of-body experiences (OBEs) refer to sensations of being outside of one's body, a perception often occurring during NDEs. OBEs may include the experience of seeing one's physical body from an "out-of-body" perspective or traveling through space feeling outside one's body. NDEs and OBEs are thought to have recurring core elements existing in all cultures. Irwin (1994: 209) lists the phenomenological characteristics of NDEs as (a) an overwhelming feeling of peace and well-being (b) impression of being located outside one's physical body, (c) floating or drifting through darkness, (d) becoming aware of a golden light (e) encountering a spiritual "presence" (f) having a rapid succession of one's past (g) experiencing a spiritual world, perhaps meeting spirits of deceased relatives. Moody (1975), Ring (1980), and Greyson (1983) provide alternate lists of core features, useful for creating scales to quantify the incidence of NDEs. Although researchers have not reached complete consensus regarding exact descriptions of these universal elements, they generally agree that such elements exist. Although most NDEs do not contain all listed elements, an account must contain a threshold of these elements to be considered an NDE. Comparisons of accounts from American, European, Middle Eastern, African, Indian, Asian, Pacific, and Native American peoples indicate that respondents in all these societies report NDEs with similar core elements (Becker, 1981, 1984; Kellehear, 1996, 2001; McClenon, 1991, 1994; Murphy, 2001; Wade, 2003; Zaleski, 1987).

Cross-Cultural Analysis of Experiential Accounts

The consistency argument, that NDE core features are similar around the world and throughout history, has led theorists to argue that (1) NDEs indicate survival of the soul after death (Ring, 1980) (2) NDEs have physiological basis (Blackmore, 1993) (3) NDEs (and certain other forms of anomalous experience) shape culture in similar directions all over the world (Hufford, 1982). These theories are not mutually exclusive and can be interpreted within social scientific and biological paradigms. Using the Darwinian paradigm, we can argue that humans evolved with physiologically-based capacities to perceive reality. If they are able to perceive, directly, an afterlife (theory 1), it is logical to assume that this capacity is physiologically based (theory 2). Such capacities would shape cultures all over the world in similar directions (theory 3). Theory 1 is a form of folk tradition, frequently advocated by NDErs. Theories 2 and 3, interpreted within the Darwinian paradigm, coincide with the ritual healing theory, a model describing how genes allowing OBEs, NDEs, and other anomalous experiences became more prevalent (McClenon, 1997, 2002).

The consistency argument is supported by comparisons of NDEs from a wide variety of cultures. For example, NDEs from both medieval Europe and Asia mention being outside the body, traveling through darkness, meeting spiritual beings, encountering a bright light, reviewing one's past, and seeing the spiritual world where deceased relatives reside (Becker, 1981, 1984; McClenon, 1991, 1994). Yet individual NDEs also have characteristics reflecting their host culture (McClenon, 1991, 1994; Zaleski, 1987). Christians, for example, describe meeting Jesus while Buddhists are greeted by the Buddha. In addition, the organizational structures of the spiritual domain, witnessed by the experiencer, tend to reflect his/her culture. Medieval Chinese and Europeans, for example, whose societies contained hierarchical structures, perceived heavenly realms with similar organizational layers – reflecting the experiencers' bureaucratic society. NDEs from non-technological societies lack hierarchical structures (McClenon, 1991, 1994).

The incidence of specific NDE core features varies among cultures. Pasricha and Stevenson (1986) report that Indian NDE accounts did not include panoramic life reviews or OBE impressions of the physical body but tend to focus on travel with a "messenger" to a transcendental realm. Counts (1983) reports that Melanesian NDE cases lacked OBE impressions and feelings of peace/well-being. Kellehear's (1993) survey of the cross-cultural literature suggests that the tunnel effect and panoramic life review are culture-specific features of the NDE. These findings are controversial. Although non-technological societies do not report tunnel experiences, Athappilly, Greyson, & Stevenson (2006) provide evidence implying that societal conceptions of NDEs do not significantly influence the phenomenology of these experiences. McClenon (1991, 1994), comparing medieval and modern accounts from Europe, American, Japan, and China, found both universal features and cultural influences. Rodabough (1985: 107) argues that claims regarding uniformities within NDEs are overstated. Although some theorists seek to prove survival after death by finding universal NDE features, scientific research is unable to resolve this issue (Blackmore, 1993).

The existence of some core features within NDEs implies a physiological basis. Blackmore (1993) reviews studies suggesting that NDEs occur as a result of the brain shutting down (the dying brain theory). Although others argue that dying brain theories are inadequate (Ring, 1980), physiological research has a cumulative quality. Studies of OBEs suggest a physiological basis for the perception of being out-of-body (Blanke, et al., 2002, 2004). Explanations of OBEs could be used to explain, in part, the incidence of many NDEs since many NDEs include OBEs.

Most researchers agree that NDEs have the capacity to change experiencers' attitudes regarding life after death (Fox, 2003; Greyson, 2000; Kellehear, 1996; Moody, 1975; Moody & Perry, 1988; Morse & Perry, 1992; Ring, 1980, 1984; Sutherland, 1992; Zaleski, 1987). NDErs tend to believe that their experience is what it appears to be – a journey to the spiritual world. NDEs contribute to similar notions regarding immediate life after death with the afterlife having characteristics similar (or superior) to normal life. The rhetorical powers of NDE accounts are enhanced by NDErs' tendency to regard their perceptions as "more real than real." Experiencers also report that their personalities were changed or transformed. This propensity for change also occurs on the social level; NDEs shape beliefs all over the world regarding spirits, souls, and life after death (McClenon, 1994, 2002).

This observation coincides with folklorist David Hufford's (1982) experiential source theory. Hufford developed this argument in opposition to a prevalent social scientific assumption, which he labels the cultural source theory. This theory specifies that culture shapes people's experiences by affecting their interpretations of perceptions. As a result, many scientists assume that anomalous perceptions are cultural products – perceptions created by the experiencer's preconceptions (Hufford, 1982). This line of thinking coincides with Durkheim's (1995) position that religion is an expression of people's feeling of being in a group. Durkheim argues that religion represents culture since, when people worship, they are actually affirming their collectivity. Durkheim believes that people in groups experience a social "effervescence" which gives rise to religious sentiment. Various arguments derived from this position mock belief in the authenticity of NDEs and other forms of anomalous experience. Experiencers are portrayed as unsophisticated, deluded, and naïve – unable to realize that they are misinterpreting their experiences. NDEs and OBEs are regarded as unworthy of scientific consideration since they have been explained through Durkheim's social scientific paradigm (Hufford, 1982).

Hufford (1982) hypothesizes that certain experiential forms, such as sleep paralysis and NDEs, do not always coincide with cultural expectations. These experiential episodes are not merely products of culture. He argues that it is logical for people to believe that NDEs represent an afterlife since the anomalous perception seems logically compelling. In general, NDErs evaluate their perceptions and have grounds for belief in them. As an alternative to the cultural source theory, he presents an "experiential source theory" - the argument that certain experiences are not merely products of culture but have the capacity to change culture. He notes that these experiential forms, such as NDEs, affect folk beliefs all over the world in common directions.

The experiential source theory can be tested through cross-cultural comparison of impacts of anomalous experience. The finding of core features within experiential forms partially supports the theory. Researchers can also document the ways that reports of certain experiences have affected folk religious beliefs.

My research includes surveys of random samples of students at three colleges in the People's Republic of China, one college in Japan, and three colleges in the USA (McClenon, 1991, 1993, 1994, 2000, 2002). Respondents were asked about major forms of anomalous experience (extrasensory perception, contact with the dead, and out-of body experience) as well as an open-ended question: "If you have had an extremely unusual experience, would you describe it briefly?" Over the years, I have assembled over 2000 experiential accounts from a wide variety of societies and have found recurring experiential forms. These forms include apparitions, waking extrasensory perceptions, paranormal dreams, out-of-body and near-death experiences, and psychokinesis (McClenon, 1994, 2002). This body of evidence suggests that certain forms of anomalous experience have core features that shape folk religious beliefs in common directions – toward belief in spirits, souls, life after death, and magical abilities. People perceiving apparitions of deceased relatives, for example, come to believe in spirits and life after death. Those experiencing frequent ESP often feel that they can harness this capacity and, as a result, develop beliefs in magical abilities. People having OBEs and NDEs tend to come to believe in souls.

Paranormal Theories

Some anomalous experiences have paranormal qualities. This tendency supports the experiential source theory since this feature provides rhetorical power for shaping folk belief. NDE/OBE accounts may provide paranormal information regarding hospital procedures, distant events, or information pertaining to diseased individuals. Moody (1975) refers to this as collaboration, an element he regards as a core feature of the NDE. The NDE literature is filled with example cases. A man under anesthesia during his surgery reported leaving his body and seeing complex medical procedures of which he had no previous knowledge. A woman reported traveling spiritually to a distant location and seeing her relatives doing an unusual task – later this was verified. A woman believed that she left her body and learned information from her deceased relatives – this information was later verified. These people described their experiences to friends and relatives, creating a form of oral folklore supporting belief in souls and life after death.

Some parapsychologists argue that these NDErs gained information through use of extrasensory perception (ESP); they believe that NDEs are not an indication of life after death, as experiencers could have used a form of ESP to gain the previously unknown information. This argument is termed the super-ESP hypothesis (Irwin, 1994). Skeptics reject both the survival after death and super-ESP hypotheses, suggesting that paranormal claims are the result of fabrication, delusion, or coincidence (Blackmore, 1993).I provide an example case from my collection to illustrate these arguments and the impact of collaborative features:

> One night I was sleeping and I woke up…but when I looked at my bed my body was still lying there. I thought I was crazy so I ran out of my house and went to my girlfriend's house and knocked on her door…she didn't hear me but I knew she was awake. I went to her window and saw she was watching T.V….I ran back to my house and just got back in the bed even though I was scared to death. I called my girlfriend the next day and told her what happened. I told her that she was watching some movie about animals and she was wearing a blue nightgown and was eating some ice cream, then she said, "Baby, that's strange because you are exactly right" and you know that scared me. We never understood how or why it happened but it really messed my head up. (Narrative #19)

Although the storyteller could be sufficiently familiar with his girlfriend's behavior that he correctly guessed her evening activities and attire, the story illustrates the experiential source theory. The storyteller feels that his experience violated his preconceptions ("it really messed my head up."). NDErs often portray forms of skepticism and include elements within their accounts to express their own doubts.

Although Greyson (2000: 338-342) and Sabom (1998) review well-documented cases that defy normal explanation, this body of evidence has had little impact on mainstream scientists. NDE researchers have no paradigm that allows a steadily growing body of knowledge regarding NDEs, and, as a result, engage in a form of deviant science (McClenon, 1984). Collaboration, a core feature of OBEs and NDEs, does not prove paranormal claims but does support the experiential source hypothesis. It is logical for people who gained knowledge paranormally to ponder the meaning of their NDEs and to feel these events have special meaning. Unlike skeptical observers, the story teller, aware of his previous knowledge of his girlfriend, noted the "we never understood why it happened." The implication of the story is that it is possible to gain information after leaving your body and that magical events are possible (shamanic performance). This perception was not merely the result of his preconceptions but was derived from his experience.

People reporting many anomalous experiences appear particularly changed by them. I provide a second example case to illustrate this point. A respondent reported floating out of his body while perceiving the "brightest white light you could imagine."

> I was convinced that I was dying and was so happy, unafraid, and accepting. I felt that I was in the process of going to heaven to see Jesus. The instant I graciously accepted this fact, the whole floating upward process speeded up dramatically and I said to myself, "This is really happening." [Then he felt panic and returned to his body]. Since this occurrence, I have had this same thing happen to me several times. From these experiences, I feel that it is possible that the dying process may have some human choice involved in it. I feel that it may allow you to ultimately control your final destiny. (Narrative #22)

People who report frequent experiences, particularly OBEs, often feel that they can gain control over these perceptions. Irwin (1985: 100) reports that 46% of those within his survey of OBEs claimed they could control the content of their experience in some way. Some experiencers visit spiritual realms whenever they wish – equivalent to shamans.

Shamans feel they leave their bodies and visit spiritual realms. They gain information valuable for performing rituals that benefit others. Grey (1985), and many others, note that NDEs are associated with psychic experiences and spiritual healing – fundamental features of shamanism. In general, those reporting frequent anomalous experiences, particularly those with performance skills, take on shaman roles, providing placebo and hypnotic suggestions to those seeking their aid (McClenon, 2002).

In summary, cross-cultural analysis of experiential accounts supports the consistency argument – people all over the world report similar elements within their NDEs. This argument supports the claim that NDEs have physiological basis and that these experiences shape folk religious belief in a similar direction all over the world – the experiential source theory.

The consistency and experiential source hypotheses could be evaluated through analysis of anomalous experiences from any society. The hypotheses predict that any society's literature will describe apparitions, paranormal dreams, waking extrasensory perceptions, psychokinesis, OBEs, and NDEs and that these episodes lead to belief in spirits, souls, life after death, and magical abilities. Evidence from Japan, China, medieval Europe, Congo, and the USA support consistency and experiential source hypotheses (McClenon, 1991, 1994, 2006, 2008).

Comparisons of Out-of-Body and Near-Death Accounts

Comparison of OBEs to NDEs sheds light on the physiological processes related to these episodes. NDEs may occur as a result of various brain centers closing down due to oxygen deprivation or other physiological processes - the dying brain theory (Blackmore, 1993). OBEs, in parallel fashion, may be due to sudden shifts in physiological state such as intrusions of right-hemisphere brain processes into the left hemisphere or the disruption of normal functions in a particular brain area (Irwin, 1994: 241-242). Cognitive processes that maintain a stable body image (being in the body) could be disrupted so that a person perceives an alternate perspective (being out-of-body).

Content analysis of collections of OBE and NDE accounts allow evaluations of the dying brain hypotheses. Gabbard, Twemlow, and Jones (1981) solicited letters from people claiming OBEs and NDEs (also discussed in Gabbard and Twemlow, 1984). They found that NDErs were more likely to hear noises during the early stage of the experience, to see a tunnel and a brilliant light, to sense a non-physical being, and to feel their life was changed by the experience. Although they found no differences between death and non-death-related cases and feeling peace/serenity or having a life review, the differences they did find between these categories contributed to Blackmore's (1993) dying brain theory.

Fox (2003) analyzed 91 NDE-like narratives selected from the 6000 case collection of religious experiences at the Religious Experience Research Center, University of Wales, Lampeter, Great Britain. Unlike the previous study, the original collection methodology did not focus directly on OBEs or NDEs. Fox identified 32 crisis cases (related to danger or death) and 59 non-crisis cases (not related to danger or death) in his sample of "NDE-like" accounts. Moody (1975) provided a 15-item list of NDE elements thought to constitute the essence of the experience. Fox determined that "the average number of Moody's original fifteen NDE elements in the crisis and non-crisis accounts examined were 3.3 and 2.9 respectively, a difference of only 0.4" (Fox, 2003: 325). These results reduce faith in the dying brain theory since the non-crisis OBEs were just as much like NDEs as the crisis accounts. Although a dying brain may affect the content of NDEs, there is no reason to believe that dying generates its core features.

McClenon (2006) analyzed 28 NDE-like accounts selected from 1832 anomalous experience narratives collected from a predominately African-American population in northeastern North Carolina. Although these respondents were markedly different culturally from those in Fox's (2003) study, the methodology was parallel in that cases were gathered without direct focus on OBEs or NDEs. Methodology differed in that undergraduate students solicited oral accounts from friends, relatives, and neighbors. Coders, instructed in Fox's (2003) system of classifying crisis and non-crisis accounts, identified 22 crisis and 5 non-crisis cases (one case was a death-bed vision). Cases were evaluated, based on previous studies, regarding incidence of NDE core features using systems devised by Moody (1975), Ring (1980), and Greyson (1983).

An example evaluation illustrates how coders counted NDE core features. Narrative #21 illustrates a crisis NDE:

> One day I woke up very sick. I was throwing up blood, sweating and having really bad cramps in my stomach. So I went to the hospital and the doctor told me that I was bleeding internally. I was losing so much blood that I blanked out. While I was out, I stared feeling as if I was dead. I looked around and I noticed I was in heaven. Everything was white and so beautiful. This place seemed so peaceful. I had heard of the gate to heaven, so I started to approach it. As I got closer, I noticed some women. One was a member of my church who had passed a long time ago. She was waving at me, as if she were saying, "Come on in." I started walking towards her when something hit me. I started thinking about my family and kids that needed me and I turned around. When I regained conscience, I was on a hospital bed. I was told that I had died and that the doctors brought me back (Narrative #21).

This crisis account includes 3 of the 15 Moody (1975) elements (peace/quiet, meeting others, and coming back), 1 of 5 Ring (1980) features (feeling peace), and 4 of 16 Greyson (1983) elements (feeling peace, encounters with apparently unearthly realm, visible spirits, and a barrier or point of no return). This story is clearly a NDE rather than an OBE.

Analysis of a non-crisis OBE example illustrates the degree that non-emergency OBEs can be similar to NDEs:

> I had worked real hard that day and felt asleep on the sofa. Then I thought I got right back up and I started walking around. I noticed someone lying on my sofa. I thought about calling 911 but the person seemed to be harmless. I walked over to it and it was me. I started panicking because I thought I was dead. I screamed and it felt like something was pulling me very fast throughout the house. I blinked my eyes and when I opened them I was in hell. I saw many people there that I knew and they were burning, screaming, and asking me for help. I was yelling for a while until I realized that I was not burning. As soon as I realized I was not burning I felt another pull and this time, when I opened my eyes, I was in heaven. I was in the middle of a forest but no ordinary forest. I saw no grass or dirt on the ground. If it was dirt, it looked as though it was golden. Then I felt another pull and this time I ended up in a foggy tunnel. I heard an echo saying my name: "A_____, you have a choice. You either follow your Lord and Savior Jesus Christ or death comes unto you." Then I went back into my body and I

was awake [the respondent goes on to state that her experience caused her to become a Christian and the interviewer noted that the respondent was a reputable member of her church – Case #23].

This account includes 5 of Moody's (1975) 15 NDE elements (out-of-body experience, tunnel, meeting others, coming back to the body and effects on life). It includes 2 of 5 Ring (1980) elements: (body separation and entering the darkness) and 3 of 16 Greyson (1983) elements (out-of-body experience, encounters with apparently unearthly realm, and a mystical being).

Table 1. Comparison of NDE Core Features within Crisis and Non-Crisis Experiences Using Three NDE Scales*

Scale	Coder scores mean (n=27)	Average St. Dev. (9 coders)	Coefficient of variation (St.dev./ Mean)	Average R among Coders (n=36)	Crisis experience mean (n=22)	Non-crisis experience mean (n=5)	T (crisis vs. non-crisis)	df	Prob. of T**
Moody (1975)	2.83	.73	.26	.85	2.81	2.87	-0.06	25	.95
Ring (1980)	1.16	.33	.29	.70	1.18	1.07	0.48	25	.64
Greyson (1983)	3.78	1.16	.31	.87	3.69	4.13	-0.32	25	.76

*Table reproduced from McClenon (2005) and used with permission of the editor, Journal of Near-Death Studies.

**Small sample sizes make inferential tests of significance problematic. Relatively large differences in means are required to achieve statistical significance. For example, if the five non-crisis Greyson NDE scores were proportionally reduced so that their mean was 1.32, or increased to create a mean of 6.96, the associated T would achieve significance at the .05 level (2 tailed test).

My data replicates Fox's findings; the crisis and non-crisis accounts have equivalent numbers of NDE features (see Table 1). Because students' evaluations of the number of NDE features did not always agree, coefficients of variation (standard deviation/mean) and average Pearson's Product Correlations (R) among coders are provided to portray the degree of agreement. The data indicate that crisis and non-crisis average scores do not differ significantly. The non-crisis averages on the Moody and Greyson scales were actually slightly higher than the crisis averages. In other words, non-crisis OBEs have slightly more NDE features than did the actual NDEs. The data imply that NDEs are not the result of a dying brain but of physiological processes equivalent to those creating OBEs.

Although there were insufficient cases to conduct valid tests of statistical significance, trends did not coincide with those noted by Gabbard, Twemlow, and Jones (1981). Non-emergency experiencers reported hearing noises, seeing tunnels, and feeling that the experience affected their lives more often than did emergency experiencers (opposite of Gabbard, Twemlow, & Jones (1981) results). Among emergency experiencers, 14% reported life reviews and 32% reported peace/quite while no non-emergency experiencers reported these elements (Gabbard, Twemlow, & Jones (1981) found no differences). Within the North Carolina data, 27% of emergency experiencers encountered others while only 20% of the non-emergency encounters perceived others – one of the few patterns also found by Gabbard,

Twemlow, and Jones (1981). These differences in findings imply that NDE/OBEs are affected by culture. As with dreams, the content of these perceptions seem creatively shaped by the experiencer. NDEs are probably created through cholinergic systems, governed by acetylcholine, which allows dreaming. Differences in patterns among studies probably reflect cultural differences. The cholinergic system allows sleep, dreams, visions, and altered states of consciousness and involves special forms of uncritical, imaginative thinking (Hobson, 1994). During normal consciousness, the aminergic system produces normal awareness, predominant during wakefulness. During a normal cycle, waking consciousness is replaced by the cholinergic system, and sleep with dreams result. This is not to say that NDEs are invalid but that dream-like processes shape these episodes. NDEs are like dreams in that they have a creative quality, reflecting imagination. Like paranormal dreams, they sometimes include elements that seem to exceed scientific explanation. The cholinergic hypothesis argues that NDEs do not originate due to the dying of the brain, but involve shaman-like processes. Like NDErs, shamans use cholinergic processes to go into trance, visit spirit worlds, and bring back information of value to their communities.

Variables Correlated with the Incidence of NDEs and OBEs

Variables correlated with the incidence of NDE/OBEs coincide with the cholinergic hypothesis. The incidence of NDEs are not correlated with age, gender, socioeconomic level, marital status, or race within the USA (Irwin, 1994: 217) but with hypnosis, absorption, dissociation, fantasy proneness and other forms of anomalous experience (Greyson, 2000, 2003). Although correlations are not always strong or consistent, the patterns are relatively clear. These variables are correlated with each other, coinciding with the idea that NDEs are related to shamanism.

Much research supports these claims. People reporting NDEs more often show a capacity for absorption as measured by Tellegen and Atkinson's (1974) absorption scale (Irwin, 1985; Twemlow & Gabbard, 1984). NDErs tend to be better hypnotic subjects, to remember their dreams more often, and to be more adept at using mental imagery (Council & Greyson, 1985; Greyson, 2000; Irwin, 1985). They tend to report more childhood trauma and dissociative tendencies (Ring, 1992).

The patterns surrounding NDEs led Ring (1992) to develop the concept of the encounter-prone NDE personality. He argues that NDErs tend to have experienced abuse and trauma during childhood. As a result, they developed dissociative tendencies and the capacity to become absorbed in alternate realities. When exposed to danger or trauma, such people perceive NDEs.

Wilson and Barber (1983) discuss fantasy proneness, characterized as a strong investment in a fantasy life coupled with hallucinatory ability. Fantasy prone people are more likely to report NDEs, OBEs, religious visions, apparitions, and to claim psychic abilities. Council and Greyson (1985) also found that NDErs have tendencies toward fantasy proneness and absorption.

The variables correlated with OBEs are equivalent to those correlated with NDEs. "Overall, the best predictors of the OBE seem to be some cognitive variables that are intercorrelated, namely dissociation, hypnotic susceptibility, absorption, and fantasy proneness" (Alvarado, 2000: 193-4). The incidence of OBEs is also positively correlated with claims of spontaneous paranormal and mystical experiences: apparitions, extrasensory perception, and specific dream variables (Alvarado, 2000: 194-5). OBE developmental variables are parallel to NDE variables: traumatic childhood events, sexual abuse, isolation from friends and playmates, and factors supporting development of hypnotic suggestibility such as encouragement of fantasy, absorption, and dissociation (Ring, 1992). Although the incidence of OBEs has not been strongly related to most forms of psychopathology, McCreery and Claridge (1995, 2002) found OBEs related to schizotypy scores among psychologically healthy individuals. Schizotypy encompasses a range of personality traits related to psychosis and schizophrenia, varying over a normally distributed continuum from psychological good health to psychological ill health.

All in all, the findings regarding correlates of NDEs and OBEs imply that similar mechanisms govern the incidence of these overlapping experiential forms. McClenon (2002) reviews evidence showing correlations between the major forms of anomalous experience (which include OBE/NDEs) and hypnotizability, propensity for anomalous experience, belief in the paranormal, fantasy proneness, temporal-lobe signs (measured by questionnaire items associated with temporal lobe epilepsy – Persinger & Makarec, 1993), temporal lobe lability (measured by EEG), thinness of cognitive boundaries (measured by Hartmann's, 1991, boundary questionnaire), and transliminality (the degree to which there is a gap in the barrier or gating mechanism between the unconscious and conscious mind; Thalbourne & Delin, 1994, 1999).

These correlations imply the existence of what might be referred to as the shamanic syndrome (McClenon, 2002). This syndrome includes high hypnotizability, high absorption, high dissociative capacity, fantasy proneness, thinness of cognitive boundaries, temporal lobe lability, transliminality, and propensity for anomalous experience. Anthropologists have noted special biographies associated with shamanism coinciding with these propensities (McClenon, 2002). Some people, exposed to stressful events during childhood, develop dissociation and absorptive skills as a result. Another pathway to development of these skills is through socialization; many societies have religious systems that help people learn how to go into trance. Those demonstrating trance performance skills can become shamans. Within the context of a trance ritual, the shaman provides therapeutic suggestions. Clients who are more open to suggestions have greater probability of benefiting from these rituals. This process results in profound forms of faith. People healed within a particular ritual system develop powerful beliefs and may become healers themselves. Anthropologists observe this pattern in societies all over the world. People with unique propensities experience profound healing, develop powerful faiths, and perform rituals that heal others with similar propensities (McClenon, 2002).

OBE and NDEs in an Evolutionary Context

Darwin's theory of evolution provides a paradigm useful for understanding the processes contributing to the incidence of OBE/NDEs and other forms of anomalous experience. All societies have people with high capacity for anomalous experience, and a recurring folklore motif describes these propensities as family based (McClenon, 1994, 2002). We would predict that propensities for recurring forms of anomalous experience have a genetic basis. According to the experiential source theory, anomalous experiences, such as NDE/OBEs, lead to belief in spirits, souls, life after death, and magical abilities. People who have frequent experiences develop certainties about the spirit world that allow them to become shamans. Shamans go into a trance, visit spiritual worlds, bring back information, and use this knowledge to perform rituals that benefit those open to hypnotic and placebo suggestion. Within this process, those with genes allowing hypnotic and placebo response have survival advantages – they are more likely to benefit from shamanic rituals. Over the millennia, genes associated with shamanic treatment have become more numerous and, as a result, the human propensity for religious sentiment has come into being.

The ritual healing theory is supported by evidence derived from a variety of fields (McClenon, 2002). It is testable within anthropology, sociology, psychology, folklore, and evolutionary physiology. The variables within the theory can be measured using standard methods. These variables include hypnotizablity (Fromm & Nash, 1992), absorption (Tellegen & Atkinson, 1974), dissociation (Carlson, et al., 1993), cognitive boundaries (Hartmann, 1991), temporal lobe lability (Persinger & Makarec, 1993), and propensity for anomalous experience (McClenon, 2002). The ritual healing theory specifies that these shamanic syndrome variables are correlated in all societies due to their genetic basis. Cooper and Thalbourne (2005), conducting research in Australia, confirmed many of the hypothesized correlations specified by the ritual healing theory.

Because the shamanic syndrome variables provide a degree of protection from mental disorder, we should find that they are correlated with the incidence of mental disorder symptoms. This relationship exists because the same environmental conditions (trauma and stress) "turn on" genes related to both mental disorder and the shamanic syndrome, a set of propensities that have evolved to protect humans from mental disorder. This hypothesis can be tested within both medical and social scientific paradigms.

Anthropological investigations of shamanism and spiritual healing can evaluate the ritual healing theory. Clients who benefit from ritual healing are hypothesized to have greater capacity for hypnosis and the other shamanic syndrome variables. They are more likely to report OBE/NDEs and other anomalous experiences. Researchers could test this hypothesis by evaluating people benefiting from ritual healing. This research has practical applications. People likely to benefit from ritual healing should be directed to practitioners whose methods fit their needs.

Folklorists, sociologists, anthropologists, and historians can examine anomalous experience accounts found in the anthropological, historical, and folklore literature. The ritual healing theory hypothesizes that accounts from any society contain core features equivalent to those in other societies. Experiences should also have parallel effects on experiencers - increasing belief in spirits, souls, life after death, and magical abilities.

A study of the history and anthropology of the Congo provides an example of this type of research (McClenon, 2006, 2008). Congo religious history describes recurring cycles of innovative religious practitioners experiencing NDE-like events that launch their careers. They then perform rituals benefiting those with hypnotic/dissociative capacity. These practitioners and their followers report anomalous perceptions whose forms coincide with those found all over the world (McClenon, 2008). Researchers could focus on a particular form of anomalous experience, such as NDEs. Eight Congo NDEs include descriptions of leaving the body, journeying to after-life realms, encountering boundaries, and communicating with spiritual beings – recurring elements within the NDE literature. Congo emergency NDEs and non-emergency experiences have equivalent percentages of NDE core features (McClenon, 2006). This evidence supports the ritual healing hypothesis; NDEs are similar all over the world due to their physiological basis and these perceptions lead to belief in spirits, souls, and life after death.

The ritual healing theory can be evaluated within the realms of medical research, anthropology, sociology, psychology, folklore studies, and genetic research. This research paradigm does not depend on philosophical speculation but builds on studies associated with the experiential source theory and Darwin's theory of evolution.

References

Alvarado, C. S. (2000). Out-of-body experiences, in E. Cardeña, S. J. Lynn, & S. Krippner (Eds.), *Varieties of anomalous experience: Examining the scientific evidence*, Pp. 183-218, Washington, DC: American Psychological Association.

Athappilly, G. K., Greyson, B., & Stevenson, I. (2006). Do prevailing societal models influence reports of near-death experiences? A comparison of accounts reported before and after 1975. *Journal of Nervous and Mental Disease, 194,* 218-222.

Becker, C. B. (1981). The centrality of near-death experience in Chinese Pure Land Buddhism. *Anabiosis, 1,* 154-171.

Becker, C. B. (1984). The Pure Land revisited: Sino-Japanese meditations and near-death experiences of the next world. *Anabiosis, 4,* 51-68.

Blackmore, S. (1993). *Dying to live*, Buffalo, NY: Prometheus Books

Blank, O., Ortigue, S., Landis, T., & Seeck, M. (2002). Stimulating illusory own-body perceptions. *Nature*, *419,* 269-270.

Blanke, O., Landis, T., Spinelli, L., & Seeck, M. (2004). Out-of-body experience and autoscopy of neurological origin. *Brain, 127(2),* 243-258.

Carlson, E. B., Putnam, F. W., Ross, C. A., Torem, M., Coons, P. Dill, D.L., Loewenstein, R. J. & Braun, B. G (1993). Validity of the Dissociative Experiences Scale in screening for multiple personality disorder: A multicenter study. *American Journal of Psychiatry, 150,* 1030-1036.

Cooper, G. & Thalbourne, M. (2005). McClenon's ritual healing theory: An exploratory study. *Journal of Parapsychology, 69,* 139-151.

Council, J. R., & Greyson, B. (1985). Near-death experiences and the "fantasy-prone" personality: Preliminary findings. Paper presented at the *93rd Annual Convention of the American Psychological Association*, Los Angeles.

Counts, D. A. (1983). Near-death and out-of-body experiences in a Melanesian society. *Anabiosis*, *3,* 115-135.

Durkheim, E. (1995). *The elementary forms of religious life.* Translated by K. E. Fields. New York: Free Press, Simon and Schuster. Original edition, 1912.

Fox, M. (2003). Religion, spirituality and the near-death experience. New York, Routledge.

Fromm, E. & Nash, M. R. (Eds.) (1992). *Contemporary hypnosis research.* New York : Guilford.

Gabbard, G. O. & Tremlow, S. W. (1984) *With the eyes of the mind.* New York: Praeger.

Gabbard, G. O., Tremlow, S. W., & Jones, F. C. (1981). Do "near-death experiences" occur only near death? *Journal of Nervous and Mental Disease, 169,* 374-7.

Grey, M. (1985) *Return from death,* London, Arkana.

Greyson, B. (1983). The near-death experience scale: Construction, reliability, and validity. *Journal of Nervous and Mental Disease, 171,* 369-375.

Greyson, B. (2000). Near-Death experiences. In E. Cardeña, S. J. Lynn, & S. Krippner (Eds.), *Varieties of anomalous experience: Examining the scientific evidence,* Pp. 315-352, Washington, DC: American Psychological Association.

Greyson, B. (2003). Incidence and correlates of near-death experiences on a cardiac care unit. *General Hospital Psychiatry, 25,* 269-276

Hartmann, E. (1991). *Boundaries in the mind: A new psychology of personality,* New York: Basic Books.

Hobson, J. A. (1994). *The chemistry of conscious states: How the brain changes its mind.* Boston: Little, Brown.

Hufford, D. (1982). *The terror that comes in the night: An experience-centered study of supernatural assault traditions.* Philadelphia, PA: University of Pennsylvania Press.

Irwin, H. J. (1985). *Flight of mind: A psychological study of the out-of-body experience.* Metuchen, NU: Scarecrow Press.

Irwin, H. J. (1994). *An Introduction to parapsychology.* Jefferson, NC: McFarland.

Kellehear, A. (1993). Culture, biology, and the near-death experience. *Journal of Nervous and Mental Disease, 181,* 148-156.

Kellehear, A. (1996). *Experiences near death: Between medicine and religion.* Oxford: Oxford University Press.

Kellehear, A. (2001). An Hawaiian near-death experience. *Journal of Near-Death Studies, 20,* 31-35.

McClenon, J. (1984). *Deviant science: The case of parapsychology.* Philadelphia, PA: University of Pennsylvania Press.

McClenon, J. (1991). Near-death folklore in medieval China and Japan: A comparative analysis. *Asian Folklore Studies, 50,* 319-42.

McClenon, J. (1993). Surveys of anomalous experience in Chinese, Japanese, and American samples. *Sociology of Religion, 54,* 295-302.

McClenon, J. (1994). *Wondrous events: Foundations of religious belief,* Philadelphia, PA: University of Pennsylvania Press.

McClenon, J. (1997). Shamanic healing, human evolution, and the origin of religion. *Journal for the Scientific Study of Religion, 36,* 345-54.

McClenon, J. (2000). Content analysis of an anomalous memorate collection: Testing hypothesis regarding universal features. *Sociology of Religion, 61,* 155-69

McClenon, J. (2002). *Wondrous healing: Shamanism, human evolution, and the origin of religion.* Dekalb, IL: Northern Illinois University Press.

McClenon, J. (2005). Content analysis of a predominately African-American near-death experience collection: Evaluating the Ritual Healing Theory. *Journal of Near-Death Studies, 23,* 159-181.

McClenon, J. (2006). Kongo near-death experience: Cross-cultural patterns. *Journal of Near-Death Studies, 25,* 21-34.

McClenon, J. (2008). Miracles in Kongo religious history: Evaluating the ritual healing theory. In J. Harold Ellens, (Ed.) *Miracles: God, science, and psychology in the paranormal*, pp. 176-197, Westport, CN: Praeger.

McCreery, C. & Claridge, G. (1995). Out-of-the-body experiences and personality. *Journal of the Society for Psychical Research, 60,* 129-148.

McCreery, C., & Claridge, G. (2002). Healthy schizotypy: The case of out-of-the-body experiences. *Personality and Individual Differences, 32,* 141-154.

Moody, R. (1975). *Life after life*, Atlanta: Mockingbird.

Moody, R. and Perry, P. (1988) *The light beyond: The transforming power of near-death experiences*, London: Macmillan.

Morse, M. and Perry, P. (1992) *Transformed by the Light: The powerful effect of near-death experiences on people's lives.* London: Piatkus.

Murphy, T. (2001). Near-death experiences in Thailand. *Journal of Near-Death Studies, 19,* 161-78.

Pasricha, S. and Stevenson, I. (1986). Near-death experiences in India. *Journal of Nervous and Mental Disease, 174,* 165-170.

Persinger, M. & Makarec, K. (1993). Complex partial epileptic signs as a continuum from normal toepileptics: Normative data and clinical populations, *Journal of Clinical Psychology, 49,* 33-45.

Ring, K. (1980). *Life at death: A scientific investigation of the near-death experience.* New York: Coward, McCann and Geoghegan.

Ring, K. (1984). *Heading Toward Omega: In search of the meaning of the near-death experience.* New York: William Morrow.

Ring, K. (1992). *The Omega project: Near-death experiences, UFO encounters, and mind at large.* New York: Morrow.

Rodabough, T. (1985). Near-death experiences: An examination of the supporting data and alternative explanations. *Death Studies, 9,* 95-113.

Sabom, M. (1998). *Light and death: One doctor's fascinating account of near-death experiences.* Grand Rapids, MI: Zondervan.

Sutherland, C. (1992). *Reborn in the light: Life after near-death experiences,* New York: Bantam.

Tellegen, A., & Atkinson, G. (1974) Openness to absorbing and self-altering experiences ("absorption"), a trait related to hypnotic susceptibility. *Journal of Abnormal Psychology, 83,* 269-277.

Thalbourne, M. A. & Delin, P. S. (1994). A common thread underlying belief in the paranormal, creative personality, mystical experience, and psychopathology, *Journal of Parapsychology, 58,* 3-38.

Thalbourne, M. A. & Delin, P. S. (1999). Transliminality: Its relation to dream life, religiosity, and mystical experience. *International Journal for the Psychology of Religion, 9,* 35-43.

Twemlow, S. W. and Gabbard, G. O. (1984). The influence of demograhic/psychological factors and preexisting conditions on the near-death experience. *Omega, 15,* 223-235.

Wade, J. (2003). In a sacred manner we died: Native American near-death experiences. *Journal of Near-Death Studies, 22,* 83-115.

Wilson, D. S. (2002). *Darwin's cathedral: Evolution, religion, and the nature of society,* Chicago: University of Chicago Press.

Wilson, S. C. & Barber, T. X. (1983). The fantasy-prone personality: Implications for understanding imagery, hypnosis, and the parapsychological phenomena. In A. A. Seikh (Ed.), *Imagery: Current theory, research, and application* (pp. 340-390). New York: Wiley.

Zaleski, C. (1987). *Otherworld journeys: Accounts of near-death experiences in medieval and modern times,* Oxford: Oxford University Press.

In: Psychological Scientific Perspectives on Out of Body… ISBN: 978-1-60741-705-7
Editor: Craig D. Murray

Chapter 10

THE 'URASHIMA EFFECT': A CULTURAL ILLUSION? A JAPANESE PERSPECTIVE ON DEATH, LIFE AND THE NEAR-DEATH EXPERIENCE

Ornella Corazza

ABSTRACT

This chapter explores near-death experiences (NDEs) in a way which contrasts with those reported in Western literature on the topic. It will analyze the near-death phenomenon from a cross-cultural point of view and discuss a small-scale study on NDEs in Japan. Introducing a Japanese perspective on life and death, it will also present for the first time, a middle way between reductionist and dualist theories that have been used until now to explain the near-death phenomena. It is concluded that there is a need to develop a more integrated and extended view of embodiment in order to understand more fully the significance of this unique set of experiences.

INTRODUCTION

A popular tale in Japan tells the story of a fisherman who decided to visit the depths of the sea (Kawauchi, 1997). His name was Urashima Taro. One day, he stepped out from his boat and went down the waters until he reached the bottom of the sea. This was as Taro had always imagined it, alive with thousands of brightly colored fish of every shape and size, whose movements filled the water with shining, swirling bubbles, with wonderful flowers that bloomed on rocks and cliffs. Wonderful as it was, however, it wasn't long before Taro began to miss his home and decided to 'go back' to his island. Oddly enough, however, he didn't seem to recognize what he saw. While he had been enjoying life in a timeless realm, hundreds of years had gone by on land. Urashima Taro looked slowly up to the sky. His life in the depths of the sea – had it all been a dream? Or was he dreaming now?

In Japan this story is a reminder that one can live the ordinary everyday life and travel in other realms, or dimensions of reality. This also known as the 'Urashima effect'. In some ways, the Urashima effect recalls the experience of those who had a near-death experience (NDE).

NDEs as a Developing Topic of Study

As Raymond Moody has first pointed out, the most common feature of the NDEs are: (1) the difficulty of expressing in words an experience of such a nature, or ineffability; (2) the feeling of dying; (3) moving through darkness or a tunnel, a cave, a cylinder, or a valley; (4) the sense of joy, love, and peace; (5) encountering the presence of deceased loved ones and other entities; (6) visions of beings of lights, guardian spirits, and so on – communication with these beings occurs without words, by the power of mere thought; (7) the perception of separation of the physical body, or out-of-body experience; (8) a life review, or a panoramic view of the proper life, or specific events that had happened in life; (9) certain sounds (such as noise, buzzing, ringing sounds); and, finally, (10) the decision of conscious return. Often an NDE does not incorporate all or even most of these features. As Moody confirmed: 'I have found no one person who reports every single component of the composite experience' (Moody, 1975: 23). There is a continuing debate about what the diagnostic criteria for an NDE might be.

Further those who reported an NDE are absolutely sure that what happened was a real experience. They will describe it as one of the most important experiences in their life (Greyson, 1993; Fenwick & Fenwick, 1995; Fox, 2003), which incorporated a strong sense of unity, a typical element of what Paul Marshall classified as 'universal mystical experience' because it is 'suggestive of contact with the universe as a whole' (Marshall, 1992: 63).

'I tried the experience of death. I was going down a tunnel. I saw the planet Earth. I could feel the relationship between the human soul, Earth and the planets. I thought I was a doll, you know the matryoshka? I was the matryoshka of the entire system. I understood that earth is inside something else. I felt its gravity. All this is embraced within a system. I was nothing, but I knew that my place was on Earth' (Corazza, 2008: 91).

The person who reported the above experience didn't face the threat of dying but he was under the influence of a 'dissociative anesthetic' called ketamine (Green et al., 1996; Parke-Davis, 1999-2000; Bell et al., 2006). Further, he was one of the few individuals who reported an NDE both in a near-death circumstance (suicide) and after the administration of ketamine. Evidence has shown that NDEs can occur under the effects of sub-anesthetic doses (10-25% of a surgical dosage) of this substance (Jansen, 1989; Bonta, 2003; Corazza & Schifano, in press), and in many other situations, such as in people who were extremely tired, during rapid acceleration during training of fighter pilots (Whinnery & Whinnery, 1990), during electro-stimulation of the temporal lobe (Persinger, 1983), after prolonged isolation and sensory deprivation (Comer et al., 1967), occasionally while carrying out everyday activities, while dreaming, amongst some others. In addition to these, similar experiences have been described as a result of shamanic (Eliade, 1964; Harner, 1980) or meditative practices (see, for instance, Becker, 1993), where these experiences do not seem to be as unusual as they are in Western countries.

NDEs are rather common experiences. The first extensive survey in this sense was conducted by the Gallup Poll organization in 1982 (Gallup, 1982), in which 15 per cent of a representative sample of American population reported an NDE. Other national studies were carried out in Germany, where 4 per cent of a representative sample of population reported an NDE (Knoblauch, Schmied, & Schnetller, 2001) and in Australia, where 8 per cent had an NDE (Perera *et al.* 2005). Badham (2005) has suggested that these results should be related to the frequency of spiritual experiences among the population in general. For instance, according to David Hay, 76 per cent of the population in Britain in 2001 described having 'an awareness of a transcendental reality' (in Badham, 2005: 202). This evidence has been supported by another study carried out at the University of London. Researchers, asked passers-by in Trafalgar Square, 'What kind of things have made you feel most sublime?' Findings showed that 65 per cent of those interviewed had had an experience, which could be defined 'as religious, spiritual, ecstatic, sacred, paranormal or mystical' (Pupynin & Brodbeck, 2001: 8).

NDE as a Cross-Cultural Topic of Research

Cross-cultural study of the NDE is a relatively new and complex field of investigation. Some researchers hold the view that the NDE is a universal experience, which has basically the same structure around the world, although cultural and religious beliefs influence various details and the way the NDE is interpreted. For example, it has been shown that an Indian person is more likely to see Yama, the King of Death, or his messengers called Yamdoots (Pasricha & Stevenson, 1986), rather than Christ or Madonna. On the contrary, others, like Cherie Sutherland, have reported cases where the content of the experience was actually different from the cultural or religious background of the person who reported the experience (Sutherland, forthcoming).

Allan Kellehear suggests that the idea that the NDE is a universal experience is particularly appealing to those who support a biological explanation of the phenomenon and he considers this kind of conclusion premature on the basis of the limited existing data in non-Western countries (Kellehear, 1996). In order to support his view, he offered a systematic comparison of near-death experiences reported in India, China, Western New Britain, Guam, Native America, and New Zealand. He came to the conclusion that only two features are universal: (1) the transition into a period of darkness; and (2) the meeting with 'other beings', once arrived in the 'other world'. Other aspects, like a 'life review', are nearly always absent in non-Western accounts. It is important to observe how the concept of 'transition into a period of darkness' is rather different from the vision of a tunnel (also known as the 'tunnel effect'). The latter, following Kellehear, is socially constructed: This darkness is then subject to culture-specific interpretations: a tunnel for Westerners, subterranean caverns for the Melanesians, and so on. NDErs who do not report a period of darkness may not view this aspect of the experience as an important part of their account or narrative (Kellehear, 1996: 35–6).

River of no Return: NDEs in Japan

Very little work has been done on NDE in Japan. Two major studies emerged from my investigation. The larger one has been carried out by Takashi Tachibana, an esteemed journalist in the country, who made a popular survey of four hundred individuals who had survived in life-threatening circumstances. In his work entitled Near-Death Experience (1994), he argues that the most common features of a Japanese NDE are the visions of long, dark rivers and beautiful flowers.

Of greater academic relevance is probably a study carried out by Yoshia Hata and his research team at the University of Kyorin (Hata et al., in Hadfield, 1991). Researchers interviewed 17 patients, who recovered from a situation where there had been minimal signs of life. Most of them had suffered heart attacks, asthma attacks, or drug poisoning. Eight of them reported memories during unconsciousness (47 per cent). Nine had no memories at all (53 per cent). Of the eight who had an experience, clear visions of rivers or ponds largely prevailed. Such elements have also been emphasized in Takashi Tachibana's survey. Probably the most interesting finding of Hata's study is that five of the eight participants (62.5 per cent) reported negative experiences, dominated by fear, pain or suffering. So it was for a 73-year-old lady, who had an NDE as a consequence of a cardiac arrest. She said: 'I saw a cloud filled with dead people. It was a dark, gloomy day. I was chanting sutras [This is a rather common practice among Buddhists. The term 'sutras' refers to the oral teachings of the Buddha]. I believed they could be saved if they chanted sutras, so that is what I was telling them to do' (Hadfield 1991: 11). Negative NDEs seem not to be that common in Western accounts, although as Peter and Elizabeth Fenwick observed, they are probably underreported because they are less likely to be communicated to others than positive experiences (Fenwick & Fenwick, 1995).

A Small-Scale Study in Japan

In 2004-5, I carried out a small-scale study in Japan in collaboration with the 21st Century COE Program on the 'Construction of Death and Life Studies Concerning Culture and Value of Life' at the University of Tokyo. The main objective of this program is to explore a variety of issues on 'Life' and 'Death' studies, which in Japanese are called shiseikan (or 'perspective on Death and Life') (Shimazono, 2004).

Case 1

Mrs O., a 66-year-old Tai Chi Master, had a very powerful near-death experience which changed her life. Sixteen years before the interview, she was very sick. She lost consciousness and was resuscitated in the emergency care unit of a hospital in Tokyo. The doctor told her later that her heart had stopped beating for a while and that she was considered clinically dead for an unknown period of time (she couldn't remember). She described having a vision of a river which separated her side from that of the Realm of Dead (or 'Yomi'). She said: 'As I got closer, at the very end of the other side of the river, I saw my mother who passed away 18 years ago. I could see only her face because a group of children monks, dressed in white and black, masked the rest of her body. The children were very noisy. I moved closer, to see my mother. She looked very worried and she said: 'Don't come here! Go back!' So I turned back and regained consciousness in the hospital. At that very moment, I heard a nurse calling my name' (Corazza, 2008: 60).

Case 2

Mrs C. was 66 years old at the time of the interview. She studied Tai Chi and became a Grand Master (the highest level in the discipline). She had an NDE in October 1975 following a long period of sickness. She was considered clinically dead for an unknown period of time. She had a vision of a river which separated her side from that of the 'spirit world'. A rainbow bridge connected the two sides of the river. Once she regained consciousness she gave the following account: 'My father came to greet me. We walked together for a little while and then he left me and crossed over a 'rainbow bridge'. I was about to follow him but he told me not to do so. He said to me: 'Go home, go home!' Then, I woke up' (Corazza, 2008: 61).

Case 3

The third person interviewed was Mr. C., a 41-year-old musician. He studied classical music and became a professional guitarist. He reported an NDE in December 1981 as a consequence of a terrible car accident. He described the vision of an empty and strange place: 'No one was there. No living things were around me. I remember that I felt serene but lonely. I was amazed at how vast the space was! It was neither too bright nor too dark. It was just there was no living thing there.' He wandered around and reached a wall of bright and magnificent Light in his path. He said: 'I saw something glittering in the distance and went to it. Next thing I knew there was a bright huge wall standing in my way. It was made of golden light. There was something I had to go across between the wall and me. I believe there was no river, no bridge or nothing specifically. The wall, which shone gold softly, was made of pure glory and I was sure that there existed whole in it. I moved towards it, being gravitated to it. I have a feeling that I saw many things in this something. Everything happened very quickly. I remember that I saw everything I had experienced. The sense of gravitation toward the light was so strong that I gradually began to lose the sense of distinguishing myself from the light. I was filled with everything. Then I thought something like: 'Would I be dead if the trend continues?' but 'I have done nothing in this life!'. Then I realized that I had developed a strong feeling of resistance towards this gravitation and the melting into the light. I remember nothing else. The next thing I knew was that I was lying in a hospital bed, and pain and that I was in pain and suffering'.

Results

Interestingly, all those interviewed were absolutely sure that what happened wasn't an illusion but a true experience. No pain or suffering was reported. One participant felt 'serene, but lonely'. This contrasts with the research results of Hata and his team at the University of Kyorin (Hata, in Hadfield, 1991) where five out of seven participants had a negative experience.

Sense of Emergence into Another 'Place'

In all three cases the individuals reported a sense of emergence into another place (or dimension of reality). Two of them recognized it as the 'Realm of the Dead'. They described it as a place of incredible beauty, full of gardens and scented flowers. In both cases, the landscape was described as being particularly bright. According to Mrs O.: 'the ground was filled with beautiful yellow flowers, like a sort of carpet'. She couldn't tell what kind of flowers there were but she noticed the colors were very unusual and very bright. Similarly, Mrs C. said: 'I was in a place filled with inexplicable gentle light and nice fragrances, as well as beautiful flowers. Then I heard a beautiful voice and music.'

As has been reported in previous studies (Hata, in Hadfield, 1991; Tachibana, 1994), this kind of vision of a beautiful place seems to be a recurrent feature in Japanese NDEs. One reason could be that nature is strongly connected with spirituality in Japan. The Japanese tendency to have NDEs related to the natural environment could be related to their intimate relationship with nature. This phenomenon has been called 'biophilia,' (Wilson, 1984).

Vision of a River

Interestingly, two out of three participants described a vision of a river which divided the world of the living from that of the dead. For both of them, to cross the river meant acceptance that they would die. A similar conclusion also emerged from previous studies (Hata, in Hadfield, 1991; Tachibana, 1994). The vision of the river has a strong link with Shinto beliefs where the element of the river has the significance of purification (Corazza, 2004; Kasulis, 2004).

Meeting with Others

Two out of three of the participants met other beings. Both Mrs O. and Mrs C. met respectively their dead mother and father, who told them 'do not cross the river' and to go back. Moreover, Mrs O. saw a group of child monks who were with her mother on the other side of the river.

Vision of the Light

One participant, Mr. C., had a powerful vision of a wall made of Light and had a form of non-verbal communication with it. He also described a sense of gravitation towards this Light, as if he was melting into it. The other two participants didn't see the Light, but they spoke about bright colors. To illustrate this point, Mrs O. made me look at the flowers in her garden, which were incredibly yellow. Mrs C. said that she was in a place filled with inexplicable, gentle, bright light and lovely fragrance. No one reported a tunnel effect or a transition through a period of darkness, which, following Kellehear (1996), is also one of the two most common elements in NDE from a cross-cultural point of view. Only one participant (Mr. C.) referred to a sense of transition, but not in the darkness. He told me he was (1) flying (2) up and (3) at great speed. Both (1) and (2) are quite unusual elements in Western NDE, where people usually are going down along a tunnel, rather than flying up. A common element is the high speed (3).

Life Review

No one reported a life review. The only exception might be represented by the musician (Mr. C.), who said that he saw everything he had experienced in the wall of Light in front of him. Nevertheless, he couldn't remember what it was. This result is in common with findings in previous studies (Hata, in Hadfield, 1991; Tachibana, 1994).

Out-of-Body Experiences

No one reported an out-of-body experience. Such a result was also reported in previous studies (Hata, in Hadfield, 1991; Tachibana, 1994). However, I have recently learnt during a personal correspondence of the case of an 87-year-old Japanese woman who had a very powerful OBE. She was considered clinically dead by the doctors. She described her amazement when she found herself out of her body and looking at her family members crying at her deathbed. Although she tried many ways to attract their attention and to communicate with them (in an attempt to tell them that she was not dead), she did not succeed. She also rang the bell of the ancestors' altar in her house. Her family members heard the sound of the bell and turned towards the altar but they were not able to see her. Finally, after many attempts, she lay down on her corpse and miraculously she came back to life. This was indeed a surprise for everyone! Accounts like these are always fascinating, but some researchers consider these experiences highly controversial and claim that they require careful replication under rigorous scientific conditions (see, for instance, French, 2005).

Border or a Point of no Return

All three NDErs came to a clear point or border of no return, which was a major component of their experience. For all of them, to cross these points meant that they would die and that they accepted this. Two of them were sent back by their dead relatives either (1) because they had a mission to accomplish in life, or (2) because their time had not yet come. Similar experiences have been widely reported in Western NDE. For instance, we currently know that in India, people tend to be sent back because of a mistake in their identities (Pasricha & Stevenson, 1986). A similar phenomenon has been described in the Tibetan *delok*, a phenomenon which literally means 'returned from the dead', and refers to the name given to people who seemingly 'die' as a result of an illness, and find themselves traveling in the Bardo, before returning to life again (Soyal Rinpoche, 1992).

On Cultural Comparison

The cultural comparison between NDEs in different countries is a very difficult topic of investigation, especially in the absence of extensive data. From a phenomenological point of view there are certain cognitive structures (or 'eidetic essences') that are common to all cultures. That is to say that the basis of any NDE is found in the same energy or power, independent of what has been experienced. Eastern traditions have grasped this concept in various ways. For example, we find the idea of Purusa in Yoga, Atman in Vedanta, Tao in Taoism, which all refer to the field, which is called 'authentic self' (Nishida, 1990).

Teachings from the Sakura

Some other interesting results emerged in terms of the study of what in Japanese is called shiseikan, or perspective on death and life (Shimazono, 2004). According to the Japanese tradition there is no clear distinction between life and death. The concept has been well expressed by Kato, who commented that in Japan 'there is a continuum between the living and the dead that make it difficult to draw clear lines' (Kato, in Martinez, 2004: 207). In other terms, as Kasulis has pointed out, for a Japanese person 'death' is present in a new born as much as 'life' is present in a sick old man (Kasulis, 2004). Such a strict interrelation between life and death appears even clearer by observing Japanese everyday life. A notable example is that of the 'cherry blossom festival', which is one of the most important events of the year in Japan. People gather together in parks to celebrate the blossoming of cherry ('sakura') and plumb trees. As Drazen, has pointed out, the blossom is also an important moment of reflection on life and death: 'An ultimate reminder that human life is very impermanent, but that, for the short time it is here, it can also be very beautiful (Drazen, 2003: 208-219). Further, the perception of life and death in the country emerges even clearer from the very peculiar way in which the Japanese deal with the problem of the abortion with images of Jizō, the protector of children. Small statues of the size of little children are placed in cemeteries to apologize to a fetus to be aborted, and as focus of prayers that the soul of the fetus will be reborn into better circumstances (Corazza, 2007a).

POSSIBLE INTERPRETATIONS OF AN NDE

There are currently various scientific explanations for the near-death experience (Fontana 2005). These could be classified into three main approaches, which, however, are not mutually exclusive: (1) the mind/brain identity (or neuroreductionist) theory; (2) psychological explanations; and (3) the transcendental (or 'survivalist') approach.

Mind and Brain Identity Theories

Also defined as 'neuro-reductionism' (Varela, 1996), this approach tends to confine human existence in terms of brain functions and sees consciousness as a mere product of the brain. Various physiological explanations have been proposed to account for the near-death experience. These include oxygen depletion in the brain (or 'cerebral hypoxia'), which is common in a dying brain (Blackmore & Troscianko, 1988), but, as we have seen, the NDE can also be experienced in other situations. Others have implicated neurotransmitters such as endorphins (Carr, 1982; Sotelo *et al.*, 1995), glutamate (Jansen, 1989; 2001), serotonin pathways (Morse *et al.*, 1986), activation of the limbic system and temporal lobe anoxic seizures, but none has yet been shown to be responsible for the phenomenon.

The methodological presuppositions of the neuro-reductionist approach have been considered as a violation of our human experience by an increasing number of scholars (see, for instance, Varela, 1996; Damasio, 1999). The main problem with this approach is that the 'objective' measurements of the brain do not allow investigation of the 'subjective' aspects of the human experience. As Leder has put it: 'By not including the "subjective" side of the experience in the reflection, we assume only a partial reflection and our question becomes disembodied' (Leder, 1990: 7). The argument has been well explored by Thomas Nagel in his article entitled 'What is it like to be a bat?' (1974), where he deals with the 'what it is like' ('subjective') character of human experience (Nagel, 1974).

Psychological Explanations

There are various psychological explanations of the NDE. One of these was formulated by Noyes& Kletti (1976), who state the NDE should be seen as a form of depersonalization, which occurs as a defense mechanism against the perceived threat of dying. Another psychological theory considers the near-death experience to be analogous to birth, while the 'tunnel effect' and the emergence into a bright light have been interpreted as a symbolic re-living of the birth process. This theory was promoted by the late astronomer Carl Sagan, who was influenced by the work on death and dying carried out by Grof & Halifax (1977). However, according to Susan Blackmore, a newborn infant would not see anything like a tunnel as it is being born. This is because the birth canal is stretched and compressed and the baby is usually forced through it with the top of the head and not with the eyes (which are closed anyway) (Blackmore, 1993). In order to test her theory, Blackmore carried out a study where she interviewed some people born normally and others delivered by Caesarean section. Almost exactly equal percentages of both groups had a tunnel experience (36 per cent) during an NDE (ibid.). Other objections have been proposed by Carl Becker. He observed: "The newborn's eyes are generally blurred by tears. They are often closed, either from relaxation, napping, or blinking . . . Even if their eyes are open and free of tears, they are often completely devoid of attention, like adults who may be momentarily oblivious to their physical surroundings even when their eyes are open" (1993: 113).

Transcendental Hypothesis

This approach, also known as the 'survivalist hypothesis', strongly supports the view that a detachable soul leaves the body at the moment of the near-death experience and that this provides evidence of our survival after the death of the body (see, for, instance, Badham & Badham, 1982; Sabom, 1982). Implicit in the survivalist hypothesis is a dichotomic way of thinking according to which soul and matter are two separate and incompatible entities. Even this approach has its own limitations. The most remarkable one is that by losing sight of mind–body wholeness, the mind is considered a disembodied entity, which is totally unrelated to the rest of the body. Further, as discussed NDEs can also occur in non life-threatening circumstances.

The Middle Way: A Non-Reductionist, Non-Dualistic View

Finally, I would like to emphasize a non-reductionist, non-dualistic view, which is inspired by a Japanese understanding of the body-mind connection. As argued above, this approach does not only assume a more integrated view of body and mind (Nagatomo, 1992; Yuasa, 1993), but also strongly emphasizes the relationship between the body and space, or place (in Japanese basho). The idea is implicit in one of the Japanese terms used to describe an individual, *ningen,* which literally means between one person and another person rather than an individual subject. In other terms, such a definition of opens up a ground for both (a) the individual and (b) the universal aspects of who we are (Nagatomo, 1992; Corazza, 2005).

The relationship between the body and space, or better 'place', has been extensively studied by Hiroshi Ichikawa (1979). In his book The Body as the Spirit, Ichikawa proposed a threefold classification of the human body. The first category is called the 'innate body-space'. This can be defined as the body delimited by the skin that we see reflected when we look at ourselves in a mirror. The second category is the 'semi-definite body-space'. This is the body that expands through the use of tools. A classic example is the stick in the hand of a blind person. In this case, the stick becomes an extension of the blind person's arm. At the same time, a pen is an extension of a finger, a telephone is an extension of the voice. When you drive your car, you may perceive the car as an extension of your legs, or when you wear your clothes, you may perceive them as an extension of your skin, and so on. According to this approach, we humans work via extensions. The third category is the 'indefinitely varying body-space'. Going far beyond the previous two body-spaces, it has three main characteristics: (1) it is always changing; (2) it is temporary; and (3) it is non-habitual.

The spatial element of place is also fundamental to Japanese understanding of transcendental states of consciousness and thus even more relevant to our discussion.

Interestingly, Hiroshi Motoyama called the state of Samadhi 'The World of Places' (Motoyama, 1991; in press). The underlying idea is that our daily reality has an invisible, deeper layer, which is different in dimension and is disclosed by the object-subject relation. Nishida called this deeper level of consciousness 'Invisible Place' (Nishida 1990). Evidence for this idea has emerged from NDEs studies, where the only common feature that seems to be present in all the experiences that we have collected so far is the spatial element, that is, to be in a specific place, as if consciousness could not be separated from space or place (Corazza, 2007b; 2008).

It can be observed that current Japanese thinking, particularly as articulated in the thought of Tetsuro Watsujii (1988), Hiroshi Ichikawa (1979) and Yasuo Yuasa (1993), provides a broader understanding of what it means to be a person, and this may allow data such those provided through near-death and other dissociative experiences to be integrated in a revised framework. Within such a wider and more comprehensive, or 'holistic', notion of the body, the near-death experience no longer challenges one's understanding of what it means to be human.

Conclusions

The 'Urashima effect' seems to be much more than cultural illusion. The cross-cultural study of the NDE is a rather new and fascinating topic of study, and it will probably be one line of enquiry to develop in future research. In many ways, at the core of this approach is a better understand of the human body and the potential that lies latent within us. As Michael Murphy has pointed out in The Future of the Body (1992), the body is endowed with extraordinary capacities, the manifestation of which makes us aware of our general lack of awareness about the reaches of human nature. Scientific discoveries have contributed to a deeper knowledge of the self and the universe around us, however the challenge of the future will be to collect evidence of our extraordinary ability to connect with the universe, so that it can be seen and known as a whole. Evidence for this has emerged from the accounts of those who had profound universal experiences such as NDE. In many ways, the value of these experiences goes far beyond the question of a scientific proof of an afterlife and brings us directly to our immediate experience of the 'here-and-now' and the sense of meaning and purpose that we may experience in this life. It also goes beyond reductionism and the attempt to locate consciousness in some part of the brain. Even more profoundly, these experiences can suggest to us that what we label 'I' is only a small part of a deeper intelligence that is immanent within all creation. They invite us to recognize and seek out this intelligence or power that seems to reach within and extend beyond the physical body.

References

Badham, P. (2005). The experiential grounds for believing in God and a future life. *Modern Believing, 46(1),* 197–208.

Badham, P. & Badham, L. (1982). *Immortality or extinction*? London: SPCK.

Becker, C.B. (1993). *Paranormal experience and survival of death.* New York: State University of New York Press.

Bell, R., Dahl, J., Moore, R. & Kalso, E. (2006). Perioperative ketamine for acute postoperative pain. *Emergency Medicine Australasia, 18(1),* 37– 44.

Blackmore, S.J. (1993). Near-death experiences in India: they have tunnels too. *Journal of Near-death Studies, 11,* 205–17.

Blackmore, S.J. & Troscianko, T. (1988). The physiology of the tunnel. *Journal of Near Death Studies*, 8, 15–28.

Bonta, I.L. (2003). Schizophrenia, dissociative anaesthesia and near-death experience: three events meeting at the NMDA receptor. *Medical Hypotheses, 62,* 23–8.

Carr, D. (1982). Pathophysiology of stress induced limbic lobe dysfunction: a hypothesis for NDEs. *Journal of Near Death Studies, 2,* 75–89.

Comer, N.L., Madow, L. & Dizon, J.L. (1967). Observation of sensory deprivation in a life-threatening situation. *American Journal of Psychiatry, 124(2),* 164–9.

Corazza, O. (2004). The varieties of the near-death experience: a study in Japan, in F. Cariglia (Ed.) *Echi d'altrove*. San Marino: Repubblica di San Marino, pp. 33–8.

Corazza, O. (2005). Space and embodiment: a Japanese understanding of human beings. Paper presented at conference, *Embodiment and the environment*, 5–8 July, Oxford Brooks University, Oxford.

Corazza, O. (2007a). The Spirit of Place: Visions of the afterlife in Japan, in F. Cariglia (Ed.) *Sopravvivere. Il velato destino della personalita*, Proceedings of the 11th International Congress on NDE, San Marino, pp. 23– 8.

Corazza, O. (2007b). Extended Body: how do we think and feel about the body in the 21st century?' In D. Janes (Ed.), *Does the body have a future?* Cambridge: Scholar Press.

Corazza, O. (2008). *Near-death experiences: exploring the mind-body connection.* London/New York: Routledge.

Corazza, O., Schifano F. (in press). A prospective study on the emergence of near-death states among a group of 50 ketamine recreational users. *Substance Use and Misuse.*

Damasio, A. (1999). *The feeling of what happens: body, emotion and the making of consciousness*. London: Harcourt Brace.

Drazen, P. (2003). *Anime explosion! the what? why? wow! of Japanese animation.* Berkeley. CA: Stone Bridge Press.

Eliade, M. (1964). *Shamanism: An archaic technique of ecstasy.* Princeton, NJ: Princeton University Press.

Fenwick, P. & Fenwick, E. (1995). *The truth in the light: an investigation of over 300 near-death experiences.* London: Hodder Headline.

French, C. (2005). Near-death experiences in cardiac arrest survivals. *Progress in Brain Research, 150,* 351–67.

Fontana, D. (2005). *Is there an afterlife? a comprehensive overview of the evidence*. Ropley, Hants: O Books.

Fox, M. (2003). *Religion, spirituality and the near-death experience*. New York: Routledge.

Gallup, G. (1982). *Adventures in immortality: a look beyond the threshold of death.* New York: McGraw-Hill.

Green, S.M., Clem, K.J. & Rothroc, K.S.G. (1996). Ketamine safety profile in the developing world: survey of practitioners, *Acad. Emergency Medicine, 3(6),* 598–604.

Greyson, B. (1993). The variety of the near-death experiences. *Psychiatry, 56,* 390–9.

Grof, S. & Halifax, J. (1977). *The human encounter with death.* New York: E.P. Dutton.

Hadfield, P. (1991). Japanese find death a depressing experience. *New Scientist, 132 (1797),* 11.

Harner, M. (1980). *The way of the shaman.* New York: HarperCollins.

Ichikawa, H. (1979). *Seishin toshite no Shintai* (The Body as the Spirit). Tokyo: Keisdshdbd.

Jansen, K.L.R. (1989). Near-Death experiences and the NMDA receptor. *British Medical Journal, 298,* 1708.

Jansen, K.L.R (2001). *Ketamine: dreams and realities.* Sarasota: MAPS.

Kasulis, T.P. (2004). *Shinto; the way home.* Honolulu: University of Hawaii Press.

Kawauchi, S. (1997). *Once upon a time in japan.* Tokyo: Kodansha International Ltd.

Kellehear, A. (1996). *Experiencing near-death: beyond medicine and religion.* Oxford: Oxford University Press.

Knoblauch, H., Schmied, I., & Schnetller, B. (2001). Different kinds of near-death experiences: A report on a survey in Germany. *Journal of Near-Death Studies, 22,* 21-22.

Leder, D. (1990). *The absent body.* Chicago: The University of Chicago Press.

Marshall, P. (1992). *The living mirror: images of reality in science and mysticism.* London: Hampshire Press.

Martinez, P. (2004). *Identity and ritual in a japanese diving village: the making and becoming of person and place.* Honolulu: University of Hawaii Press.

Moody, R.A. (1975). *Life after Life.* Atlanta, GA: Mockingbird Books.

Morse, M.L. Castillo, P., Venecia, D., Milstein, J. & Tyler, D.C. (1986). Childhood near-death experiences. *American Journal of Diseases of Children, 140,* 1110–14.

Motoyama, H. (1991). *The correlation between psi energy and ki.* Tokyo: Human Science Press.

Motoyama, H. (in press). *The metaphysical logic: a synthesis of religions east and west.* trans. S. Nagatomo and J. Krummel. Encinitas, CA: California Institute for Human Science.

Murphy, M. (1992). *The future of the body.* New York: Penguin Putman Inc.

Nagatomo, S. (1992). *Atonement through the body.* Albany, NY: State University of New York Press.

Nagel, T. (1974). What is it like to be a bat? *Philosophical Review, 83,* 435–50.

Nishida, K. (1990). *An inquiry into the good*, trans. M. Abe and C. Ives. New Haven, CT: Yale University Press

Noyes, R. & Kletti, R. (1976). Depersonalisation in the face of life-threatening danger: a description. *Psychiatry, 39,* 19–30.

Parke-Davis product information sheet (1999–2000). *Ketalar®, ABPI Compendium of Data Sheets and Summaries of Product Characteristics, 1999–2000.* Datapharm Publications, pp. 1120–2.

Pashricha, S. & Stevenson, I. (1986). Near-death experiences in India: a preliminary report. *Journal of Nervous and Mental Disease, 174,* 165–70.

Perera, M., Padmasekara, G., & Belanti, J. (2005). Prevalence of Near-Death Experiences in Australia. *Journal of Near-Death Studies, 24 (2),*

Persinger, M. (1983). Religious and mystical experiences as artefacts of temporal lobe function: a general hypothesis. *Perceptual and Motor Skills, 57,* 1255–62

Pupyin, O. & Brodbeck, S. (2001). *Religious experience in London*, Second Series Occasional Paper 27. Oxford: Religious Experience Research Centre.

Sabom, M.B. (1982). *Recollection of death: a medical investigation.* New York: Harper & Row.

Sagan, C. (1979). *Broca's brain.* New York: Random House.

Shimazono, S. (2004). *From salvation to spirituality.* Melbourne: Trans Pacific Press.

Soyal Rinpoche (1992). *The Tibetan book of the living and the dying.* London: Routledge, pp. 330–6.

Sotelo, J., Perez, R., Guevara, P. & Fernandez, A. (1995). Changes in brain, plasma and cerebrospinal fluid contents of B-endorphin in dogs at the moment of death. *Neurological Research, 17,* 223.

Sutherland, C. (forthcoming). *Trailing clouds of glory: the near-death experiences of western children and teens.*

Tachibana, T. (1994). *Near death experience.* Tokyo: Bungei Shunju (Japanese only).

Varela, F.J. (1996). Neurophenomenology: a methodological remedy for the hard problem. *Journal of Consciousness Studies, 3(4),* 330– 49.

Watsuji, T. (1988). *Climate and culture*, trans. G. Bownas. New York: Greenwood Press, Inc.

Whinnery, J.E. & Whinnery, A.M. (1990). Acceleration-induced loss of consciousness', *Archives of Neurology, 47,* 764–76.

Wilson, E.O. (1984). *Biophilia: the human bond with others species.* Cambridge, MA: Harvard University.

Yuasa, Y. (1993). *The body, self-cultivation, and ki-energy.* Albany, NY: State University of New York Press.

In: Psychological Scientific Perspectives on Out of Body... ISBN: 978-1-60741-705-7
Editor: Craig D. Murray

Chapter 11

Out-of-Body and Near-Death Experiences as Evidence for Externalization or Survival[1]

John Palmer

Abstract

The author reviews research studies of out-of-the body experiences (OBEs) and near-death experiences (NDEs) that could be seen as providing evidence for survival of death, either directly (NDEs) or indirectly through separation of the mind from the body (OBEs). Two operational criteria for justifying these claims are distinguished. The first is evidence for extrasensory (ESP) perception or psychokinesis (PK) of a type that occurs only in a survival context, e.g., during an OBE. The second is evidence of cognition or behavior in a person whose brain processes are too degraded to support such activity. Three OBE experiments are reviewed in which a selected participant is asked to travel to a remote location and observe a target (ESP) or influence a physical detector (PK). Although ESP or PK was demonstrated in each case, it was never of a type unique to survival contexts. For NDEs, the main example is a famous case in which a surgery patient had an NDE while presumably brain dead as a result of induced hypothermic cardiac arrest, but it is unclear if the NDE actually occurred during the period of brain death. Despite these deficiencies, the NDE evidence increases the subjective probability of survival.

Introduction

The question of whether humans survive the death of the body is one of the most longstanding and controversial issues in parapsychology. Although there is general agreement among parapsychologists that psi[2] has been demonstrated to be real, at least as a genuine communication anomaly, there is no such consensus on the survival issue.

---

[1] This paper is a truncated version of an Invited Address presented at the 49th Parapsychological Association Convention, Stockholm, Sweden, August, 2006.

[2] Psi is a generic term used to cover ESP and PK, which are defined in footnotes 3 and 5 respectively.

The traditional approach to the survival question has been to demonstrate psi in what I call a survival context. By that I mean a circumstance that, when taken at face value, involves the participation of a discarnate entity. This entity generally fulfills the role of the ostensible psi source. This approach is most apparent in mediumship research, where the crucial question (provided we can accept that the psi is genuine) is where the information comes from. Does it come, as it seems on the surface, from a discarnate entity? Or is the source more mundane, for example, the mind (or brain) of a living relative of the deceased, or a document or newspaper story? Thus, the survival problem is a special case of what I consider the most important as well as the most difficult challenge facing modern parapsychology, namely, the source-of-psi problem. The other major example of the source-of-psi problem is the psi-based experimenter effect, which refers to the possibility that experimenters contribute their own psi to the results of their experiments (Palmer, 1989, 1997).

I have taken the position that such evidence is suggestive of survival to the degree that the particular type of psi manifested is limited to survival contexts (Palmer, 1975). I think most parapsychologists take it for granted that the source of psi in nonsurvival contexts is not a discarnate entity. When there is nothing in the context that suggests survival, there is no positive reason to postulate a new entity to account for it. In such a situation, it is appropriate to appeal to the parsimony principle, which tells us that we should attribute psi in both contexts to the potential source for which we have the most independent evidence.

The second approach to demonstrating survival has gained prominence in parapsychology only recently. It has been argued for forcefully in the recent book by Kelly et al. (2007). The multiple authors of this volume discuss a wide range of parapsychological and nonparapsychological phenomena and abilities that appear to transcend the capabilities of the human brain as accepted by mainstream neuroscientists. If a phenomenon or ability transcends the limits of the brain, then the brain cannot be the cause of it. As no other body part is a plausible candidate either, some kind of nonphysical mind is the only viable alternative.

In the remainder of this chapter I will review survival-relevant parapsychological research in two related areas: out-of-body experiences (OBEs) and near-death experiences (NDEs). Research in OBEs has generally used the first approach discussed above (psi in survival contexts), whereas the strongest piece of survival evidence from NDEs represents the second approach (transcending brain limitations).

OUT-OF-BODY EXPERIENCES (OBEs)

I define an OBE as a sequence of internal images or sensations that creates the immediate subjective impression that one's center of consciousness is located outside one's physical body. Note in particular that this judgment is sudden and made without reflection; it is not the opinion one arrives at later, after giving the matter some thought. Note that this definition does not include anything about the content of the experience or the particular types of imagery involved. The extent to which such characteristics are present in OBEs as defined above should be, and to some extent has been, determined empirically, most notably by Alvarado (1984). I chose this definition because I think the attribute that makes the OBE interesting to parapsychologists is indeed this subjective experience of externalization. That is what defines the experience as occurring in a survival context and qualifies it, along with objective evidence of psi, as potential survival evidence. To classify OBEs as survival evidence, we also must assume that whatever leaves the body has mental capacities, most notably consciousness, and does not possess characteristics such as weight that would cause it to be classified as physical. Once this conceptual hurdle is overcome, it is not a much further leap to suggest that it can function independently of the body, which in turns means that it could survive the death of the body. Still, the evidence for this last point is not as strong as it would be if the physical body was "dead" or demonstrably nonfunctional at the time of the experience, which is the case with a veridical NDE. That is why, all else being equal, NDEs potentially provide stronger survival evidence than OBEs.

Below, I will briefly review several experiments in which attempts were made to demonstrate externalization in OBEs. In all these cases, it is either stated or can be reasonably inferred that the OBEer had the subjective experience of externalization at roughly the time the psi effect manifested. Thus, they meet the conditions of psi occurring in a survival context. However, to meet the more rigid test I have proposed above, an additional requirement must be met: the *type* of psychic phenomenon that occurred (cf., Gauld, 1982) is unique to survival related contexts. I will restrict myself to experiments with selected participants who claim the ability to induce OBEs voluntarily, and where it is relatively clear that a psi effect occurred. How well do these candidates meet the more rigorous criterion?

Miss Z

The first major experimental attempt to test for ESP[3] during an OBE was a single trial conducted with a percipient who was referred to anonymously as Miss Z (Tart, 1968). The participant went to bed at night with electrodes attached to measure EEG and eye movements. On a shelf above the bed was placed a card with a randomly selected five-digit number written on it. Miss Z was to leave her body during the night, view the number from above, and memorize it so she could report it the next morning. At that time she correctly identified the number ($p = .0001$).

Although no one was in the room with Miss Z during the night, any attempt to get up and view the number with the eyes would have been detected, because it would have led to extreme fluctuations in the EEG recording. No such extreme deflections were noted. However, it was later discovered that there was a clock face in the room that could conceivably have reflected an image of the number into Miss Z's eyes as she was lying in bed. Given the location of the clock and the available light, this artifact is highly unlikely, but not impossible. It is also possible that she cheated by sneaking a pocket mirror into the lab room.

Assuming these artifacts did not occur, can we conclude that the type of psi demonstrated by Miss Z is unique to survival contexts? The answer is no. It is obvious that the ability Miss Z demonstrated is essentially the same as card guessing, which has been demonstrated numerous times by participants in normal states of consciousness. It has frequently been

3 *ESP* is the acronym for extrasensory perception. It means the acquisition of information about an external object or event (mental or physical; past, present, or future) in some way other than through any of the known sensory channels.

argued in cases of mediumship that one should also give weight to effects that are unique to survival contexts with respect to their magnitude as well as their type (e.g., Gauld, 1982). This argument does not impress me, because unlike type, magnitude represents a continuum. It just seems too likely that extreme values on continua such as degree of belief or alteration of consciousness could be the crucial correlate of extreme psi scores, rather than externalization, which seems best conceptualized as qualitatively distinct from internalization. Also, there are cases in the remote-viewing[4] literature demonstrating a magnitude of psi at least as great as Miss Z's (e.g., May, 1995). In remote viewing, viewers generally do not consider themselves to be externalized.

Harary's Kitten

This experiment was conducted with a college student, Keith Harary, who claimed the ability to have OBEs at will (Morris, Harary, Janis, Hartwell, & Roll, 1978). At a randomly selected time, he projected to a room in an adjacent building in which several detectors were located. One of these detectors was another person, who was blind to the projection time. Also in the room were several physical detectors measuring various kinds of electromagnetic activity. The last detector was one of two kittens the staff had bought for Harary as pets. The test kitten was located in a cage with a grid floor, and the activity of the kitten could be measured by counting the number of different squares traversed over a specified period of time. In each of two independent trials, the kitten, as predicted, was significantly less active and meowed less during the randomly selected projection periods than at adjacent control times. In a second study of similar design, the kitten, when active, oriented its body in the direction of the externalized OBEer significantly more often than in the other directions. There were no significant results with the human or physical detectors.

As with Miss Z, the kind of psi discussed here is quite similar in kind to ordinary telepathy, which has been demonstrated with animals as well as humans in nonsurvival contexts. Perhaps the best example with animals is a series of experiments by Sheldrake (1999) in which dogs behaviorally anticipated the randomly selected times that their owner was about to leave for home.

Tanous and the Optical Image Device

Another person who claimed the ability to have OBEs at will was the psychic Alex Tanous. In a rather elaborate experiment, Tanous was asked to leave his body and peek through a hole in a special box called an optical image device (Osis & McCormick, 1980). Inside the box were three stimuli, each of which could be in any one of four orientations. One target, for example, was a circular disk divided into four different colored quadrants. Each target choice was positioned such that the three together could only be correctly observed by someone looking through the hole. In other words, people looking through the hole would be

[4] *Remote viewing* is another term for ESP. It is used especially in an experiment wherein a "viewer" attempts to describe a geographically remote location.

able to correctly determine the juxtaposition of the three targets with their eyes. Also, adjacent to the box was a strain gauge, which is designed to detect physical pressure.

First, it should be noted that the experimenters implicitly made an odd and seemingly gratuitous assumption about the nature of the externalized body, namely, that it has "sense organs" corresponding to the physical eye and that's its information-gathering capacities are restricted by the physical laws of optics. Although I don't think one can go so far as to say that the assumption contradicts the tenet that whatever leaves the body is nonphysical, it certainly does not seem very compatible with it. It must be said that the OBE literature in general is not very explicit about how the externalized self acquires information, but the most reasonable guess is that this mechanism is the same as that used for ESP in the living. In other words, the nonphysical self functions the same way whether it is located inside or outside the body. From an evolutionary perspective, this observation in turn raises the question (to my knowledge never addressed) of what evolutionary advantage there would be for the nonphysical self to have the ability to leave the physical body. There is little evidence that psi is adversely affected by distance (Palmer, 1978), and at the risk of jumping the gun about the conclusions of this chapter, there is little evidence that information acquisition is better when the nonphysical self is presumably outside the body than when it is presumably inside the body. In other words, there is little evidence that the physical body somehow inhibits the functioning of the nonphysical body when the two are "attached."

Returning to the experiment itself, the main finding was a significant tendency for the strain gauge to show the greatest deflections when Tanous achieved hits on the ESP targets. However, the support this finding provides for the authors' theory is undercut by the fact that the hits entered into the correlation were hits on the individual targets rather than on the three together. The whole point of using the optical image device was to prove that the nonphysical self was looking through the hole by showing that it would get a significant excess of hits on the whole target system, that is, on all three of its components together.

The bottom line, however, is the same as in the previous cases. The success that Tanous achieved with the optical device is quite analogous to the standard forced-choice ESP demonstrated countless times in nonsurvival contexts. Likewise, influencing strain gauges is an example of macro-PK[5]. Apparent PK influence of strain gauges has also been demonstrated in nonsurvival contexts (Hasted, 1981).

Converging Evidence and the Wilmot Case

However, there is one point in favor of the Osis and McCormick (1980) experiment as evidence for externalization. I am referring to the demonstration of ESP and PK occurring simultaneously. I am not aware of such an effect occurring in a nonsurvival context, but this could be because it has rarely been sought in such a context. Further experiments of this type would be welcome in their own right, because if "successful" they would provide stronger,

5 PK is the acronym for psychokinesis, the influence of mind on a physical system that cannot be entirely accounted for by the mediation of any known physical energy. Macro-PK refers to a PK effect that does not require statistical analysis for its demonstration. It also is sometimes used to refer to PK on a target system that is larger than those involving quantum mechanical processes. PK on quantum mechanical systems is referred to as micro-PK.

although not conclusive, evidence that ESP and PK are two expressions of the same underlying mechanism.

Such convergence can also be found in the spontaneous case literature on OBEs. A relatively well-documented case that deserves some evidential weight is the famous Wilmot case (Sidgwick, 1891–1892), in which the converging phenomena are ESP during an OBE and the roughly simultaneous "perception" by two individuals of the OBEer. Mrs. Wilmot went to bed concerned about the safety of her husband who was traveling home aboard a ship. During the night, she had a spontaneous OBE in which she traveled to the state room on the ship where her husband and another passenger, Mr. Tait, were sleeping. Mr. Tait first awoke to notice a "strange woman" in the cabin. The following morning, Mr. Wilmot noted that he had had a dream that corresponded to Mr. Tait's apparitional experience. Written reports were provided by the Wilmots, but not by Mr. Tait. However, the main weakness of the case is that the testimonials appeared in writing more than 20 years after the event.

Near-Death Experiences (NDEs)

Whereas OBEs are defined by the OBEer's immediate reaction to the experience of externalization, NDEs are defined by the circumstances under which the experience takes place, i.e., imminent death. Thus, an experience that occurred when a person is facing the prospect of imminent death could be classified as an NDE even if the person did not immediately interpret the experience as representing survival of death. However, the immediate reaction of NDEers is invariably to interpret their experience as a glimpse of the afterlife, so the difference is not of great practical importance. In contrast to the case with OBEs, there has been a great deal of research leading to the identification of a sequence of stages that characterize what is called the classical NDE. Not every stage occurs in every NDE, but the experience tends to begin the same way and the stages tend to follow in the same order as described in the classical NDE. The experiences differ primarily in how many stages they traverse before they end. One set of stages, adapted from Ring (1980), is as follows:

[1] Sense of being dead
[2] Feelings of peace and well-being
[3] Leaving the body
[4] Entering the darkness (often a tunnel)
[5] Encountering a presence or hearing a voice
[6] Taking stock of one's life (past-life review)
[7] Seeing or being immersed in a bright light
[8] Encountering spirits (usually of deceased relatives or religious figures)
[9] Returning to the body

It is obvious from a review of these stages that one component, and I would say the major component, of the classical NDE is the OBE, and this is what most clearly defines the relationship between the OBE and the NDE. Like OBEs in other contexts, the OBEs that occur in near-death contexts are qualitatively very vivid and realistic, and they do not have the subjective quality of ordinary dreams. Also, they lead to the immediate conviction that the nonphysical self, which in the case of NDEs we might better call the soul, actually did externalize. Indeed, this conviction tends to be very strong in NDEers, and they often lose their fear of death as a result (Ring, 1980).

The Pam Reynolds Case

Arguably the strongest single piece of evidence for survival in the NDE literature is the Pam Reynolds case (Sabom, 1998), so I will discuss it here in some detail. It is an example of the recent emphasis on the manifestation of cognitive processes or behavior that transcends the known capacities of the brain as evidence for survival. Reynolds was a 35-year-old woman suffering from an aneurism in the basal artery. As the standard neurosurgical procedures were unavailable at this time at her location in Atlanta, Georgia, a rather extreme alternative was chosen. The surgery required that Pam's body temperature be reduced markedly, at which point the blood was drained from her head. Technically, this procedure is referred to as inducing hypothermic cardiac arrest. As a result, Pam's heartbeat and breathing stopped and her EEG was flat: by standard clinical criteria, she was dead.

The Procedure

At 7:15 AM, Pam was wheeled into the operating room. Her arms and legs were tied down to the operating table and her eyes taped shut. Various detectors were applied to her body to measure brain activity, blood flow from the heart, heart rate, blood oxygenation, and temperature of the core body and brain. The brain stem was periodically stimulated by 100 dB clicks applied from molded speakers inserted in both ears, such that any brain stem activity would appear as evoked potentials on the EEG. During this period, a general anesthetic (presumably Pentothal) was gradually introduced intravenously.

At 8:40 AM the surgery began. The skull was opened with a pneumatically-powered bone saw that made a loud buzzing noise. Beginning at 10:50, blood was pumped from Pam's body through the femoral artery into a cardiopulmonary bypass machine, cooled, and pumped back into the body. At 11:00, cardiac arrest was induced by massive intravenous doses of potassium chloride. At 11:20 her body temperature had descended to 60° F, and the vital signs became absent. At 11:25, the blood was drained from Pam's body and the process to remove the aneurism began. At an unspecified time before 12:00 noon, warm blood began to be pumped back into Pam's body and her vital signs began to return. At 12:00, a problem, ventricular fibrillation, was detected and corrected by the application of 100 joules of electricity through two defibrillation pads. By 12:32 the body temperature had recovered to 89.6° F. Pam was wheeled to the recovery room at 2:10 PM.

The NDE and Related Veridical Experiences

After the procedure, Pam reported that during the surgery she had a classical NDE. She was pulled from her body through a vortex into an expanding, very bright light. While immersed in the light she saw a number of deceased relatives who looked like they did when they were alive. They communicated with her by a process that seems akin to telepathy and also "fed" and "nourished" her through some undefined means. They would not permit her to go further into the light and indeed insisted that she return to her body. After some internal struggle she agreed that this was the best course. As she completed her journey back, through what is now called a tunnel rather than a vortex, she saw her physical body lying on the operating table. The combination of the tunnel pushing and the body pulling drove her back into her body and she gradually returned to waking consciousness.

Pam also reported experiences that accurately reflected various stages of the actual operating procedure as she was leaving her body. It is not clear whether these experiences occurred while she was in the vortex or before. She saw some of the equipment and overheard some of the conversations of the surgical team. However, her most notable experience was hearing the loud buzzing sound of the saw used to open her skull; she also gave a generally accurate description of the saw.

Analysis

In Sabom's (1998) account of Pam's NDE, excerpts from her verbal report of her experiences are inserted at places in the narrative of the medical procedure where they would fit logically. For example, her report of the buzzing sound immediately followed the description of the saw being used to open the skull. Her description of moving out of her body through the vortex immediately followed the account of blood being drained from her body, a time at which her vital signs indicated clinical death. The problem is that we are given little basis to conclude that this is exactly when these experiences occurred. All this happened at a time when Pam was under a great deal of stress. The changes in her vital signs that preceded the flat EEG, for example, would be sufficient for us to assume that the cognitive faculties were degraded to the point that she might not accurately register in long-term memory when various aspects of the experience occurred. The well-known fact that people seek to see the world in a way that makes sense suggests that if she had to "fill in the gaps" of what she accurately remembered, it would be in the direction of creating a "sensible" narrative: i.e., the events occurring in coordination with the corresponding stages of the medical procedure. It also is not clear how much of Sabom's (1998) description of the NDE came from what Pam reported immediately after the procedure and how much from his interview with her three years later. The material from Sabom's interview is even more susceptible to "logical" reconstruction than the earlier report. In short, we cannot be confident that any of these experiences in fact occurred during the part of the procedure in which Pam was clinically dead.

As for the veridical experiences, Pam could have noticed the saw on the table before her eyes were taped shut, without remembering it. It also is far from established that the earpieces, even with the clicks, fully eliminated Pam's ability to hear the sounds made by the saw. Pam described the sound as "humming at a relatively high pitch and the all of a sudden it went Brrrrrrrr! like that [italics in original]. High-pitch sounds are relatively easy to block, but low-pitch ones are not, and the "Brrrrrrrrr" may well have been low-pitch. Moreover, such a sound could have been felt as a vibration. If there was a sufficient time interval between each click, the sound of the saw possibly could have been heard during these intervals, even if the clicks themselves blocked it. This matter could still be settled if one could find one of these devices and test it with an earpiece and clicks of the type used in the surgery.

Finally, in the chaotic world of parapsychology, it is possible that Pam obtained the veridical information by precognition, perhaps even before she entered the operating room. It is far from clear, and in fact highly unlikely, that there is no temporal gap between the time information enters the unconscious mind and the time it appears in consciousness, including the nonwaking consciousness Pam presumably experienced during the surgery. In any event, the fact that these veridical experiences occurred before the period of clinical death weakens these experiences as evidence for survival, even if they were paranormal.[6]

Anesthesia and NDEs

Do the kinds of anesthetics used in surgery degrade brain-mediated cognitive processes enough to preclude an NDE? If so, then Pam's experiences would rise enormously in value as evidence for survival, and the many NDEs reported in cases of surgery not as extreme as Pam's would suddenly carry evidential weight as well. A study relevant to this question was reported by John et al. (2001), who collected quantitative EEG (QEEG) data from 176 hospital patients under anesthesia. On average, there was a reduction in gamma frequencies and an increase in theta and delta frequencies. The reduction in gamma could be taken as a deterioration of the kinds of brain activity needed to maintain cognitive activity, thereby supporting the survivalist interpretation of the NDE. However, a closer examination of John's report suggests a possible loophole in this thesis. John reported a slight increase in gamma relative to baseline during the early stages of unconsciousness, particular in the occipital lobe (specifically, O1), which is associated with visual imagery. Also, no variance data were reported. If this variance was nonnegligible, it is possible that the mean shift was attributable to a small percentage of patients in whom gamma elevated substantially during this period, enough (probably in conjunction with other, unknown factors) to support the relevant cognitive activity. This limiting assumption is reasonable in that only a small percentage of surgery patients report NDEs or other forms of imagery as having occurred during surgery. The gamma effect is particularly noteworthy in light of a report of increased gamma at O1 among Brazilian Indians under the influence of the hallucinogen Ayahuasca (Don et al., 1998).

Nonetheless, more data are needed to draw any firm conclusions about the physiological possibility of NDEs under anesthesia. It would be particularly interesting to learn if occipital gamma similar to what John found during the early unconsciousness phase in the patients he evaluated could be identified during voluntarily induced OBEs.

Looking Ahead

What if it could be established that Pam's NDE did occur when she was "brain dead"? Whereas the surgical team's measures captured activity in the cerebral cortex and the brain stem, they probably did not detect much subcortical activity. However, based on what we currently know about brain function, it does not seem possible that this part of the brain alone could account for the cognitive activity that Pam reported. The prospect of an NDE being

---

[6] Since presenting my lecture in 2006, I became aware of a critique of the Reynolds case by Augustine (2007), followed by rebuttals from Sabom (2007) and Tart (2007). Augustine states categorically that "Reynolds did *not* have her NDE during any period of flat EEG" (p. 217; italics in original), but his subsequent argument is remarkably deficient in supporting such a strong assertion. His main point is that Pam's experience of the surgeons talking occurred prior to the flat EEG. That is indeed what Sabom's report indicates, although, as I note in the main text, one cannot be too confident even about that. However, the crux of the matter, as Sabom (2007) noted in his rebuttal, is that the principal part of her NDE [seemed to] occur later, when her EEG *was* flat. The only justifiable conclusion about the veridicality of Pam's NDE is neither "atheism" nor "belief" but "agnosticism."

caused even in part by some nonphysical entity would be anathema to the many neuroscientists for whom materialism is a philosophical premise that borders on a self-evident truth. If they were ever confronted with such a situation, my guess is that they would say that the subcortical brain regions not reflected in the surgeon's measurements had been shown to have previously unrecognized capacities. This would be a bitter pill to swallow in its own right, as it would require revamping theoretical propositions that theretofore had been considered well established, but it probably would be considered preferable to changing the metaphysics.

Unfortunately, it is unlikely that the Reynolds case, or any similar case, will ever force neuroscientists into this corner. It is highly unlikely that a situation would arise in which surgeons would be willing to detect all possible brain activity during surgery of the type Pam underwent. It might even be a practical impossibility in an operating room setting. Even if that somehow could be accomplished, we still have the problem of determining whether the NDE really took place during "brain death." Perhaps someday we could figure out how to overcome these technical and ethical problems, but it is not likely anytime soon. In the meantime, it is important to keep in mind that in many areas of science, including parapsychology, evidence is often a matter of degree (Palmer, 1987). By this standard, I think we can say that evidence from the Reynolds case, as well as other evidence reviewed by Kelly et al. (2007) of cognitive feats that appear to transcend the limits of the brain's capabilities, has raised the probability that we do in fact survive death. For instance, Pam Reynold's NDE *might* have occurred during brain death, and that is certainly what the narrative implies. How much this evidence has raised the probability of survival must be determined by each reader, based on his or her own worldview, (subjective) antecedent probabilities, and critical but fair-minded evaluation of the empirical evidence.

REFERENCES

Alvarado, C.S. (1984). Phenomenological aspects of out-of-body experiences: A report of three studies. *Journal of the American Society for Psychical Research, 78,* 219–240.

Augustine, K. (2007). Does paranormal perception occur in near-death experiences? *Journal of Near-Death Studies, 25,* 203–236.

Don, N.S., McDonough, B.E., Moura, G., Warren, C.A., Kawanishi, K., Momita, H., et al. (1998). Effects of "Ayahuasca" on the human EEG. *Journal of Phytomedicine, 5,* 87–96.

Gauld, A. (1982). *Mediumship and survival: A century of investigations.* London: William Heinemann.

Hasted, J. (1981). *The metal-benders*. London: Routledge & Kegan Paul.

John, E.R., et al. (2001). Invariant reversible QEEG effects of anesthetics. *Consciousness and Cognition, 10,* 165–183.

Kelly, E.F., Kelly, E.W., Crabtree, A., Gauld, A., Grosso, M., & Greyson, B. (2007). *Irreducible mind: Toward a psychology for the 21st century.* Lanham, MD: Rowman & Littlefield.

May, E.C. (1995). AC technical trials: Inspiration for the target entropy concept. *Proceedings of the Parapsychological Association, 38,* 193–211.

Morris, R.M., Harary, S.B., Janis, J., Hartwell, J., & Roll W.G. (1978). Studies of communication during out-of-body experiences. *Journal of the American Society for Psychical Research, 72,* 1–21.

Osis, K., & McCormick, D. (1980). Kinetic effects at the ostensible location of an out-of-body projection during perceptual testing. *Journal of the American Society for Psychical Research, 74,* 319–329.

Palmer, J. (1975). Some recent trends in survival research. *Parapsychology Review, 6*(3), 15–17.

Palmer, J. (1978). Extrasensory perception: Research findings. In S. Krippner (Ed.), *Advances in parapsychological research 2: Extrasensory perception* (pp. 59–243). New York: Plenum.

Palmer, J. (1987). Have we established psi? *Journal of the American Society for Psychical Research, 81,* 111–123.

Palmer, J. (1989). Confronting the experimenter effect. *Parapsychology Review, 20*(4), 1–4; *20*(5), 1–5.

Palmer, J. (1997). The challenge of experimenter psi. *European Journal of Parapsychology, 13,* 110-122.

Ring, K. (1980). *Life at death: A scientific investigation of the near-death experience.* New York: Coward, McCann, & Geohegan.

Sabom, M.A. (1998). *Light & death: One doctor's fascinating account of near-death experience.* Grand Rapids, MI: Zondervan.

Sabom, M.A. (2007). Commentary on "Does paranormal perception occur in near-death experiences?" *Journal of Near-Death Studies, 25,* 257–260.

Sheldrake, R. (1999). *Dogs that know when their owners are coming home: And other unexplained powers of animals.* New York: Three Rivers Press.

Sidgwick, Mrs. H. (1891–1892). On the evidence for clairvoyance. Part I. *Proceedings of the Society for Psychical Research, 7,* 30–99.

Tart, C.T. (1968). A psychophysiological study of out-of-body experiences in a selected subject. *Journal of the American Society for Psychical Research, 62,* 3–27.

Tart, C.T. (2007). Commentary on "Does paranormal perception occur in near-death experiences?" *Journal of Near-Death Studies, 25,* 251–256.

In: Psychological Scientific Perspectives on Out of Body… ISBN: 978-1-60741-705-7
Editor: Craig D. Murray

Chapter 12

ENDLESS CONSCIOUSNESS: A CONCEPT BASED ON SCIENTIFIC STUDIES ON NEAR-DEATH EXPERIENCE

Pim van Lommel[1]

ABSTRACT

Some people who have survived a life-threatening crisis report an extraordinary conscious experience. Near-death experiences (NDEs) occur with increasing frequency because of improved survival rates resulting from modern techniques of resuscitation. The content of an NDE and the effects on patients seem similar worldwide, across all cultures and all times. Several theories have been proposed to explain an NDE. The challenge to find a common explanation for the cause and content of an NDE is complicated by the fact that an NDE can be experienced during various circumstances, such as during severe injury of the brain as in cardiac arrest, as well as on occasions where the brain seems to function normally. Despite the finding that these experiences are reported during various physiological and psychological circumstances, the NDE is mostly remembered following a period of a functional loss of all functions of the brain (clinical death). But there is no scientific explanation of why only a small percentage of patients report an NDE following a critical medical situation. Since the publication of several prospective studies on NDE in survivors of cardiac arrest, with strikingly similar results and conclusions, the phenomenon of the NDE can no longer be scientifically ignored. It is an authentic experience which cannot be simply reduced to imagination, fear of death, hallucination, psychosis, the use of drugs, or oxygen deficiency, and people appear to be permanently changed by an NDE during a cardiac arrest of only some minutes duration. According to these studies, the current materialistic view of the relationship between the brain and consciousness held by most physicians, philosophers and psychologists is too restricted for a proper understanding of this phenomenon. There are good reasons to assume that our consciousness does not always coincide with the functioning of our brain: enhanced consciousness can sometimes be experienced separately from the body.

[1] See www.pimvanlommel.nl

Introduction

An NDE can be defined as the reported memory of a range of impressions during a special state of consciousness, including a number of special elements such as an out-of-body experience, pleasant feelings, seeing a tunnel, a light, deceased relatives, or a life review. Many circumstances are described during which NDEs are reported, such as cardiac arrest (clinical death), shock after loss of blood, traumatic brain injury or intra-cerebral haemorrhage, near-drowning or asphyxia, but also in serious diseases not immediately life-threatening, during isolation, depression or meditation, or without any obvious reason. Similar experiences to near-death ones can occur during the terminal phase of illness, and are called deathbed visions. Furthermore, so-called "fear-death" experiences are mainly reported after situations in which death seemed unavoidable like serious traffic or mountaineering accidents. The NDE is transformational, causing enhanced intuitive sensibility, profound changes of life-insight, and the loss of fear of death. The subjective nature and absence of a frame of reference for this experience lead to individual, cultural, and religious factors determining the vocabulary used to describe and interpret the experience.

According to a recent randomized inquiry the USA and in Germany about 4% of the total population in the western world experienced an NDE (Gallup & Proctor, 1982; Schmied, Knoblaub, & Schnettler, 1999). So, more than 9 million people in the USA and more than 2 million people in the UK must have had this experience. An NDE seems to be a relatively regularly occurring, and to many physicians an inexplicable phenomenon and hence an ignored result of survival in a critical medical situation. Why do we physicians hardly ever hear a patient tell about his or her near-death experience? Patients are reluctant to share their experience with others because of the negative responses they get. As a doctor you have to be open to hear about an NDE, patients must feel that you trust them, that you can listen without any comment or prejudice.

A Near-Death Experience

This is the story of a woman who experienced a near-death experience during delivery:

> "Suddenly I realise I am looking down at a woman who is lying on a bed with her legs in supports. I see the nurses and doctors panicking, I see a lot of blood on the bed and on the floor, I see large hands pressing down hard on the woman's belly, and then I see the woman giving birth to a child. The child is immediately taken to another room. I know it is dead. The nurses look dejected. Everybody is waiting. My head is knocked back hard when the pillow is pulled away. Once again, I witness a great commotion. Swift as an arrow I fly through a dark tunnel. I am engulfed by an overwhelming feeling of peace and bliss. I hear wonderful music. I see beautiful colours and gorgeous flowers in all sorts of colours in a large meadow. At the far end is a beautiful, clear, warm light. This is where I must go. I see a figure in a light garment. This figure is waiting for me and extends her hand. I feel that I am warmly and lovingly expected. We proceed hand in hand to the beautiful and warm light. Then she lets go of my hand and turns around. I feel that I am pulled back. I notice a nurse slapping me hard on my cheeks and calling me".
>
> "Once returned from that beautiful world, that beautiful experience, my reception here in this world was cold, frosty and above all loveless. The nurse I tried to share my beautiful

experience with dismissed it by saying I would soon receive some more medication so I could sleep soundly and then it would be all over. All over? I did not want that at all. On the contrary, I did not want it to be over. I wanted to go back. The gynaecologist told me I was still young, I could have plenty more children and I should just move on and focus on the future. I stopped telling my story. Just to find words for my experience was difficult enough, how could words express what I had experienced? But what else could I do? Where could I take my story? What was the matter with me? Had I gone mad? And I kept silent. I spent years dedicated to a silent search. When, eventually, I found a book in the library with a report of an NDE, I could hardly imagine that I had had such an experience. Even I had stopped believing myself. Only very, very gradually did I come to have the courage and the strength to believe myself, to trust my experience, so I could start accepting and integrating it in my life".

How it Started

As a cardiologist I had the privilege to meet many patients who were willing to share their near-death experience (NDE) with me. The first time this happened was in 1969. In the coronary care unit the alarm suddenly went off. The monitor showed that the electrocardiogram (ECG) of a patient with a myocardial infarction had become flat. The man had a cardiac arrest. After two electric shocks and a spell of unconsciousness lasting some four minutes, the patient regained consciousness, much to the relief of the nursing staff and attendant doctor. That attendant doctor was me. I had started my cardiology training that year. Following the successful resuscitation everyone was pleased, except the patient. To everyone's surprise he was extremely disappointed. He spoke of a tunnel, of colours, of a light, of a beautiful landscape and of music. He was extremely emotional. The term near-death experience did not yet exist, nor had I ever heard of people having any recollection of the period of their cardiac arrest. Whilst studying for my degree, I had learnt that such a thing is in fact impossible: being unconscious means not being aware, and that applies to people suffering a cardiac arrest or patients in a coma. In the event of a cardiac arrest, a patient is unconscious, he has stopped breathing and he has no palpable pulse or blood pressure. At such a moment, it should be simply impossible to be conscious or to have memories because all brain function has ceased.

Although I had never forgotten the successfully resuscitated patient from 1969 with his memories of the period of his cardiac arrest, I had never done anything with the experience. This changed in 1986 when I read a book by George Ritchie about near-death experiences with the title Return from Tomorrow (Ritchie, 1978). When suffering double pneumonia as a medical student in 1943, Ritchie had experienced a period of clinical death. At the time, antibiotics such as penicillin were not yet widely used. Following a period of very high fever and extreme tightness of the chest, he passed away: he stopped breathing and his pulse had gone. He was pronounced dead by a doctor and covered with a sheet. But a male nurse was so upset by the death of this medical student that he managed to persuade the attendant doctor to administer an adrenalin injection in the chest near the heart – a most unusual procedure in those days. Having been 'dead' for more than nine minutes, George Ritchie regained consciousness to the immense surprise of the doctor and nurse. It emerged that during his spell of unconsciousness, the period in which he had been pronounced dead, he had had an extremely deep experience of which he could recollect a great many details. At first he was quite unable and afraid to talk about it. Later he wrote his book about what happened to him in those nine minutes. And after graduation, he shared his experiences with medical students in psychiatry lectures. One of the students attending these lectures was Raymond Moody, who was so intrigued by this story that he started looking into experiences that may occur during critical medical situations. In 1975 he wrote the book Life after Life (Moody, 1975), which became a global best-seller. In this book Moody first used the term near-death experience (NDE).

After reading George Ritchie's book I kept asking myself how someone can possibly experience consciousness during cardiac arrest and indeed whether this is a common occurrence. That is why, in 1986, I started systematically asking all the patients at my out-patient clinic who had ever undergone resuscitation whether they had any recollection of the period of their cardiac arrest. I was more than a little surprised to hear, within the space of two years, 12 reports of such a near-death experience among just over 50 survivors of cardiac arrest. Since that first time in 1969, I had not heard any other such reports. I had not enquired after these experiences either, because I had not been open to them. But all these reports I was hearing now roused my curiosity. After all, according to current medical knowledge it is impossible to experience consciousness when one's heart has stopped beating.

Questions

For me it all started with curiosity. With asking questions; with seeking to explain certain objective findings and subjective experiences. The phenomenon of near-death experience raised a number of fundamental questions. An NDE is a special state of consciousness that occurs during an imminent or actual period of physical, psychological or emotional death. But how and why does an NDE occur? How does the content of an NDE come about? Why does a person's life change so radically after an NDE? I was unable to accept some of the answers to these questions, because they seemed incomplete, incorrect or unfounded. I grew up in an academic environment in which I had been taught that there is a reductionist and materialist explanation for everything. And up until that point, I had always accepted this as indisputably true.

Some scientists do not believe in questions that cannot be answered, but they do believe in wrongly formulated questions. The year 2005 saw the publication of a special anniversary issue of the journal *Science*, featuring 125 questions that scientists have so far failed to solve (Kennedy & Norman, 2005). The most important unanswered question, What is the universe made of?, was followed by: What is the biological basis of consciousness? I would reformulate this second question as follows: Is there a biological basis of consciousness (at all)? We can also distinguish between both temporary and timeless aspects of our consciousness. This prompts the following question: Is it possible to speak of a beginning of our consciousness and will our consciousness ever end?

In order to answer these questions, we need a better understanding of the relationship between brain function and consciousness. We shall have to start by examining whether there is any indication that consciousness can be experienced during sleep, general anaesthesia, coma, brain death, clinical death, the process of dying and, finally, after confirmed death. If the answers to any of these questions are positive, we must look for scientific explanations and scrutinise the relationship between brain function and consciousness in these different situations. By studying everything that has been thought and written about death throughout history, in all times, cultures and religions, we may be able to form a different or better picture of death. But we may achieve the same on the basis of findings from recent scientific research into near-death experiences. It has emerged that most people lose all fear of death after an NDE. Their experience tells them that death is not the end of everything and that life goes on in one way or another. According to people with an NDE, death is nothing other than a different way of being with an enhanced and broadened consciousness, which is everywhere at once because it is no longer tied to a body. This is what someone wrote to me after his NDE:

> 'It is outside my domain to discuss something that can only be proven by death. However, for me personally this experience was decisive in convincing me that consciousness endures beyond the grave. Death turned out to be not death, but another form of life.'

The Dutch Prospective Study on NDE in Survivors of Cardiac Arrest

In order to obtain more reliable data to corroborate or refute the existing theories on the cause and content of an NDE, we needed a properly designed scientific study. This was the reason why in 1988 Ruud van Wees and Vincent Meyers, both psychologists who wrote their doctoral theses on NDE, and I, a cardiologist with an interest in the subject, started designing a prospective study in the Netherlands (van Lommel, van Wees, Meyers, & Elfferich, 2001). At that point, no large-scale prospective studies into NDE had been undertaken anywhere in the world. Our study aimed to include all consecutive patients who had survived a cardiac arrest in one of the 10 participating Dutch hospitals. In other words, this prospective study would only be carried out among patients with a proven life-threatening crisis. All of these patients would have died of their cardiac arrest had they not been resuscitated within five to ten minutes. This kind of design also creates a control group of patients who have survived a cardiac arrest but who have no recollection of the period of unconsciousness. In a prospective study such patients are asked, within a few days of their resuscitation, whether they have any recollection of the period of their cardiac arrest, i.e. of the period of their unconsciousness. All patients' medical and other data are carefully recorded before, during and after their resuscitation.

We had a record of the electrocardiogram, or ECG, for all patients included in our study. An ECG displays the electrical activity of the heart. In cardiac arrest patients this ECG record always displays a normally lethal arrhythmia (ventricular fibrillation) or an asystole (a flat line on the ECG). In the event of resuscitation outside the hospital we were given the ECG done by the ambulance staff. Following successful resuscitation we carefully recorded the demographic data of all patients, including age, sex, education, religion, foreknowledge of NDE and whether or not they had had an earlier NDE. They were also asked whether they had been afraid just before their cardiac arrest. Likewise, we carefully recorded all medical information, like: what was the duration of the actual cardiac arrest? What was the duration of unconsciousness? How often did the patient require resuscitation? What medication, and in what dosage, was administered to the patient before, during and after resuscitation? We also recorded how many days after resuscitation the interview took place, whether the patient was lucid during the interview and whether his or her short-term memory was functioning well.

Within four years, between 1988 and 1992, 344 successive patients who had undergone a total of 509 successful resuscitations were included in the study. In other words, all the patients in our study had been clinically dead. Clinical death is defined as the period of unconsciousness caused by lack of oxygen in the brain (anoxia) because of the arrest of circulation, breathing or both, as caused by cardiac arrest in patients with an acute myocardial infarction. If, in this situation, no resuscitation is initiated, the brain cells will be irreversibly damaged within five to ten minutes and the patient will always die.

A longitudinal study into life changes was based on interviews after two and eight years with all patients who had reported an NDE and who were still alive, as well as with a control group of post-resuscitation patients who were matched for age and sex, but who had not reported an NDE. The question was whether the customary changes in attitude to life after an NDE were the result of surviving a cardiac arrest or whether these changes were caused by the experience of an NDE. This question had never been subject to scientific and systematic research before. The Dutch study was published in *The Lancet* in December 2001(van Lommel, van Wees, Meyers, & Elfferich, 2001).

If patients reported memories from the period of unconsciousness, the experiences were scored according to a certain index, the WCEI, or "weighted core experience index" Ring, 1980). The higher the number of elements reported, the higher the score and the deeper the NDE. Our study found that 282 patients (82 per cent) had no recollection of the period of their unconsciousness, whereas 62 patients – 18 per cent of the 344 patients – reported an NDE. Of these 62 patients with memories, 21 patients (6 per cent) had some recollection; having experienced only some elements, they had a superficial NDE with a low score. And 42 patients (12 per cent) reported a core experience: 18 patients had a moderately deep NDE, 17 patients reported a deep NDE and 6 patients a very deep NDE.

Half of the patients with an NDE were aware of being dead and had positive emotions, 30 per cent had a tunnel experience, observed a celestial landscape or met with deceased persons, approximately a quarter had an out-of-body experience, communication with 'the light' or perception of colours, 13 per cent had a life review and 8 per cent experienced the presence of a border. In other words, all the familiar elements of an NDE were reported in our study, with the exception of a frightening or negative NDE.

Are there any reasons why some people do but most people do not recollect the period of their unconsciousness? In order to answer this question we compared the recorded data of the 62 patients with an NDE to the data of the 282 patients without an NDE. To our big surprise we did not identify any significant differences in the duration of the cardiac arrest, no differences in the duration of unconsciousness and no differences in whether or not intubation was necessary for artificial respiration in seriously ill patients who remained in a coma for days or weeks after a complicated resuscitation. Nor did we find differences in the thirty patients who had a cardiac arrest during electrophysiological stimulation (EPS) in the catheterization laboratory and whose heart rhythms were always re-established via defibrillation (an electric shock) within fifteen to thirty seconds. So we failed to identify any differences between the patients with a very long or a very brief cardiac arrest. The degree or gravity of the lack of oxygen in the brain (anoxia) appeared to be irrelevant. Likewise, it was established that medication played no role. Most patients suffering a myocardial infarction receive morphine-type painkillers, while people who are put on a respirator following complicated resuscitation are given extremely high doses of sedatives. A psychological cause such as the infrequently noted fear of death does not affect the occurrence of an NDE either, although it did affect the depth of the experience. Whether or not patients had heard or read anything about NDE in the past made no difference either. Any kind of religious belief, or indeed its absence in non-religious people or atheists, was irrelevant and the same was true for the standard of education reached. Factors that do affect the frequency of an NDE are an age below 60 and if patients required several resuscitations during their stay in hospital, the chances of an NDE report were greater. Remarkably, we found that patients who had had an NDE in the past also reported significantly more frequent NDEs in our study. A complicated resuscitation can result in a long coma and most patients who have been unconscious on a respirator for days or weeks are more likely to suffer short-term memory defects as a result of permanent brain damage. These patients reported significantly fewer NDEs in our study. This suggests that a good memory is essential for remembering an NDE.

We were particularly surprised to find no medical explanation for the occurrence of an NDE. All the patients in our study had been clinically dead and only a small percentage reported an enhanced consciousness with lucid thoughts, emotions, memories, and sometimes perception from a position outside and above their lifeless body while doctors and nursing staff were carrying out resuscitation. If there were a physiological explanation, such as a lack of oxygen in the brain (anoxia), for the occurrence of this enhanced consciousness, one might have expected all patients in our study to have reported an NDE. They had all been unconscious as a result of their cardiac arrest, which caused the loss of blood pressure and the cessation of breathing and all physical and brain-stem reflexes. And it is well established that people without any lack of oxygen in the brain like in depression or meditation also can experience an 'NDE'. Likewise the gravity of the medical situation, such as long-term coma after a complicated resuscitation, failed to explain why patients did or did not report an NDE, except in the case of lingering memory defects. The psychological explanation is doubtful because most patients did not experience any fear of death during their cardiac arrest as it occurred so suddenly they failed to notice it. In most cases they were left without any recollection of their resuscitation. This is borne out by Greyson's (2003) study, which only collected the subjective data of patients after their resuscitation and showed that most patients did not even realise they had had a cardiac arrest. This is similar to fainting. When people regain consciousness they have no clear idea of what happened. A pharmacological explanation could be excluded as well, as the medication had no effect on whether or not patients reported an NDE.

The later interviews in the longitudinal study were conducted using a standardised inventory featuring 34 life-change questions Ring, 1984). Among the 74 patients who consented to be interviewed after two years, 13 of the total of 34 factors listed in the questionnaire turned out to be significantly different for people with or without an NDE. The second interviews showed that in people with an NDE fear of death in particular had significantly decreased while belief in an afterlife had significantly increased. We then compared these 13 factors, which had been so significantly different between the two groups with and without NDE after two years, in the same patients after eight years. It struck us that after eight years the people without NDE were also undergoing unmistakable processes of transformation. Nevertheless, clear differences remained between people with and without NDE, although by now these differences had become a little less marked. We were also surprised to find that the processes of transformation that had begun in people with an NDE after two years had clearly intensified after eight years. The same was true for the people without NDE. In summary, we could say that eight years after their cardiac arrest all patients had changed in many respects, showing more interest in nature, the environment and social justice, displaying more love and emotions and being more supportive and involved in family life. Nevertheless the people who had experienced an NDE during their cardiac arrest continued to be clearly different. In particular, they were less afraid of death and had a stronger belief in an afterlife. We saw in them a greater interest in spirituality and questions about the purpose of life, as well as a greater acceptance of and love for oneself and others. Likewise, they displayed a greater appreciation of ordinary things, whereas their interest in possessions and power had decreased. The conversations also revealed that people had acquired enhanced intuitive feelings after an NDE, along with a strong sense of connectedness with others and with nature. Or, as many of them put it, they had acquired 'paranormal gifts'. The sudden occurrence of this enhanced intuition can be quite problematic, as people suddenly have a very acute sense of others, which can be extremely intimidating, and also experience clairvoyance, prophetic feelings and visions. This intuitive sense can be quite extreme, with people 'sensing' feelings and sadness in others, or having the sense of knowing when someone will die – which usually proved to be accurate. The integration and acceptance of an NDE is a process that may take many years because of its far-reaching impact on people's pre-NDE understanding of life and value system. Finally, it is quite remarkable to see a cardiac arrest lasting just a few minutes give rise to such a lifelong process of transformation.

Only the large-scale Dutch study allowed for statistical analysis of the factors that may determine whether or not an NDE occurs. It thus ruled out the aforementioned possible physiological, psychological and pharmacological explanations for the occurrence of an NDE. Our study was also the first to include a longitudinal component with interviews after two and eight years, which allowed us to compare the processes of transformation between people with and without an NDE. We identified a distinct pattern of change in people with an NDE and revealed that integrating these changes into daily life is a long and arduous process. And we reached the inevitable conclusion that patients experienced all the aforementioned NDE elements during the period of their cardiac arrest, during the total cessation of blood supply to the brain. Nevertheless, the question how this could be possible remained unanswered.

Other Prospective Studies on NDE

Bruce Greyson, who published a prospective study in 116 survivors of cardiac arrest in the USA, found that 15.5 per cent of the patients reported an NDE: 9.5 per cent reported a core NDE and 6 per cent a superficial NDE (Greyson, 2003). He writes that "no one physiological or psychological model by itself could explain all the common features of an NDE. The paradoxical occurrence of a heightened, lucid awareness and logical thought processes during a period of impaired cerebral perfusion raises particular perplexing questions for our current understanding of consciousness and its relation to brain function. A clear sensorium and complex perceptual processes during a period of apparent clinical death challenge the concept that consciousness is localized exclusively in the brain." (Greyson, 2003: p.275)

The British prospective study by Sam Parnia and Peter Fenwick (Parnia, Waller, Yeates, & Fenwick, 2001) included 63 patients who survived their cardiac arrest. They found in their study that 11 per cent reported an NDE: 6.3 per cent reported a core NDE, and 4.8 per cent a superficial NDE. They write that the NDE-reports suggest that the NDE occurs during the period of unconsciousness. This is a surprising conclusion, in their view, because "when the brain is so dysfunctional that the patient is deeply comatose, those cerebral structures, which underpin subjective experience and memory, must be severely impaired. Complex experiences such as are reported in the NDE should not arise or be retained in memory. Such patients would be expected to have no subjective experience, as was the case in the vast majority of patients who survive cardiac arrest, since all centres in the brain that are responsible for generating conscious experiences have stopped functioning as a result of the lack of oxygen." (Parnia, Waller, Yeates, & Fenwick, 2001: p.154) Another, frequently cited explanation might be that the observed experiences occur during the early phases of the cessation or during the recovery of consciousness. Parnia and Fenwick, however, claim that the verifiable elements of an out-of-body experience during unconsciousness, such as patients' reports on their resuscitation, render this extremely unlikely.

Over a period of four years Penny Sartori carried out an even smaller study into NDE in 39 survivors of cardiac arrest in the UK (Sartori, 2006). She found that 23 per cent reported an NDE: 18 per cent reported a core NDE, and 5 per cent a superficial NDE. She concludes that "according to mainstream science, it is quite impossible to find a scientific explanation for the NDE as long as we 'believe' that consciousness is only a side effect of a functioning brain." (Sartori, 2006: p.25) The fact that people report lucid experiences in their consciousness when brain activity has ceased is, in her view, difficult to reconcile with current medical opinion.

Theories about NDE

With our current medical and scientific concepts it seems indeed impossible to explain all aspects of the subjective experiences as reported by patients with an NDE during a transient loss of all functions of the brain. Scientific studies into the phenomenon of NDE highlights the limitations of our current medical and neurophysiological ideas about the various aspects of human consciousness and the relationship between consciousness and memories on the one hand and the brain on the other. The prevailing paradigm holds that memories and consciousness are produced by large groups of neurons or neural networks. For want of evidence for the aforementioned explanations for the cause and content of an NDE the commonly accepted, but never proven concept that consciousness is localised in the brain should be questioned. After all, how can an extremely lucid consciousness be experienced outside the body at a time when the brain has a transient loss of all functions during a period of clinical death, even with a flat EEG? Furthermore, even blind people have described veridical perceptions during out-of-body experiences at the time of their NDE. Another theory about NDE holds that NDE might be a changing state of consciousness (transcendence, or the theory of continuity), in which memories, self-identity, and cognition, with emotion, function independently from the unconscious body, and retain the possibility of non-sensory perception. Obviously, during NDE enhanced consciousness is experienced independently from the normal body-linked waking consciousness, during the period of cardiac arrest, during the period of apparent unconsciousness, during the period of clinical death. But how do we know that the EEG is flat in those patients with cardiac arrest, and how can we study this? Through many studies with induced cardiac arrest in both human and animal models cerebral function has been shown to be severely compromised during cardiac arrest, with complete cessation of cerebral flow (Gopalan, Lee, Ikeda, & Birch, 1999), causing sudden loss of consciousness and of all body reflexes, but also with the abolition of brain-stem activity with the loss of the gag reflex and of the corneal reflex, and fixed and dilated pupils are clinical findings in those patients. And also the function of the respiratory centre, located close to the brainstem, fails, resulting in apnoea (no breathing). The electrical activity in the cerebral cortex (but also in the deeper structures of the brain) has been shown to be absent after 10-20 seconds (a flat-line EEG) (De Vries, Bakker, Visser, Diephuis, & Huffelen, 1998; Clute & Levy, 1990; Losasso, Muzzi, Meyer, & Sharbrough, 1992; Parnia & Fenwick, 2002). In acute myocardial infarction the duration of cardiac arrest in the Coronary Care Unit is usually 60-120 seconds, in an out-of-hospital arrest it even takes much longer. So all 562 survivors of cardiac arrest in the four prospective studies on NDE must have had a flat EEG because no patient had been resuscitated within 20 seconds.

The quite often proposed objection that a flat line EEG does not rule out any brain activity, because it is mainly a registration of electrical activity of the cerebral cortex, misses the mark The issue is not whether there is any brain activity of any kind whatsoever, but whether there is brain activity of the specific form regarded by contemporary neuroscience as the necessary condition of conscious experience. And it has been proven that there is no such specific brain activity at all during cardiac arrest. Moreover, although measurable EEG-activity in the brain can be recorded during deep sleep (no-REM phase) or during general anaesthesia, no consciousness is experienced because there is no integration of information and no communication between the different neural networks (Alkire & Miller, 2005; Alkire, Hudetz, & Tononi, 2005; Massimini, Ferrarelli, Huber, Esser, Singh, & Tononi, 2005). So even in circumstances where brain activity can be measured sometimes no consciousness can be experienced. A functioning system for communication between neural networks with integration of information is essential for experiencing consciousness, and this does not occur during cardiac arrest, or not even during deep sleep or general anaesthesia.

Consciousness and Brain Function

For decades, extensive research has been done to localize consciousness and memories inside the brain, so far without success. Also we should ask ourselves how a non-material activity such as concentrated attention or thinking can correspond to an observable (material) reaction in the form of measurable electrical, magnetic, and chemical activity at a certain place in the brain. Neuro-imaging studies have shown these aforesaid activities, with specific areas of the brain becoming metabolically active in response to a thought or feeling. However, although providing evidence for the role of neuronal networks as an intermediary for the manifestation of thoughts (neural correlates), those studies do not necessary imply that those cells also produce the thoughts. A correlation doesn't elucidate anything about cause or result. And how should "unconscious" matter like our brain "produce" consciousness, while the brain only is composed of atoms and molecules in cells with a lot of chemical and electrical processes? We have to admit that it is not possible to reduce consciousness to neural processes as conceived by contemporary neuroscience, because it is still an unproven assumption that consciousness and memories emerge from brain function, and until now there is no scientific evidence for neural correlates of all aspects of subjective experience. Direct evidence of how neurons or neuronal networks could possibly produce the subjective essence of the mind and thoughts is currently lacking. We cannot measure what we think or feel. There are no known examples of neural-perceptual matches, and hence reasons to doubt the truth of the "matching content" doctrine. The assumption in the "matching content" doctrine is that following activation of special neuronal networks you always will have the same content of thoughts or feelings. This seems extremely unlikely, because neural activation is simply neural activation; it only reflects the use of structures. This could be compared with a radio: you can activate the radio by turning it on, and you can activate a certain wavelength by tuning in on a special channel, but you will not have any influence on the content of the programme you are going to hear. Activating the radio does not influence the content of the programme, and neural activation alone does not explain the content of emotions or sensations.

Most of the people who carry out research into consciousness, such as neuroscientists, psychologists, psychiatrists and philosophers, are still of the opinion that there is a materialist and reductionist explanation for consciousness. The well-known philosopher Daniel Dennett believes, and many with him, that consciousness is nothing other than matter (Dennett, 1991), and that our subjective experience that our consciousness is something purely personal and differs from someone else's consciousness is merely an illusion. According to these scientists, consciousness originates entirely from the matter that constitutes our brain. If this were true then everything we experience in our consciousness would be nothing but the expression of a machine controlled by classical physics and chemistry, and our behaviour the inexorable outcome of nerve cell activity in our brain. Obviously the notion that all subjective thoughts and feelings are produced by nothing other than the brain's activity also means that it is an illusion to believe in free will. This viewpoint has serious implications for concepts such as moral responsibility and personal freedom.

About Concepts in Science

When empirical scientific studies discover phenomena or facts that are inconsistent with current scientific theories, so-called anomalies, these new facts must not be denied, suppressed or even ridiculed, as is still quite common these days. In the event of new findings the existing theories ought to be developed or adjusted, and if necessary rejected and replaced. We need new ways of thinking and new kinds of science to study consciousness and acquire a better understanding of the effects of consciousness. Some scientists, such as the philosopher Chalmers, are more receptive and take consciousness seriously:

> 'Consciousness poses the most baffling problems in the science of the mind. There is nothing that we know more intimately than conscious experience, but there is nothing that is harder to explain.' (Chalmers, 1995: p.200).

Chalmers has specialised in the problem of consciousness and has written a first-class review of the various theories that seek to explain the relationship between consciousness and the brain (Chalmers, 2002).

In the past, too, new kinds of science developed when prevailing scientific concepts could no longer explain certain phenomena. Sir William Lawrence Bragg has said:

> "The important thing in science is not so much to obtain new facts as to discover new ways of thinking about them".

At the start of the previous century, for instance, quantum physics emerged because certain findings could no longer be accounted for with classical physics. Quantum physics upset the established view of our material world. The slow acceptance of the new insights provided by quantum physics can be attributed to the materialist worldview we have been raised with. According to some quantum physicists, quantum physics even assigns to our consciousness a decisive role in creating and experiencing the physical world as we perceive it. This not yet commonly accepted interpretation holds that our picture of reality is based on the information received by our consciousness. This transforms modern science into a subjective science with a fundamental role for consciousness. The quantum physicist Werner Heisenberg (1901-1976) formulates it as follows:

> 'Science no longer is in the position of observer of nature, but rather recognizes itself as part of the interplay between man and nature. The scientific method ... changes and transforms its object: the procedure can no longer keep its distance from the object.' (Heisenberg, 1955: p. 21)

For me science means asking questions with an open mind. Science should be the search for explaining new mysteries, rather than stick with old concepts. He, who has never changed his mind because he could not accept new concepts, has rarely learned something. We desperately need a real paradigm shift in science, and I sincerely hope that quantum physicist Max Planck was wrong when he said in 1934:

> "A new scientific truth does not triumph by convincing its opponents and making them see the light, but rather because its opponents eventually die, and a new generation grows up that is familiar with it." (Planck, 1948: 33-34).

In my opinion, current science must reconsider its hypotheses about the nature of perceptible reality, because these ideas have led to the neglect or denial of significant areas of consciousness. Current science usually starts from a reality based solely on objective, physical phenomena. Yet at the same time one can (intuitively) sense that besides objective, sensory perception there is a role for subjective aspects such as feelings, inspiration and intuition. As stated before, current scientific techniques are incapable of measuring or demonstrating the content of thoughts, feelings and emotions. A purely materialist analysis of a living being cannot reveal the content of our consciousness. I believe and hope that in the near future modern science will include research on subjective experiences like those that occur in our consciousness, and that we will accept non-local concepts to understand how we are interconnected with each other and also with nature.

Non-Local Consciousness

So it is indeed a scientific challenge to discuss new hypotheses that could explain the reported interconnectedness with the consciousness of other persons and of deceased relatives, to explain the possibility to experience instantaneously and simultaneously (non-locality) a review and a preview of someone's life in a dimension without our conventional body-linked concept of time and space, where all past, present and future events exist, and the possibility to have clear and enhanced consciousness with memories, with self-identity, with cognition, with emotion, with the possibility of perception out and above the lifeless body, and even with the experience of the conscious return into the body, which is experienced as something very oppressive. They regain consciousness in their body and realize that they are "locked up" in their damaged body, meaning again all the pain and restriction of their disease. And it is important to mention that until now it has been impossible to induce a real out-of-body experience with veridical perception from a position out and above the body by any method whatsoever, despite incorrect suggestions about this possibility in the medical literature (Van Lommel, 2007).

In some articles (Van Lommel, 2004; 2006) and in my recent book (Van Lommel, 2007) I describe a concept in which our endless consciousness with declarative memories finds its origin in, and is stored in a non-local space as wave-fields of information, and the cortex only serves as a relay station for parts of these wave-fields of consciousness to be received into or as our waking consciousness. The latter belongs to our physical body. Thus there are two complementary aspects of consciousness, which cannot be reduced one to the other, and the function of neuronal networks should be regarded as receivers and conveyors, not as retainers of consciousness and memories. In this concept, consciousness is not rooted in the measurable domain of physics, our manifest world. This also means that the wave aspect of our indestructible consciousness in the non-local space that is inherently immeasurable by physical means. However, the physical aspect of consciousness, which originates from the wave aspect of our consciousness through collapse of the wave function, can be measured by means of neuro-imaging techniques like EEG, fMRI, and PET-scan. This non-local aspect of consciousness can be compared to gravitational fields, where only the physical effects can be measured, and the fields themselves are not directly demonstrable.

Based on my NDE-research I conclude that our waking consciousness, which we experience as our daily consciousness, is only a complementary aspect of our whole and endless non-local consciousness. This consciousness is based on indestructible and constant evolving fields of information, where all knowledge, wisdom and unconditional love are present and available, and these fields of consciousness are stored in a dimension beyond our concept of time and space, with non-local interconnectedness. One could call this our higher consciousness, divine consciousness or cosmic consciousness.

Finally, an NDE is both an existential crisis and an intense lesson in life. People change after an NDE as it gives them a conscious experience of a dimension in which time and distance play no role, in which past and future can be glimpsed, where they feel complete and healed and where they experience unlimited knowledge and unconditional love. These life changes mainly spring from the insight that love and compassion for oneself, for others and for nature are major prerequisites for life. Following an NDE people realise that everything and everyone is connected, that every thought has an effect on both oneself and the other, and that our consciousness continues beyond physical death. People realise that death is not the end.

CONCLUSION

There are still more questions than answers, but, based on the aforementioned theoretical aspects of the obviously experienced continuity of our consciousness, we finally should consider the possibility that death, like birth, may well be a mere passing from one state of consciousness to another. The inevitable conclusion that that there is a continuity of consciousness because consciousness can be experienced independently of brain function might well induce a huge change in the scientific paradigm in western medicine, and could have practical implications in actual medical and ethical problems such as the care for comatose or dying patients, euthanasia, abortion, and the removal of organs for transplantation from somebody in the dying process with a beating heart in a warm body but with a diagnosis of brain death. Such understanding also fundamentally changes one's opinion about death, because of the almost unavoidable conclusion that at the time of physical death consciousness will continue to be experienced in another dimension, in which all past, present and future is enclosed. "Death is only the end of our physical aspects". However, research on NDE cannot give us the irrefutable scientific proof of this conclusion, because people with an NDE did not quite die, but they all were very close to death, and without a functioning brain. But, as I have explained, it has been scientifically proven that, during NDE enhanced consciousness was experienced independently of brain function. Quoting from a recent death announcement:

> "All what you have, falls into decay, but what you are lives on, beyond time and space".

So we have a body and we are conscious. Without a body we still can have conscious experiences. Recently someone with an NDE wrote me:

> 'I can live without my body, but apparently my body cannot live without me'.

Scientific studies on NDE challenge our current concepts about consciousness and its relation with brain function, and its conclusions are also important for many aspects in healthcare.

Regarding what we can learn from people who are willing to share their NDE with others, I would like to quote Dag Hammerskjöld (1964): "Our ideas about death define how we live our life". Because as long as we believe that death is the end of everything we are, we will give our energy towards the temporary and material aspects of our life. In our short-sightedness and our ignorance we forget to reflect on the future of our planet, where our children and our grandchildren will have to live, and survive. We forget about sustainability as we are now destroying and exhausting systematically our planet, just because we are living in a competitive and materialistic society. We should realize that the harm we cause to each other and to nature ultimately is harming ourselves, because we as humans are not only intensively interconnected ('entangled') with each other, but also with animals and plants living on our endangered earth. We should stop thinking and acting as if we are better than others, because this will always be at the expense of children and other weak and delicate creatures around the world. We should recognise that our view of the world is wrong, because we do not realize that the world, as we see it, only derives its (subjective) reality from our consciousness. Because it is only our consciousness that is determining how we see this world. If we are in love, the world around us is beautiful, when we are depressed our world is like hell, and when we are frightened (made terrified by politicians and by the press) our world will be full of terror. 'The mind in its own place, and in itself, can make a heaven of hell,' wrote John Milton even in 1667 in his poem 'Paradise Lost'. So we have to change our personal consciousness to change the world and to change the way we live now, as Ervin Laszlo (2003) clearly explains in his book 'You can change the world'. It will require a huge change in consciousness indeed. We should all feel the responsibility for this change.

REFERENCES

Alkire, M.T. & Miller, J. (2005). General anesthesia and the neural correlates of consciousness. *Progress in Brain Research, 150,* 229-244.

Alkire, M.T., Hudetz, A.G., & Tononi, G. (2008). Consciousness and anesthesia. *Science, 322 (5903),* 876-880.

Chalmers, D.J. (1995). Facing up to the problem of consciousness. *Journal of Consciousness Studies*, *3(1),* 200-219.

Chalmers, D.J. (2002). *Consciousness and its place in nature.* In: *Philosophy of mind: Classical and contemporary readings.* Oxford University Press. Also at: http://consc.net/papers/nature.html

Clute, H. & Levy, W.J. (1990). Electroencephalographic changes during brief cardiac arrest in humans. *Anesthesiology, 73,* 821-825.

Dennett, D. (1991). *Consciousness explained.* Little, Brown and Co., Boston, London.

De Vries, J.W., Bakker, P.F.A., Visser, G.H., Diephuis, J.C., & Van Huffelen, A.C. (1998). Changes in cerebral oxygen uptake and cerebral electrical activity during defibrillation threshold testing. *Anesthesia & Analgesia, 87,* 16-20.

Gallup, G., & Proctor, W. (1982). *Adventures in immortality: A look beyond the threshold of death.* New York: McGraw-Hill.

Gopalan, K.T, Lee, J., Ikeda, S., & Burch, C.M. (1999). Cerebral blood flow velocity during repeatedly induced ventricular fibrillation. *Journal of Clinical Anesthesia, 11(4),* 290-295.

Greyson, B. (2003). Incidence and correlates of near-death experiences in a cardiac care unit. *General Hospital Psychiatry, 25,* 269-276.

Hammerskjöld D. (1964) *Markings*, translated by Leif Sjöberg and W.H. Auden. London, Faber and Faber, 1964; New York, Knopf, 1964. Originally published in Swedish as *Vägmärken*. Stockholm, Bonniers, 1963.

Heisenberg, W. (1955). *Das Naturbild der heutigen Physik.* Rowohlt, Reinbeck, S. 21.

Heisenberg, W. (1958). *Physics and philosophy.* Harper and Row, New York.

Laszlo, E. (2003). You can change the world- *The global citizen's handbook for living on planet earth.* Select Books, New York.

Losasso, T.J., Muzzi, D.A., Meyer, F.B., & Sharbrough, F.W. (1992). Electroencephalographic monitoring of cerebral function during asystole and successful cardiopulmonary resuscitation. *Anesthesia & Analgesia, 75,* 12-19.

Massimini, M., Ferrarelli, F., Huber, R., Esser, S.K., Singh, H., & Tononi G. (2005). Breakdown of Cortical Effective Connectivity during Sleep. *Science, 309 (5744),* 2228-2232.

Moody, R.A. Jr. (1975). *Life after life*. Covington, G.A.: Mockingbird Books.

Kennedy, D., & Norman, C. (2005). What we don't know. *Science, 309 no. 5731,* 75.

Parnia, S. & Fenwick, P. (2002). Near-death experiences in cardiac arrest: visions of a dying brain or visions of a new science of consciousness. Review article. *Resuscitation, 52,* 5-11.

Parnia, S., Waller, D.G., Yeates, R., & Fenwick, P. (2001). A qualitative and quantitative study of the incidence, features and aetiology of near death experience in cardiac arrest survivors. *Resuscitation, 48,* 149-156.

Planck, M. (1948) *Scientific autobiography and other papers*, trans. F. Gaynor (New York, 1949), pp.33-34

Ring, K. (1980). *Life at death: A scientific investigation of the near-death experience.* New York: Coward, McCann & Geoghegan.

Ring, K. (1984). *Heading toward omega: In search of the meaning of the near-death experience*. New York: Morrow

Ritchie, G.G. (1978). *Return from tomorrow*. Grand Rapids, Michigan: Chosen Books of The Zondervan Corp.

Sartori, P. (2006). The Incidence and Phenomenology of Near-Death Experiences. *Network Review* (Scientific and Medical Network), *90,* 23-25.

Schmied, I., Knoblaub, H., & Schnettler, B. (1999). *Todesnäheerfahrungen in Ost- und Westdeutschland. Ein empirische Untersuchung. In: Todesnähe: Interdisziplinäre Zugänge zu Einem* Außergewöhnlichen Phänomen. Eds. Knoblaub H, Soeffner HG., pp. 65-99. Konstanz: Universitätsverlag Konstanz.

van Lommel P. (2007) *Eindeloos Bewustzijn. Een wetenschappelijke visie op de bijna-dood ervaring*. Ten Have. (publication in other languages will follow in 2009 (in Germany) and 2010 (in USA and UK by Harper Collins): *Endless Consciousness, A Scientific Approach to the Near-Death Experience.*)

van Lommel, P., van Wees, R. van Meyers, V., & Elfferich, I. (2001). Near-death experiences in survivors of cardiac arrest: A prospective study in the Netherlands. *Lancet 358,* 2039-2045.

van Lommel, P. (2004) About the continuity of our consciousness *Advances in Experimental Medicine and Biology, 550,* 115-132.

van Lommel, P. (2006) Near-Death Experience, consciousness and the brain: A new concept about the continuity of our consciousness based on recent scientific research on near-death experience in survivors of cardiac arrest. *World Futures, The Journal of General Evolution, 62,* 134-151.

In: Psychological Scientific Perspectives on Out of Body… ISBN: 978-1-60741-705-7
Editor: Craig D. Murray

Chapter 13

NEAR-DEATH EXPERIENCES AND THE BRAIN

Christopher C. French

ABSTRACT

This chapter presents an overview of neuroscientific approaches to the near-death experience (NDE) focusing on the possible roles of hypoxia, hypercarbia, neurochemicals such as endorphins and serotonin, unusual activity in the temporal lobes, and REM-state intrusions into wakeful consciousness. Recent claims that findings from NDE studies constitute a major challenge to the central assumptions of modern neuroscience are critically assessed. Such claims appear to be based upon a misconception of the so-called "dying-brain hypothesis" and misrepresentations of previous research. It is concluded that although the neuroscientific approach requires further refinement before a definitive and comprehensive account of NDEs can be provided, this approach holds the most promise with respect to understanding this powerful and intriguing aspect of human experience.

You thought you might be a ghost,
You thought you might be a ghost,
You didn't get to heaven but you made it close,
You didn't get to heaven but you made it close.
Lyrics from "42" by Coldplay (2008)

INTRODUCTION

Roe (2001) suggested that theoretical explanations of near-death experiences (NDEs) can be divided into three general categories. The first category he refers to as spiritual (or transcendental) theories. According to theories of this kind, the NDE is exactly what it appears to be to the person having the experience. It is evidence that consciousness (or the soul) can become separated from the physical brain under certain conditions. The NDE is seen as providing a glimpse into a spiritual realm to which souls travel after death. Most major religions maintain that all human beings possess an immaterial, immortal soul which survives bodily death and so this approach to NDEs is consistent with such beliefs. The second broad category is psychological theories such as the claim that the NDE is a psychological defense mechanism (Noyes & Kletti, 1976, 1977) which kicks in at times of great physical danger or the somewhat less plausible notion that NDEs may be based upon memories of being born (Grof & Halifax, 1977; Sagan, 1979). The third broad category is what Roe refers to as organic theories, that is to say attempts to explain the various components of the NDE in terms of neuropsychological processes. These theories are the subject of the present chapter.

It should be borne in mind that this system of classification is employed merely for presentational convenience and that in practice there is often a great deal of overlap between theories under the different headings. Following Palmer (1986), we might label theorists who favor either psychological or organic explanations for NDEs as conventional theorists. Spiritual theories, on the other hand, although they may involve aspects of both psychological and organic theories, would be viewed by their proponents as not reducible to the organic level of neuroscience. Such theories, which we might label as survivalist theories, hold that NDEs involve a soul which cannot be explained in such terms. Putting it very simply, the debate in this area is primarily focused upon whether the NDE is best conceived of as being a glimpse of an afterlife, with all the implications that that would have for parapsychology and our understanding of mind-body interaction, or as simply being the visions of a dying brain. The phrase "dying-brain hypothesis" is a convenient shorthand that is often used to refer to organic (i.e., neuropsychological) theories of the NDE. However, it is widely accepted that one does not actually need to be near to death to experience an NDE (Owens, Cook, & Stevenson, 1990) and use of the term "dying-brain hypothesis" should not be misconstrued as implying otherwise. Any comprehensive neuropsychological theory of NDEs must be able to account for the fact that NDEs can occur in brains that are not dying as well as the fact that not all brains that come close to death experience an NDE. The details of such a theory are yet to be fully developed but solid progress has been made and, arguably, these same observations present an even greater challenge to those who maintain that NDEs provides a glimpse of an afterlife.

Since the early research of Moody (1975, 1977) and Ring (1980), a consensus seems to have emerged that the prototypical NDE, in Western cultures at least, consists of a number of distinct components that usually appear in the following sequence. First, there is a feeling of peace and well-being (although it is now recognized that NDEs can occasionally cause terror and distress; e.g., Atwater, 1988; Greyson & Bush, 1992; Rawlings, 1978). Next, there is a feeling of separation from the physical body. During this out-of-body experience (OBE), the individual often reports being able to see their own physical body from an external vantage point. Before or after the OBE, a transitional region of darkness may be reported, sometimes described as being like a tunnel. Many NDErs (i.e., people experiencing an NDE) report being drawn towards a bright light which does not hurt their eyes and, upon entering the light, often perceive themselves to be in the presence of a spiritual being such as God or Jesus. A non-judgmental panoramic life review may then be experienced. The NDEr may then pass through the light into a spiritual realm, often resembling a beautiful garden, where deceased friends and relatives are encountered. A point of no return, represented by a natural border such as a river or a wall, may be reached and the decision is made to return to the physical body.

Although this is the prototypical description of NDEs in modern Western societies, it is recognized that there is a great deal of variability in the reports collected. Most NDEs, even in the West, include only a few of the components described and they do not always occur in the order presented. Ring (1980), for example, reported the results from a survey of 102 people who had come close to death, 48% of whom reported NDEs. In his sample, 60% reported peace and well-being, 37% reported separation from the physical body, around a quarter reported entering a region of darkness, 16% reported seeing a brilliant light, and 10% reported moving through the light into another realm. Typically, NDEs are reported as being the most profound and vivid experience possible, often described as being "realer than real" (Blackmore, 1993).

When cross-cultural studies are considered, even more variability is found (e.g., Kellehear, 2001; Kellehear, Stevenson, Pasricha, & Cook, 1994; but see Strubelt & Maas, 2008, for an example of drug-induced NDEs in the Iboga healing ceremony in Gabon which allegedly includes all of the typical Western components). The degree to which NDEs really are consistent within and between cultures is a hotly debated topic (Augustine, 2007a). Fox (2003) provides an insightful discussion of the degree to which such apparent consistency as there is may be a consequence of investigators unintentionally interpreting the reports they receive in terms of preconceived schemata. It is certainly the case that most neuropsychological theories to date have been developed to explain components of the prototypical Western NDE and would need to be refined somewhat in order to be applied to the range of experiences reported in other cultures. Once again, however, any variability between accounts would appear to present an even bigger challenge to those who hold that NDEs provides a glimpse of an eternal afterlife (Augustine, 2007b).

As discussed by Blackmore (1993, 1996a), widely varying estimates of the incidence of NDEs in Western society have been obtained from studies of the general population. For example, Gallup (1982) published the widely quoted estimate of 15% but this was based upon responses to the question, "Have you, yourself, ever been on the verge of death or had a 'close call' which involved any unusual experience at that time?" As Blackmore points out, this could cover situations in which people actually were medically close to death or other types of near escapes, such as narrowly avoiding being hit by a car. Also, the term "unusual experience" might cover various types of experience which are not generally considered to be part of NDEs. Even if we ask the question, "What proportion of people who come medically close to death experience an NDE?", estimates still vary widely. French (2005) reviewed four systematic studies of NDEs in cardiac arrest survivors and reported estimates ranging from 6.3% to 23%, but argued that the best estimate for such patients was probably 10-12%. The best conclusion we can draw is that NDEs are not uncommon in individuals who come close to death.

Detailed discussion of the many neuroscientific explanations proposed to account for different components of NDEs in recent decades is beyond the scope of the current chapter. Furthermore, some of the components listed above have received less consideration from conventional theorists than others, most notably the encountering of entities during an NDE, the panoramic life review, and the experience of a sudden return to the physical body. The remainder of this chapter will present an overview of conventional theories followed by a more detailed discussion of the argument that findings from studies of NDEs are a major challenge to some of the fundamental assumptions of modern neuroscience. For more detailed discussion of organic and other theories of NDEs, the reader is referred to Bailey and Yates

(1996), Blackmore (1993, 1996a), Corazza (2008), Fenwick and Fenwick (1995), Fox (2003), French (2005), Greyson (2000a), Irwin and Watt (2007), Morse (1990, 1992), Roe (2001), Ring (1980, 1992), Sabom (1982), and Woerlee (2003).

AN OVERVIEW OF NEUROSCIENTIFIC APPROACHES TO NDES

Fighter pilots sometimes experience so-called G-LOC episodes (acceleration (+Gz)-induced loss of consciousness) during certain maneuvers in which extreme acceleration causes a lack of blood flow to the brain. Whinnery (1997), on the basis of almost 1000 G-LOC episodes, drew attention to the strong similarity such episodes have with some components of the NDE including "tunnel vision and bright lights, floating sensations, automatic movement, autoscopy, out-of-body experiences, not wanting to be disturbed, paralysis, vivid dreamlets of beautiful places, pleasurable sensations, psychological alterations of euphoria and dissociation, inclusion of friends and family, inclusion of prior memories and thoughts, the experience being very memorable (when it can be remembered), confabulation, and a strong urge to understand the experience." (Whinnery, 1997, p. 245). Such evidence strongly suggests that hypoxia (i.e., reduced oxygen levels) in the brain can cause many of the symptoms of NDEs. Hypercarbia (i.e., raised levels of carbon dioxide) will often be associated with reduced oxygen supply and Meduna (1950) reported that hypercarbia can itself cause the experience of bright lights, recollection of past memories, OBEs, and mystical insights.

In addition to the likely role of blood gases, various neurotransmitters have also been suggested as being involved in the generation of NDEs. Carr (1982) proposed that the generally positive emotional tone of NDEs may be a result of the release of endorphins, neurotransmitters that are released at times of extreme physical and psychological stress and are known to reduce pain perception. Serotonin release was seen as having a more important role by Morse, Venecia, and Milstein (1989), particularly with respect to OBEs and mystical hallucinations. Endorphins are not powerful hallucinogens, but many aspects of the effects of ketamine, such as bright lights and moving through tunnels, do seem to parallel components of NDEs, leading Jansen (1989, 1997, 2001) to develop a model of NDEs based upon this observation (see also Corazza, 2008). However, in contrast to the typical NDE, the ketamine experience usually feels unreal (Fenwick, 1997) and is more likely to be frightening (Strassman, 1997).

A number of different lines of evidence strongly support the claim that the temporal lobe is involved in NDEs (Augustine, 2007a). Temporal lobe seizures in epileptics are sometimes associated with vivid OBEs (Devinsky, Feldmann, Burrowes, & Bromfield, 1989; Vuilleaumier, Despland, Assal, & Regli, 1997), with bliss and mystical feelings of oneness with the universe (French, 2005) and even visions of dead friends and relatives (Blackmore, 1993). Frenck, McCarty, and Liebeskind (1978) pointed out that hypoxia would affect both the temporal lobes and the limbic system and that the seizure threshold of both areas would be reduced by the release of endorphins. Britton and Bootzin (2004) presented further evidence of a direct link between NDEs and altered functioning in the temporal lobes. More epileptiform EEG activity was recorded from the temporal lobes of NDErs than from a control group, with this activity almost always lateralized to the left temporal lobe. It should be noted that the results of this study would have been even more compelling had the control group used consisted of individuals who had come close to death but had not experienced NDEs rather than individuals who had never come close to death. It could be argued that the results reported were a consequence of trauma and not specifically related to NDEs at all but Britton and Bootzin present reasonable arguments against such an interpretation, implying that some people are more prone to experience NDEs for physiological reasons. Fox (2003) has reported, on the basis of examination of first-hand accounts of NDEs, that many NDErs appear to exhibit hypergraphia, a compulsion to write excessively about spiritual matters, which is also known to be associated with temporal lobe epilepsy.

The notion of an NDE-prone personality was put forward by Ring and Rosing (1990), who found that a group who had experienced NDEs were more likely to report that they had had troubled childhoods compared to a control group who were interested in NDEs but had never actually experienced one. The former group was also found to score higher on a measure of dissociativity, in line with previous research supporting a link between the tendency to dissociate and childhood trauma. It is generally believed that the tendency to dissociate may serve as a defense mechanism in cases of traumatic childhood by psychologically distancing the child from the harshness of reality. Blackmore (1993) was rightly critical of Ring and Rosing's conclusion that this supported the idea of an NDE-prone personality, pointing out that the appropriate control group from which to draw such conclusions would be a group of individuals who had come close to death but not experienced an NDE, not simply a group who were interested in NDEs. However, more recent research by Greyson (2000b) has shown that people who experience an NDE do indeed show higher levels of dissociativity than those who come close to death but do not have such an experience.

Even these findings are open to the alternative interpretation that the raised levels of dissociativity are a consequence not a cause of NDEs. However, taken in the context of other research indicating that NDErs had more mystical experiences prior to their NDE than the average person (Greyson & Stevenson, 1980) and that they reported more ostensibly psychic experiences, OBEs, and intense spiritual experiences than non-NDErs (Kohr, 1983; Thomas, Cooper, & Suscovich, 1982), the evidence does now appear to favor the notion of a pre-existing proneness to NDEs. Furthermore, it is perhaps more accurate to think of this proneness as being linked not directly to personality factors but to pre-existing temporal lobe instability (Blackmore, 1993).

It has long been known that direct electrical stimulation of the temporal lobe can induce a number of experiences that also occur during NDEs including OBEs, hallucinations, and memory flashbacks (Penfield, 1955; Tong, 2003). Blanke and colleagues have recently published several reports relating to electrically induced OBEs and OBEs associated with neurological conditions (e.g., Blanke & Arzy, 2005; Blanke, Landis, Spinelli, & Seeck, 2004; Blanke, Mohr, Michel, Pascual-Leone, Brugger, et al., 2005; Blanke, Ortigue, Landis, & Seeck, 2002; Blanke & Thut, 2007; Bünning & Blanke, 2005). Blanke et al. (2004, p. 243) argue that both OBEs and autoscopy "are related to a failure to integrate proprioceptive, tactile and visual information with respect to one's own body (disintegration in personal space) and by a vestibular dysfunction leading to an additional disintegration between personal (vestibular) space and extrapersonal (visual) space." Both types of integration failure are said to be caused by paroxysmal activity of the temporo-parietal junction in a state of impaired consciousness.

It might be objected that any model of OBEs that explains the phenomenon in terms of a failure to integrate visual and vestibular sense information cannot account for cases of OBEs occurring in the blind (e.g., Ring & Cooper, 1999). However, it is clear that the blind do have a sense of extrapersonal space based upon other sensory systems and thus it would appear to be reasonable to suggest that OBEs in the blind may be based upon a similar failure to integrate personal and extrapersonal space, albeit that the latter would not involve the visual modality in the blind. Such an account is consistent with Ring's (2001) contention that the blind do not see in the same sense as the sighted during an OBE. Instead, "it is more a matter of knowing, through a still poorly understood mode of generalized awareness, based on a variety of sensory impressions, especially tactile ones, what is happening around them" (p. 69, 2001).

OBEs produced by electrical stimulation of the brain tend to differ from spontaneous OBEs in some ways (Neppe, 2002; Holden, Long, & MacLurg, 2006). For example, the former do not feel as realistic, stable and continuous as the latter but this may well reflect differences in context. Patients undergoing direct brain stimulation would be well aware of the cause of their unusual sensations. Furthermore, the electrical stimulation would be administered in short bursts unlike the unusual neural activity assumed to often underlie spontaneous OBEs. If, as has been argued, electrically induced OBEs are caused by a failure to integrate information from the visual and vestibular senses, this would seem to imply that patients would need to have their eyes open for electrical stimulation of the brain to cause an OBE. However, as described below, Blackmore (1996b) has argued convincingly that the mind can, under certain conditions, adopt a mental model of reality that is based upon imagery, memory and imagination rather than sensory input. Indeed, this assumption is central to many psychological models of the OBE. In which case, it would follow that it may be sufficient for an OBE to be induced by electrical stimulation of the brain in a patient with good imagery skills if they simply imagine their immediate environment rather than keep their eyes open. This would be a promising hypothesis to test in future research.

While many different neuroscientific explanations have been put forward to explain the various components of NDEs, most have tended to provide plausible explanations for some components at the expense of others. Some theorists, most notably Saavedra-Aguilar and Gómez-Jeria (1989) and Blackmore (e.g., 1993, 1996a), have attempted to produce integrated models drawing upon the various accounts already outlined. Arguably, Blackmore (1993) has provided the most comprehensive account to date, proposing that different components of NDEs are probably caused by different physiological processes. Thus, the precise phenomenological details of any particular NDE will depend upon the specific pattern of brain activity at the time and NDEs would be expected to vary across individuals. Full details of Blackmore's model are beyond the scope of this chapter but she essentially adopts the approach of synthesizing the most promising suggestions of other theorists along with developing novel explanations where appropriate. For example, she argues that feelings of peace and bliss during NDEs are probably the result of endorphin release, as suggested by Carr (1982). But she developed a completely novel explanation for the sensation of moving down a dark tunnel towards a bright light, based upon neuronal disinhibition in the visual cortex. Such neuronal disinhibition plays a central role in Blackmore's theorizing about NDEs and she stresses that it can have many different causes.

Blackmore's (1996b) explanation of OBEs has been particularly influential. Within cognitive psychology it is widely accepted that our mental model of reality is based upon two sources of information. First, there is the raw sensory input entering through our eyes, ears, and other senses. This "bottom-up" information is often inherently ambiguous and so perception also involves "top-down" processing, that is, the influence of our knowledge, beliefs and expectations about the world, in order to disambiguate the sensory input. As one might expect, top-down processing is more influential when the sensory information is degraded in some way. Our model of reality is constantly revised and updated on the basis of the interaction between bottom-up and top-down processing. One important aspect of our model of reality is our sense of self. Because vision is the sense that we most rely upon, the sense of self is subjectively felt to be behind the eyes for most people. In general, our model of reality is based upon incoming sensory information and so it usually matches the outside world fairly well. Under certain conditions, however, particularly if the sensory input is degraded in some way, the mind may adopt as the best model of reality one that is in fact based primarily upon memory and imagination, perhaps influenced by whatever sensory input is still available. In such circumstances, an OBE may be experienced. The world of the OBE is seen by Blackmore as being nothing more nor less than the world of the imagination. Thus, NDEs are seen to have a common core, based upon the underlying physiological causes, but the actual hallucinations experienced will be influenced by top-down processes, e.g., religious beliefs (so Christians encounter Jesus not Zeus).

An intriguing hypothesis has been put forward recently by Nelson, Mattingly, Lee, and Schmitt (2006) suggesting that some aspects of NDEs, such as the appearance of extraordinary light and inability to move (or awareness of "being dead"), might be a consequence of the REM (rapid eye movement) state intruding into wakefulness. During the REM stage of sleep, the muscles of the body are actually paralyzed, presumably to prevent the sleeper from actually physically carrying out the actions involved in a dream. During a fairly common phenomenon known as "sleep paralysis", the REM state intrudes upon normal wakeful consciousness (French & Santomauro, 2007; Santomauro & French, in press). Sleep paralysis is often associated with auditory and visual hallucinations, a strong sense of presence, and intense fear. It can be induced by deliberately interfering with the sleep cycle in order to elicit sleep-onset REM periods (Takeuchi, Miyasita, Sasaki, Inugami, & Fukuda, 1992). In a comparison between 55 NDErs and a group of matched controls, it was found that the former were much more prone to sleep paralysis as well as sleep-related hallucinations (Nelson et al., 2006), suggesting that certain individuals may be more prone to NDEs because of a physiological predisposition to REM intrusion.

It can be seen that a strong case can be made that virtually all components of NDEs are mirrored to a greater or lesser extent by similar phenomena that occur outside of the NDE context. Unless strong arguments can be presented otherwise, it would be reasonable to assume that similar neuropsychological processes underlie both NDEs components and their non-NDE counterparts. Although there is still some considerable way to go before it could be claimed that we have a definitive neuropsychological model of NDEs supported by solid empirical evidence, real progress has been made and the neuropsychological approach generates several testable hypotheses for future research. For example, if the precise details of an NDE depend upon the underlying state of the brain, we might expect that different types of close encounter with death (e.g., drowning vs. motor accidents vs. surgery) would tend to produce some differences in the distribution of the NDE components reported. Some relevant data supporting such hypotheses is already available (e.g., Blackmore, 1993) but further research is required.

NDEs: A Fundamental Challenge to Neuroscience?

A number of prominent NDE researchers have claimed that the results of recent prospective studies present a major challenge to modern neuroscience. As Parnia and Fenwick (2002, p. 8) wrote, "The occurrence of lucid, well structured thought processes together with reasoning, attention and memory recall of specific events during a cardiac arrest (NDE) raise a number of interesting and perplexing questions regarding how such experiences could arise. These experiences appear to be occurring at a time when cerebral function can be described at best as severely impaired, and at worst absent." Greyson (2003) and van Lommel et al. (2001) express similar views. In the words of the latter, "How could a clear consciousness outside one's body be experienced at the moment that the brain no longer functions during a period of clinical death with flat EEG [electroencephalogram]?" (van Lommel et al., 2001, p. 2044).

These arguments have been criticized on a number of grounds. French (2001, 2005) pointed out that it is not at all clear that NDEs actually do occur during a period of flat EEG. Even assuming that the patients in question entered a period of flat EEG, the NDE may have occurred as they entered that state or as they slowly recovered from it. Parnia and Fenwick (2002) had rejected the idea that the NDE may have occurred as the patient is becoming unconscious because this happens too quickly. But as French (2005) points out, it is unclear how much time would be required to experience an NDE and a common feature of altered states of consciousness is time distortion. This is well illustrated by the life review component of the NDE itself which, although involving a review of a person's entire life, only seems to last a very brief time.

Parnia and Fenwick (2002) also claim that the NDE could not occur as a person slowly regains consciousness as this period is characterized by confused thinking not the lucid consciousness reported by NDErs. French (2005) notes, however, that the attribution of confusion is typically made by an outside observer. The subjects themselves may not subjectively feel confused at all. In the words of Liere and Stickney (1963, p.300), "Hypoxia quickly affects the higher centers, causing a blunting of the finer sensibilities and a loss of sense of judgment and of self-criticism. The subject feels, however, that his mind is not only quite clear, but unusually keen."

Van Lommel et al. (2001, p. 2039) argue that the fact that only a minority of the patients in their study reported an NDE is a problem for neuropsychological explanations: "We do not know why so few cardiac patients report NDE after CPR [cardiopulmonary resuscitation] [...]. With a purely physiological explanation such as cerebral anoxia [i.e., absence or near absence of oxygen] for the experience, most patients who have been clinically dead should report one." Crislip (2008) criticizes the assertion that the patients involved in this study were "clinically dead". Van Lommel et al.'s (2001, p. 2040) own definition of clinical death is "a period of unconsciousness caused by insufficient blood supply to the brain because of inadequate blood circulation, breathing, or both. If, in this situation, CPR is not started within 5-10 min, irreparable damage is done to the brain and the patient will die." But, as Crislip points out, every patient in this study did receive CPR, mostly within 10 minutes, so they all had blood and oxygen delivered to their brain. Effective CPR eliminates or minimizes the risk of cerebral hypoxia or anoxia. On the basis of the data presented, there is simply no way to determine which patients in this study, if any, actually suffered from reduced oxygen to the brain but given the variability in both the effectiveness of CPR and in the time it takes for the brain to become anoxic, one most certainly would not expect "most patients" in this study to experience an NDE. As Crislip (p. 14) goes on to write: "Having your heart stop for 2 to 10 minutes and being promptly resuscitated doesn't make you 'clinically dead'. It only means your heart isn't beating and you may not be conscious."

Crislip (2008) also takes van Lommel et al. (2001) to task for their assertion (p. 2044) that "in cardiac arrest the EEG usually becomes flat in most cases within about 10 s from onset of syncope [loss of consciousness]". They cite papers by Clute and Levy (1990) and Aminoff, Scheinmann, Griffing, and Herre (1988) in support of this claim. However, the cited papers do not actually support van Lommel et al.'s claim. For example, Clute and Levy report that the average time to the *start* of EEG changes, such as slowing and attenuation, was over 10 s after the last heartbeat. No data are presented on the time taken for the EEG to become isoelectric (i.e., to "flatline").

The most robust and comprehensive rebuttal to date of the idea that NDEs present a major challenge to neuroscience is that of Braithwaite (2008). Although his criticisms are mainly directed at the study by van Lommel et al. (2001), they apply equally to other studies that are presented as supporting this position. In line with Crislip (2008), Braithwaite points out that little or no attempt was made in the van Lommel et al. study to obtain direct measures of anoxia. Furthermore, van Lommel and colleagues, along with other survivalists, appear to be basing their arguments upon the assumption that the dying-brain hypothesis asserts that anoxia/hypoxia will inevitably lead to an NDE. In fact, as Blackmore (e.g., 1993, 1996a) makes very clear, it is the precise rate of change or rate of anoxia onset that is thought to be important (see also Woerlee, 2003) and it is by no means the case that anoxia/hypoxia would always be associated with an NDE.

Braithwaite (2008), again in line with Crislip (2008), emphasizes the importance of between-brain variability. The same level of hypoxia can produce different effects on experience and behavior across different individuals as shown, for example, by the study of G-LOC syndrome already described (Whinnery, 1997). Differences in brain physiology will interact with external stressors in particular and specific ways to produce such variability. As Braithwaite goes on to point out, bearing such considerations in mind, the fact that only a minority of the patients in this study experienced an NDE would appear to be more of a problem for survivalist accounts than for the dying-brain hypothesis. Whereas considerable variability would be expected on the basis of the latter, how does a survivalist account explain the fact that only a minority of those who come near to death actually report an NDE?

The survivalists are also accused by Braithwaite (2008) of placing undue confidence in EEG measures (see also French, 2005). Survivalists generally appear to assume that a flat EEG is indicative of total brain inactivity and that therefore the experience of an NDE during such a flatline period would completely undermine the core assumption of modern neuroscience that any complex experience must be based upon a functioning neural substrate. Even assuming that NDEs actually occur during such periods, which is open to doubt as already discussed, the assumption that isoelectric surface EEG recordings are always indicative of total brain inactivity is simply wrong. Surface EEG recordings may fail to pick up activity in deeper structures such as the hippocampus or amygdala. Gloor (1986) reviews evidence indicating that inter-ictal discharges in these areas can produce complex meaningful hallucinations without the involvement of the cortex.

Another argument which, according Braithwaite (2008), relies upon misplaced confidence in surface EEG measurement was put forward by Fenwick and Fenwick (1995). They argued that, in cases where the surface EEG recording was not flat, if the NDE was a hallucinatory experience based upon disinhibition, evidence of this disinhibition should be visible in the surface EEG recorded at the time. However, data from a recent study comparing EEG recorded at the scalp with EEG recorded from electrodes surgically implanted in deep sub-cortical regions (Toa, Ray, Hawes-Ebersole, & Ebersole, 2005) show conclusively that high-amplitude seizure activity can be occurring in deep brain regions and yet be completely undetectable in the surface EEG. Even more strikingly, a study comparing surface EEG recordings with the fMRI blood-oxygen-level dependent (BOLD) response showed that the surface EEG could fail to detect seizure activity at the level of the cortex that was detected by the BOLD response (Kobayashi, Hawco, Grova, Dubeau, & Gorman, 2006).

The emphasis given to the allegedly central role of hypoxia/anoxia by survivalists is in fact a misrepresentation of the dying-brain hypothesis. This means that many of the criticisms of the hypothesis made by survivalists border on the irrelevant. It is not reduced oxygen to the brain *per se* that is the direct trigger of the NDE according to most versions of the dying-brain hypothesis, it is neural disinhibition. Hypoxia/anoxia may well trigger such disinhibition but, as Braithwaite (2008, p. 12) points out, it can also "be triggered by many [other] psychological and neurological factors such as confusion, trauma, sensory deprivation, illness, pathology, epilepsy, migraine, drug use and brain stimulation".

Braithwaite (2008) also draws attention to a severe problem that the survivalists appear not to have even noticed, let alone solved. The fact that NDErs can talk about their experiences afterwards means that a memory for the experience must have been encoded to represent the experience. The laying down of memories relies on a functioning memory system which means that the neural circuits responsible for memory must have been functioning at the time of the NDE. If that is the case, these same circuits may well have been involved in the hallucinatory experience itself. If one argues, as some survivalists do, that the brain is too unstable during the NDE to support the generation of complex hallucinatory experiences, surely it must follow that the brain would also be too unstable to encode and store memories of such experiences? How then could anyone ever *remember* NDEs?

As described above, many components of NDEs are similar to experiences caused by a range of factors in non-NDE contexts, such as "pathology, disease, illness, neurological conditions (e.g., schizophrenia, autoscopy, Charles-Bonnet syndrome, migraine aura, epilepsy aura) and direct forms of brain stimulation" (Braithwaite, 2008). Such strong similarity is taken by conventional theorists as good evidence that the related NDE components almost certainly are caused by similar underlying neural mechanisms. Survivalists, on the other hand, set great store by minor differences between the NDE component and the non-NDE equivalent. For example, van Lommel et al. (2001) comment that the recollections produced by direct cortical stimulation in epileptics prior to brain surgery are not the same as the panoramic life review of the NDE because the former are "fragmented and random" (p. 2044) and do not have life-transforming consequences such as eliminating the fear of death. As Braithwaite (2008) points out, contrary to this assertion, brain stimulation can in fact sometimes produce vivid recollections of meaningful experiences (e.g., Gloor, 1986). But even in those cases where it produces random and fragmentary memories, this can easily be accounted for in terms of the actual nature of electrical stimulation employed by surgeons prior to brain surgery, as discussed previously in the context of electrically induced OBEs.

The surgeon's aim is to identify the cortical area associated with a particular sensation or aura prior to surgery and to that end the electrical stimulation applied is brief, localized and controlled. This is very different to the large and prolonged seizure-like activity thought to underlie NDEs. Finally, it is not remotely surprising that no transformational effects are produced given the huge differences in context between the two situations. Every effort is made to ensure that patients undergoing brain stimulation are as relaxed as possible. They are fully conscious during the procedure, know exactly what to expect, and receive constant feedback and reassurance from the surgical team. This is very different to the typically traumatic situation in which an NDE is experienced, during which the NDEr may well be injured, semi-conscious, confused, and disoriented.

There are numerous reports of apparently veridical perception during the OBE component of the NDE. There is no doubt that if it could be shown that such perception really can occur during an OBE, the central assumption of modern neuroscience, that consciousness is entirely dependent upon the underlying neural substrate and cannot become separated from that substrate, would be severely undermined. Conventional theorists, however, are not convinced that such cases cannot be accounted for in terms of non-paranormal factors including "information available at the time, prior knowledge, fantasy or dreams, lucky guesses, and information from the remaining senses. Then there is selective memory for correct details, incorporation of details learned between the end of the NDE and giving an account of it, and the tendency to tell a good story." (Blackmore, 1996b, p. 480). Augustine (2007c) has recently presented a thorough critical review of the evidence from such cases and concluded that the claim that a paranormal explanation is required is not supported.

Even cases which have achieved almost mythical status as being completely immune from non-paranormal explanation, such as the NDE of Pam Reynolds, have not withstood critical scrutiny (Woerlee, 2005a, 2005b, 2007). It is worth outlining the Pam Reynolds case, first reported by Sabom (1998), in a little more detail as it is often presented as being the single strongest case in support of the survivalist position. Reynolds underwent a relatively unusual surgical procedure to remove a giant basilar artery aneurysm. The location and size of the aneurysm were such that standard neurosurgical procedures could not be used and instead a technique known as hypothermic cardiac arrest was employed. This procedure requires the patient's body temperature to be reduced to 16°C, heartbeat and breathing are stopped, brainwaves flatten, and blood is drained from the head. Following removal of the aneurysm, the patient's body is returned to its normal temperature, heartbeat and circulation are restored, wounds are closed, and the patient slowly returns to normal consciousness in the recovery room.

When Reynolds regained consciousness, she reported a detailed NDE which had apparently taken place while she was unconscious. She said that she had become aware during the early phase of the operation of the sound of a small pneumatic drill being used to open her skull. She then had an OBE during which she watched herself being operated upon from a vantage point above the neurosurgeon's shoulder, correctly reporting many details of the procedure (including a fairly accurate description of the pneumatic saw being used) and also comments made by the surgical team at the time. She then traveled through a black vortex to a realm of light, where she met deceased relatives who looked after her and helped her to return to her physical body. She was able to report that the song "Hotel California" by the Eagles was playing in the operating theatre when she returned.

Woerlee's (2007) detailed analysis of this case includes a timeline of the major events reported based upon the account provided by Sabom (1998). From this, it clear that the whole wondrous account provided by Reynolds can be explained in terms of her actually recovering consciousness at various points during the operation, even though she was still paralyzed, pain-free and sedated due to the effects of drugs administered to her. The regaining of consciousness during surgical procedures is widely acknowledged as occurring during a minority of operations. Her OBE took place during the early phase of her operation. Although her eyes were taped shut, she would be able to hear what was going on around her. Claims that this would not be possible because she was wearing earphones at the time are rejected by Woerlee on the not unreasonable grounds that we all know from personal experience that wearing earphones does not completely eliminate our ability to hear ambient sounds. Her OBE was essentially based upon visual imagery generated in response to what she could hear going on around her. Her description of the saw would be influenced by the sound it made, as the saw used was similar in appearance to the small pneumatic drills used by dentists since around 1950. Her experience of traveling through a black vortex and subsequent experiences in a realm of light may well have occurred either as she re-entered a period of unconsciousness or as she recovered from the unconsciousness that would inevitably occur as her body temperature was rapidly cooled. She clearly did regain consciousness again temporarily whilst still in the operating theatre as her ability to report the music being played clearly demonstrates. The interested reader is referred to the analysis presented by Woerlee (2007) for more detailed evaluation of this fascinating case. Recognition of the basic fact that patients can sometimes recover some degree of consciousness whilst appearing to outside observers as being totally unconscious provides a plausible explanation for many cases where accurate descriptions of events are provided during the OBE phase of an NDE (e.g., some of those presented by Cook, Greyson, & Stevenson, 1998).

Augustine (2007d) presents a compelling case that at least some NDEs are clearly hallucinatory insofar as they can be shown not to correspond to external reality at all. Such cases are probably severely under-represented in the NDE literature as survivalists will naturally focus upon the apparently veridical cases that they claim cannot be explained in non-paranormal terms. The burden of proof remains with the survivalists, however, to show that such veridical perception can occur under controlled conditions that would rule out the operation of any of the non-paranormal factors listed. A number of small-scale studies (e.g., Parnia, Waller, Yeates, & Fenwick, 2001) have attempted to achieve this by placing hidden targets in coronary care units in such a position that they can only be viewed from a vantage point near the ceiling. To date, no NDEr has reported viewing the hidden target during an OBE. However, if such results were forthcoming in future studies under conditions which ruled out alternative non-paranormal explanations, they would indeed challenge conventional neuroscience.

Conclusion

Although the neuroscientific approach to NDEs has yet to produce a comprehensive and definitive account supported by strong empirical data, it can reasonably be argued that real progress towards that goal has been achieved. A wide range of data from psychological, neuropsychological and neurological studies is consistent with such accounts which also have the benefit of generating testable hypotheses for future research. In contrast, the survivalist approach does not appear to generate clear and testable hypotheses. Because of the vagueness and imprecision of the survivalist account, it can be made to explain any possible set of findings and is therefore unfalsifiable and unscientific. By refining the neuroscientific explanations of NDE that have already been proposed, we can realistically hope for improved understanding of this fascinating phenomenon in the future.

References

Aminoff, M.J., Scheinmann, M.M., Griffing, J.C., & Herre, J.M. (1988). Electrocerebral accompaniments of syncope associated with malignant ventricular arrhythmias. *Annals of Internal Medicine, 108,* 791-796.

Atwater, P.M.H. (1988). *Coming back to life: The after-effects of the near-death experience.* New York: Dodd Mead.

Augustine, K. (2007a). Psychophysiological and cultural correlates undermining a survivalist interpretation of near-death experiences. *Journal of Near-Death Studies, 26,* 89-125.

Augustine, K. (2007b). "Psychophysiological and cultural correlates undermining a survivalist interpretation of near-death experiences" defended. *Journal of Near-Death Studies, 26,* 163-175.

Augustine, K. (2007c). Does paranormal perception occur in near-death experiences? *Journal of Near-Death Studies, 25,* 203-236.

Augustine, K. (2007d). Near-death experiences with hallucinatory features. *Journal of Near-Death Studies, 26,* 3-31.

Bailey, L.W., & Yates, J. (eds.). (1996). *The near-death experience: A reader.* New York & London: Routledge.

Blackmore, S. J. (1993). *Dying to live: Science and the near-death experience.* London: Grafton.

Blackmore, S.J. (1996a). Near-death experiences. In G. Stein (ed.), *The encyclopedia of the paranormal.* Amherst, NY: Prometheus Books. Pp. 425-441.

Blackmore, S.J. (1996b). Out-of-body experiences. In G. Stein (ed.), *The encyclopedia of the paranormal.* Amherst, NY: Prometheus Books. Pp. 471-483.

Blanke, O., & Arzy, S. (2005). The out-of-body experience, self, and the temporo-parietal junction. *The Neuroscientist, 11,* 16-24.

Blanke, O., Landis, T., Spinelli, L., & Seeck, M. (2004). Out-of-body experience and autoscopy of neurological origin. *Brain, 127,* 243-258.

Blanke, O., Mohr, C., Michel, C.M., Pascual-Leone, A., Brugger, P., Seeck, M., Landis, T., & Thut, G. (2005). Linking out-of-body experience and self processing to mental own-body imagery at the temporo-parietal junction. *Journal of Neuroscience, 25,* 550-557.

Blanke, O., Ortigue, S., Landis, T., & Seeck, M. (2002). Stimulating illusory own-body perceptions. *Nature, 419,* 269-270.

Blanke, O., & Thut, G. (2007). Inducing out-of-body experiences. In S. Della Sala (ed.). *Tall tales about the mind and brain: Separating fact from fiction.* Oxford: Oxford University Press. Pp. 425-439.

Braithwaite, J. J. (2008). Towards a cognitive neuroscience of the dying brain. [UK] *Skeptic, 21(2),* 8-16.

Britton, W.B., & Bootzin, R.R. (2004). Near-death experiences and the temporal lobe. *Psychological Science, 15,* 254-258.

Bünning, S., & Blanke, O. (2005). The out-of-body experience: precipitating factors and neural correlates. *Progress in Brain Research, 150,* 331-350.

Carr, D.B. (1982). Pathophysiology of stress-induced limbic lobe dysfunction: A hypothesis relevant to near-death experiences. *Anabiosis: The Journal of Near-Death Studies, 2,* 75-89.

Clute, H.L., & Levy, W.J. (1990). Electroencephalographic changes during brief cardiac arrest in humans. *Anesthesiology, 73,* 821-825.

Cook, E. W., Greyson, B., & Stevenson, I. (1998). Do any near-death experiences provide evidence for the survival of human personality after death? Relevant features and illustrative case reports. *Journal of Scientific Exploration, 12,* 377-406.

Corazza, O. (2008). *Near-death experiences: Exploring the mind-body connection.* London & New York: Routledge.

Crislip, M. (2008). Near death experiences and the medical literature. [US] *Skeptic, 14(2),* 14-15.

Devinsky, O., Feldmann, E., Burrowes, K., & Bromfield, E. (1989). Autoscopic phenomena with seizures. *Archives of Neurology, 46,* 1080-1088.

Fenwick, P. (1997). Is the near-death experience only N-methyl-D-aspartate blocking? *Journal of Near-Death Studies, 16,* 43-53.

Fenwick, P., & Fenwick, E. (1995). *The truth in the light: An investigation of over 300 near-death experiences.* London: Headline.

Fox, M. (2003). *Religion, spirituality and the near-death experience.* London & New York: Routledge.

French, C.C. (2001). Dying to know the truth: visions of a dying brain, or false memories? *Lancet, 358,* 2010-2011.

French, C. C. (2005). Near-death experiences in cardiac arrest survivors. *Progress in Brain Research, 150,* 351-367.

French, C.C., & Santomauro, J. (2007). Something wicked this way comes: Causes and interpretations of sleep paralysis. In S. Della Sala (ed.). *Tall tales about the mind and brain: Separating fact from fiction.* Oxford: Oxford University Press. Pp. 380-398.

Frenk, H., McCarty, B. C., & Liebeskind, J. C. (1978). Different brain areas mediate the analgesic and epileptic properties of enkephalin. *Science, 200,* 335-337.

Gallup, G. (1982). *Adventures in immortality.* New York: McGraw Hill.

Gloor, P. (1986). Role of the limbic system in perception, memory, and affect: Lessons from temporal lobe epilepsy. In B. K. Doane & K. E. Livingstone (eds.). *The limbic system: Functional organisation and clinical disorders.* New York: Raven Press.

Greyson, B. (2000a). Near-death experiences. In E. Cardeña, S. J. Lynn, & S. Krippner (eds.), *Varieties of Anomalous Experiences: Examining the Scientific Evidence.* Washington: American Psychological Association. Pp. 315-352.

Greyson, B. (2000b). Dissociation in people who have near-death experiences: out of their bodies or out of their minds? *Lancet, 355,* 460-463.

Greyson, B. (2003). Incidence and correlates of near-death experiences in a cardiac care unit. *General Hospital Psychiatry, 25,* 269-276.

Greyson, B., & Bush, N. E. (1992). Distressing near-death experiences. *Psychiatry, 55,* 95-110.

Greyson, B., & Stevenson, I. (1980). The phenomenology of near-death experiences. *American Journal of Psychiatry, 137,* 1193-1196.

Grof, S., & Halifax, J. (1977). *The human encounter with death.* New York: Dutton.

Holden, J. M., Long, J., & MacLurg, J. (2006). Out-of-body experiences: All in the brain? *Journal of Near-Death Studies, 25,* 99-107.

Irwin, H.J., & Watt, C.A. (2007). *An introduction to parapsychology.* 5th ed. Jefferson, NC: McFarland & Co.

Jansen, K. L. R. (1989). Near-death experience and the NMDA receptor. *British Medical Journal, 298,* 1708-1709.

Jansen, K. L. R. (1997). The ketamine model of the near-death experience: A central role for the N-methyl-D-aspartate receptor. *Journal of Near-Death Studies, 16,* 79-95.

Jansen, K. L. R. (2001). *Ketamine: Dreams and realities.* Sarasota, FL: Multidisciplinary Association for Psychedelic Studies (MAPS).

Kellehear, A. (2001). An Hawaiian near-death experience. *Journal of Near-Death Studies, 20,* 31-35.

Kellehear, A., Stevenson, I., Pasricha, S., & Cook, E. (1994). The absence of tunnel sensation in near-death experiences from India. *Journal of Near-Death Studies, 13,* 109-113.

Kobayashi, E., Hawco, C. S., Grova, C., Dubeau, F., & Gorman, J. (2006). Widespread and intense BOLD changes during brief focal electrographic seizures. *Neurology, 66,* 1049-1055.

Kohr, R. L. (1983). Near-death experiences, altered states, and psi sensitivity. *Journal of Near-Death Studies, 3,* 157-176.

Liere, E. J., & Stickney, J. C. (1963). *Hypoxia.* Chicago: University of Chicago Press.

Meduna, L. J. (1950). *Carbon dioxide therapy.* Springfield, Illinois: Charles C. Thomas.

Moody, R. A. (1975). *Life after life.* New York: Bantam Books.

Moody, R. A. (1977). *Reflections on life after life.* St. Simon's Island, GA: Mocking Bird Books.

Morse, M. (1990). *Closer to the light.* London: Souvenir.

Morse, M. (1992). *Transformed by the light: The powerful effect of near-death experiences on people's lives.* New York: Ballantine.

Morse, M. L., Venecia, D., & Milstein, J. (1989). Near-death experiences: A neurophysiological explanatory model. *Journal of Near-Death Studies, 8,* 45-53.

Nelson, K. R., Mattingly, M., Lee, S. A., & Schmitt, F. A. (2006). Does the arousal system contribute to near death experience? *Neurology, 66,* 1003-1009.

Neppe, V. M. (2002). "Out-of-body experiences" (OBEs) and brain localisation: A perspective. *Australian Journal of Parapsychology, 2,* 85-96.

Noyes, R., & Kletti, R. (1976). Depersonalisation in the face of life-threatening danger: an interpretation. *Omega, 7,* 103-114.

Noyes, R., & Kletti, R. (1977). Depersonalisation in the face of life-threatening danger. *Comprehensive Psychiatry, 18,* 375-384.

Owens, J. E., Cook, E. W., & Stevenson, I. (1990). Features of "near-death experience" in relation to whether or not patients were near death. *Lancet, 336,* 1175-1177.

Palmer, J. (1986). Progressive skepticism: A critical approach to the psi controversy. *Journal of Parapsychology, 50,* 29-42.

Parnia, S., & Fenwick, P. (2002). Near death experiences in cardiac arrest: visions of a dying brain or visions of a new science of consciousness. *Resuscitation, 52,* 5-11.

Parnia, S., Waller, D. G., Yeates, R., & Fenwick, P. (2001). A qualitative and quantitative study of the incidence, features and aetiology of near death experiences in cardiac arrest survivors. *Resuscitation, 48,* 149-156.

Penfield, W. (1955). The role of the temporal cortex in certain psychical phenomena. *Journal of Mental Science, 101,* 451-465.

Rawlings, M. (1978). *Beyond death's door.* Nashville: Thomas Nelson.

Ring, K. (1980). *Life at death: A scientific investigation of the near-death experience.* New York: Coward, McCann, and Geoghegan.

Ring, K. (1992). *The Omega Project.* William Morrow, New York.

Ring, K. (2001). Mindsight: Eyeless vision in the blind. In D. Lorimer (ed.), *Thinking beyond the brain: A wider science of consciousness.* Edinburgh: Floris. Pp. 59-70.

Ring, K., & Cooper, S. (1999). *Mindsight: Near-death and out-of-body experiences in the blind.* Palo Alto, CA: William James Center for Consciousness Studies.

Ring, K., & Rosing, C. J. (1990). The Omega Project: An empirical study of the NDE-prone personality. *Journal of Near-Death Studies, 8,* 211-239.

Roe, C. A. (2001). Near-death experiences. In R. Roberts & D. Groome (eds.), *Parapsychology: The science of unusual experience.* London: Arnold. Pp. 141-155.

Saavedra-Aguilar, J. C., & Gomez-Jeria, J. S. (1989). A neurobiological model of near-death experiences. *Journal of Near-Death Studies, 7,* 205-222.

Sabom, M. B. (1982). *Recollections of death: A medical investigation.* London: Corgi.

Sabom, M. B. (1998). *Light and death: One doctor's fascinating account of near-death experiences.* Grand Rapids, Michigan: Zondervan.

Sagan, C. (1979). *Broca's brain: Reflections on the romance of science.* New York: Random House.

Santomauro, J., & French, C. C. (in press). Terror in the night: The experience of sleep paralysis. *The Psychologist.*

Strassman, R. (1997). Endogenous ketamine-like compounds and the NDE: If so, so what? *Journal of Near-Death Studies, 16,* 27-41.

Strubelt, S., & Maas, U. (2008). The near-death experience: A cerebellar method to protect body and soul – lessons from the Iboga healing ceremony in Gabon. *Alternative Therapies, 14,* 30-34.

Takeuchi, T., Miyasita, M., Sasaki, Y., Inugami, M., & Fukuda, K. (1992). Isolated sleep paralysis elicited by sleep interruption. *Sleep, 15,* 217-225.

Thomas, L. E., Cooper, P. E., & Suscovich, D. J. (1982). Incidence of near-death and intense spiritual experiences in an intergenerational sample: An interpretation. *Omega, 13,* 35-41.

Toa, J. X., Ray, A., Hawes-Ebersole, S., & Ebersole, J. S. (2005). Intracranial EEG substrates of scalp EEG interictal spikes. *Epilepsia, 46,* 669-676.

Tong, F. (2003). Out-of-body experiences: From Penfield to present. *Trends in Cognitive Sciences, 7,* 104-106.

van Lommel, P., van Wees, R., Meyers, V., & Elfferich, I. (2001). Near-death experience in survivors of cardiac arrest: a prospective study in the Netherlands. *Lancet, 358,* 2039-2045.

Vuilleaumier, P., Despland, P. A., Assal, G., & Regli, F. (1997). Voyages astraux et hors du corps: héautoscopie, extase et hallucinations expérientielles d'origine épileptique [Out-of-body and astral journeys: Heautoscopy, ecstasis and experimental hallucinations of epileptic origin]. *Revue Neurologique, 153,* 115-119.

Whinnery, J. E. (1997). Psychophysiologic correlates of unconsciousness and near-death experiences. *Journal of Near-Death Studies, 15*, 231-258.

Woerlee, G. M. (2003). *Mortal minds: A biology of the soul and the dying experience.* Utrecht: de Tijdstroom.

Woerlee, G. [M.] (2005a). An anaesthesiologist examines the Pam Reynolds story. Part 1: Background considerations. [UK] *Skeptic, 18(1)*, 14-17.

Woerlee, G. [M.] (2005b). An anaesthesiologist examines the Pam Reynolds story. Part two: The experience. [UK] *Skeptic, 18(2)*, 16-20.

Woerlee, G. M. (2007). *The unholy legacy of Abraham.* Leicester: Matador.

In: Psychological Scientific Perspectives on Out of Body... ISBN: 978-1-60741-705-7
Editor: Craig D. Murray

Chapter 14

FINDING MEANING IN NEAR-DEATH EXPERIENCES

Craig D. Murray, David J. Wilde and Joanne Murray

ABSTRACT

Near-death experiences (NDEs) have become a topic of increasing interest to medical and psychological researchers over the last 35 years. During the course of this research agenda, several studies have focused on the phenomenology of the experience and its after-effects, mostly from a nomothetic stance. This chapter reports on the experience of having an NDE and the meanings attributed to that experience and its resultant after-effects by taking an idiographic, phenomenological approach. Here we detail how individuals may choose elements of an experience which are most personally meaningful for them and how this is incorporated into their later lives. Of particular interest here is how participants came to new understandings of their lives as a result of their NDE. A process of integration is helped or hindered by physical and psychological factors concomitant at the time of the NDE. Also evident are the challenges the NDE, or elements therein, have on the individual's sense of self and how they maintain and develop that self in the years following the event.

INTRODUCTION

Near-death experiences have become a topic of increasing research interest over the last 35 years. These are defined by Greyson (1994, p. 460) as "profound subjective event[s] with transcendental or mystical elements that many people experience on the threshold of death." The majority of studies have profiled the experient as a healthy, well-adjusted individual (Greyson, 2000; Irwin, 1999), and identified the occurrence of the NDE as being without demographic differentiation (Greyson, 1996; Ring, 1980; Sabom, 1982). It is found to be a mostly positive, life-affirming experience (Ring, 1993) that can happen at anytime during the lifespan (Atwater, 2003). Although not all NDEs are pleasant journeys; some have been reported to be quite frightening (Bush, 2002; Greyson & Bush, 1992).

During the course of this research agenda, several studies have focused on the phenomenology of the experience and its after-effects. Raymond Moody (1975, 1977) was the first researcher to compile a list of commonly reported features occurring during the NDE (e.g. feelings of peace and joy, ineffability and having an out-of-body experience or OBE). These features have been reported in many studies conducted since then (e.g. Fenwick & Fenwick, 1995; Ring, 1980; Sabom, 1982), with some features (e.g. tunnels, a sense of peace and joy) appearing more frequently than others (e.g. experiencing cities of light or supernatural rescues). Yet, despite the fact that Moody noted that no two NDEs are identical, and that some NDEs will not contain all of the features he identified, the repeated findings of these features gave rise to the idea that there is universality to the phenomenon. However, Ring (1993) has challenged this idea, suggesting that research into this facet of the NDE is currently too underdeveloped to concretize this proposal. Although, some support for this counter-argument has come from studies that have found cultural variations within NDE accounts (e.g. Knoblauch, Schmied, & Schnettler, 2001; Murphy, 2001; Pasricha & Stevenson, 1986).

NDEs and other transcendent experiences can radically and permanently transform the experient's, attitudes, beliefs and lifestyle, changing their lives forever (Greyson, 1996). Some of the reported positive after-effects are; a concern for others, a greater interest in spiritual matters, enhanced appreciation of, or renewed sense of purpose to life, a reduced fear of death, increased belief in an after life or survival of the soul, less interest in materialism and competitiveness, and a greater importance placed on values such as love and being of service to others (Flynn, 1982; Grey, 1985; Greyson, 2000; Noyes, 1980; Ring, 1980; Sabom, 1982).

The unpredictable and profound nature of the NDE can often leave a person ill-equipped to deal with any subsequent spiritual awakenings; leaving them with fears for their mental health, an inability or difficulties in communicating their experience to family, friends and health professionals, and sometimes with symptoms akin to Post-Traumatic Stress Disorder (PTSD) (Greyson, 1996; 2001). Many experients may also have to cope with these changes over and above whatever health issues led them to the point of near-death in the first place, for instance, cardiac arrest.

The majority of the above work has been nomothetic in nature, usually taking the form of survey studies (e.g. Athappilly, Greyson, & Stevenson, 2006; Groth-Marnat & Summers, 1998; Knoblauch, Schmied, & Schnettler, 2001). This approach has provided a wealth of data about how the average experient integrates their NDE, modifies their attitudes and values, and undergoes spiritual transformation and growth. However, missing from this approach is the ability to specify any detail about the particular nuances of any one person's transformative processes. For instance, when someone is said to have acquired a 'greater interest in spiritual matters' after an NDE, what exactly does that mean or entail for that person? It is without question that the transformative effects described above happen to individuals and as such are highly personal matters. In order to understand more deeply how the individual person experiences these life changes, it is necessary to employ qualitative methods, which are more receptive to investigating these "pluralisation of life worlds" (Flick, 2002, p. 2).

Some qualitative studies (or studies with qualitative components) have been conducted with a focus, or partial focus, on the transformational experiences of people following their NDE. For instance, Blackmore (1993) conducted a study of NDEs in India. As part of the study she examined the detailed written accounts provided by experients about their NDEs and the after-effects they experienced.

Morris and Knafl (2003) conducted interviews with patients in the USA who had reported NDEs during recovery from cardiac arrest. The study utilized a naturalistic enquiry method to explore the nature and meaning of their NDEs. Initially, patients went through a period of confusion about what had happened and if the experience was actually real or not. The extent to which this was initially integrated also depended upon how their NDE account was received by their health care professionals.

Once it has occurred, the NDE remains a unique and fixed memory for the remainder of a person's life – memories which have been found to be resilient to the usual embellishments and distortions (Greyson, 2007; van Lommel, van Wees, & Meyers, 2001) as a result of elapsed time (Estes, 1997) or emotional pressure (Schooler & Eich, 2000) – and an event which connects old and new patterns of daily living in which the individual strives to piece together the meaning and significance of the experience.

While this previous work has added substantially to our understanding of the NDE, a closer examination of the longitudinal after-effects experienced by people who have them, the nature of those after-effects, and the temporal, social and psychological factors that may impinge on the integration process, and in particular, the person's sense of self or identity is needed. The present chapter reports our work (see Wilde & Murray, 2009) on this topic using a phenomenological, idiographic approach in which participants are interviewed in depth about their experiences. To date there has been no in-depth examination of the lived experience of having an NDE and what meaning NDErs attribute to that experience within such a framework.

Study Detail

The work reported here is part of a wider study examining the occurrence, phenomenology and psychological correlates of out-of body and near-death experiences. Here we focus on interviews with three participants who had experienced a near-death experience. The aim is to develop an understanding of these experiences as lived, rather than to focus on issues of veridicality or underlying causal mechanisms. The particular theoretical and philosophical approach we take is that of Interpretative Phenomenological Analysis (see Wilde & Murray, 2009, and Wilde & Murray, in press), an established qualitative framework for eliciting accounts and making sense of the meaning making which the experient is engaged in. In what follows we summarize the salient themes identified in this work along with the implications of participants' experiences.

NDEs Within a Biographical Context

The NDE occurs within the evolving context of a person's life. As with any other major life event, there are after-effects to the NDE which serve as way finders and indicators to how a person might interpret and find meaning in the experience, and how this may influence who they become. Within this theme, each of the three participant's stories is presented, briefly detailing their lives and personalities prior to and after their NDEs. Later themes will examine in more depth the transformative aspects of the experience.

Jane's Story

Jane's life prior to her NDE was that of a twenty-something young woman who had few aspirations beyond finding a partner and settling down into a family way of life. At the time of her NDE she had already married. She recalled having no particularly strong religious or spiritual values, no real belief in God or an after-life and claimed not to have previously known anything about NDEs. She talked about having an uneasy relationship with her parents at the time of her NDE, particularly with her mother, which she described as one of conflict. Her NDE happened in hospital during an operation on a burst stomach. Her pre-operative condition was one of physical, mental and emotional turmoil. She was in extreme physical pain and scared of dying:

> "I had Peritonitis. I was in a lot of pain…I asked the nurse "am, am I going to die?", and the nurse sort of hesitated slightly before she answered…so I had got myself in the state of mind where I had been prepared really just to be obliviated…although it was quite scary, but I had actually given myself over it."

Her NDE was distinguished by very strong emotions; fear, anger, anxiety, isolation and remorse, each played out against a backdrop of several distinct motifs, which had seminal ramifications in the process of integrating her NDE. The most powerful of these motifs appeared near the end of the experience, when Jane found herself falling down into darkness towards a globe of light below her, at the same time she remembered hearing a chant and felt "filled by the recognition" of it. She claimed to have heard this chant before, during an operation at the age of 10, but it seemed even more intimate to her than that:

> "I just knew I'd heard this, this chant hundreds of times before…I knew it was really significant…a major and powerful experience…this is the sound that happens when you die."

At the end of her fall, Jane encountered a group of discarnate beings she described as very gentle and loving and "glowing from within". She began a dialogue with the beings and the exchange took the form of a disagreement about whether or not she would remember the chant, which she assumed would be the key to people accepting that her experience was real. She felt anger towards these beings who challenged her. Yet, despite her fury, they offered their understanding and told her that she would hear the chant again during her lifetime. They asked her why she wanted to go back to her life to which she replied that she wanted to have children and watch them grow up.

As this exchange ended, Jane found herself in another dark and lonely place; a place she felt as though she was never going to leave, where she was left alone to reflect about the relationships with her friends and parents, and the times she had said and done bad things in her life. This motif was characterized by feelings of inadequacy. Amidst this heavy, lonely feeling she heard a voice say to her, "don't be too hard on your self", and at that point she returned to her body and awoke from the operation. Jane felt that her life changed dramatically after the NDE. Ultimately, the experience was a pivotal point in her life and development as a human being. The insights gained from her time in this dark void seeded and gradually flourished. She spoke about the initial changes in her world view and attitudes this part of the experience held for her:

> "It absolutely changed me into being a sort of just living for, a normal life to seriously thinking about life…quite er, deep serious thinker about life, and, and philosophy."

Her early post-NDE life was marked by feelings of confusion and attempts to make sense of her experience; in particular certain elements of the experience were identified as meaningful, but challenging for her to comprehend their significance. For instance, she related how she picked out one element of the NDE – falling towards a sphere of light – and began her quest to understand it:

> " I started reading science fiction quite a bit after…that, was the first thing I did…it *[the NDE]* seemed to me that it was so much larger than just, just this planet…it didn't get me anywhere in particular…that was where my interest was."

Later, as the perceived meaning of her experience began to germinate, she took an interest in psychology and religion, and later, trained to be a counselor and an interfaith minister.

Margaret's Story

Margaret had her NDE whilst in hospital for the birth of her first child. She was 21 years old. She described herself as living a hippy kind of lifestyle; a carefree, happy-go-lucky kind of person, with no real outlook on life and no plans made for the future other than to one day get married and have children. Margaret had been admitted to hospital a week prior to the birth. Everything seemed to be going normally until she was told that her baby had died shortly after her labor had begun. Despite numerous attempts to inform the medical staff at the hospital of a known allergy to Suxamethonium, a drug used in anesthetics, she was given an anesthetic containing this drug during the birth of her child. She then underwent an extremely painful and protracted labor until finally collapsing after being administered the anesthetic:

> "The pain was so hideous and inescapable…by the end of the first evening I was quite happy if they would've come and kill me, death seemed a really good idea…I was screaming… it's an image of being tortured in my mind…so, I went from that feeling…straight into another form of consciousness."

Once under the anesthetic, Margaret found herself out of her body, seemingly without physical form, inhabiting a place of vast blackness, which she felt she was "leaking" into. She felt contentment and peace and was relieved to have escaped the excruciating pain she had just been in. She said that if she could have drawn a picture of herself it would have been of a "huge smile". During this time, she felt her attention had split into two; one part had begun a dialogue with a male, disembodied voice, which she understood to be the voice of her just deceased child, but at the same time, something extremely wise and all-knowing. The voice talked to her about how life works and she felt instinctively she was hearing the truth. The remainder of her attention was focused on a gradually approaching light, to which she was becoming increasingly adverse to its presence. This sense of foreboding eventually overcame her and she related her trepidation to the voice:

> "The voice said to me, what's wrong?...And I said...I don't want to go in the light...I won't cease to exist, but my ego will have gone, my character, my personality, the thing that makes me the individual I am will be gone."

Margaret then found herself out of the darkness and saw her husband and how upset he was hearing that she had collapsed and that the baby had died. She then saw her parents being told of her death and again saw how it saddened them. When she contemplated the amount of grief her death would cause, she began falling again and then awoke.

Margaret had two major issues to deal with post-NDE. Firstly, following the death of her baby, she had become very suspicious and deeply mistrusting of the hospital authorities and the staff who operated on her that day. She believed that they had made mistakes that caused the death of her baby and put her through an agonizingly painful experience. Secondly, there was the issue of the NDE and trying to come to terms with what had happened during the experience and what it had all meant. Above all, she really wanted to find someone who had had the same experience as she had and felt deep feelings of "isolation and alienation".

Margaret's later attempts to find connection and empathy were characterized by struggle, distrust and a pervading sense of separation. Yet, despite the difficulties, she had endured and made a success of her life. Similarly to Jane, she believed her NDE was positive in nature and outcome. Since the NDE she believed she had become more creative in life and felt that her creativity stemmed directly in some way from her NDE:

> "It seems to me that it was a bit of a gift, to have an experience, that it has colored my life ever since...I think I have become more creative, erm, the jobs I've had are all jobs that I've created for myself...since having that experience *[the NDE]*."

Deborah's Story

Deborah described her everyday childhood as being surrounded by people who were "very intuitive, very clairvoyant" and so was familiar with anomalous phenomena, such as NDEs, from an early age. She used to have nocturnal out-of-body experiences (OBEs) between the ages of 5 and 11 years during which she would leave her body and travel to forests and "other realms".

Her NDE happened in hospital whilst living in Dhahran, Saudi Arabia. She was having an operation, which was going smoothly until at some stage her heart rate and blood pressure began falling. The surgical team fought to restore her vital signs, including using a defibrillator to restart her heart. In the midst of this, she found herself floating on the operating theatre ceiling. She was in a state of pure bliss and could see the theatre, the equipment, the staff and her own body below her. She recognized her friend, the anesthetist, and tried to communicate with her by tapping her on the shoulder, but her friend did not acknowledge her presence. She then found herself leaving the hospital and flying peacefully along a tunnel towards a blue light. She saw a hand descending out of the light and reaching towards her. She felt that if she had taken the hand she would have died. At this point she began a short dialogue with what she believed was the voice of God:

> "As I got there, I turned round and said, I don't want to go yet…My baby's a couple of months old and I was still feeding, I can't leave my children, I want to see them grow old…I want to be a grandmother…and, in answer to this, 'ok, you can go back', and…I had made promises…'cos that power to me is God…and I'd said to him…I'll go and do your work for you."

At this point she returned to her body and awoke from under the anesthetic.

Deborah's story differered from Margaret's and Jane's, where the latter two had no real spiritual or religious inclinations, or experience of leaving their bodies, prior to their NDEs, Deborah had grown up with the notions of clairvoyance and other anomalous phenomena during her childhood. She had already learned to meditate, had an active interest in spirituality and anomalous phenomena, and already had experiences of leaving her body prior to having her NDE. Having made a promise to God, Deborah was quite certain of the path she was embarked upon; one of service to humankind. It was something she had embraced wholeheartedly in her everyday life ever since, and which had formed a core set of beliefs and attitudes underpinning some devoted practices and difficult life changes and decisions. She recalled how she first noticed changes manifesting after her NDE:

> "I've always been a twenty-four seven mother, homemaker…so I've always had time to myself to meditate and to do my yoga…and I think after this *[NDE]* I got more into my yoga and into my meditation and, er, I started meditating twice a day."

Common to all three participant's stories was that each in some way each came to a new understanding in their lives as a result of their NDE. Not all participant's subsequent life changes and decisions can be attributed to their NDEs alone. Yet, the deeper understandings they discovered about themselves and their reasons for being, which they gleaned from that experience, once acknowledged and understood, became the platforms for their future personal development and growth.

Developing New Understandings Following the NDE

Jane's story is illustrative of this theme. One of the most significant motifs in her NDE came towards the end where she experienced being 'trapped' in a form of limbo; a dark, isolating place in which she had a tangible sense of being in a space where time had no meaning; an eternity in a void where nothing got resolved and no help was forthcoming while she worked through her personal dilemmas, until finally realizing the nature of her problems. During this time she contemplated the relationships she had with different people, in particular her relationship with her mother. This was a desperately remorseful and melancholic experience for her:

> "I started thinking…particularly relationships with my parents were so bad and how I hadn't been a good enough daughter I hadn't been the way my mother had wanted me to be

> and, erm, I was really feeling pain because of all the horrible things I'd said, y'know as a teenager as you do…and then a voice said…'don't be too hard on yourself'. It was a very powerful sentence."

Having reached this awareness, Jane was essentially 'freed' from the void to return to her body. Within this most profound part of her NDE, Jane reached a new understanding about her relationships with other people. Having returned from her experience, this realization forced her to confront the importance of working through her relationship issues, something she carried through, not only on a personal level, but in a professional capacity as well when she later trained as a relationship counselor for the organization, RELATE. The ascription between the NDE and her later behavior was made clear by Jane:

> "Well, 'don't be too hard on yourself' was very, proved later to be very meaningful to me…that has remained with me as, as my guideline really."

Some of the defining characteristics of Margaret's NDE and, indeed, the more complicated parts of her life since that experience, had been a persistent sense of separation, of being alienated and not understood or listened to. She had nurtured a belief that the world was a difficult place to live in and that life was a struggle and that struggle had an educational purpose, defining the person, who ultimately saw the value of it all in the process. She felt that through her experience losing the baby in hospital, and the challenges she had endured whilst trying to integrate her NDE, she had faced her own struggles. However, she saw her NDE as a gift, something which has given her an understanding of the world, a philosophy and a theory about the truth of one's existence, from which she could draw comfort.

Since her NDE she had looked to scientific theories she believed might explain the totality of her experience. She placed great faith in these theories to discover the answers to the questions she had about her experience. It had also provided her with a potential solution to the enigma of why she felt so isolated from other people who she perceived as unable to understand her experience, and the radical shift between the person she was prior to the NDE and the post-NDE Margaret:

> "Sometimes I think that when I fell back from that experience I fell back to a different place…certainly the girl who climbed onto that table *[operating table]* was not the same person who got up off it…the change was so dramatic in my way of thinking that my younger self…it's like waking up in a universe where people talk in a different language to you somehow, and you try to say something and it's like, no they ain't getting it, they don't understand what I'm saying so I'll shut up."

The key feature of Deborah's NDE was the promise she made to do God's work when she returned. Given her previous experience and interest in spiritual matters, her interpretation of the meaning of her NDE is unequivocal. Post-NDE she found a strengthened, clearer purpose in her life and the experience appeared to have renewed and refreshed her intentions to commit to a spiritual journey:

> "After that, that changed my life…because I'm very much, erm, I dunno what you might call it, into spirituality for years…I'm in service for others…God sent me home so I've got to start doing some work…that's when I found my guru, my spiritual master."

Since her NDE, Deborah had adopted an attitude and position of service to others. This has been reflected by her commitment to practicing ethically, to pass on her knowledge and skills to others, and to help those who are most in need of help:

> "...I was teaching at the *[psychic college]* for nine years actually, Kundalini yoga...I was just planting seeds...I don't teach so much now, that's not where I'm at 'cos I'm not there to earn money...I'm on my path...I did past life therapy, I did that for some time but...I'm not gonna do a past life on you because it's not, it's not, a fun thing. If you want to come here because you've got a medical problem, then we'll look at it."

SELF-ACTUALIZATION FOLLOWING THE NDE

The final theme presented here compliments and builds upon some of the changes participants had experienced from the time of their NDE. Signs of the influence of Jane's NDE began soon after and were characterized by a general feeling of having been exposed to information which necessitated a re-alignment of her personal beliefs and values about such issues as life after death, religion and her relationships with her friends/family and with God:

> "It was such a big change for me because y'know I suddenly had to think about my, what my beliefs were suddenly again."

Jane felt lucky to have had her NDE and that, because of it, much of her life had not been wasted. The alterations in her beliefs and attitudes were succeeded by some major life changes as she found herself gradually becoming absorbed in developing herself personally and spiritually. Interpersonal relationships became of primary importance to her. In order to make further sense of this, she gravitated to reading about psychology, in particular self-help books about relationships, and eventually worked as a Samaritan and trained as a relationship counselor. She took up the challenge of changing and improving relationships for other people, and of those in her own life:

> "I ended up accepting myself for the person that I was...knowing that I was loved and loveable...I've never really succeeded because my, actually my friends were pretty screwed up people, so I, I, it's just accepting them and accepting the best possible solutions for day-to-day relationships went on."

Jane's growth continued to find deeper meaning in her views about relationships, death and dying, and the importance of giving and receiving forgiveness:

> "Because the people left behind are the ones hanging on to stuff and there's no way to resolve it...Forgiveness is very important I mean not forgiveness to benefit the other person but forgiveness to help yourself really."

Post-NDE, she took an active interest in learning about different religions, particularly Christianity. Again, her shift in attitudes and beliefs towards religion was underpinned by significant behavioral changes:

> "I did some other courses as well…to do with religion and er, studied that and then I did interfaith er, minister erm, training as well, this was after I left RELATE."

Jane perceived her NDE as a new beginning and was no longer afraid of dying. She confessed it was hard to say what influences could be attributed directly to the NDE, however, she didn't think she would have become a counselor without having had that experience.

Margaret, too, underwent great changes in the personal, emotional and spiritual domains of her life. Her initial efforts to make sense of her NDE were met with diverse and sometimes extreme reactions. She found some support from her husband whom she told soon after the experience and who was accepting. However, in further attempts to share the experience, she began communicating with the leader of a spiritual group based in India, hoping to find some wisdom and empathy with her experience:

> "I had a letter from the Guru in India…he said well, did this happen while you were having an operation…and he said, well that would be the anesthetic, and he just, he was saying that was a dream state, that wasn't real, and that made me very cross, that he would deny my experience, without having had it himself."

After this she turned to internet discussion forums about NDEs, again only to be rebuffed regarding the authenticity of her experience. She believed her attempts to make her NDE accessible to other people had been frustrated by the ineffability of the experience itself:

> "Sometimes there aren't words available to describe a nebulous experience…you end up using clichéd words that make you feel as if you are talking madness or you know about supernatural events that are, that are risible and laughable."

Having had to contend with people who had either not believed her NDE or had out rightly dismissed it as false, and allied to her belief that the hospital covered up a medical accident that resulted in her baby's death, Margaret had developed a deep distrust of whom she would tell her story to for fear of further reproach, selectively sharing it with trusted people who have belief in her experience.

As with Jane, Margaret believed that post-NDE she had experienced a range of psychological and behavioral changes in her life. She thought that she had undergone an expansion in her psychic, creative and mental abilities, such as the gaining the gift of foresight. She believed that she had become more empathic; an empathy extending beyond human-to-human empathy to empathizing with animals, alive or dead. She termed this development as having "evolved to the next stage". These enhanced abilities she believed were additional reasons why she has felt a sense of separateness from other people.

Like Margaret, Deborah also received a mixed reaction to the disclosure about her NDE. However, her negative reactions came closer to home. In the years following her NDE, both she and her husband noticed that her behavior and personality were changing. These transformations had a profound impact on her relationships with her husband and her children. Her husband was an Armenian man, Greek Orthodox in religion, and considered her talk of NDEs, and some of her spiritual practices, as "evil". These divisions eventually contributed to the couple divorcing. With hindsight, she believed this was necessary; a consequence in part because of "his fear", but also that getting divorced was an ingredient of her spiritual growth. However, she did find support and acceptance from her children regarding her spiritual life and her NDE:

> "I've progressed…I think that's something that, erm, I've have given my children…one chapter of my life has closed, because now I'm on the next part is my spiritual journey with my children."

She viewed the NDE as having confirmed to her the validity of her spiritual path and that it had strengthened her resolve to discuss her spiritual beliefs. Since her NDE, Deborah's devotion to service had impacted on her decision making and the choices she has had to make regarding what she brought into her life that would best honor her commitments:

> "There are different types of yoga, and I wanted mine spiritual…then after a few years I left the psychic college…they always just want money out of you and if you do this course, and of course I found I don't need to go back and do another, so I passed all that and moved on."

In terms of the promises she made to God, she admitted that she never remembered exactly what she promised to do, but periodically she was reminded of them when he needed her to take on some new task, such as her latest work on her path:

> "Sometimes the conversation *[with God]* comes back and I think, ahh, I've done this. That's what I've done for you, thank you…I do a lot of work in India, and I, I have a spiritual master there and we feed five hundred people a day, and so now that's where I my path is."

Discussion

The above analysis has shown the NDE to be a major life transition event; one which can exert lasting social, affective and psychological tensions on the individual in terms of the evolution of their selves and identities in their quest for meaning. In this section of the paper we will discuss these findings within a theoretical context.

One of the main aims of this study was to carry out an examination of the lived experience of having an NDE and what meaning NDErs attribute to that experience. Corbett (1996) considered the meaning of an event as having "dispositional power" over the experient in what they will do or think afterwards. The results from this study show that NDEs can be considered as critical life events (Dougherty, 1990) in terms of the transitions experienced afterwards that affect the development of the person's self, their identities, their relationships and general life directions. The 'dispositional power' of the critical life event has been previously acknowledged by various authors (Baltes & Danish, 1980; Brim & Ryff, 1980; Pearlin, 1980).

What our results have been successful in emphasizing is the psychological, social and affective tensions experienced by our participants throughout the process of these transitions.

Jane's response to her NDE was similar in nature to one described by Bush (2002) – called 'the turnaround' – the main meaning behind the NDE is seen as a kind of caveat; a forewarning of an ill-advised direction in life that must be heeded. Jane does 'hear' the warning she is been given and makes changes in her life in accordance. Despite her confusion and angst, she seemed to have overcome and resolved the underlying message of her experience.

The overall meaning of Margaret's NDE was complicated and hence her assimilation of her experience had taken an uneasy trajectory. The shock and pain of the death of her baby, as well as her harrowing experience giving birth to a still-born child, was irrevocably intertwined with the experience of communicating with him in an out-of-body state during her NDE. As her life progressed beyond that critical point, the influences of both events vied for psychological attention in Margaret's everyday living space. Sometimes they coalesced in periods of psychological contraction and introversion; substantiated by her thoughts of alienation and separation, and protracted communication difficulties with hospital authorities and in trying to combat the perceived illegitimacy of her NDE by other people. More than a need for social bonding, on the one hand, she had a burning desire to find acceptance and peace in some form of public acknowledgement of her NDE, and on the other, an admission of negligence on behalf of the hospital staff.

Whilst the most linear of the three narratives is the story of Deborah's NDE, there are tensions evident in how she resolved the conflict between her autonomous self and her connected self. The progression along a spiritual path is often viewed through modern eyes as a fulfilling and constantly enriching experience, yet historically it has been strongly linked with struggle and dark nights of the soul; a lonely journey where difficult and painful situations are often the most profound providers of spiritual wisdom (Corbett, 1996; Eichmann, 1991). Throughout the interview, Deborah repeatedly evoked this symbolic image of the 'path' and the 'journey', underwriting her determination, autonomy and responsibility to honor her pledge. This process leads to the creation of her own spiritual ego-ideal and self-image (Downton, 1980; Sacks, 1979). Many of her decisions and choices were streamlined to aid the fulfilment of that mission and some of these impact upon her relational self (e.g. Hine, 1970; Lofland & Stark, 1965). This kind of social re-balancing has also been noted by Downton (1980). For instance, she spoke about the split from her husband after 30 years of marriage as a necessary step in her spiritual evolution, citing religious difference and personal changes as the main drivers behind the split. Yet, she also mentioned a strong wish to feel connected, grounded to her children as companions along the path, a self desiring a connection to another self or selves, another which shares similar goals and understandings.

CONCLUSION

The qualitative findings presented here add to existing knowledge of NDEs in showing that to more deeply understand the impact of NDEs it is crucial to consider how the experience fits within the biographical context of an individual's life. This differs from much of the previous work to date, which has largely considered the NDE as a separate entity and in so doing has lost how individuals respond to such a unique critical life event and the transformative processes it can thrust upon them. As our data have shown, rather than being an overall influence on personal and spiritual growth, people will choose elements of an experience which are most personally meaningful for them and take that into their later lives.

As their lives change, and in the light of new information and experiences, so may their interpretation of their NDE.

The idiographic, phenomenological approach taken in this research has been instrumental in highlighting the subtle affective, social and psychological mediating factors that influenced how the NDE was interpreted and integrated during the course of daily living. In addition, concomitant physical and psychological events can also intertwine in vastly complex ways, which may aid or hinder the individual's resolution of the underlying meaning of the NDE. What it has also shown is the challenges the NDE, or elements therein, have on the individual's sense of self and how they maintain and develop that self in the years succeeding the event.

ACKNOWLEDGEMENTS

The work reported here was supported by a grant awarded by the Bial Foundation and a Parapsychological Association Research Endowment. The authors would like to express their gratitude for this support.

REFERENCES

Athappilly, G.K., Greyson, B., & Stevenson, I. (2006). Do prevailing societal models influence reports of ndes? a comparison of accounts reported before and after 1975. *The Journal of Nervous and Mental Disease, 194(3),* 218-222.

Atwater, P.M.H. (2003). *The new children and near-death experiences.* Rochester, Vermont: Bear & Company.

Baltes, P. B., & Danish, S. J. (1980). Intervention in life span development and aging: issues and concepts. In R. R. Turner & H. W. Reese (Eds.), *Lifespan developmental psychology intervention.* New York, NY: Academic Press.

Blackmore, S. J. (1993). Near-death experiences in India: They Have Tunnels Too. *Journal of Near-Death Studies, 11(4),* 205-217.

Brim, O. G., & Ryff, C. D. (1980). On the properties of life events. In P.B. Baltes & O. G. Brim (Eds.), *Life-Span development and behavior.* New York, NY: Academic Press.

Bush, N. E. (2002). Afterward: Making meaning after a frightening near-death experience. *Journal of Near-Death Studies, 21(2),* 99-133.

Corbett, L. (1996). *The Religious function of the psyche.* London, England: Routledge.

Dougherty, C.M. (1990). The Near-death experience as a major life transition. *Holistic Nursing Practice, 4(3),* 84-90.

Downton, J.V. (1980). An Evolutionary theory of spiritual conversion and commitment: the case of divine light mission. *Journal for the Scientific Study of Religion*, 19(4), 381-396.

Eichmann, W. C. (1991). Meeting the dark side in spiritual practice. In C. Zweig & J. Abrams (Eds.), *Meeting the shadow: The hidden power of the dark side of human nature.* Los Angeles, CA: Tarcher/Perigee.

Estes, W. K. (1997). Processes of memory loss, recovery, and distortion. *Psychological Review, 104,* 148-169.

Fenwick, P., & Fenwick, E. (1995). *The truth in the light.* London: Headline.

Flick, U. (2002). *An introduction to qualitative research* (2nd ed.). London: Sage Publications Ltd.

Flynn, C. P. (1982). Meanings and implications of NDEr transformations: Some preliminary findings and implications. *Journal of Near-Death Studies, 2,* 3-13.

Grey, M. (1985). *Return from death: An exploration of the near-death experience. London: Arkana.*

Greyson, B. (1994). Near-death experiences. In R. Corsini (Ed.), *The Encyclopedia of psychology* (pp. 460-462). New York: Wiley.

Greyson, B. (1996). The Near-death experience as a transpersonal crisis. In B. Scotton, A. B. Chinen & J. R. Battista (Eds.), *Textbook of transpersonal psychiatry and psychology.* New York: Basic Books.

Greyson, B. (2000). Near-death experiences. In E. Cardeña, S. J. Lynn & S. C. Krippner (Eds.), *Varieties of anomalous experience: Examining the scientific evidence* (pp. 315-352): American Psychological Association.

Greyson, B. (2001). Post-traumatic stress symptoms following near-death experiences. *American Journal of Orthopsychiatry, 71(3),* 368-373.

Greyson, B. (2007). Consistency of near-death experience accounts over two decades: are reports embellished over time? *Resuscitation, 73,* 407-411.

Greyson, B., & Bush, N. E. (1992). Distressing near-death experiences. *Psychiatry, 55,* 95-110.

Groth-Marnat, G., & Summers, R. (1998). Altered beliefs, attitudes, and behaviors following near-death experiences. *Journal of Humanistic Psychology, 38,* 110-125.

Hine, V. (1970). Bridge burners: Commitment and participation in a religious movement. *Sociological Analysis, 31,* 61-66.

Irwin, H. J. (1999). Near-death experiences. In *An introduction to parapsychology* (3rd ed., pp. 199-217): McFarland & Company.

Knoblauch, H., Schmied, I., & Schnettler, B. (2001). Different kinds of near-death experience: A report on a survey of near-death experiences in Germany. *Journal of Near-Death Studies, 20(1),* 15-29.

Lofland, J., & Stark, R. (1965). Becoming a world-saver: A theory of conversion to a deviant perspective. *American Sociological Review, 30,* 862-875.

Moody, R. A. (1975). *Life after life.* Covington, GA: Mockingbird Books.

Moody, R. A. (1977). *Reflections on life after life.* St. Simon's Island, GA: Mockingbrid Books.

Morris, L. L., & Knafl, K. (2003). The nature and meaning of the near-death experience for patients and critical care nurses. *Journal of Near-Death Studies, 21(3),* 139-167.

Murphy, T. (2001). Near-death experiences in Thailand. *Journal of Near-Death Studies, 19(3),* 161-178.

Noyes, R. (1980). Attitude change following near-death experience. *Psychiatry*, 43, 234-242.

Pasricha, S., & Stevenson, I. (1986). Near-Death experiences in India: A Preliminary Report. *Journal of Nervous and Mental Disease, 174(3),* 165-170.

Pearlin, L. I. (1980). Strains and Psychological distress among adults. In N. J. Smelser & E. H. Erickson (Eds.), *Themes of work and love in adulthood.* Cambridge, Mass.: Harvard University Press.

Ring, K. (1980). *Life at death: A scientific investigation of the near-death experience.* New York: Coward, McCann & Geoghegan.

Ring, K. (1993). The Near-death experience. In R. Walsh & F. Vaughan (Eds.), *Paths Beyond Ego: The transpersonal vision.* New York: Jeremy P.Tarcher/Putnam.

Sabom, M. (1982). *Recollections of death: A medical investigation.* New York: Harper & Row

Sacks, H. L. (1979). The Effect of Spiritual Exercises on the Integration of Self-System. *Journal for the Scientific Study of Religion, 18(1),* 46-50.

Schooler, J. W., & Eich, E. (2000). Memory for emotional events. In E. Tulving & F. I. M. Craik (Eds.), *The Oxford handbook of memory* (pp. 379-392): Oxford University Press.

van Lommel, P., van Wees, R., & Meyers, V. (2001). Near-death experiences in survivors of cardiac arrest: A Prospective Study in the Netherlands. *The Lancet, 358,* 2039-2045.

Wilde, D.J. and Murray, C.D. (2009). The evolving self: finding meaning in near-death experiences using Interpretative Phenomenological Analysis. *Mental Health, Religion & Culture, 12,* 223-239.

Wilde, D.J. and Murray, C.D. (in press) Interpreting the anomalous: finding meaning in out-of-body and near-death experiences. *Qualitative Research in Psychology*

Notes on Contributors

Jane Aspell is a postdoctoral researcher in the Laboratory of Cognitive Neuroscience in the Brain Mind Institute of the Swiss Federal Institute of Technology in Lausanne, Switzerland. Her research investigates the neural bases of bodily perception and self-consciousness and focuses on the role of multisensory integration in the representation of the bodily self. Email: jane.aspell@epfl.ch

Carlos S. Alvarado, Ph.D., is Assistant Professor of Research at the Department of Psychiatry and Neurobehavioral Sciences of the University of Virginia. He has conducted research on the psychology and the features of out-of-body experiences, and has published papers about the history of parapsychology. Alvarado has been twice President of the Parapsychological Association. Currently he is Adjunct Faculty at the Institute of Transpersonal Psychology, Associate Editor of the Journal of Scientific Exploration, and a member of the editorial Board of the Journal of the Society for Psychical Research. Email: csa3m@virginia.edu

John Belanti, BSW, MAASW, works as a Social Worker and is a Team Leader in a Community Mental Health Team. Key research areas include prevalence of near-death experiences in Australia, and phenomenology of cross cultural near-death experiences. Email: belantijf@yahoo.com.au

Olaf Blanke is Associate Professor of Cognitive Neuroscience and Director of the Laboratory of Cognitive Neuroscience at the Swiss Federal Institute of Technology in Lausanne, Switzerland and Consultant Neurologist at the University Hospital, Geneva. Olaf''s research focuses on cognitive and systems neuroscience and the role of different sensory systems and the motor systems in self-consciousness. His most recent research on bodily self-consciousness has integrated full-body tracking and other technologies from the field of virtual reality and robotics with cognitive science and neuroimaging. Email: olaf.blanke@epfl.ch

Etzel Cardeña is Thorsen Professor of Psychology at Lund University, Sweden. He is past president of SCEH and Division 30 of the American Psychological Association and current president of the Parapsychological Association. His around 180 scientific publications include the book Varieties of Anomalous Experience. Email: etzel.cardena@psychology.lu.se

Dr. Ornella Corazza is a Medical Anthropologist who has been researching the near-death and ketamine experiences at the School of Oriental and African Studies (SOAS), University of London. She also spent time as a Research Fellow at the 21st Century Centre of Excellence (COE) Program on the Construction of Death and Life Studies at the University of Tokyo, Japan, in the course of which she studied near-death experiences among the Japanese.

She also teaches an MA course on Japanese Philosophy of the Body at the University of Wales, Lampeter. She is the author of a number of academic publications and Near-Death Experiences: Exploring the Mind-body Connection (2008). Her current interest of research is on cross-cultural understanding of health. E-mail: oc1@soas.ac.uk

Renaud Evrard is a clinical psychologist and a doctoral student preparing a PhD in clinical and differential aspects of exceptional experiences at the University of Rouen, France. He has been an active member of the Student Group of Institut Métapsychique International since 2004, and a student affiliate of the Parapsychological Association since 2007. In 2007 he co-founded the Service for Orientation and Help of People with Exceptional Experiences in Paris. Email: evrardrenaud@gmail.com

Chris French is a Professor of Psychology and Head of the Anomalistic Psychology Research Unit in the Psychology Department at Goldsmiths. He has published over 100 articles and chapters covering a wide range of topics within psychology. His main current area of research is the psychology of paranormal beliefs and anomalous experiences. He frequently appears on radio and television casting a skeptical eye over paranormal claims. He is the editor of The Skeptic magazine (UK version). Email: c.french@gold.ac.uk

Dr. Kathryn Gow is a Senior lecturer at Queensland University of Technology. Her primary areas of interest are psychology and psychiatry, including hypnosis, OBEs and NDEs. Email: K.gow@qut.edu.au

Harvey J. Irwin completed a Ph.D. in psychology at the University of New England in Australia and has been a member of the School of Psychology in that university for over thirty years. Currently he is an Honorary Research Fellow at the University of New England. His research interests include the nature and psychological functions of belief in the paranormal; the phenomenology of parapsychological experiences; the psychology of out-of-body and near-death experiences; parapsychological research within the context of the sociology of science; the origins of dissociative disorders; the impact of childhood trauma on psychological development; criminalistic psychology; eating disorders; and bereavement therapy. In 2002 the Parapsychological Association presented him with an Outstanding Research Contribution Award in recognition of his empirical and theoretical work in parapsychology over 25 years. E-mail: hirwin2@une.edu.au

Karuppiah Jagadheesan, MBBS, MD, FRANZCP, is a Consultant Psychiatrist with research interests in the phenomenology, neurobiology and psychopharmacology of psychiatric disorders and near-death experiences. E-mail: kuruppiah.jagadheesan@nh.org.au

Pascal Le Maléfan is a Lecturer in psychopathology at the University of Rouen, France. He has research interests in child and adolescent psychopathology, near death experiences, and the history of psychopathology. Email: pascal.lemalefan@wanadoo.fr

James McClenon, Ph.D., LCSW, works as a social work therapist at the Virginia Beach Psychiatric Center. He is the author of three books: Deviant Science: The Case of Parapsychology, Wondrous Events: Foundations of Religious Belief, and Wondrous Healing: Shamanism, Human Evolution, and the Origin of Religion. His published journal articles pertain to spiritual healing, religion, human evolution, and anomalous experience. Current research involves psychotherapy in Iran. Email: beingthere@gmail.com

Dr. Craig Murray is a Senior Lecturer in Psychology in the School of Health and Medicine at Lancaster University, UK. He has published widely on the topics of disability, health and illness, parapsychology, and technology. He is editor of the forthcoming book

Amputation, Prosthesis, and Phantom Limb Pain: An Interdisciplinary Perspective, to be published by Springer. Email: c.murray@lancaster.ac.uk

Joanne Murray is a research associate in the School of Health and Medicine at Lancaster University, UK. Email: joannemurray24@yahoo.c.uk

John Palmer, Ph.D., is Director of Research at the Rhine Research Center and Editor of the Journal of Parapsychology. He is a past President of the Parapsychological Association. He has published numerous research articles in professional journals and is co-author of the book Foundations of Parapsychology. His research has focused primarily on psychological factors associated with ESP performance in the laboratory. Email: john@rhine.org

Mahendra Perera, MBBS, PhD, MD, MRCPsych, FRANZCP, FAChAM, is a Consultant Psychiatrist at the Albert Road Clinic, Melbourne, Australia. Her areas of research interest are attention deficit hyperactivity disorder (ADHD) in adults, near-death experiences, and the philosophy of science. Email: relax101@gmail.com

Devin Blair Terhune is a doctoral candidate in the Department of Psychology at Lund University in Lund, Sweden. His research interests include the cognitive neuroscience of executive attention, hypnosis, and anomalous experiences. Email: devin.terhune@gmail.com

Jerome J. Tobacyk received the Ph.D. in personality psychology from the University of Florida in 1977 and is professor of psychology at Louisiana Tech University. He has twice been awarded a Fulbright professorship to Poland. His research interests include: the nature and functions of paranormal beliefs, psychological type theory, philosophical psychology, and consumer/organizational processes-especially from cross-cultural perspectives. He is the author of a widely used paranormal belief assessment instrument-the Revised Paranormal Belief Scale. Email: Jerryt@latech.edu

Pim van Lommel, M.D., recently retired as cardiologist from Hospital Rijnstate, an 800 beds Teaching Hospital in Arnhem, the Netherlands, and is now doing full-time research on the mind-brain relation. He graduated in 1971 at the University of Utrecht, and finished his specialization in cardiology in 1976. He published several articles on cardiology, but since he started his research on near-death experiences (NDE) in survivors of cardiac arrest in 1986 he is the author of over 20 articles, one book and several chapters about NDE. See also www.pimvanlommel.nl . Email: pimvanlommel@gmail.com

David Wilde gained his undergraduate Degree in Psychology with Human Physiology at the University of Sunderland in 1996. Following that he graduated with an MSc in Environmental Psychology at the University of Surrey in 1997. More recently, in 2005, he attained a Diploma in Consciousness and Transpersonal Psychology from Liverpool John Moore's University. He has research publications in the areas of palliative care and anomalous experiences. David is currently a PhD candidate at the University of Manchester, UK, investigating the occurrence and phenomenology of out-of-body experiences, funded by the Bial Foundation. Email: David.J.Wilde@manchester.ac.uk.

INDEX

A

abortion, 152, 184
absorption, 1, 9, 10, 11, 14, 33, 37, 39, 40, 42, 47, 49, 50, 54, 58, 60, 61, 64, 65, 66, 67, 68, 69, 70, 84, 96, 137, 138, 139, 142
academics, 2
acceleration, 146, 190
accident victims, 119
accidental, 55, 71
accidents, 8, 74, 112, 172, 193
accounting, 30
acetylcholine, 137
activation, 93, 95, 97, 153, 181
acute, 103, 118, 126, 156, 176, 178, 180
adaptation, 115
ADHD, 223
adjustment, 21
administration, 146
adolescence, 63
adolescents, 50
adult, 48, 107
adulthood, 218
adults, 41, 154, 218, 223
advertisements, 29
aetiology, 126, 186, 202
affective dimension, 66
affective disorder, 115
affective experience, 94
African-American, 135, 141
age, 41, 43, 45, 46, 50, 107, 108, 110, 125, 137, 175, 176, 177, 208, 210, 218
agent, 4, 5
aging, 217
agnosia, 91
aid, 28, 97, 134, 210, 212, 216, 217
air, 74
alienation, 210, 216
allergy, 209
alpha, 42
altered state, 1, 9, 10, 12, 14, 20, 23, 24, 36, 49, 69, 96, 104, 137, 194, 201
alternative, 23, 28, 30, 32, 33, 54, 71, 132, 142, 160, 165, 191, 198
alternatives, 9
ambulance, 175
American Psychological Association, 14, 63, 67, 99, 140, 141, 200, 218, 221
amnesia, 39, 102, 103
amplitude, 196
Amputation, 223
Amsterdam, 87
amygdala, 195
anaesthesia, 156, 174, 180
analgesia, 94, 103
analgesic, 103, 125, 200
analytical psychology, 7, 18
anesthetics, 123, 167, 168, 209
aneurysm, 197
anger, 208
Anglo-Saxon, 71
animal models, 180
animals, 133, 162, 169, 184, 214
anomalous, vii, 2, 4, 10, 14, 20, 62, 63, 67, 69, 70, 90, 97, 99, 105, 106, 111, 113, 114, 115, 129, 130, 131, 132, 133, 134, 135, 137, 138, 139, 140, 141, 210, 211, 218, 219, 222, 223
anoxia, 123, 176, 177, 194, 195, 196
anoxic, 153, 195
antagonist, 122
antecedents, 17, 49
anthropological, 139
anthropology, 139, 140
antibiotics, 173

anxiety, 9, 92, 94, 103, 106, 123, 208
application, 22, 51, 60, 71, 77, 107, 143, 165
Arabia, 210
Argentina, 14, 15
argument, 4, 18, 41, 130, 131, 132, 134, 153, 162, 167, 189, 196, 206
Armenia, 16
arousal, 10, 18, 19, 33, 34, 47, 88, 90, 94, 201
arrest, 4, 22, 123, 126, 148, 156, 159, 165, 171, 172, 173, 174, 175, 176, 177, 178, 179, 180, 185, 186, 189, 194, 195, 197, 200, 201, 202, 206, 207, 219, 223
arrhythmia, 175
arrhythmias, 199
artery, 165, 197
articulation, 60
artificial intelligence, 35
ASCs, 23, 24, 33, 34
Asia, 130
Asian, 130, 141
aspartate, 200, 201
asphyxia, 172
assault, 8, 104, 141
assessment, 19, 21, 50, 57, 95, 129, 223
assimilation, 216
assumptions, 5, 57, 65, 187, 189
asthma attacks, 148
asynchronous, 78, 79, 80, 82
asystole, 175, 186
Atlas, 124
atoms, 180
attacks, 148
attitudes, 10, 11, 17, 20, 49, 101, 131, 206, 208, 211, 213, 218
attribution, 77, 82, 88, 194
audition, 85
aura, 14, 196
Australasia, 156
Australia, 41, 118, 124, 126, 139, 147, 157, 221, 222, 223
authenticity, 131, 214
automatization, 94
autonomy, 216
awareness, 15, 38, 41, 69, 70, 74, 77, 85, 89, 90, 92, 93, 95, 97, 99, 119, 125, 137, 147, 155, 178, 192, 193, 212

B

back, 2, 12, 28, 30, 31, 33, 47, 73, 78, 79, 80, 81, 107, 118, 119, 121, 133, 135, 136, 137, 139, 149, 150, 151, 152, 165, 166, 172, 173, 199, 208, 212, 215
banks, 69
barrier, 115, 135, 138
basilar artery, 197
battery, 60
beating, 148, 174, 184, 195
beef, 122
behavior, 4, 28, 32, 35, 50, 62, 73, 91, 94, 96, 102, 103, 106, 133, 159, 165, 195, 212, 214, 217
behavioral change, 84, 213, 214
belief systems, 124
beliefs, 6, 17, 57, 70, 101, 106, 109, 113, 115, 120, 121, 129, 131, 132, 138, 147, 150, 188, 193, 206, 211, 213, 215, 218, 222, 223
bell, 151
benefits, 26, 97, 114
bereavement, 222
binding, 86
biometric, 50
bipolar, 112, 115
bipolar disorder, 112
birth, 7, 8, 17, 107, 153, 172, 184, 209, 216
bleeding, 135
blindness, 40, 53, 91
blood, 85, 135, 165, 166, 172, 173, 177, 178, 185, 190, 194, 196, 197, 210
blood flow, 165, 185, 190
blood pressure, 85, 173, 177, 210
blood supply, 178, 194
body concept, 31
body image, 7, 8, 9, 10, 11, 19, 21, 25, 27, 47, 54, 55, 58, 62, 66, 68, 88, 90, 92, 95, 99, 102, 103, 134, 199
body schema, 2, 90, 100
body temperature, 165, 197, 198
BOLD, 196, 201
bonding, 216
Boston, 20, 141, 185
bottom-up, 27, 29, 58, 97, 193
brain, 2, 3, 4, 24, 25, 26, 53, 55, 60, 75, 79, 83, 84, 86, 87, 103, 104, 118, 122, 123, 125, 126, 131, 134, 135, 136, 137, 141, 153, 155, 158, 159, 160, 165, 167, 168, 171, 172, 173, 174, 176, 177, 178, 179, 180, 181, 184, 186, 187, 188, 190, 192, 193, 194, 195, 196, 199, 200, 201, 202, 223
brain activity, 165, 167, 168, 179, 180, 192
brain damage, 75, 177
brain functioning, 123
brain functions, 153
brain injury, 75, 172
brain stem, 76, 165, 167, 180
brain structure, 103, 123
Brazil, 15
Brazilian, 167

breakdown, 28, 31, 32, 64, 69, 74
breathing, 165, 173, 176, 177, 180, 194, 197
Britain, 14, 134, 147
bubbles, 145
Buddha, 130, 148
Buddhism, 122, 124, 140
buildings, 29
burning, 135, 216
bypass, 165

C

candidates, 161
cannabis, 88
car accidents, 74
carbon, 123, 125, 190, 201
carbon dioxide, 123, 190
cardiac arrest, 4, 22, 123, 126, 148, 156, 159, 165, 171, 172, 173, 174, 175, 176, 177, 178, 179, 180, 185, 186, 189, 194, 195, 197, 200, 201, 202, 206, 207, 219, 223
cardiologist, 118, 173, 175, 223
cardiology, 173, 223
cardiopulmonary bypass, 165
cardiopulmonary resuscitation, 186, 194
case study, 88, 124
casting, 222
catalyst, 112
catheterization, 176
causality, 82
cave, 146
cell, 181
census, 125
central nervous system, 75
cerebral cortex, 167, 180
cerebral function, 180, 186, 194
cerebral hypoxia, 153, 194
cerebrospinal fluid, 158
channels, 161
chest, 79, 80, 81, 107, 173
chicken, 122
childhood, 39, 40, 48, 49, 63, 107, 137, 138, 191, 210, 211, 222
children, vii, 7, 10, 15, 118, 149, 152, 158, 173, 184, 208, 209, 211, 214, 215, 216, 217
Chile, 121
China, 131, 132, 134, 141, 147
chloride, 165
cholinergic, 137
Christianity, 122, 213
Christians, 130, 193
circulation, 176, 194, 197
classical, 149, 164, 165, 181, 182
classical physics, 181, 182
classification, 15, 44, 86, 154, 188
clients, 93
clinical approach, 71
clinical disorders, 200
clinical examination, 84
clinician, 91
clinics, 88
clouds, 158
clusters, 49
coding, 86
cognition, 17, 21, 48, 64, 87, 93, 159, 179, 183
cognitive activity, 167
cognitive function, 96
cognitive map, 24, 29, 30, 34
cognitive process, 10, 11, 31, 38, 47, 57, 89, 104, 165, 167
cognitive processing, 10, 47
cognitive psychology, 12, 24, 53, 192
cognitive science, 221
cognitive style, 115
cognitive system, 9, 23, 27, 31, 34, 53, 64, 71
cognitive variables, 137
coherence, 33
collaboration, 132, 133, 148
college students, 50
colleges, 132
colonization, 121
colors, 150, 151
coma, 173, 174, 176, 177
communication, 19, 21, 32, 39, 113, 146, 151, 159, 169, 176, 180, 216
communities, 137
community, 20, 50
compassion, 113, 183
competitiveness, 206
complexity, 26, 30, 32, 101, 103
complications, 21
components, 2, 40, 64, 66, 84, 90, 118, 163, 188, 189, 190, 192, 193, 196, 206
composition, 122, 123
compounds, 202
compulsion, 191
computing, 88
concentration, 30, 33
conceptualization, 2, 38
conditioning, 10, 47
conductance, 79
confabulation, 190
confidence, 109, 195, 196
conflict, 7, 100, 208, 216
conformity, 106
confusion, 72, 194, 196, 207, 209, 216

Congress, 70, 156
congruence, 80, 82, 83
conjecture, 13
connectivity, 89, 96, 100, 101
conscious experiences, 179, 184
consciousness, 2, 4, 1, 2, 9, 10, 12, 14, 15, 16, 18, 20, 21, 22, 23, 24, 34, 35, 36, 37, 38, 41, 47, 49, 53, 55, 56, 60, 61, 63, 64, 67, 69, 73, 74, 78, 80, 82, 84, 85, 86, 87, 89, 91, 95, 96, 99, 101, 102, 103, 104, 111, 113, 118, 120, 123, 126, 137, 148, 149, 153, 154, 155, 156, 160, 161, 166, 167, 171, 172, 173, 174, 175, 177, 178, 179, 180, 181, 182, 183, 184, 185, 186, 187, 190, 191, 193, 194, 195, 197, 198, 201, 202, 209, 221
consensus, 75, 130, 159, 188
consent, 42
constraints, 26, 29, 34, 83
construction, 7, 9, 25, 31, 32, 40, 58, 85
contingency, 43
continuity, 179, 184, 186
control, 23, 28, 30, 32, 34, 54, 65, 91, 94, 95, 97, 100, 101, 104, 107, 108, 109, 111, 133, 162, 175, 176, 190, 191
control condition, 97
control group, 54, 92, 94, 97, 175, 176, 190, 191
convergence, 164
conversion, 91, 101, 102, 103, 217, 218
conversion disorder, 92, 103
conviction, 5, 165
corneal reflex, 180
correlation, 20, 32, 40, 45, 61, 66, 88, 113, 157, 163, 180
correlation coefficient, 45
correlations, 44, 45, 137, 138, 139
cortex, 56, 75, 76, 78, 86, 95, 96, 97, 102, 123, 126, 167, 180, 183, 192, 195, 196, 202
cortical stimulation, 196
costs, 51
covering, 222
CPR, 194
creative personality, 142
creativity, 210
creep, 27
critically ill, 123
criticism, 23, 106, 194
cross-cultural, 4, 124, 126, 131, 132, 134, 145, 151, 155, 189, 222, 223
cross-cultural comparison, 132
crying, 151
cues, 25, 79, 80, 82, 83, 84, 98
cultivation, 158
cultural differences, 137
cultural influence, 131
cultural perspective, 124, 125, 223
culture, 2, 17, 117, 118, 119, 121, 122, 130, 131, 137, 147, 158
curiosity, 74, 174
currency, 69
cycles, 139

D

daily living, 207, 217
danger, 129, 134, 137, 157, 188, 201
Daniel Dennett, 181
Darwin's theory, 138, 140
database, 107
debates, 5
debt, vii
decay, 184
decision making, 215
decisions, 26, 211, 216
decoupling, 96
defects, 177
defence, 102
defense, 153, 188, 191
defibrillation, 165, 176, 185
defibrillator, 210
deficiency, 171
deficit, 40, 46, 223
deficits, 77
definition, 4, 9, 12, 38, 154, 160, 194
degenerate, 28
degradation, 66
degrees of freedom, 44
delivery, 172
delusion, 7, 133
delusions, 7, 99, 115
demand characteristic, 98
demographic data, 175
denial, 16, 30, 35, 182
dentists, 198
dependent variable, 45
depersonalization, 11, 13, 22, 38, 39, 43, 47, 49, 50, 94, 103, 105, 153
depressed, 55, 185
depression, 172, 177
deprivation, 9, 30, 64, 74, 134, 146, 156, 196
detachment, 62, 95, 97, 113
developmental psychology, 217
deviation, 43, 136
diagnostic criteria, 146
dichotomy, 32
Dienes, 91, 99
differentiation, 205
direct measure, 195

disability, 1, 222
discharges, 195
discipline, 149
disclosure, 105, 112, 114, 115, 214
discreteness, 30
discrimination, 112
diseases, 75, 172
disinhibition, 106, 123, 192, 196
disorder, 20, 21, 49, 50, 78, 92, 103, 112, 115, 139, 140, 223
dissociation, 3, 1, 4, 8, 9, 10, 12, 13, 14, 17, 21, 37, 38, 39, 40, 41, 42, 43, 44, 45, 46, 47, 48, 49, 50, 57, 58, 59, 60, 61, 62, 63, 64, 65, 66, 67, 68, 69, 70, 71, 72, 75, 84, 87, 91, 92, 95, 99, 100, 101, 102, 129, 137, 138, 139, 190
dissociative disorders, 8, 38, 50, 58, 68, 103, 222
dissociative identity disorder, 50
distance learning, 111
distortions, 8, 55, 64, 123, 207
distress, 61, 119, 188, 218
distribution, 39, 193
diversity, 102
diving, 157
dizziness, 94
doctors, 135, 151, 172, 177
dogs, 158, 162
dominance, 82
dosage, 146, 175
draft, vii
dream, 1, 3, 5, 14, 33, 35, 54, 65, 108, 137, 138, 142, 145, 164, 193, 214
dreaming, 18, 33, 35, 64, 137, 145, 146
drowning, 172, 193
drug use, 64, 196, 209
drug-induced, 118, 189
drugs, 24, 27, 30, 171, 198
DSM-II, 8
duration, 74, 171, 175, 176, 180
dynamic factors, 1

E

ears, 165, 193
earth, 33, 119, 146, 184, 185
earthquake, 62, 127
eating, 133, 222
eating disorders, 222
ecological, 62
ecstasy, 3, 15, 156
EEG, 24, 101, 138, 161, 165, 166, 167, 168, 179, 180, 183, 190, 194, 195, 196, 202
EEG activity, 190
EEG patterns, 24
ego, 7, 8, 210, 216
elaboration, 34
election, 123
electricity, 165
electrocardiogram, 173, 175
electrodes, 161, 196
electroencephalogram, 194
electroencephalography, 103
electrographic seizures, 201
electromagnetic, 162
emotion, 91, 156, 179, 183
emotional, 12, 90, 99, 119, 129, 173, 174, 190, 207, 208, 214, 219
emotional reactions, 12
emotions, 8, 11, 21, 62, 123, 124, 176, 177, 178, 181, 182, 208
empathy, 112, 210, 214
employment, 41
encephalitis, 75
encouragement, 138
endorphins, 122, 123, 153, 187, 190
energy, 1, 152, 157, 158, 163, 184
engagement, 94
England, 14, 41, 56, 86, 217, 222
enterprise, 107
enthusiasm, 3
entropy, 168
environment, 5, 10, 24, 47, 62, 83, 94, 95, 98, 107, 122, 150, 156, 174, 178, 192
environmental awareness, 93
environmental conditions, 139
environmental factors, 62
epidemiology, 21
epilepsy, 55, 75, 86, 107, 108, 110, 123, 138, 191, 196, 200
episodic memory, 102
epistemological, 3
ERPs, 100
estrangement, 119
etiology, 124
euphoria, 190
Euro, 119, 124
Europe, 130, 131, 134
Europeans, 120, 130
euthanasia, 184
evening, 133, 209
evil, 214
evoked potential, 165
evolution, 16, 138, 140, 141, 215, 216, 222
examinations, 2, 84
excitability, 3
excitation, 3, 123
exclusion, 43, 54, 69

execution, 96
executive functions, 91, 96
exercise, 29
exposure, 90, 99
externalization, 160, 161, 162, 163, 164
extinction, 155
eye, 9, 23, 28, 29, 31, 54, 161, 163, 193, 222
eye movement, 161, 193
eyes, 17, 25, 54, 56, 65, 67, 86, 95, 119, 121, 135, 141, 153, 161, 163, 165, 166, 188, 192, 193, 198, 216

F

fabrication, 133
factor analysis, 50
factorial, 42
failure, 55, 57, 64, 123, 191, 192
fainting, 9, 177
faith, 70, 111, 135, 138, 212
family, 108, 109, 111, 112, 135, 139, 151, 178, 190, 206, 208, 213
family life, 178
family members, 109, 151
fanaticism, 3
FBI, 78, 82, 84
fear, 7, 8, 30, 72, 74, 110, 111, 113, 119, 148, 165, 171, 172, 175, 176, 177, 193, 196, 206, 208, 214, 215
fears, 3, 206
feedback, vii, 197
feeding, 211
feelings, 5, 38, 77, 83, 87, 93, 108, 114, 117, 118, 124, 131, 172, 178, 181, 182, 190, 192, 206, 208, 209, 210
feet, 74
fetus, 152
fever, 173
fibrillation, 165, 175, 185
films, 54
fish, 145
five-factor model, 14
flashbacks, 123, 191
float, 29
floating, 2, 9, 10, 47, 62, 64, 73, 77, 81, 93, 94, 107, 123, 130, 133, 190, 210
flow, 165, 180, 185, 190
fluctuations, 161
fluid, 158
fMRI, 101, 183, 196
focusing, 4, 62, 66, 106, 187
folklore, 122, 132, 138, 139, 140, 141
forests, 210
forgiveness, 119, 213
Fox, vii, 9, 11, 12, 19, 57, 58, 65, 66, 68, 84, 88, 92, 102, 119, 125, 131, 134, 140, 146, 156, 189, 190, 191, 200
fragility, 62
France, ii, 222
free will, 181
freedom, 44, 111, 119, 181
frequency distribution, 45
frontal lobe, 91, 96, 100
frustration, 108
functional imaging, 103
functional magnetic resonance imaging, 86
functional separation, 38

G

Gabon, 189, 202
Gallup, 117, 125, 146, 156, 172, 185, 189, 200
Gallup Poll, 146
gas, 122, 123
gases, 190
gauge, 93, 163
gender, 41, 43, 44, 45, 46, 137
general anesthesia, 74, 76, 87
generation, 182, 190, 196
genes, 4, 129, 130, 139
Geneva, 221
Georgia, 165
Germany, 117, 125, 147, 157, 172, 186, 218
gift, 210, 212, 214
gifted, 8, 21
glutamate, 153
goals, 216
God, 34, 122, 142, 155, 188, 208, 211, 212, 213, 215
gold, 149, 222
goodness of fit, 43
grain, 34
grandparents, 110
grass, 135
gravitation, 149, 151
gravitational field, 183
gravity, 146, 176, 177
Great Britain, 134
grief, 210
group membership, 43
groups, 39, 43, 48, 65, 78, 92, 97, 131, 153, 177, 179
growth, 206, 211, 213, 215, 216
Guam, 147
guardian, 146
guessing, 161
Guillain-Barre syndrome, 86
gyrus, 55, 91, 95, 123

H

habituation, 24, 27, 62
hallucinations, 1, 4, 5, 6, 7, 10, 11, 14, 16, 19, 27, 55, 74, 76, 77, 83, 85, 86, 87, 91, 92, 93, 94, 95, 96, 98, 100, 103, 123, 190, 191, 193, 195, 202
hands, 25, 86, 87, 172
hanging, 206, 213
happiness, 113
harm, 184
Harvard, 158, 218
Hawaii, 157
healing, 4, 21, 63, 109, 110, 129, 130, 134, 138, 139, 140, 141, 142, 189, 202, 222
health, 1, 18, 51, 62, 100, 105, 106, 107, 114, 115, 138, 206, 207, 222
health care, 51, 207
health care costs, 51
health care professionals, 207
health locus of control, 100
healthcare, 184
hearing, 108, 118, 136, 164, 166, 174, 208, 209, 210
heart, 148, 165, 173, 174, 175, 176, 184, 195, 210
heart attack, 148
heart rate, 165, 210
heartbeat, 85, 165, 195, 197
heating, 26
height, 123
Heisenberg, 182, 185
Helix, 16
hemisphere, 75, 97, 134
heritability, 48
high scores, 42, 59
high-level, 27
highways, 120
hippocampal, 125
hippocampus, 195
hospital, 8, 10, 107, 132, 135, 148, 149, 167, 175, 177, 180, 208, 209, 210, 212, 214, 216
hospitalized, 19
hospitals, 175
host, 130
house, 158, 202
household, 118
human, 2, 5, 61, 74, 86, 94, 111, 113, 115, 125, 133, 139, 141, 146, 152, 153, 154, 155, 156, 157, 158, 160, 162, 168, 179, 187, 200, 201, 208, 214, 217, 222
human brain, 61, 160
human experience, 2, 5, 74, 115, 153, 187
human nature, 155, 217
humans, 25, 73, 88, 130, 139, 154, 159, 162, 184, 185, 200
husband, 164, 210, 214, 216
hyperactivity, 223
hypercarbia, 187, 190
hypersensitive, 92
hypnagogic state, 12
hypnosis, 4, 5, 6, 12, 22, 38, 51, 62, 63, 70, 71, 89, 90, 91, 92, 93, 94, 95, 96, 97, 98, 99, 100, 101, 102, 103, 104, 129, 137, 139, 140, 143, 222, 223
hypnotherapy, 93, 102
hypnotic, 5, 6, 11, 19, 50, 51, 68, 71, 89, 90, 91, 92, 94, 95, 96, 97, 98, 99, 100, 101, 102, 103, 134, 137, 138, 139, 142
hypothesis, 32, 60, 65, 77, 96, 124, 132, 133, 137, 139, 140, 141, 154, 156, 157, 187, 188, 192, 193, 195, 196, 200
hypoxia, 187, 190, 194, 195, 196, 201
hypoxic, 123
hysteria, 16, 49, 101, 102

I

ice, 133
identification, 56, 71, 72, 78, 79, 80, 164
identity, 9, 31, 38, 41, 50, 71, 84, 85, 91, 112, 153, 179, 183, 207
idiographic approach, 207
idiosyncratic, 1, 2
Illinois, 141, 201
illumination, 26
illusion, 4, 3, 4, 5, 55, 56, 78, 82, 86, 88, 123, 150, 155, 181
illusions, 77, 83, 84, 85, 87, 92
imagery, 1, 5, 7, 10, 11, 12, 13, 14, 15, 16, 22, 30, 32, 33, 47, 51, 54, 55, 56, 65, 67, 68, 71, 75, 84, 88, 93, 96, 99, 137, 143, 160, 167, 192, 198, 199
images, 4, 5, 6, 7, 8, 26, 29, 31, 67, 100, 117, 152, 157, 160
imagination, 3, 4, 5, 9, 23, 24, 25, 29, 30, 31, 32, 33, 34, 54, 61, 64, 137, 171, 192, 193
imaging, 86, 103, 180, 183
imaging techniques, 183
immortal, 187
immortality, 156, 185, 200
impulsiveness, 106
in situ, 129
incidence, 4, 19, 43, 54, 61, 88, 91, 92, 103, 125, 126, 130, 131, 135, 137, 138, 139, 186, 189, 202
inclusion, 3, 43, 98, 190
incompatibility, 26
independent variable, 43, 45, 46
indexing, 41
India, 118, 120, 121, 124, 126, 142, 147, 152, 156, 157, 201, 206, 214, 215, 217, 218

Indian, 121, 130, 147
Indians, 167
indication, 61, 132, 174
indicators, 207
individual differences, 60, 63, 101
individuality, 119
Indo-Pacific, 70
induction, 4, 5, 11, 16, 24, 39, 65, 84, 86, 89, 90, 91, 92, 93, 94, 96, 97, 98, 99, 100, 101, 103
infarction, 173, 176, 180
infections, 75
infinite, 34
informed consent, 42
inhibition, 96, 97, 108, 111
inhibitory, 97
injection, 173
injury, 75, 171, 172
innovation, 11
insight, 106, 172, 183
inspiration, 182
instability, 191
instruments, 57
integration, 2, 4, 40, 57, 66, 75, 77, 82, 84, 88, 89, 91, 95, 96, 105, 112, 178, 180, 191, 205, 207, 221
integrity, 43
intelligence, 20, 35, 155
intentions, 212
interaction, 4, 7, 9, 61, 62, 90, 91, 188, 193
interaction process, 4
interactions, 9, 11
interdisciplinary, 71
interference, 77
intergenerational, 202
internal processes, 25
internalization, 162
internet, 214
interval, 166
intervention, 217
interview, 108, 148, 149, 166, 175, 216
interviews, 60, 176, 177, 178, 207
intimidating, 178
intoxication, 75
intravenous, 165
intrinsic, 38, 100
introversion, 216
intrusions, 77, 134, 187
intuition, 178, 182
investigations, 75
investigative, 64
investment, 1, 19, 137
ipsilateral, 95
Iran, 222
island, 145
isolation, 27, 93, 94, 108, 138, 146, 172, 208, 210

J

Japan, 122, 126, 127, 131, 132, 134, 141, 145, 148, 150, 152, 156, 221
Japanese, vi, 4, 122, 140, 141, 145, 148, 150, 151, 152, 154, 155, 156, 157, 158, 221
Jefferson, 16, 18, 20, 49, 61, 67, 101, 141, 201
jobs, 210
judgment, 120, 121, 160, 194
jumping, 163
Jung, 7, 17, 18
Jungian, 7
justice, 178
justification, 38, 41

K

ketamine, 146, 156, 190, 201, 202, 221
kinesthetic, 9, 10, 38, 41, 47
King, 112, 114, 147

L

labeling, 56
labor, 92, 209
laboratory studies, 11
land, 118, 145
landscapes, 119
language, 42, 119, 122, 124, 212
large-scale, 175, 178
later life, 106, 108, 110
laws, 163
leadership, 70
learning, 24, 111, 213
left hemisphere, 134
lens, 79
lesion, 76
lesions, 77
life changes, 176, 183, 206, 211, 213
life cycle, 120
lifespan, 3, 2055, 217
lifestyle, 206, 209
life-threatening, 10, 47, 148, 154, 156, 157, 171, 172, 175, 201
lifetime, 24, 60, 69, 74, 85, 208
likelihood, 43
limbic system, 123, 153, 190, 200
limitation, 5, 95, 118
limitations, 30, 62, 97, 98, 123, 154, 160, 179
linear, 48, 216

linear model, 48
links, 73
listening, 25, 107
localised, 179
localization, 89, 90, 101
location, 4, 5, 6, 20, 28, 31, 73, 74, 75, 78, 79, 80, 81, 82, 83, 84, 90, 92, 94, 132, 159, 161, 162, 165, 169, 197
locus, 90, 93, 94, 97, 100
London, 4, 14, 15, 16, 17, 19, 20, 21, 35, 36, 56, 85, 87, 102, 115, 125, 141, 142, 147, 155, 156, 157, 158, 168, 185, 199, 200, 201, 202, 217, 218, 221
long period, 149
longitudinal study, 176, 177
long-term memory, 166
Los Angeles, 18, 140, 217
loss of consciousness, 158, 180, 190, 195
Louisiana, 223
love, vii, 8, 110, 119, 122, 146, 178, 183, 185, 206, 218
lying, 33, 62, 73, 107, 133, 135, 149, 161, 166, 172

M

magnetic, iv, 3, 84, 86, 180
magnetic resonance imaging, 86
magnetism, 15
mainstream, 133, 160, 179
maintenance, 24, 65
males, 107
malignant, 199
manipulation, 4, 78, 84, 89, 92, 94
marijuana, 74
marital status, 137
marriage, 216
material activity, 180
materialism, 168, 206
matrix, 44
meanings, 5, 107, 119, 205
measurement, 12, 49, 50, 102, 196
measures, 46, 48, 49, 57, 58, 59, 60, 66, 78, 80, 103, 106, 112, 167, 195
media, 55
medial prefrontal cortex, 95
mediation, 163
medical care, 123
medical student, 173
medication, 107, 108, 123, 173, 175, 176, 177
medicine, 3, 125, 141, 157, 184
meditation, 12, 34, 54, 62, 63, 172, 177, 211
melancholic, 211
Melanesia, 120
Melanesian, 120, 125, 131, 140
melting, 149, 151
membership, 43, 60
memory, 3, 4, 9, 23, 24, 25, 27, 28, 29, 31, 33, 54, 56, 61, 64, 69, 91, 102, 123, 126, 166, 172, 175, 177, 179, 191, 192, 193, 194, 196, 197, 200, 207, 217, 219
memory loss, 217
men, 41
meningitis, 75
mental disorder, 139
mental health, 105, 107, 115, 206
mental illness, 106, 112, 114
mental image, 75, 84, 137
mental imagery, 75, 84, 137
mental model, 53, 192
mental processes, 38, 40
mental representation, 5
messengers, 120, 147
metaphors, 36
Middle East, 130
migraine, 75, 87, 196
mind-body, 22, 124, 156, 188, 200
mind-body problem, 22
minority, 194, 195, 198
mirror, 17, 41, 72, 154, 157, 161
misconception, 187
misconceptions, 5
misidentification, 99
misinterpretation, 66
MIT, 56, 86, 87
modalities, 8, 11, 13, 82, 85
modality, 83, 99, 192
modeling, 24, 25, 27, 34, 53
models, 3, 9, 13, 23, 24, 25, 26, 27, 28, 29, 32, 33, 34, 35, 48, 61, 62, 64, 69, 71, 89, 100, 115, 140, 180, 192, 217
modules, 111
modus operandi, 21
molecules, 180
money, 70, 213, 215
monks, 121, 122, 149, 150
Monroe, 65, 67, 71
mood, 106, 113
mood states, 113
Moody's, 118, 134, 136
morning, 161, 164
morphine, 176
motor system, 77, 221
movement, 9, 12, 26, 90, 93, 190, 193, 218
MRI, 87
multiple personality disorder, 20, 140
multiple regression analysis, 45
multivariate, 13, 43, 46, 50

multivariate statistics, 50
muscle relaxant, 77
muscles, 193
music, 54, 107, 149, 150, 172, 173, 198
myocardial infarction, 173, 176, 180
mystical experiences, 54, 64, 69, 123, 138, 157, 191

N

narratives, 100, 118, 119, 120, 121, 134, 135, 216
Nash, 12, 19, 90, 93, 94, 95, 97, 99, 100, 101, 102, 104, 139, 140
Native American, 126, 130, 142
natural, 32, 35, 58, 120, 150, 188
natural environment, 150
naturalization, 58
nausea, 94
negative experiences, 148
neglect, 40, 182
negligence, 216
nerve, 181
nervous system, 75, 77
Netherlands, 22, 49, 50, 175, 186, 202, 219, 223
network, 96, 109, 111
neural mechanisms, 196
neural networks, 179, 180
neurobiological, 4, 82, 117, 122, 123, 124, 202
neurobiology, 222
neuroimaging, 77, 85, 221
neuroleptic, 103
neurological condition, 191, 196
neurons, 61, 179, 181
neuropathology, 18
neurophysiology, 4, 89
neuropsychology, 3
neuroscience, 3, 5, 53, 54, 75, 100, 101, 102, 180, 187, 188, 189, 194, 195, 197, 198, 200, 221, 223
neuroscientists, 160, 168, 181
neuroticism, 106
neurotransmitters, 122, 153, 190
New England, 41, 56, 86, 222
New Jersey, 126
New South Wales, 70
New York, 13, 15, 16, 17, 18, 19, 20, 21, 22, 35, 36, 48, 49, 50, 51, 56, 63, 67, 71, 72, 86, 102, 115, 124, 125, 126, 127, 140, 141, 142, 143, 156, 157, 158, 169, 185, 186, 199, 200, 201, 202, 217, 218, 219
New Zealand, 22, 51, 102, 115, 147
NMDA, 122, 125, 156, 157, 201
NMDA receptors, 122
N-methyl-D-aspartate, 200, 201
noise, 27, 146, 165
non-emergency, 4, 129, 135, 136, 140
non-reductionist, 154
nonverbal, 10, 47
normal, 2, 8, 9, 18, 19, 25, 28, 30, 31, 33, 34, 38, 39, 40, 50, 54, 58, 60, 65, 66, 69, 73, 74, 83, 102, 106, 131, 133, 134, 137, 142, 161, 179, 193, 197, 209
normal distribution, 39
North America, 14, 40, 88, 120
North Carolina, 68, 135, 136
nurse, 149, 172, 173, 208
nurses, 126, 172, 218
nursing, 173, 177

O

observations, 11, 126, 188
occipital cortex, 76
occipital lobe, 167
omission, 29, 30
opioid, 122
opposition, 131
optical, 162, 163
optics, 163
oral, 132, 135, 148
orbitofrontal cortex, 97
organic, 40, 91, 101, 188, 189
organism, 9, 28
orientation, 10, 47
oscillations, 104
oscillatory activity, 96
out-of-hospital, 180
outpatient, 49
ownership, 73, 77, 78, 82, 86, 87, 90
oxygen, 123, 134, 153, 171, 176, 177, 179, 185, 190, 194, 196
oxygenation, 165

P

Pacific, 70, 130, 158
pain, 30, 40, 42, 94, 113, 119, 122, 148, 149, 150, 156, 183, 190, 198, 208, 209, 212, 216
palliative care, 223
paradigm shift, 182
paradoxical, 1, 178
paralysis, 76, 92, 98, 100, 101, 104, 107, 108, 110, 131, 190, 193, 200, 202
paranoia, 7
parents, 108, 119, 208, 210, 211
parietal cortex, 86
parietal lobe, 75

parieto-occipital cortex, 76
Paris, 15, 16, 19, 20, 21, 49, 62, 63, 87, 222
passenger, 164
passive, 9, 10, 47, 64
pathology, 2, 16, 72, 196
pathophysiology, 123
pathways, 61, 112, 153
patients, 10, 19, 39, 75, 76, 77, 83, 84, 85, 87, 92, 100, 103, 118, 123, 148, 167, 171, 172, 173, 174, 175, 176, 177, 178, 179, 184, 189, 192, 194, 195, 197, 198, 201, 207, 218
peer, 3
peers, 2, 109
penicillin, 173
Pennsylvania, 141
perception, 2, 6, 8, 17, 19, 20, 24, 25, 26, 28, 29, 53, 56, 64, 72, 78, 87, 90, 92, 93, 94, 99, 102, 129, 131, 132, 133, 138, 146, 152, 159, 161, 164, 168, 169, 176, 177, 179, 182, 183, 190, 193, 197, 198, 199, 200, 221
perceptions, 3, 6, 8, 11, 13, 21, 25, 54, 56, 57, 62, 77, 85, 93, 99, 106, 107, 112, 119, 124, 125, 129, 131, 132, 133, 134, 137, 139, 140, 179, 199
perfusion, 178
peripheral nervous system, 77
permit, 165
personal communication, 32, 39
personality, 2, 6, 7, 8, 10, 12, 14, 17, 18, 20, 21, 22, 37, 39, 47, 50, 51, 57, 58, 60, 61, 64, 67, 69, 70, 71, 101, 105, 113, 115, 137, 138, 140, 141, 142, 143, 191, 200, 202, 210, 214, 223
personality characteristics, 47, 60
personality disorder, 20, 50, 106, 140
personality factors, 191
personality measures, 60
personality traits, 105, 138
PET, 103, 183
pets, 162
pharmacological, 177, 178
phenomenology, 4, 2, 9, 21, 23, 30, 31, 38, 39, 47, 63, 74, 84, 88, 89, 92, 95, 96, 100, 103, 118, 121, 131, 201, 205, 207, 221, 222, 223
Philadelphia, 15, 20, 141
philosophers, 4, 171, 181
philosophical, 15, 25, 53, 60, 113, 140, 168, 207, 223
philosophy, 185, 209, 212, 223
physical world, 34, 182
physicians, 4, 126, 171, 172
physicists, 182
physics, 181, 182, 183
physiological, 4, 3, 9, 10, 24, 40, 79, 129, 130, 131, 134, 136, 140, 153, 167, 171, 177, 178, 191, 192, 193, 194
physiology, 16, 34, 84, 88, 139, 156, 195
pilot study, 101, 103
pilots, 146, 190
pitch, 166
placebo, 134, 139
planets, 146
planning, 96
plants, 184
plasma, 158
platforms, 211
play, 7, 32, 61, 64, 85, 183
pleasure, 122
pneumonia, 107, 173
poisoning, 148
Poland, 223
politicians, 185
poor, 105
population, 18, 21, 38, 39, 50, 65, 67, 74, 84, 90, 91, 102, 115, 117, 135, 147, 172, 189
Portugal, 100
positive correlation, 61, 66
positive emotions, 176
positive mood, 113
positive relation, 11, 43, 69
positive relationship, 11, 69
postoperative, 156
posttraumatic stress disorder, 103
posture, 82, 90
potassium, 165
power, 71, 132, 142, 146, 152, 155, 178, 211, 215, 217
powers, 24, 131, 169
pragmatic, 89
predictability, 45, 60
prediction, 31, 32, 46, 80, 97
predictor variables, 43, 45
predictors, 43, 46, 60, 137
predisposing factors, 60
pre-existing, 66, 84, 191
prefrontal cortex (PFC), 95, 96, 97, 98, 102
pregnant, 110
prejudice, 172
premotor cortex, 86
president, 221
press, 2, 12, 14, 33, 80, 88, 107, 115, 146, 155, 156, 157, 185, 193, 202, 207, 219
pressure, 85, 107, 163, 173, 177, 207, 210
primate, 86
prior knowledge, 111, 113, 197
probability, 4, 138, 159, 168
problem solving, 70
producers, 6
production, vii, 96

program, 111, 148
proposition, 123
protection, 139
protocol, 78, 98
prototype, 72
PSS, 43, 45
psyche, 6, 40, 217
psychiatric disorders, 222
psychiatrist, 126
psychiatrists, 39, 181
psychobiology, 35, 36
psychological development, 222
psychological functions, 222
psychological health, 62
psychological illnesses, 113
psychological processes, 9, 11, 62, 112, 121
psychological stress, 190
psychological variables, 13
psychological well-being, 113, 114
psychologist, 8, 222
psychology, 1, 2, 3, 1, 2, 7, 8, 12, 13, 16, 18, 19, 20, 22, 24, 35, 41, 53, 58, 63, 64, 69, 139, 140, 141, 142, 168, 192, 209, 213, 217, 218, 221, 222, 223
psychopathology, 13, 22, 49, 51, 61, 63, 64, 88, 102, 103, 106, 115, 138, 142, 222
psychopharmacology, 222
psychosis, 18, 86, 105, 112, 115, 138, 171
psychosomatic, 40, 99
psychotherapy, 222
psychotic, 72
PTSD, 206
public, 2, 216
Puerto Rican, 14
pulse, 173
punishment, 121
pupils, 180
purification, 150

Q

qualitative research, 218
quantum, 163, 182
questioning, 118
questionnaire, 19, 37, 41, 42, 55, 65, 67, 68, 80, 113, 114, 115, 118, 138, 177
questionnaires, 41, 81, 84

R

race, 137
radio, 181, 222
rain, 123, 134, 174
random, 123, 132, 196
range, 1, 42, 46, 65, 66, 70, 91, 105, 138, 160, 172, 189, 196, 198, 214, 222
ratings, 42
reading, 69, 121, 174, 209, 213
realism, 10, 47, 65, 109
reality, 2, 3, 9, 23, 24, 25, 26, 27, 28, 29, 30, 31, 32, 33, 34, 35, 54, 55, 61, 62, 64, 69, 70, 71, 84, 93, 95, 130, 145, 150, 155, 157, 182, 185, 191, 192, 198, 221
reasoning, 194
recall, 14, 31, 87, 113, 194
recalling, 54
reception, 172
receptors, 122
recognition, 72, 208, 222
recollection, 3, 33, 64, 173, 174, 175, 176, 177, 190
reconcile, 179
reconstruction, 166
recovery, 109, 110, 115, 165, 179, 197, 207, 217
recreational, 156
recurrence, 108
reductionism, 153, 155
redundancy, 27
refining, 199
reflection, 27, 114, 122, 152, 153, 160
reflexes, 177, 180
regional, 103
regression, 8, 43, 45, 46, 60
regression analysis, 43, 45, 46
regression equation, 44, 45, 46
regulation, 99, 103
relationship, 4, 7, 10, 13, 22, 32, 61, 62, 68, 69, 70, 90, 91, 98, 102, 109, 110, 139, 146, 150, 154, 164, 171, 174, 179, 181, 208, 211, 212, 213
relationships, 11, 66, 115, 208, 211, 212, 213, 214, 215
relatives, 113, 119, 121, 130, 132, 135, 152, 164, 165, 172, 183, 188, 190, 197
relaxation, 30, 64, 92, 94, 99, 154
relevance, 3, 41, 49, 71, 82, 103, 106, 148
reliability, 42, 48, 67, 97, 141
religion, 17, 117, 122, 125, 131, 141, 142, 157, 175, 187, 209, 213, 214, 222
religiosity, 142
religious belief, 120, 121, 129, 132, 134, 141, 147, 177, 193
religious beliefs, 120, 121, 129, 132, 147, 193
REM, 18, 33, 76, 86, 180, 187, 193
removal of organs, 184
replication, 21, 39, 48, 49, 58, 103, 151
reporters, 58, 59, 60
research design, 46

resistance, 1, 2, 149
resolution, 217
resources, 9, 37
respiration, 176
respirator, 176
respiratory, 180
resuscitation, 171, 173, 174, 175, 176, 177, 179, 186, 194
retention, 123
returns, 64, 197
Reynolds, 3, 165, 167, 168, 197, 198, 203
rhythms, 176
right hemisphere, 75, 97
rigidity, 26
risk, 51, 163, 194
rivers, 38, 148
robotics, 84, 221
robustness, 4
Royal Society, 124
rubber, 78, 82, 86, 88

S

sacred, 142, 147
sadness, 178
safety, 156, 164
sample, 21, 41, 43, 44, 49, 59, 60, 65, 66, 68, 69, 95, 103, 118, 119, 123, 134, 136, 147, 189, 202
sand, 34
Saudi Arabia, 210
scalp, 196, 202
schema, 2, 72, 90, 100
schizophrenia, 55, 105, 106, 112, 114, 138, 156, 196
schizotypal personality disorder, 106
schizotypy, 1, 11, 19, 63, 105, 106, 113, 115, 138, 142
scientific knowledge, 111
scientific method, 60, 65, 182
scientific understanding, 2, 3, 73, 75
scores, 39, 42, 45, 46, 59, 80, 112, 136, 138, 162
SCRs, 100
search, 71, 112, 126, 142, 173, 182, 186
secular, 17
sedatives, 176
seeds, 213
seizure, 15, 91, 101, 122, 123, 190, 196, 197
seizures, 86, 101, 153, 190, 200, 201
selecting, 26, 32
selective memory, 197
self, 3, 18, 19, 37, 56, 78, 79, 82, 85, 87, 213, 219
self-concept, 31
self-consciousness, 56, 73, 74, 78, 80, 82, 84, 85, 87, 99, 101, 111, 221
self-esteem, 109, 111, 112
self-help, 213
self-identity, 31, 179, 183
self-image, 25, 216
self-knowledge, 63
self-observation, 11
self-regulation, 99
self-report, 41, 48, 84, 91
seller, 174
semantic, 101
sensation, 9, 61, 69, 71, 82, 91, 118, 120, 192, 197, 201
sensations, 2, 5, 6, 10, 14, 47, 65, 77, 81, 107, 124, 129, 160, 181, 190, 192
sense organs, 1, 163
sensitivity, 112, 201
sensory functioning, 92
sensory modalities, 8, 11, 13
sensory systems, 55, 192, 221
separateness, 214
separation, 4, 3, 38, 40, 69, 136, 146, 159, 188, 189, 210, 212, 216
sequelae, 96, 97
series, 39, 57, 66, 91, 98, 119, 162
serotonin, 153, 187, 190
sex, 175, 176
sexual abuse, 138
sexual assault, 8
shamanism, 129, 134, 137, 138, 139
shape, 130, 131, 132, 134, 137, 145
shaping, 119, 121, 132
shares, 216
sharing, 109, 112, 214
shock, 110, 172, 176, 216
shocks, 173
short-term, 10, 47, 175, 177
short-term memory, 175, 177
shoulder, 197, 210
sign, 112
signaling, 77
signals, 10, 47, 76, 83
signs, 29, 138, 142, 148, 165, 166, 210
similarity, 11, 50, 190, 196
sites, 29
skeptics, 68, 69
skills, 10, 32, 33, 35, 47, 54, 65, 67, 68, 108, 134, 138, 192, 213
skin, 79, 154
skin conductance, 79
sleep, 3, 18, 27, 33, 35, 66, 76, 86, 92, 100, 107, 108, 110, 131, 137, 173, 174, 180, 193, 200, 202
sleep paralysis, 76, 92, 100, 107, 108, 110, 131, 193, 200, 202

social anxiety, 92, 103, 106
social factors, 105
social justice, 178
social network, 109, 111
social relationships, 115
social skills, 108
social work, 222
socialization, 138
socioeconomic, 137
sociologists, 139
sociology, 3, 139, 140, 222
software, 43, 45, 50
somatic symptoms, 46
somatization, 51
Somatoform, 40, 42, 44, 45, 49, 59, 66, 99, 102
somatosensory, 25, 30, 55, 76, 99, 123
sounds, 1, 146, 166, 198
South America, 120
spatial, 32, 65, 66, 69, 73, 74, 75, 78, 79, 80, 82, 83, 85, 88, 89, 90, 93, 154
spatial location, 75, 82, 83, 90
specialization, 223
species, 158
spectrum, 50, 106
speculation, 61, 140
speed, 151
spinal cord, 76
spiritual, 55, 112, 115, 121, 129, 130, 131, 133, 134, 139, 140, 147, 187, 188, 191, 202, 206, 208, 211, 212, 214, 215, 216, 217, 222
spiritual awakening, 206
spirituality, 112, 125, 140, 150, 156, 158, 178, 200, 211, 212
SPR, 4, 6, 7
SPSS, 43, 45, 50
stability, 26, 30, 32, 103
stabilize, 29, 33
stages, 164, 166, 167
standard deviation, 43, 59, 136
standard error, 44
statistical analysis, 163, 178
statistics, 43, 45, 50, 58
stereotypes, 10, 47
stigma, 112, 115
stigmatized, 112
stimulus, 48, 79, 95, 97
stock, 164
stomach, 135, 208
storage, 29
strain, 163
strategies, 35, 69, 100, 108
stream of consciousness, 56
strength, 83, 173
stress, 8, 9, 21, 23, 27, 46, 64, 103, 113, 122, 124, 139, 156, 166, 190, 200, 218
stressful events, 138
stressors, 195
stress-related, 46
students, 11, 15, 17, 21, 37, 41, 48, 50, 67, 68, 103, 132, 135, 174
subcortical structures, 76
subgroups, 58, 60
subjective, 4, 6, 10, 16, 20, 47, 48, 51, 60, 66, 67, 81, 86, 88, 115, 153, 159, 160, 161, 165, 168, 172, 174, 177, 179, 181, 182, 185, 205
subjective experience, 60, 66, 160, 161, 174, 179, 181, 182
subjectivity, 5, 87
substrates, 102, 122, 126, 202
suffering, 77, 119, 148, 150, 165, 173, 176
suicide, 86, 146
supernatural, 115, 122, 141, 206, 214
supply, 71, 178, 190, 194
suppression, 102
surgeons, 167, 168, 196
surgery, 85, 107, 132, 159, 165, 166, 167, 168, 193, 196
surgical, 146, 166, 167, 197, 198, 210
surprise, 8, 54, 151, 173, 176
survival, 2, 4, 16, 129, 130, 131, 133, 139, 154, 156, 159, 160, 161, 164, 165, 167, 168, 169, 171, 172, 200, 206
survival rate, 171
surviving, 176
survivors, 4, 22, 123, 126, 127, 171, 174, 178, 179, 180, 186, 189, 200, 202, 219, 223
susceptibility, 11, 46, 50, 68, 71, 101, 103, 138, 142
sustainability, 184
Sweden, 159, 221, 223
switching, 97
Switzerland, 221
symbolic, 72, 153, 216
symbols, 120
symptom, 15, 40, 46, 47
symptoms, 42, 46, 49, 88, 91, 94, 139, 190, 206, 218
synapses, 61
synchronization, 96, 97
synchronous, 78, 79, 80, 81
syndrome, 77, 85, 86, 123, 138, 139, 195, 196
synthesis, 157

T

tangible, 211
Taoism, 152
targets, 8, 163, 198

taste, 55
teaching, 213
teens, 158
telephone, 154
television, 42, 222
temperature, 165, 197, 198
temporal, 56, 75, 82, 83, 112, 123, 126, 138, 139, 146, 153, 157, 167, 187, 190, 191, 200, 202, 207
temporal lobe, 123, 138, 139, 146, 153, 157, 187, 190, 191, 200
temporal lobe epilepsy, 138, 191, 200
test-retest reliability, 42
Thailand, 120, 121, 126, 142, 218
theoretical assumptions, 57
therapy, 125, 201, 213, 222
theta, 167
thinking, 2, 5, 9, 22, 25, 26, 27, 33, 38, 69, 84, 131, 135, 137, 154, 155, 180, 181, 182, 184, 194, 209, 211, 212
thinking styles, 22
Thomas Nagel, 153
threat, 8, 9, 31, 92, 126, 146, 153
threatening, 10, 47, 79, 117, 118, 123, 148, 154, 156, 157, 171, 172, 175, 201
three-dimensional, 99
threshold, 122, 123, 125, 130, 156, 185, 190, 205
tics, 40
timing, 100
tinnitus, 55, 83
title, 3, 124, 173
Tokyo, 126, 127, 148, 157, 158, 221
tolerance, 45
tonic, 92
top-down, 27, 58, 95, 97, 106, 193
torture, 71, 120
tracking, 26, 221
tradition, 7, 10, 54, 130, 152
traffic, 172
training, 30, 71, 146, 173, 214
traits, 22, 105, 138
trajectory, 216
trans, 157, 158, 186
transcendence, 35, 118, 119, 179
transcranial magnetic stimulation, 84
transcripts, 108
transference, 4, 7, 20, 119
transformation, 5, 9, 16, 45, 47, 177, 178, 206
transformations, 87, 91, 95, 214, 218
transition, 147, 151, 215, 217
transitions, 215
translation, 124
transmission, 20
transparent, 29, 107
transplantation, 184
trauma, 11, 13, 39, 40, 49, 62, 68, 90, 137, 139, 191, 196, 222
traumatic brain injury, 75, 172
traumatic experiences, 50
travel, 2, 3, 16, 29, 67, 118, 130, 145, 159, 187, 210
trees, 29, 152
trial, 161
triggers, 66, 96, 97
trust, 108, 172, 173
Tsunami, 120
twins, 50
typology, 59, 117

U

undergraduate, 135, 223
underreported, 148
unfolded, 57
uniform, 98
universality, 206
universe, 146, 155, 174, 190, 212
university students, 15, 21, 37, 68, 103
unusual experiences, 61, 124
updating, 27, 82

V

validation, 48, 50
validity, 42, 48, 67, 141, 215
values, 11, 162, 206, 208, 213
variability, 46, 59, 189, 195
variables, 7, 10, 11, 12, 13, 24, 41, 43, 45, 46, 61, 62, 70, 101, 119, 129, 137, 139
variance, 40, 45, 61, 167
variation, 4, 13, 77, 117, 136
vehicles, 6
velocity, 185
ventricular arrhythmias, 199
ventricular fibrillation, 165, 175, 185
Vermont, 217
vibration, 107, 166
victims, 119
village, 157
violent, 8
virtual reality, 55, 84, 221
visible, 135, 196
vision, 4, 11, 14, 20, 25, 26, 56, 80, 82, 83, 85, 119, 121, 135, 147, 148, 149, 150, 151, 190, 193, 202, 219
visual environment, 95
visual field, 123

visual modality, 192
visual perception, 6, 28, 87, 90, 94
visual stimuli, 11
visual system, 57
visuospatial, 10, 47
vocabulary, 172
voice, 107, 121, 150, 154, 164, 208, 209, 210, 211, 212
vortex, 165, 166, 197, 198

W

waking, 6, 33, 97, 107, 132, 134, 137, 166, 179, 183, 212
Wales, 70, 134, 222
walking, 135
War on Terror, 70
watches, 82
water, 122, 145
weakness, 164
wealth, 65, 206
wear, 154
well-being, 106, 112, 113, 114, 115, 130, 131, 164, 188, 189
Werner Heisenberg, 182
Western countries, 146, 147
Western culture, 17, 119, 122, 188
Western societies, 189
William James, 202
windows, 29
wisdom, 183, 214, 216
withdrawal, 9
women, 41, 135
workplace, 108
worldview, 107, 168, 182
worry, 107, 111
writing, 2, 7, 26, 121, 164

Z

Zen, 54

Same structure, but change the reaction one decision to "imagination" and include her.

Imagination = B